DARK SOULS

Dark Souls. Beyond the Grave. Volume 2
by Damien Mecheri and Sylvain Romieu
edited by Third Éditions
32, rue d'Alsace-Lorraine, 31000 Toulouse
contact@thirdeditions.com
www.thirdeditions.com

Follow us:
🐦: @Third_Editions
f: Facebook.com/ThirdEditions
👻: ThirdÉditions
📷: ThirdÉditions

Edited by: Nicolas Courcier and Mehdi El Kanafi
Editorial assistants: Damien Mecheri and Clovis Salvat
Texts by: Damien Mecheri and Sylvain Romieu
Proofreading: Thomas Savary, Claire Choisy, Yves Choisy and
Jean-Baptiste Guglielmi (copy preparation);
Zoé Sofer and Jérémy Daguisé (proofs).
Translated from French by: Elise Kruidenier (ITC Traductions)
Illustrations: Hubert Griffe
Layout: Émilie Truong
Cover assembly: Frédéric Tomé
Classic cover: Jan-Philipp Eckert
Collector's edition cover: Hubert Griffe

This book aims to provide information and pay homage to the great *Dark Souls*
video game series.
In this unique collection, the authors retrace a chapter in the history of the *Dark
Souls* video games, by identifying the inspirations, background and contents of these
games through original reflection and analysis.

English edition, copyright 2018, Third Éditions.
All rights reserved.
ISBN 978-2-37784-038-0

Damien Mecheri and Sylvain Romieu

Foreword by **Kévin «Moguri» Cicurel**
Afterword by **Benoît «ExServ» Reinier**

DARK SOULS

ダークソウル

BEYOND THE GRAVE

VOLUME 2

03rd.

THIRD
éditions

Table of Contents

DARK SOULS

ダークソウル

BEYOND THE GRAVE

FOREWORD

I T MAY SEEM glaringly obvious that the *Souls* series was very influential on the video game world and its consumers, but we would do well to remember that this was not always the case. Only in hindsight did many of us grasp its full impact. It wasn't so much that *Demon's Souls* and *Dark Souls* were poorly received at the outset. In fact, they were relatively well received by critics and the public alike. However, they were considered niche games intended for players who were looking for despair and a good butt-kicking. But the *Souls* games have always been more than that. If they were simply very good games, we would surely not still be writing books about them today.

We should not feel too ashamed of our delayed full appreciation, since one of the greatest feats of the series was its bold cryptic approach, at a time when all other games were working towards ever-greater clarity and immediacy. When *Demon's Souls* was released in 2009, and the first *Dark Souls* in 2011, we were simply not capable of fully grasping all of their many facets or of discovering all of their secrets. First, we needed to watch as players from around the world took to the Internet to pool their extensive research and begin to give form to the story of the first *Dark Souls*. Then, we had to witness its success, and see the number of studios—independent and giant alike—sing the praises of the game, or draw inspiration from it directly or indirectly, in order to acknowledge the great impact it has had on the whole industry. Finally, we saw the game commended by the speedrun and streaming community, and knew that we were dealing with a potentially immortal game, which will take its place beside the traditional *Zelda* or *Castlevania* games popular in GDQs[1] and other similar events.

Today, of course, it's become a little ridiculous to say that the *Souls* games have had an effect on video games. The lapalissade principle has set in: everyone sees this as obvious, and there's really no use in stating it. In just a few years, the series went from a strange, vaguely sadistic and obscure entity to a hip piece of pop culture. Now,

1. GDQs (AGDQs or SGDQs for Awesome/Summer Games Done Quick) are American charitable events where a number of players work one after the other to finish various games in record time, while raising funds for organizations such as Doctors Without Borders or the Prevent Cancer Foundation.

even if you don't play the game, it's still good form to recognize the importance of the *Souls* games and the impressive way in which they have percolated throughout the medium. For those who have been fans of the series from the beginning, it's certainly good to see, but it's perhaps also a little unfair to other games. In our lives, we are all constantly missing out on a great number of things. There are no doubt dozens of dormant *Dark Souls* equivalents waiting to be discovered in a variety of cultural arenas, and our first judgments are sometimes so powerful that they prevent us from fully appreciating the things that contain more than they appear to at first glance. This is a rather frightening idea: the *Souls* games quickly gained public recognition, but other games may not.

Perhaps it is out of guilt, or pride—and surely a little bit of both—that we strive to not miss out on any of the different ways that *Dark Souls* manifests its impact on video games. Even if this sometimes means that we get a little off track. We look for (and always find, if we really want to) references, homages and direct inspiration, even in places where they don't actually exist. At this point, finding *Dark Souls* references everywhere is practically a meme.[2] *Dark Souls* is brought up at every turn, when playing *Thumper*,[3] or even during a game of *Zelda: Breath of the Wild*, as players quickly forget the immense legacy that the original *Zelda* games left for *Dark Souls*. This doesn't do justice to the FromSoftware series either, or to the games that strive to present themselves as its offshoots. It simplifies the very complex relationships of influence and—to top it all off—we risk missing out on new experiences that have more going for them than a basic and vague resemblance to the *Souls* games.

In the same vein, the father of the series, Hidetaka Miyazaki, confided to the Japanese magazine *Famitsu* that his goal is not to create new games similar to *Dark Souls*.[4] In some ways, we do want him to be able to free himself from his own games: this could only lead to good things. He could just work on producing games he himself likes, and we could hope for new formulas and striking new universes. We must work to remember that video games (FromSoftware's or others) can also take us by surprise, and we should be mindful of what they may offer. This is the best lesson we can take away from the minor neglect we were guilty of towards the *Souls* series.

In the meantime, maybe it is worth turning our focus back to the series itself, even at the risk of spotting *Dark Souls'* influence all over, since it is always interesting to dig a bit and ask some questions. Maybe, instead of wondering what legacy *Dark Souls* has left for video games, we can let its effects distill naturally over time and begin by

---

2. This is especially the case on the @xmeetsdarksouls Twitter account: although it is increasingly moving away from its original concept, it still compiles excessive comparisons with *Dark Souls*.
3. A musical game developed by Drool, released in October 2016, and often called "the *Dark Souls* of rhythm games," due to its difficulty and oppressive environment.
4. Translated from Japanese: http://gematsu.com/2017/03/dark-souls-iii-director-not-concerned-whether-not-next-game-resembles-dark-souls.

considering what *Dark Souls* did for *Dark Souls*. In other words, we can try to analyze and study the more or less subtle permutations of the series within its own scope.

What consequences did the staggering success have on the series, which started out as a single game that even FromSoftware saw as doomed from the beginning? How did *Dark Souls III* handle the end of the narrative and game cycle? How did *Bloodborne* assimilate a formula now familiar to us all, and turn it into an entirely different universe? The latter two games are all the more interesting to analyze because they signal a return–after the embryo of *Demon's Souls*, the first *Dark Souls*, and particularly the orphan *Dark Souls II*–to a creation of Hidetaka Miyazaki, who in the meantime had been promoted to CEO of FromSoftware.

And this turn of events worked out well for us, since Damien and Sylvain now propose to dissect these two monuments of the cycle now known as "*Soulsbourne*."

Kévin Cicurel

Kévin "Moguri" Cicurel

After several years spent working as a specialized videogame journalist for magazines such as *Gameplay RPG*, *Role Playing Game* and *Consoles +*, and reporting for the *Nolife TV* channel, Moguri constantly wonders if he has successfully transformed his passion into a job, or if it's the other way around.

DARK SOULS

ダークソウル

BEYOND THE GRAVE

PREFACE

C OVERING *Bloodborne* in a book entitled *Dark Souls: Beyond the Grave* may seem a little odd. Anyone who has taken on the FromSoftware Gothic masterpiece will have noticed clear similarities with the *Souls* games. The kinship is undeniable: not only do the works have similar traits, they also share the same DNA: that of Hidetaka Miyazaki, of course—the meticulous and obsessive designer, who pushes his teams to give all they have and makes sure he never rests on his laurels.

In *Bloodborne*, the designer retained the essence of the *Souls* games, while setting it apart with thoroughly redesigned battle mechanics, and a similar yet very different atmosphere. With *Dark Souls III*, on the other hand, he preferred to come full circle and reach an apotheosis, an end to his dark fantasy series, even if that meant sticking with old ideas.

In the first *Dark Souls: Beyond the Grave* book, we discussed *Demon's Souls* in a similar way: it served as a mold for the subsequent series. We felt that *Bloodborne* was just as essential to our analysis here. It took the major elements from the *Souls* games and transformed them, and serves as a fascinating reflection of the series' evolution. It allows us to shine light on the constituent elements of the series and better understand the exceptional success of these works, as well as the impact they had on players who were looking for new, challenging experiences, both from a gameplay and artistic standpoint.

Bloodborne and *Dark Souls III* also marked a leap towards a new generation of consoles. The new machines' performance freed the talents of the different artists working on the project, while the greater budget allocated to FromSoftware definitively put the series into the "AAA" production category. These logistical and material upheavals were underscored by FromSoftware's general use of subcontractor studios, with an evident impact on the technical style of the games, although they did not suffer any real artistic compromise.

In this second volume on the fascinating *Souls* and *Bloodborne* games, we invite you to continue exploring their cryptic stories, and to deepen the study of their aesthetic approaches and their gaming philosophy.

For clarity's sake, *Bloodborne* and *Dark Souls III* will first be discussed separately, in two distinct "books," which will focus on the behind-the-scenes development, story analysis, the themes, and the soundtrack for each game. The third and final "book" is devoted to decoding the two games, both in relation to the series itself, and from the perspective of related topics that were not covered in the first volume, from artistic influences and marketing, to a look at how the games have evolved.

Bloodborne and *Dark Souls III* are both different and complementary. It is rewarding to see what they reveal about FromSoftware's creations and Miyazaki's process, as well as the overall videogame market and the nature of the medium. We thought we had covered these topics from all angles in the first volume, but these two additional games opened up new avenues for reflection. We hope that this work will pique your curiosity and your thirst for knowledge, and demonstrate once again how much the *Souls* games and *Bloodborne*, these dense, terrifying and melancholic action-RPGs, have unprecedented richness, with unparalleled meticulousness equal only to the level of trust they place in players.

⚜ The Authors

Damien Mecheri

Passionate about films and video games, Damien joined the writers team of *Gameplay RPG* in 2004, writing several articles for the second special edition on the *Final Fantasy* saga. He continued his work with the team in another publication called *Background*, before continuing the online adventure in 2008 with the site *Gameweb.fr*. Since 2011, he has come aboard Third Éditions with Mehdi El Kanafi and Nicolas Courcier, the publisher's two founders. Damien is also the author of the book *Video Game Music: a History of Gaming Music*. For Third Éditions, he is actively working on the "Level Up" and "Année jeu vidéo" collections. He has also written or co-written several works from the same publisher: *The Legend of Final Fantasy X*, *Welcome to Silent Hill: a Journey into Hell*, *The Works of Fumito Ueda: a Different Perspective on Video Games* and, of course, the first volume of *Dark Souls: Beyond the Grave*.

Sylvain Romieu

Curious by nature, a dreamer against the grain and a chronic ranter, Romieu is also a passionate traveler of the real and the unreal, the world and the virtual universes, always in search of enriching discoveries and varied cultures. A developer by trade, he took up his modest pen several years ago to study the characteristics and richness of the marvelously creative world of video games. He writes for a French video game site called *Chroniques-Ludiques*, particularly on the topic of RPGs, his preferred genre.

DARK SOULS

ダークソウル

BEYOND THE GRAVE

BOOK I
BLOODBORNE

DARK SOULS

ダークソウル

BEYOND THE GRAVE

CHAPTER ONE
CREATION

D URING the summer of 2012, as FromSoftware was polishing up the *Artorias of the Abyss* DLC for the first *Dark Souls*, the development studio was contacted by Sony. Sony had learned its lesson from *Demon's Souls*; the long-lasting success of the FromSoftware work was phenomenal. With the hope of forging a similarly fruitful partnership, Sony once again offered the studio an exclusive contract. In IGN's "making of" video, Masami Yamamoto (head of external development for Sony Japan Studio) provides some context: "Usually, developers come to us with their ideas to start a new project. *Bloodborne* was a bit of a special case, as we had a strong desire to work with Miyazaki-san, we brought the idea to FromSoftware."

From the start, however, it was never a question of making a *Demon's Souls 2*.[5] Although it may have been tempting to capitalize on an already successful game, the pull towards innovation was greater.

Project Beast

FromSoftware and Sony agreed on one important thing: the game would be designed for the next generation of consoles: namely, for PlayStation 4. Hidetaka Miyazaki was unreservedly assigned to head the project. In it, he saw an opportunity to design a game along the same lines as the *Souls* games, but in a different world, directly inspired by Gothic novels—with Bram Stoker's *Dracula* in mind—and the unnerving themes from H. P. Lovecraft's stories. For years, Miyazaki had dreamed of creating an environment inspired by Gothic and Victorian architecture. He felt, however, that this level of detail could only be achieved using superior technology, an advantage promised by PlayStation 4.

The concept of the game had been kicking around in his head for some time, as he told IGN in 2015: "The game mechanics, or the Gothic theme for example, those were some areas or concepts that were always brewing, and one of the areas that

---

5. In one of the alpha versions of *Bloodborne*, a bug allowed players to battle Gascoigne. He would use the expression "*Umbasa*" in one of his dialogues, an intriguing direct reference to *Demon's Souls*.

I always wanted to achieve in my career." However, he also recognized the great weight on his shoulders, following the success of *Demon's Souls* and *Dark Souls*. He knew that fans were just waiting for him to trip up.

The project, christened *Project Beast*, began soon after the *Astorias of the Abyss* DLC was released in August 2012. At the time, FromSoftware was also beginning to build *Dark Souls II*, its cash cow. Miyazaki kept his distance from this sequel, which was handed off to Tomohiro Shibuya and Yui Tanimura, with support from the FromSoftware president and creator of *King's Field*, Naotoshi Zin, who supervised the game system.

On his end, Hidetaka Miyazaki formed a trusted team of regular collaborators, such as lead programmer Jun Itô (who had already filled this role for *Demon's Souls* and *Dark Souls*), composer and lead sound designer Tsukasa Saitô (*Armored Core* games), and most of his regular artists: Daisuke Satake, Masanori Waragai and Hiroshi Nakamura. The success of *Demon's Souls*, and the even greater success of *Dark Souls*, allowed FromSoftware to grow its ranks significantly. In total, no fewer than fifty programmers participated in the project, along with around twenty game system designers and fifty people working on visual creation (animation, scenery, characters, etc.). Thanks to financial support from Sony, many Japanese, Chinese and Taiwanese studios were sub-contracted during the production to help with graphics and visuals.

All in all, a particularly large team worked on *Project Beast* to make it a major PlayStation 4 exclusive. It relied heavily on the *Souls* community as a foundation for success, with the hope of attracting new players to the new and exciting game world. Maintaining a close eye on every detail of his work, Hidetaka Miyazaki had to work twice as hard to lead such a large team, in particular when his status within the company radically changed.

Previously majority-owned by shareholder Transcosmos, FromSoftware was bought out in April 2014 by Kadokawa Corporation, which acquired eighty percent of FromSoftware stock. This led to some major upheavals in the studio, particularly with the nomination of Hidetaka Miyazaki as company president. The promotion rewarded his total investment in the company since being hired in 2004, along with the financial boon he had brought the studio through the sale of the *Souls* games. However, though Miyazaki was happy with the new position, his top priority was to continue as a creator: there was no way he was going to leave his role as creative director. His conditions were accepted, and he therefore maintained his role as head of *Project Beast*, while naming Kazuhiro Hamatani (*Ninja Blade, Metal Wolf Chaos*) as lead game designer in order to reduce his workload. Miyazaki was appointed president on May 21, 2014, the official date that FromSoftware was purchased, at a time when the first rumors of *Project Beast* were reaching the public. The initial images showed significant common features with *Souls*, in particular a wall of fog that must be crossed to reach a boss.

In June 2014, at E3, FromSoftware officially announced the game and its true title, *Bloodborne*. It was presented in a computer-animated trailer, later used in the title screen of the final game. A few days later, another trailer was leaked with gameplay elements, which left the Internet teeming with excitement.[6] Although it is bloodier and more dynamic than its *Souls* predecessors, *Bloodborne* is nonetheless their direct descendant, also sharing their horror imagery.

On the Hunt for Nightmares

In the beginning, the *Bloodborne* project revolved around two major concepts: "exploring the unknown" and "fighting for one's life." At first glance, these themes could define any one of the *Souls* games, but the new game lent them new meaning. Miyazaki's goal was to produce more energetic battles, requiring players to take a more aggressive stance than in the *Souls* games. Equipment weight would no longer be taken into account, to encourage rolling and dodging. Armor was therefore replaced with clothing: the character became lighter and faster, but this also reinforced the player's feeling of vulnerability. The shield also no longer played much of a role.[7]

To make up for this lack of protection, *Bloodborne* introduced guns. Miyazaki explained this difficult choice in 2015 to *4Gamer*: "When I thought about how we could express this idea of more active battles in the game, I thought that guns could be effective. However, I didn't want to turn the game into a shooter. I wanted the guns to show their true usefulness in close quarters combat." By allowing players to interrupt enemy attacks at the right time with a well-placed shot, and then following up with a devastating ("visceral") counter-attack, guns act as a replacement for the *Souls* shield by serving as a "parry." This option must be used sparingly, however, due to the limited number of bullets available, which means that in spite of the guns, *Bloodborne* does not qualify as a "shooter."

Bloodborne adopts the same philosophy as the other FromSoftware games: players are thrown into a hostile environment laden with formidable challenges, and triumphing over the game's abominations gives players the same feelings of elation.

From Miyazaki's perspective, the interest lies in the way players make the experience their own. The choice of weapons and items is in line with the role-playing and customization logic. *Bloodborne* offers fewer weapons than *Souls*, which was

---

6. The leaked video also showed elements that eventually changed during production: the presence of new weapons and the location of Ebrietas, who was then located in the Grand Cathedral, where players fight Amelia in the final game.
7. The description of the wooden shield makes intentions obvious: "A crude wooden shield used by the masses who have arisen to join the hunt. Hunters do not normally employ shields, ineffectual against the strength of the beasts. Shields are nice, but not if they engender passivity."

intentional on Miyazaki's part. In 2015, he explained the following to *PlayStation Blog*: "In a way, the variety is still there, but it's absorbed down on a customization level, rather than in the quantity of actual weapons."[8] There are nevertheless many similarities between *Bloodborne* and the *Souls* games: Blood Vials stand in for the Estus Flask for healing, with a return to consumable items as in *Demon's Souls* and *Dark Souls II*; "blood echoes" are similar to souls, allowing players to level up by speaking with the Plain Doll at Hunter's Dream, whose role also mirrors that of the Maiden in Black in *Demon's Souls*, or the Emerald Herald from *Dark Souls II*.

Insight points replace *Dark Souls*' humanity points: they are used in the same way to interact online, with notable differences unique to the *Bloodborne* universe.

With the support of Sony's studios and experience, FromSoftware worked to define each piece of the battle mechanics to offer an experience that best reflects the feeling of "fighting for one's life." Pushing players to melee fight increases difficulty. To reward the fortitude of players during fights, the team came up with a system that would allow players to regain health over a short time after being hit by attacking the enemy. Miyazaki returned to this point in the official guide: "The regain system was something we came up with to encourage the sense that you're fighting a life-and-death struggle, one of the themes supporting this game's battle system. It changes the concept of your defense to something proactive, and it invites you to take a more fatalistic approach to fighting, encouraging that to-the-death feel. That was both the inspiration for, and the aim of, the regain system."

Miyazaki never saw difficulty as an aim in itself, but rather a method for producing the ever-important sense of achievement, which he had emphasized since the time of *Demon's Souls*. During an interview for *PlayStation LifeStyle* in October 2014, producer Masaaki Yamagiwa was quick to remind players that the key to success lies in strategy and patience: "We want to make sure that our message gets across that when you play the game, it doesn't require super reflexes or super finger movements. As long as you study the situation and learn the AIs, you can overcome the enemies." This was an obvious marketing pitch to reassure potential players, but also a reflection of the subtle approach to difficulty.

As in the *Souls* games, Miyazaki wanted to make sure that enemies inspire fear in *Bloodborne* players. The feeling of a fight to the death is heightened by the blood splattering that punctuates the fights. This was a risky aesthetic choice, since the creative director was anxious to keep this profusion of blood from becoming ridiculous. The attention paid to the art direction and frightening approach to the universe prevented this from happening.

---

8. Game mechanics and control vary greatly depending on the weapons, all of which can be used in two ways by toggling using the L1 button, to produce different hits and damage.

Mazes of terror

Hidetaka Miyazaki explained the appeal of horror to *PlayStation Blog*: "Whether it be nature or society, it's often a harsh and unkind environment—so that translates into my games." However, he tempered this statement by explaining that his interest in Lovecraftian horror above all supports the game's underlying approach: "It's not like horror is something we specifically go for, but it's important to have that sense of fear and terror because it directly ties into the player overcoming that and enhancing their sense of achievement."[9]

The *Bloodborne* universe, as we've seen, draws from Lovecraft's works and Gothic literature, which led the FromSoftware teams to go to Romania and the Czech Republic to draw inspiration from local architecture. There are also some Victorian touches to the medieval decor, such as the characteristic street lamps. With these elements, Miyazaki did not so much want to evoke 19th century London as the cities farther from the capital, by mixing architecture from old Gothic cities with that of the small towns that could have existed during the Victorian era. PS4 allowed the designers to achieve a high level of detail, as lead programmer Jun Itô explained in the making of: "I don't think the basic process for creating a game has changed much, but the memory storage and the number of CPU cores had much bigger increases during the transition from PS3 to PS4 versus the transition from PS2 to PS3." With his team of programmers, he focused on textures and the appearance of clothing: "We spent a lot of CPU power on simulating fabric, so all our time and effort as programmers will be rewarded if players feel the world has a softness to it."

The characters' appearance is also directly tied to the Victorian era through a number of clothing details. "While creating these designs, I thought about how to bring these hunters to life in different ways, through their unique expertise and personal preferences," explained artist Tetsu Takahashi in the making of, highlighting the importance of endowing each piece of the game with visual attributes that are both easily identifiable and coherent.

To immerse players in this universe, the designers aimed to bring together the most successful exploration aspects of *Demon's Souls* and *Dark Souls*. From the former, *Bloodborne* maintained the "hub" concept (here, Hunter's Dream) that can be accessed at any time using warp points spread out through the level; from the latter, it kept the idea of a world where areas are interconnected and shortcuts can be unlocked between them. When all is said and done, this element is less pronounced than

---

9. An interview from *IGN* in 2015 also highlights the fact that the *Souls* creator was not just interested in morbid worlds: "I've always had an interest in doing something colorful or heartwarming, but no one believes me," he said with a smile. However, in the official guide, he admits that he's "a little jealous of people who are scared of the dark."

in *Dark Souls*, due to the many levels of reality in *Bloodborne*: dream, main world, nightmare, etc.

As meticulous as ever about the creation of his levels, Miyazaki himself drew all of the maps for the game's areas.[10] His method of design and supervision had not changed: he wanted to make sure that the smallest details were in place, and that they lived up to his visual criteria, between sophistication and elegance. In 2015, he explained FromSoftware's current philosophy to 4Gamer.net: "When it comes to game design, our style is to not have a 'lead designer,' but instead have the director work directly with the individual designers."[11] Most of his team members were now used to working with him and knew his approach, particularly those in the art department who learned to decode the keywords he would give them to spark their creativity.

This time, Miyazaki chose to convey the fear of the unknown found in Lovecraft's terrifying stories. This objective inspired the concept artists, like Tetsu Takahashi: "I tried to depict the fear or panic people feel when faced with the unknown or something they don't understand. [...] Also, I tried to depict the darkness that is born from a damaged psyche."

A Sprawling Story

Miyazaki's cryptic method of narration—which requires decoding through close attention to item descriptions, listening to each character and observing the scenery—reaches its full potential here. In the official *Bloodborne* guide, he admits to his penchant for difficult-to-decode stories: "I kind of have a virtual pendulum in my mind. Generally, every other game I make is inscrutable and interpretive, then the next one is easier to understand. *Armored Core 4* was my first game as a director. That was really hard to understand, but then my next one, *For Answer*, was a lot more approachable. Then *Demon's Souls* was inscrutable, *Dark Souls* more approachable, and now we have *Bloodborne*."

His top priority is to leave players great leeway for interpretation: he loves to read the different theories and analyses floating around online. Although he writes the full stories himself, he asks for input from his team.[12] When development begins, he creates a forum in which he lays out all of his ideas, which are then discussed.[13]

---

10. With the exception of the Chalice Dungeons.
11. That said, in reality, there is always a "lead designer" in essential departments: sound, graphics, game system, etc. The difference here was that Miyazaki himself gave the directions to each department, coordinating and checking everything.
12. The same goes for item names, which he loves to choose himself: "I consider things like word origins, how it sounds in expressions, regional considerations, the whole thing." He remains receptive to suggestions from his team and from Frognation, the company charged with English localization since *Demon's Souls*.
13. As an anecdote, his favorite characters include the scholars such as Freke the Sage from *Demon's Souls*, and Iosefka and Willem from *Bloodborne*; he has expressed his disappointment that the latter are not very popular.

Bloodborne revolves around intellectual transcendence and the repression of impulses, as he specifies in the game's official guide: "The urge to transform into a beast is in conflict with the basic sense of humanity we all have. That humanity serves as a kind of shackle, keeping the transformation in its place. The stronger the shackle keeping that urge to transform in place, the larger the recoil once that shackle is finally broken." The *Bloodborne* creator sometimes draws inspiration from his new daily reality, as he mentioned humorously in 2015 to *The Guardian*: "Now I'm president, I get to meet a lot of other company presidents. They're such weird people. I'm fascinated by them. I use some of them as enemy characters in our games."

However, although he maintains full creative freedom, Miyazaki sometimes removes elements from the final game judged by his team to be much too dark, or crazy. He does not hesitate to acknowledge FromSoftware members who have developed ideas that impressed players. In the official guide, for instance, he notes that designer Masaru Yamamura implemented the Plain Doll's responses to players' gestures.

A Shared Experience

While the free online mode in PS3 led him to imagine the revolutionary asynchronous multiplayer model in *Demon's Souls*, Miyazaki had to rack his brains to come up with a new idea for *Bloodborne*. The online functionalities were certainly very similar to the *Souls* games (messages on the ground left by other players, the ability to invade or be invaded, factions, etc.), but the Chalice Dungeons represent a noteworthy new addition.

Inspired by PlayStation 4's "Share Play" feature, and by the increasing buzz among the Souls community,[14] Miyazaki came up with the concept for these dungeons that can be randomly generated and shared among players. The goal is to give players the constant pleasure of rediscovering the game. With access to "unlimited content," Miyazaki hopes that players will share as much information as possible and help one another to complete the dungeons. For him, the idea was not so much to draw inspiration from rogue-likes (with random dungeons as one of their traditional characteristics), but rather to encourage discussion between players. As with the online mode of *Dark Souls II* being developed at the same time, FromSoftware responded to the numerous requests from fans by facilitating connections between players in *Bloodborne*.

---

14. The series creator confided the following in *PlayStation Blog*: "I'll go online and enjoy reading what [the players] have to say." He even says that he's happy every time people ask why he decided to make difficult games. The thing that surprised him most were the speedruns, an approach that he had not planned for at all when designing the games.

Victory and Extensions

The final months of the design process were devoted to multiple test sessions to root out bugs, while an entire team worked to balance the level of difficulty. The FromSoftware and Sony teams did what they could to optimize the game, while aiming for an average of thirty frames per second. Their goal was to achieve the best compromise between the smoothness required by the fights and the many elements that needed to be displayed. Although Miyazaki has said that the PS4 proved to be easy to program, allowing for the design of complex architectures and highly detailed animations, the final result was not as perfect as was hoped.

In its worldwide release from March 24-27, 2015,[15] *Bloodborne* suffered very long loading times and occasional drops in frame rate, a problem that had already affected *Dark Souls* at times. FromSoftware quickly did what it could to release patches, a situation that frustrated Miyazaki, but which he believed necessary: "I'm sure users would prefer it if we released something free of imperfections from the get-go, and that's a perfectly reasonable expectation to have, but realistically speaking, I think patches are a necessary thing."

Despite these problems, the game received almost unanimous positive reviews from critics and the public alike. Over one million copies sold in less than a month, and sales broke the two-million mark during the summer of 2015: a big success, surpassing the already high expectations of Sony and reaching the same heights as the *Souls* games. *Bloodborne* thus established itself as one of the major PS4 exclusives, but also as one of the most popular games for the new generation of consoles. And for the first time in the history of the series, the game was dubbed into several languages (English, French, Spanish, Japanese, etc.), while the previous episodes had only been produced in English.

Soon, a DLC was in production, taking advantage of this success and giving players an extension of the *Bloodborne* world. According to producer Masaaki Yamagiwa, two DLCs were originally planned, but FromSoftware soon decided to meld them into one single adventure, to be called *The Old Hunters*. Miyazaki wanted to take the opportunity to clear up some confusion about the plot, by suggesting some origins for the Plain Doll and the Hunter's Dream, along with the story of one of the Great Ones referenced in the game, Kos.

Based on player feedback that there were not enough weapons in the original game, the FromSoftware team also decided to supplement the DLC with over ten new weapons with varied characteristics. *The Old Hunters* was created with great care,

---

15. The release date had initially been set for February 6, 2015, but in November 2014, the date was pushed back by a month and a half in order to fix some details and problems noticed by players during closed alpha testing, which took place in three-hour test sessions on October 1, 3 and 5, 2014.

introducing three additional areas and five new bosses. Thanks to support from Sony, the DLC had a high enough budget to record new music with an orchestra, so that it wouldn't clash with the *Bloodborne* soundtrack.[16]

The Old Hunters was released on November 24, 2015, and was greeted with praise similar to that of the original game. This was in spite of some criticism regarding the difficulty of one boss (a tad too difficult), and the scarcity of items used to optimize the new weapons.[17] These reservations were minor compared to the positive aura surrounding *Bloodborne*. Hidetaka Miyazaki had prevailed: he had successfully completed an original work without the name "*Souls*," but with the same spirit as these other games. This victory confirmed what was said of him in the "making of" by Masami Yamamoto (head of external development for Japan Studio): "[Miyazaki-san] creates games which resonate with people regardless of the fact that they were made in Japan or that there are cultural differences between Japan and other countries."

---

16. The soundtrack for the first *Dark Souls*' DLC, *Artorias of the Abyss*, was not recorded with real instruments as in the original game. For more information on *Bloodborne*'s music and a behind-the-scenes look at its creation, check out the chapter on this topic.
17. The patch 1.09 fixed this problem, allowing players to exchange a Blood Rock for sixty insight points.

DARK SOULS

ダークソウル

BEYOND THE GRAVE

CHAPTER TWO
UNIVERSE

Introduction to new themes

Demon's Souls and *Dark Souls* explored the themes of death and souls, and *Bloodborne* strayed little from this approach, building its universe and story around other themes just as rich in symbolism: blood, madness, the moon, and the hunt (and by extension, bestiality), this time at the heart of the plot. The plot is complex, much more so than that of the *Souls* games, tackling a wide array of subjects, such as species evolution and different planes of existence, while also touching on the unquenchable desire to create life. This complexity is heightened by the use of proper nouns with strange spellings, such as "Byrgenwerth" and "Pthumeru," and above all by the lack of precision regarding many of the essential elements in the *Bloodborne* universe. Ironing out the story therefore requires more conjecture and interpretation than the *Souls* games did. No matter! Hidetaka Miyazaki's singular narration invites us to do just that. Hints are tucked away in every nook and cranny, within every description and the shortest dialogue, in the attire worn by the characters, and even sometimes in their voices or gestures, along with the music and the placement of items. *Bloodborne* brilliantly builds on the narrative legacy of the *Souls* games, transcending them with its new themes.

The Universe's Principles

Before presenting the story behind *Bloodborne*, it's worth taking some time to look at the universe's guiding principles, which are quite different from the genre's classics.

Humans and Great Ones

First, we need to start by distinguishing the different types of beings found in *Bloodborne*. Humans are the game's primary species, or at least serve as its focal point. The story revolves around the human city of Yharnam and its surrounding areas. Other far-off lands are referenced in the game, without much detail—we don't often meet humans from these parts.

Besides the residents of Yharnam, the game also refers to the Pthumerians, subjects of a lost ancient kingdom. Vestiges of their mysterious civilization were discovered long ago within the labyrinths buried beneath Yharnam. Archaeological research has shown that the Pthumerians possess strange powers, derived from divine entities known as the "Great Ones."

The Great Ones are *Bloodborne*'s gods,[18] or at least are viewed as such by humans, who are fascinated by the immortality and power of these mysterious superior beings. Their occult power is difficult and dangerous to wield: anyone who comes into contact with it for too long will lose their mind. The Great Ones are scornful of humans, but envy them for their fertility: any child born to a Great One is stillborn. There are actually several species of Great Ones, some of whom are met by the player. For instance, the Amygdalas are a relatively common type of Great One. Their shape is unusual: that of a giant spider crossed with an anthropomorphic skeleton. These beings live in another plane of existence, which generally remains invisible and inaccessible. However, this unseen dimension interferes with that of the humans on rare occasions:

---

18. These Great Ones are similar to the "Great Old Ones" from Howard Phillips Lovecraft's works, down to their very name. Later, we'll look more closely at the parallels between the game and this author's writings.

when the moon turns red, an event we will discuss in further detail. Other Great Ones appear to be unique individuals, through their shape or habits, such as the Moon Presence, Kos, or Formless Oedon.

Planes of Existence

There are several different planes of existence in the *Bloodborne* universe. Although most of these planes remain independent, some intertwine at times, leading to unexpected apparitions or changes in the mental or physical state of the residents in one of these planes. For example, as we noted above, the red Blood Moon reveals the many Amygdalas; they can be found peacefully perched atop the buildings around the city of Yharnam. When players accrue more than forty Insight points, they can see these monstrosities squatting on the city's roofs, long before the Blood Moon appears. This detail proves that the other plane exists, invisible to most mortals.

There are other planes of existence, such as the Cosmos. Several Great Ones draw some of their powers from the Cosmos, or even originate there. Ebrietas, for instance, is known as the Daughter of the Cosmos. When the One Reborn boss appears, summoned by the bells rung by the magicians from the ramparts, we can quickly spot a nebula with a starry backdrop. According to the description of the Choir Bell "that projects an arcane sound across planes of existence," it is possible to establish communication with these planes using carillons: we can call other players, invade them, or as in the example of the One Reborn, summon a superior being.

We will note a final, distinct type of plane of existence: that of dreams and nightmares, where the most powerful Great Ones live.

Dreams and Nightmares

There are levels that take place within dreams and nightmares, where some universal laws from the real world seem not to apply. The Hunter's Dream, the Hunter's Nightmare (in *The Old Hunters* DLC) and the Nightmare of Mensis are the three known dream- or nightmare-like locations in *Bloodborne*. In these twisted, phantasmagorical reflections of previously visited locations, the normal laws of physics apply, so that players can explore them like other real worlds. Yet some details remind us that this is a dream world. For example, once the area's boss has been defeated, the normal "Prey Slaughtered" is replaced by "Nightmare Slain." Furthermore, dreams do not contain the chronological indications of the game's main quest: the progression that begins with twilight, then the small moon at nightfall, then the majestic full moon, and finally the blood-red moon. Dreams and nightmares are also associated with the moon, but the moon's light is constant, no matter the stage of the game, as if time stands still. A final, unusual characteristic of dreams and nightmares is that they were created by Great Ones: the Hunter's Dream was made by the Moon Presence; Kos created the Hunter's Nightmare, and the Nightmare of Mensis ends when Mergo's Wet Nurse is defeated. Some Great Ones, such as the Amygdalas, are not present in dreams, perhaps due to a hierarchy between the different Great Ones. Players must still face one of these beings in an ethereal, surreal location, the Nightmare Frontier. We will come back to each of these dreams and nightmares, along with their creators, in our presentation of the game's story, but it is worth noting that these surreal locations belong to the Great Ones, while the real world is essentially occupied by human beings.

It seems likely that these different planes of existence, including dreams and nightmares, are built in layers one on top of the next. There are some hints throughout the adventure that suggest this. Our primary clue is that from some areas, you can glimpse parts of different locations. For instance, from the Fishing Hamlet, you can view the tops of the Yharnam buildings emerging from the depths of the ocean. But the city has never been flooded—it is simply located in the lower layer, in the Yharnam plane of existence. Above the Fishing Hamlet (in the Hunter's Nightmare created by Kos), there is the location called the Nightmare Frontier. From here, it is possible to spot the masts of ships clashing far below, from the dizzying heights upon which the Frontier floats: of course, these are the ships from the Fishing Hamlet. Finally, the outline of the Nightmare of Mensis castle appears far off, above in the fog of the Nightmare Frontier. This vertical structure is more obvious when sounds[19] are heard, deeply disturbing certain residents of these worlds. The noise made by a neighbor directly above or below will be much more noticeable (and irritating in the long term) than a far-off racket.

Blood and Insight

Before diving head first into the fascinating *Bloodborne* universe, there are a couple of final concepts to cover: Blood and Insight. Humans use Blood or Insight to attain the "eldritch Truth," a superior stage in their evolution, equivalent to that of the Pthumerians. However, Blood and Insight have opposing properties. Blood stirs up beasthood, and by extension, physical power and skill, while Insight inflames the spirit and knowledge, thus intellectual abilities. When a human takes on too much Blood, their level of Insight goes down, and they transform into a "blood-starved beast." On the other hand, gaining too much Insight brings them to the status

19. In certain conditions, it is possible to hear a baby's cries. We'll come back to this detail later on.

of a Lumenwood or a Celestial, similar to the occult power of the Great Ones, which unfortunately may lead to madness. Humans must be moderate in their consumption of Blood and Insight. However, many have tried to attain the power of the Great Ones, and players will cross swords with a number of the resulting beasts and celestials throughout the adventure.

Backstory

Although a chronological approach would start with the ancient Pthumerian civilization, and then follow the series of events that caused it to fall, we prefer to retrace the game's story from the viewpoint of the city of Yharnam. The first events recounted in *Bloodborne* are indeed related to the city of Yharnam, or rather to its surroundings. The story begins with a strange discovery made by researchers from Byrgenwerth...

Byrgenwerth, Back to the Discovery

Byrgenwerth College was a major site of higher learning not far from central Yharnam, between the edges of the Forbidden Woods and the shores of Moonside Lake. Scholars at the college conducted productive research, which put the school on the map. One day, archaeologists from Byrgenwerth discovered the vestiges of an ancient civilization below Yharnam: the Pthumerians. The exploration of the first underground labyrinths, and then the catacombs, would change the fate of Yharnam's inhabitants forever. Their destiny rested on the shoulders of three individuals, with fates as different as they were tragic.

Willem, Laurence and Gehrman were all originally at Byrgenwerth College. Respectively representing wisdom, strength and agility, the three very different companions shared one common goal: the archaeological study of the people of Pthumeru. Who were these people? How did they live? And what caused this fascinating civilization to fall? These questions remained unanswered, until a new discovery blew everything else away. Some remains led them to believe that the Pthumerians were actually superhuman beings. This unexpected revelation presented humans with the possibility that they, too, could attain a higher level of being, and Pthumeru became the focus of study at Byrgenwerth.

Continued excavation led the scholars to discover the existence of the Great Ones, superior beings worshipped by the people of Pthumeru—the Pthumerians even called themselves the "Guardians of the Great Ones." Archaeologists eventually found an ancient blood sample (known as the "Old Blood") containing the Great Ones' power. This blood was researched meticulously in the hope of discovering how to raise the current human species to the same level as the Pthumerians. This transcendence was given the name "eldritch Truth."

Following this incredible archaeological discovery, some hostile creatures, beasts, began to appear. Gehrman, who was well versed in combat (unlike his associates), took it upon himself to eradicate this menace. He became the First Hunter, isolating himself from the scholarly world of Byrgenwerth. In Yharnam, Gehrman set up in the Workshop, where he trained other hunters in his special techniques and fight moves to employ against the savage violence of their enemies. However, Willem was the first to draw the connection between the appearance of the beasts and the research conducted on the old blood. He felt that these creatures presented too great a danger, and that the research should be halted. This led to the long disagreement between Willem and Laurence, who remained convinced of the merits of studying the blood.

When looking for sources of information on the Great Ones other than this insidious ruby-colored substance, Willem and his disciples focused their research on sites other than the Pthumerian crypts, outside of Yharnam. Their curiosity and hard work led them to a fishing hamlet, where they discovered the remains of a Great One that was different from those worshipped by the Pthumerians, and hitherto unknown by the Byrgenwerth researchers. This Great One, known as Kos, was closely tied to the ocean, where its strength seemed to originate. The fishermen began worshipping this Great One, and over time started losing touch with reality: the hamlet grew more isolated and its inhabitants began morphing into deformed creatures, as pale as the moon.

No one knows exactly what took place between Willem and the fishermen, but the accusations of the hamlet's priest suggest that Willem committed sacrilege towards Kos (or "Mother Kos," as the villagers call it), which was pregnant. The Great Ones were never able to reproduce, however, and all of their offspring were stillborn. On every newborn cadaver, one third of an umbilical cord remained, which soon became known as the "Cord of the Eye."

It seems that Willem stole the cord from Kos. This discovery would radically change the researcher's approach to his study of the human species and its fate. The cord was exactly what he had been looking for since he had given up experimenting on the Old Blood: it represented a new means of attaining the eldritch Truth. He thus discovered "Insight," which considerably increased his own wisdom and intelligence, allowing him to near the power of the Great Ones. The One Third of Umbilical Cord gave him "eyes on the inside," and provided him with a superhuman mind.

Armed with this discovery, Willem returned to see Byrgenwerth. During his absence, Laurence had continued to supervise the research and experiments conducted on the Old Blood. The beasts multiplying throughout Yharnam had begun to pose a serious problem for the city's residents. The scholars of Byrgenwerth feared the blood as much as it fascinated them. One of them pilfered a sample and fled to Cainhurst Castle, where he founded the clan of the Vilebloods, composed of nobles who became vampires—immortal, bloodthirsty monsters that had never before existed in this world. With everything that was happening, the population's fears continued to grow.

"Fear the old blood." Before becoming the characteristic saying of Byrgenwerth, this sentence was voiced by the man who became known as Master Willem. His work on the eyes and Insight, which seemed to be more effective and safer than the blood research, made him the college's uncontested authority. However, Laurence felt differently. Although he had maintained deep respect for his former friend Willem, he decided to leave Byrgenwerth and recommence his studies on the Old Blood. In Yharnam, he founded a new institution: the Healing Church.

The Foundation of the Healing Church

The Healing Church was founded with the same ambitions as those associated with Oedon,[20] known as "The Formless." This new institution and the Great One in question shared the same mission. One of the churches built was named the Oedon Chapel, which attests to the close ties that the Healing Church maintained with blood. In the Yharnam Cathedral Ward, the priests began to distribute free therapeutic blood that could be ministered to those who were ill. This blood was different from the Old Blood, which contaminated humans: it was created by Laurence following changes to the original blood, and showed incredible healing powers, giving those who took it a highly unexpected vital force. Invalids began flocking to the doors of the Healing Church, begging for blood to ease their sufferings. The Church grew quickly and began to take on a new structure, with the creation of the ranks of Vicar, Blood Saint and Church Hunter.

Laurence became the First Vicar, some kind of quasi-supervisor known for their gold pendant with Willem's famous adage engraved on it: "Fear the old blood." In spite of his attachment to the blood, Laurence had not forgotten the warning of his old friend from Byrgenwerth.

The Blood Saints, for their part, served as living sources of the Blood Ministration: the women continually provided the blood used by the Healing Church. The first of the Blood Saints was named Adeline, held prisoner in the Church's laboratories.

20. "Both Oedon, and its inadvertent worshippers, surreptitiously seek the precious blood," reads the Formless Oedon Rune. Oedon is a Great One known for its interest in the blood, which aligns with the Healing Church's mission.

She was kept tied to a chair, with a syringe constantly implanted in her arm to withdraw her precious blood, which would then be sent to Yharnam to heal illnesses. The horrifying experiments conducted by the priests were kept secret, and the laboratories were set up far from the old city, not far from the miserable Fishing Hamlet, where Willem robbed Kos of the Cord of the Eye. Due to the danger presented by the Old Blood, a new formula had to be developed. A curious interaction was discovered between the blood and the Celestial Water, which came from the ocean where Kos had arisen. The water contained unique properties from this Great One, in particular Insight. The laboratories were then supervised by the benevolent Maria, who was admired by her experiment subjects. Sadly, the research conducted on this new blood had catastrophic effects. The heads of the unfortunate test subjects blew up like balloons, and they eventually went totally mad. By adjusting the dose, she managed to produce a relatively stable mixture. As the first survivor to truly produce blood, Adeline was declared a saint. But this miracle came at the cost of hundreds of horribly mutilated victims, including Saint Adeline herself, with her giant, misshapen head. Ironically for Laurence and his Healing Church, this new formula of blood and Kos's Celestial Water resulted from research that was actually very similar to the work done by Willem on the eyes and Insight.

Experiments were conducted in the laboratories on other people, which led them to transform into new creatures. Although these individuals remained human-like and two-legged, they were no longer human beings due to their blueish skin, and above all the monstrosity of their bodies and limbs. Their heads were frightfully deformed: some even looked like a cluster of thick, short branches, which earned them the name "Lumenwood."[21] They drew their power from the Cosmos, and were the first "phantasms" to appear since the fall of Pthumeru. Described as the confidants[22] or messengers[23] of the Great Ones, the Lumenwood were the first form of humanity to be elevated towards the dark powers of the Great Ones,[24] in contrast to the beasts, who formed due to the blood's impact on the primitive part of the bestiality inherent to every human being.

---

21. The description of the Milkweed Rune indicates that he who becomes a Lumenwood "peers towards the sky, feeding phantasms in its luscious bed." The density of the "luscious bed," a generous metaphor for their atrocious head deformities, depends on the Lumenwood's strength. The "Living Failure" boss fight pits the avatar against a group of Lumenwoods within a glowing garden of sunflowers. Moreover, we note that the giant floral form at the center of the arena recalls the head of the avatar when he acquires the Milkweed Rune. The avatar becomes a Lumenwood, and his head morphs into… broccoli.
22. The game provides the following description of the Empty Phantasm Shell: "Empty invertebrate shell that is said to be a familiar of a Great One."
23. In the description of the Augur of Ebrietas, Phantasms are described as "the invertebrates known to be the augurs of the Great Ones."
24. The Celestials, created later by the Choir, are a second example. They have the same scientific origins as Lumenwoods (humans subjected to experiments) and similar physical traits, as well as a close relationship with the Cosmos. We'll come back to this.

Even though the laboratory research produced a formula that balanced Blood and Insight, to produce a fluid perfect for the Blood Ministration, it was not used in most cases. The laboratories were abandoned after the premature death of Maria, and because it was impossible to produce enough high-quality blood for all of the Yharnam invalids. Added to this, only Saint Adeline had remained sane. The Healing Church decided to halt its research due to the cost (in experiments subjects, and Celestial Water) and limited quality of blood produced. The church resolved to use less rich,[25] yet more dangerous blood, which was likely to cause patients to transform into beasts. These beasts therefore continued to multiply throughout the streets of Yharnam.

Laurence, the First Vicar of the Healing Church, put together a team of Pursuers to slow the proliferation of beasts. The hunters of the Healing Church, also known as the Holy Blades, swapped the traditional lightweight hunting items used formerly by Gehrman for heavy arms and armor, which offered them better protection and greater effectiveness against the beasts. These specific items were designed and produced by the Healing Church Workshop, created for the occasion.

Thus assembled and better equipped than simple hunters, these new paladins, led by the charismatic Ludwig, soon restored order in the darkest corners of the city. The weakest of the invalids who had become dependent on the Blood Ministration and succumbed to beasthood were eliminated. The Healing Church built up its power day by day. This relative peace did not last, however, because a merciless curse would soon strike the city: the Beastly Scourge.

The Beastly Scourge

The Beastly Scourge began with the appearance of the Ashen Blood, a monstrous poison that affected many of Yharnam's inhabitants. The epidemic's victims swarmed to the doors of the Healing Church to receive the Blood Ministration,[26] which was in fact poor-quality blood, as we have already seen. Soon, almost the entire population was under the power of this blood, which of course meant that the number of beast transformations also skyrocketed.

The number of beasts grew so high that the Church Hunters, who were greatly undermanned, had to recruit many Pursuers, primarily from the population. The recruits were inexperienced and weakened, and even with weapons they were not

25. This "cheaper" blood would be produced by the other Blood Saint we meet in the game: Adella. It is possible to obtain blood samples from Saint Adeline and Adella; by comparing them, we can see that Saint Adeline's blood is indeed much more effective than that of Saint Adella.
26. We should note that the Blood Ministration is administered using impressive syringes. Was this how the epidemic spread? Since "Bloodborne" means "transmitted by the blood," the game's title could simply refer to the origin of the Beastly Scourge, the event that led to the downfall of humanity.

especially effective against the beasts. Worse still, most of these recruits eventually lost their minds, and many were lost to the Hunter's Nightmare.[27] The Healing Church was well aware of this chaotic situation, but kept this a secret,[28] continuing to extend its reach by dispensing the Blood Ministration to as many people as it could.

Yharnam's inhabitants were not the first to face the Beastly Scourge. As archaeological evidence would show in the land of Loran, the Pthumerians were also afflicted by this scourge following peculiar medical experiments similar to the Healing Church's Blood Ministration. This similarity suggests a cyclical rise and fall of human civilizations.

Exactly why the Pthumerians disappeared remains a mystery. Nevertheless, the vestiges of the ancient people suggest to believe that they went down an almost identical path to that of the Yharnamites: discovery of the power of the Great Ones, desire for the eldritch Truth, experimental medications, appearance of the Beastly Scourge, and later on (we'll come back to this), the attempt of a Great One to have a child with a human. The major steps of rise and fall can be found in both civilizations, and Pthumeru's ruins did not bode well for Yharnam, which would never recover from the Beastly Scourge and eventually succumbs totally to confusion and madness.

The Occult Rituals of the School of Mensis

Although the Healing Church was always opposed to the philosophy of Byrgenwerth, and even prohibited entry to Byrgenwerth College from the city's districts, some of the church's members did not share this point of view. This was why certain scholarly priests, followed by some researchers from Byrgenwerth, decided to join the School of Mensis.

Led by the eccentric Micolash, the School of Mensis was created within Yahar'gul, known as the Unseen Village. The research here was different from that conducted by the Healing Church (on blood) and by Byrgenwerth (on eyes, or Insight), but their primary objective was still to enter directly into contact with a Great One. To do this, the School of Mensis gathered many test subjects. They recruited vile mercenaries and charged them with kidnapping as many people as they could by pretending to be benevolent hunters; their unfortunate victims were then taken to the prisons of Yahar'gul.[29]

---

27. In the first area of the DLC, players face some of these former hunters who fell prey to the nightmare.
28. A shameful secret, often mentioned in the DLC, particularly in the dialogue of Simon, a former Church Hunter.
29. Throughout the adventure, players meet some of these kidnappers. Players may even wind up in a cell of the Unseen Village if they are "killed" by one of them. This provides an alternate way to visit this area earlier in the game—since access is denied until later—, or to meet and free the Blood Saint Adella.

The experiments of the School of Mensis remained secret; no one knew their true nature or extent. Some were partially successful: many Amygdalas began wandering around the roofs and facades of Yahar'gul's buildings, intrigued by the powerful rituals performed in this area.

Micolash, however, was not satisfied with these first rituals. Could he see all of the Amygdalas, the Great Ones invisible to humans, in a dimension that only appears when the moon turns red? The statues of Amygdalas found in Yahar'gul prove that the members of the School of Mensis at least knew what they looked like, but maybe they never actually saw how many of these creatures there were, unaware that what they were searching for was right in front of them the whole time. Their rituals only intensified. At the same time, the Mensis Cages were built, with great dark power: they were placed around the head of their test subjects, allowing a handful of individuals to enter into contact with the Great Ones. No one survived this, however, and their desiccated bodies were eventually strewn throughout the roads of Yahar'gul with their Mensis Cages still bolted to their heads. Micolash was one of them. Through the ritual, he was able to make contact with Mergo's Wet Nurse in the Nightmare of Mensis, and it agreed to take in Micolash, who was nevertheless dead in the real world. Micolash's ritual had some major consequences on what followed, including the disastrous Beastly Scourge, with the appearance of the Blood Moon, exposing even more humans to their beasthood.[30] At a time when the number of beasts was already skyrocketing, the Mensis ritual led to a veritable catastrophe, sealing the fate of the Unseen Village, now in the hands of monsters.

Along with the expansion of the School of Mensis, a similar organization known as the Choir began to amass a worrying amount of power.

---

30. Throughout the adventure, the player can find inscriptions referring to Mensis, beasts and the blood moon in the cells of Yahar'gul and in Byrgenwerth College. One such inscription reads, "Madmen toil surreptitiously in rituals to beckon the moon," where the "madmen" in question are members of the School of Mensis, accused of summoning the Blood Moon, associated with the multiplication of beasts. This correlation is also found in the following two inscriptions: "When the red moon hangs low, the line between man and beast is blurred," and "The Mensis ritual must be stopped, lest we all become beasts."

The Audience of the Choir

Like the School of Mensis,[31] the masked society of the Choir primarily consists of scholars, while remaining attached to the Healing Church. Its members were among the elite of the ecclesiastic order: high-ranking priests along with scholars who wished to continue Byrgenwerth's work. Although members of the church, they remained close to Willem's school of thought, also focusing on Insight over Blood to reach the eldritch Truth. The method they used was what distinguished them from other organizations. The group had decided to recommence the archaeological research conducted in the Pthumerian Catacomb labyrinth. They eventually unearthed a series of chalices with surprising properties. Then, they made an extraordinary discovery, the first since those of Byrgenwerth many years earlier: the Great Isz Chalice, which the members of the Choir brought back with them. Following extensive research on the precious chalice, they were able to obtain an audience with a Great One, Ebrietas, Daughter of the Cosmos.

Ebrietas agreed to share some of its knowledge with members of the Choir: knowledge heretofore inaccessible to humans. This revelation would change the group's mission, as they turned their attention towards the Cosmos and the divine, and thus towards the eldritch Truth.[32]

The knowledge shared by Ebrietas allowed members of the Choir to create Celestials from human subjects. The skin of these subjects turned blue, and their heads ballooned out, though they remained less monstrous than their predecessors from the Healing Church, the Lumenwoods. They grew similar to the Great Ones, gaining a dark power both formidable and mysterious. Most of the test subjects were children: the Upper Cathedral Orphanage was a focal point for the Choir members' experiments. The resulting Celestials were kept secret, including the Choir's masterpiece, the Celestial Emissary; all of the places where the Choir conducted its tests were strewn with caskets, smaller than those found on every Yharnam street corner. A final clue indicating the origins of the Celestials is their small size: they all have

---

31. The Choir and the School of Mensis were in competition. In the Nightmare of Mensis, Edgar, a spy for the Choir, attacks players when they cross the bridge that leads to the main section of the castle: the moonlit setting makes for an unforgettable duel. Edgar's presence in this nightmare attests to the rivalry between the two organizations. The Choir monitored the School of Mensis's movements; after Micolash's ritual succeeded, Edgar found himself trapped in the Great One's nightmare. In a passage that leads to the fight against Ebrietas, in the Choir's quarters, it is possible to summon a man named Damian from the School of Mensis.

32. Members of the Choir had a Cosmic Eye Watcher Badge, in the shape of an eye, which contained a glimpse of the Cosmos where the iris would normally be. "The eye signifies the very Cosmos," explains the item's description. "The Choir stumbled upon an epiphany, very suddenly and quite by accident. Here we stand, feet planted in the earth, but might the Cosmos be very near us, only just above our heads?" Beyond the sky, and invisible to the human eye, the Cosmos appears from time to time throughout the game: when the One Reborn is summoned, for example, or when the Lumenwoods or Celestials use their magic and a meteor shower rains down through the dimensions to pelt the player.

a child-like frame. Never had humans been so close to attaining the eldritch Truth. Experiments on Insight and eyes had also begun to bear fruit.

On his end, Willem had continued to research the Cord of the Eye he had stolen from the Great One Kos years earlier in the Fishing Hamlet.

Rom, or the Elevation of Byrgenwerth

The departure of Laurence for Byrgenwerth following his disagreements with Willem marked the beginning of the end for the college. Faced with the inconsistency of his school's teachings[33] and the insanity of his most faithful collaborators,[34] Willem eventually isolated himself to focus on his "eyes on the inside," a considerable source of Insight, which he had obtained from the Cord of the Eye.[35] The Healing Church ordered for access to Byrgenwerth to be closed off or restricted by a password, thus sealing Willem's fate.

The Byrgenwerth provost continued to take in a great amount of Insight. He saw the "eyes on the inside" as an inestimable gift, and their hold over his mind eventually led him to cover his own eyes with a metal mask. He continued to rise towards the eldritch Truth, but not as much as one of his protégés who had remained by his side: Rom.[36] According to Micolash, from the School of Mensis, Kos gave Rom many eyes. Rom's face is indeed covered with eyes, recalling the Amygdalas. Rom's transformation brought it closer to the Great Ones. Its mind was elevated in the way of the Celestials, until the power of the Great Ones caused it to lose its sanity. It was reduced to a hollow shell, so to speak, earning it the name of the "Vacuous Spider."

---

33. "The focus not on knowledge, or thought, but on pure pretension would surely bring Master Willem to despair, if only he knew": this we read on the Student Uniform, referring to the degradation of the Byrgenwerth education.
34. "Willem kept two loyal servants back at Byrgenwerth. When they were sent into the labyrinth they encountered the eldritch Truth and went mad. One became the password gatekeeper, while Dores became a graveguard of the forest. Both remained loyal, even in madness," explains the description of the Graveguard Mask. In spite of their ravaged minds, Willem's most faithful followers therefore continued to do his bidding. The password gatekeeper guarded access to Byrgenwerth, only allowing those who would whisper the correct password ("Fear the old blood") to enter, through the massive door that separates the Cathedral Ward from the Forbidden Woods. Dores, the "graveguard," met a gruesome end, to judge by his set, which can be found scattered in the Forbidden Woods, not far from the cemetery that he once guarded. Willem's faithful servant was no doubt attacked by one of the colossal boars in the area (known fittingly as "maneater boars" in the official guide).
35. "Eyes symbolize the truth Master Willem sought in his research. Disillusioned by the limits of human intellect, Master Willem looked to beings from higher planes for guidance, and sought to line his brain with eyes in order to elevate his thoughts," explains the Eye Rune. After gaining "eyes on the inside" using the Cord of the Eye taken from Kos, Willem could no longer live without the eyes and Insight. Insight served as a means of spiritual elevation and pushed the limits of the human mind, which profoundly changed his vision of the world.
36. Rom's exact identity remains a mystery; however, this person, or thing, would stay with Willem until the very end. Did he discover Rom in the Pthumerian crypts, or was Rom once a member of an overly zealous group of students? No one knows.

Willem would soon discover what happened to his protégé. He began to see the futility of his search for the eldritch Truth. No matter how close one may get to the knowledge of the Great Ones, humans would remain small specks of dust compared to these superior entities. It was pointless to think humans could ever reach their level.

Then, up in the sky, appeared a red moon. Micolash had successfully completed his ritual: the veil was lifted from another dimension, and humans had never known such a danger. Now, they were in the grips of their darkest bestiality. Aware of the threat posed by the Blood Moon, Willem called upon the dark powers of Rom to create a barrier of protection to hide this other dimension. Rom was confined to the Moonside Lake, where it would spend its life working to preserve humanity. Although it could not save humanity from the Beastly Scourge, its sacrifice allowed it to slow the species' extinction.

Learning the Eldritch Truth

The various organizations we've seen so far were all working to learn the eldritch Truth: the elevation of the human species to a higher state of being and thought. However, they all used different methods in the hope of reaching this objective: Byrgenwerth, with Willem, aimed to expand the mind through the accumulation of Insight, in particular by using the eyes taken from the Great One Kos, and widespread use of the Madman's Knowledge and Great One's Wisdom; the School of Mensis and Micolash tried to enter directly into contact with a Great One; the members of the Choir relied primarily on the knowledge passed on to them by Ebrietas, which allowed them to create the Celestials from humans, who achieved a status almost as elevated as that of the Great Ones, drawing their power from the Cosmos; finally, the Healing Church and Laurence focused their efforts on researching blood.

Although research on blood did not solve the issue of the eldritch Truth, the Healing Church continued to use it, but with a new objective: increasing its power over the population and making the people dependent on the Blood Ministration. The Choir's experiments produced the Celestials, but this was another failure. Although these creatures were powerful, with ties to the Cosmos, they were not Great Ones, and never would be. Finally came Byrgenwerth College and the School of Mensis: they were able to find a concrete path to the eldritch Truth. Willem and Rom obtained the "eyes on the inside" from Kos, and Micolash gave them the opportunity to inhabit a Great One's nightmare. Micolash's ritual led to the appearance of the Blood Moon, a disastrous event for his fellow men: a critical situation stopped at the very last moment by Willem. Although chagrined by the limitations of the human species, he found the courage to halt human extinction using Rom, leaving humanity's fate up in the air... that is, until the game's events begin.

The Encounter Between Gehrman and the Moon Presence

No one knows exactly when Gehrman decided to withdraw from Yharnam. Perhaps the massive Beastly Scourge had crushed all of his hope of seeing his people escape the darkness. Or perhaps he isolated himself due to the death, in the Healing Church laboratories, of his former student Maria, with whom Gehrman was very close. Either way, he was no longer seen in his Old Workshop, which was soon totally abandoned. The new hunters were recruited by other groups: the Powder Kegs, the Vilebloods of Cainhurst, the League, the Holy Blades of Ludwig, or the Executioners of Logarius. All of these groups were so involved in local goings-on that they had almost forgotten their original mission: to eradicate the beasts and protect the population.

Gehrman, the First Hunter, one of the original trio of friends with Laurence and Willem, he who had played such an important role in the history of Yharnam, no longer had a place in the world. Although the circumstances are unclear, Gehrman had dealings with the Moon Presence. This two-legged, scraggy Great One with red and black flesh is distinctive by its many tentacles sprouting from its head, like a monstrous, sprawling head of hair. The Moon Presence was one of the Great Ones to live in the dream and nightmare dimension. Probably after having captured Gehrman, it set up the backdrop for the Hunter's Dream to satisfy the desires of its "guest"[37] by recreating the First Hunter's Workshop.[38] It also gave Gehrman's Doll consciousness: this doll was the result of very fine craftsmanship, created based on the model of Gehrman's former student Maria. She would therefore keep him company in this surreal place, separated from the world. On the other hand, Gehrman had to recruit excellent hunters for a peculiar mission, in addition to the normal pursuit of beasts: it entailed ending the Nightmare of Mensis, where Micolash now lived—a curious objective that we will aim to explain later on.

The Night of the Hunt

The player's avatar sets out in the middle of a large-scale Night of the Hunt in the streets of Yharnam. Of course, the event gets its name from its vocation of hunting and exterminating beasts; however, it also draws its structure from the phases of the nighttime, which are visible throughout the game as the twilight, night, and the full moon. There are too few hints to determine exactly how much time has passed since Willem and Rom placed their protective barrier over the world. However, it is certain that several Nights of the Hunt took place in

---

37. "The Great Ones that inhabit the nightmare are sympathetic in spirit." (Moon Rune)
38. When players discover the Abandoned Old Workshop, they receive the Source of the Dream trophy.

the meantime. For years, hunters had methodically pursued beasts, but they continued to appear indefinitely.

However, the Night of the Hunt in which players participate seems to be exceptional and grandiose. As with the Undead in Dark Souls, who was unique among millions of others (thought we don't know exactly why), the story emphasizes the game's particular context without giving too much away.

Although most hunters land in the Hunter's Nightmare when they die or first begin to show signs of frenzy, players go to Gehrman's Hunter's Dream. This dream is a welcoming, otherworldly place, with a large house similar to the Workshop atop a wooded hill, bathed in the soft light of an eternally full moon. A number of tombs can also be found in this area, embellished with white flowers. This location feels like a peaceful retreat amidst the chaos of the Night of the Hunt.

Two characters live here: first there is an animated, human-sized doll that can speak, who allows players to level up; although she is a puppet, she is one of the only kind, warm presences in this world. Her features and voice are that of Maria, the former disciple of the First Hunter. Gehrman is therefore in this location as well. Now an invalid, he is wheelchair bound, and struggles to greet his new guest or even to provide advice.

The player's avatar is therefore one of the hunters selected by Gehrman to carry out the hazy plans of the location's true creator. At this stage, however, we still know nothing about the Moon Presence, the past of the First Hunter, or of the old city of Yharnam, which will soon be explored as players tackle the perilous Night of the Hunt. There, we discover vestiges of the Healing Church and the ravages of the Beastly Scourge as twilight makes way for the dark night. Then the moon appears, full and magnificent. Players follow their path to Byrgenwerth, where they meet Willem, who feebly points his stick towards Moonside Lake below, at the foot of the college. Following an impressive leap into the void, reflecting the player's determination, the Hunter meets Rom and slays the creature.

The cutscene following Rom's death reveals a woman on the waters of Moonside Lake. She wears an impressive white dress, covered in an unsettling bloodstain from her stomach to her lower abdomen. Then, a baby's cry echoes out, as the avatar turns to see where the woman is looking: the Blood Moon hangs above us—frightening and overwhelming—and even the camera framing in this sequence does not show us its full extent. The scene is as short as it is gripping, provoking new questions without any obvious ties to the first part of the game. Who is this woman? Why the baby's cries? What are the consequences of this red moon?

Yharnam and Mergo

The woman in white is none other than the former Pthumerian Queen. She was na-med Yharnam, like the city that was eventually built atop the remains of her civilization.

Her greatest misfortune was to be chosen to carry a Great One's child; as the bloods-tains suggest, the birth was not a successful one because children of the Great Ones are always stillborn. Queen Yharnam lost her baby, Mergo. However, when players defeat Rom and the Pthumeru sovereign appears, a baby's cries can be heard. Does this mean the baby actually lived? Anxious, but maybe also affected by the cries of her infant, the sovereign looks up at the Blood Moon, the cause of all suffering.

First, the Blood Moon signifies that the barrier has fallen away. Whenever this hap-pens, a Great One comes to inseminate a human (this happens only rarely, thankful-ly).[39] Queen Yharnam was once a victim of the Great Ones. Then, we must remember that this barrier had disappeared following Micolash's ritual, and this is why Rom put a new protective veil in place, in order to contain the catastrophe. Players' questions are answered in the Nightmare of Mensis, which now appears accessible by going to Yahar'gul, the Unseen Village, where the School of Mensis is located. In Yahar'gul, we find the following note: "Ritual secret broken. Seek the nightmare newborn." Although short, it confirms that players must focus their attention on the newborn.

Players then enter the Nightmare of Mensis using a dead body (no doubt Micolash[40]) wearing a Mensis Cage, surrounded by dozens of similar bodies, in an especially grim setting. Later on, the victory against Micolash will not end the nightmare. Players must climb to the top of the castle, a focal point for the otherworldly level, to find Queen Yharnam a second time. She has the same stance as when she previously ap-peared on Moonside Lake, now directing her despondent gaze towards a mysterious cradle (that of Mergo), guarded by the nightmare's final boss: Mergo's Wet Nurse.

Mergo's Wet Nurse is the nameless Great One who no doubt created the Nightmare of Mensis, just as the Moon Presence is behind the Hunter's Dream, and Kos the Hunter's Nightmare. During his ritual, Micolash was able to enter into contact with Mergo's Wet Nurse, who invited or forced him to be the host of her nightmare, an ancient dream that may have originated when the Pthumerian Queen gave birth. Indeed, one of the Cords of the Eye provides the following information: "Every Great One loses its child, and then yearns for a surrogate." The surrogate in question, for

---

39. A note found in Byrgenwerth College describes the consequences of the Blood Moon: "When the red moon hangs low, the line between man and beast is blurred. And when the Great Ones descend, a womb will be blessed with child."

40. An interesting note: in the game, interaction with the corpse is called "Inspect Mummy." Although the cadaver is perfectly preserved, it is not especially clear why the term "mummy" is used here. The term could suggest another meaning, however: it is also an affectionate British term for "mother." Could the leader of the School of Mensis, in his madness, have made his followers refer to him as "Mummy"?

Mergo's Wet Nurse, was the creation of a dream where Mergo lies in its cradle, alive. The newborn's cries echo throughout the planes of existence,[41] and they were likely heard by the Moon Presence.

The Moon Presence's schemes

The story that follows necessarily relies on a set of interpretations and extrapolations, because the story works to maintain the mystery surrounding the Moon Presence's actions. A number of clues sprinkled throughout the game nonetheless invite us to advance some potential theories.

First, it seems highly likely that it was Mergo's stillbirth that led to the creation of the Nightmare of Mensis. So could it be that the Great One's nightmares all arose from these tragic deaths? In *The Old Hunters* DLC, the final Hunter's Nightmare sequence shows Kos bringing the "Orphan of Kos" into the world, named thus because his creator dies soon after his birth. Since this takes place within a nightmare, the reality must have been different (as with Mergo, which is still alive in the Nightmare of Mensis, but died in the real world): it is likely that Kos's child was also stillborn. We also mustn't forget that Willem previously stole One Third of Umbilical Cord from the Fishing Hamlet (where Kos washes up in the nightmare).[42] This item, also found on the body of Mergo and on Arianna's newborn,[43] is also associated with a crystal clear description: "Every infant Great One has this precursor to the umbilical cord."

As players explore the Abandoned Old Workshop, where Gehrman previously lived with his disciples, they find another One Third of Umbilical Cord. This is a surprising discovery, leading to questions about the First Hunter's past. This suggests that either a Great One's child was born in the Workshop, or that the Cord of the Eye was brought there afterwards. In both cases, it draws a connection between Gehrman and this Great One's child. The Hunter's Dream may have arisen following a tragedy related to this baby, who would therefore have belonged to the Moon Presence. We're just left to imagine who the mother could have been.

Everything about the doll who lives in the Hunter's Dream along with Gehrman recalls the deceased Maria. Her features and voice[44] are that of Maria. She is in the exact image of the First Hunter's student, and was very precious to him. The hair

---

41. If we have more than sixty Insight points, we occasionally hear the infant's cries, no matter where we are located (outside of dreams and nightmares), from the very beginning of the game. Once the Blood Moon appears, no matter the avatar's Insight level, the baby's cries can be heard now and then.
42. This item is also called the "Cord of the Eye."
43. Arianna is a descendant of the Cainhursts. At the end of the game, and if all of the quest's conditions are met, she will be impregnated by Oedon and give birth to a stillborn infant, under the chapel named after this Great One. It is an abominable scene, recalling the despair and suffering of the Pthumerian Queen.
44. The two characters share a single voice actor, whose name appears in the end credits: Evetta Muradasilova.

ornament and set we find in the Abandoned Old Workshop also suggest an emotional bond between the Workshop's founder (Gehrman) and his Plain Doll ("Maria"). The Master's feelings for his pupil therefore seem clear. Whether or not these two hunters ever had a romantic relationship, it was nipped in the bud or ended when the Moon Presence came to impregnate Maria,[45] who would give birth to a stillborn infant. Traumatized, the Cainhurst huntress left to join the Healing Church, leaving her mentor, or lover, behind in his now vacant Workshop. Seeking a surrogate after the death of its child, the Moon Presence would imprison Gehrman in its dream; out of "kindness," it gives consciousness to the doll made by the First Hunter, to provide a pleasant companion.

Although the Great Ones' motives remain elusive, the Moon Presence's desire for a child gives us a glimpse of its state of mind. The nightmare created to freeze the day when Mergo was born, with its cries that echo throughout the planes of existence all the way to the Hunter's Dream, disturbed the Moon Presence, which had also experienced a loss according to our hypothesis. There is even a note in the Unseen Village that suggests that players "find one, and silence its harrowing cry." A "harrowing cry" for a being such as the Moon Presence, which was also unable to produce viable offspring: the Mergo that lives eternally in this other Great One's nightmare was a disturbing anomaly that needed correcting. This is why Gehrman was charged with finding a strong enough hunter to fight Rom and access the Nightmare of Mensis, where this hunter would find and silence Mergo.

Players often complete this scenario without considering why. Manipulated by the Moon Presence, and by Gehrman's intervention, they remain oblivious. This story suggests that the Great Ones exist in a higher sphere, inaccessible to humans, inferior beings whom they scorn. However, the Moon Presence's deep-seated motivations—its frustration, search for a surrogate, and its desire for something inaccessible to those in its condition—seem to reduce it to the level of a common human. In some ways, these beings who supposedly incarnate divine magnificence, in possession of the much-coveted eldritch Truth, are actually driven by the same desires. A cruel irony, which underscores the complexity of Miyazaki's characters in *Bloodborne*.

---

45. Maria is originally from the Cainhurst clan, like Arianna, and was also victim to a Great One's desire to reproduce.

Conclusions

It seems that we have enough information to understand the different endings presented in this game. There are three of them. The first two endings are somewhat traditional, while the last one—the most difficult to obtain—continues the idea of satisfying the Great Ones' desire to bear children.

Once Mergo's Wet Nurse has been defeated, the Hunter's Dream transforms: the Workshop goes up in flames, and Gehrman waits for the player in a majestic field of white flowers that was previously inaccessible. Seated under a giant tree, a compelling symbol of cycles and rebirth, he greets the avatar with the words:

"Good Hunter, you've done well, the night is near its end. Now I will show you mercy. You will die, forget the dream, and awake under the morning sun. You will be freed from this terrible Hunter's Dream."

If the player accepts this fate, Gehrman rises from his seat, grasping his scythe (the Grim Reaper's famous weapon from modern folklore) to decapitate the Hunter. The Hunter will then wake up at dawn in the streets of Old Yharnam, like the Hunter Djura.[46] The Night of the Hunt is over.

On the other hand, the player's refusal leads to a staggering duel with Gehrman. However, after defeating the First Hunter, the Moon Presence approaches and defeats the avatar, powerless. Then, he takes over for Gehrman in his wheelchair, accompanied by the Doll, ready to look for new hunters on behalf of this dream's Great One.

Finally, players can choose to fight the Moon Presence, as long as they have consumed three One Third of Umbilical Cords or Cords of the Eye. If victorious, players experience a third and final conclusion. In reality, there are four umbilical cord thirds. Here they are, in order of birth:

 ‣ that of Mergo, the earliest known stillbirth, child of the Pthumerian Queen Yharnam and an unknown Great One, perhaps Mergo's Wet Nurse (since we get the cord after defeating her);

 ‣ that of the Orphan of Kos (with a unknown mother), found by Byrgenwerth, passed along to the Choir, and then to Imposter Iosefka, a member of the Choir who continues her research on the Celestials in her sordid clinic, where we can find this cord;

 ‣ that of the Workshop, left by Maria and the Moon Presence's child, which we find in the Abandoned Old Workshop, set back from the Healing Church;

 ‣ that of the son of Arianna, impregnated by Formless Oedon, a cord that we find in the sewers of the Oedon Chapel, on the still-warm body of the deformed infant.

---

46. Djura, who we meet in Old Yharnam, suggests that he still has some memory of the Hunter's Dream and the Doll. At one time, therefore, he was one of these hunters from the dream, before meeting his gruesome fate.

When consumed, the Cords of the Eye give players a maximum level of Insight and "eyes on the inside." Consuming three thirds, or a whole, regrows the Moon Presence and unlocks a game-ending fight, in a climax where a human triumphs over a god: "Nightmare slain" (as when the Orphan of Kos or Mergo's Wet Nurse were eliminated), and the screen goes black. The final cutscene, only about thirty seconds long, begins: outside the Workshop, which no longer burns but once again looks like new, the Plain Doll takes a larva in her arms, as if holding a newborn, and says softly, "Oh, good hunter,"[47]

If we simply look at the trophies, we can read the "Childhood's Beginning" description, obtained through this ending: "You became an infant Great One, lifting humanity into its next childhood." By ingesting the cords and defeating the Moon Presence, the Hunter has finally become a Great One, and a Great One's child at that. This previously seemed to be impossible and unnatural, and introduces new unknowns to the game's universe. In some ways, the avatar reaches a new form of eldritch Truth, after being raised to such heights that he is reborn as a Great One. No longer a human, the avatar is now a child of the gods. The *Bloodborne* story contains a final irony: now that the longed-for child is finally born, it no longer has a parent: a joyless birth without family, which could lead the child to search for a surrogate parent, perhaps in the Doll. She is kind, yes, but is no more than a simulacrum.

---

47. Isn't it a little disturbing that the game ends with a comma?

Characters

As we've seen: in addition to its very cryptic narration, the *Bloodborne* story is quite complex. The storyline takes shape primarily as we discover the various characters' pasts. In order to maintain some clarity in our presentation of the story, we have saved some less significant information related to various characters for this chapter. Protagonists who were already presented in detail, such as the Doll or Master Willem, will not be presented again here.

The Hunters

Most NPCs in the game are hunters. However, they belong to different clans, with a variety of denominations and philosophies. Sometimes, animosity develops between some factions, or even a deep hatred such as that between the Executioners and the Vilebloods.

☙ Gehrman and the Crows

The hunt began in response to the appearance of the first beasts, after the archaeologists dug up the Pthumerian ruins. Gehrman was the very first hunter. He took some apprentices under his wing to assist him in the hunt. Gehrman gathered his students in a location called the Workshop, which contained many tools designed to help hunters defeat beasts. We will not spend much time looking at the Blood Gem Workshop, which is simply used to strengthen weapons using blood (a substance with impressive properties we have already seen). The Rune Workshop is more interesting to examine. By etching certain runes into their mind, hunters can attain considerable strength. These runes were created by a student of Byrgenwerth named Caryll, who was highly esteemed by Master Willem, at least before he began to work on runes tied to the word "blood". These are actually transcriptions of utterings, and in particular the voices of the Great Ones. Caryll created many of these runes, with a variety of properties. Some were inhuman sounds or words from the Great Ones, particularly Formless Oedon, or monstrous roars: the hunters had all sorts of powers available to them. No one knows what happened to Caryll, but his work would be used for several generations, up until the time the game takes place. In addition to the blood gems and runes, many famous weapons were forged in the First Hunter's Workshop, and a wide variety of effective, quick hunting techniques were developed, and then taught. After laying the foundations for the hunt, Gehrman disappeared quickly from Yharnam.[48]

Before he meets the player, Gehrman has taken advantage of his position within the Hunter's Dream to recruit several hunters. Two more notable hunters: Djura, formerly a member of the Powder Kegs faction, who (sadly) retains very little information about his time spent in the dream, and Eileen, who has a stronger memory, and gives the player a few snippets of this far-off past. Eileen is one of the Crows[49]—strange, charismatic characters who hunt the hunters who have fallen into madness or turned into beasts, in order to "save" them by killing them and offering redemption: a salvation to spare them from an eternity of suffering in the Hunter's Nightmare.[50] The hunters' suffering has given way to peace, which emanates from the tombs in the Hunter's Dream. Although the primary function of this place was to fulfill the Moon Presence's mission, it feels as though it was co-opted to become a refuge for the damaged hunters' souls. The First Hunter understood his "heirs" like no one else: a merciful man,[51] who, without overindulging in Blood or Insight, took advantage from the power of a Great One to improve the fates of his fellow men.

This is another clue that could suggest that Gehrman created the Crows: the Hunter we meet in the Grand Cathedral during the first part of the game (an optional fight, but notable for its difficulty and the class of the enemy) is called "Bloody Crow of Cainhurst" in the official guide. It turns out that this mysterious character uses and abuses Gehrman's techniques. Moreover, his affiliation with Cainhurst (he wears their armor, at least) suggests ties with Maria, and ties him to the First Hunter. The case of the Bloody Crow of Cainhurst seems strange, however. He wounds Eileen, his counterpart, as if he has lost his mind and renounced his ties to the Crows. Once players

---

48. See his encounter with the Moon Presence in the previous chapter.

49. Eileen's Beak Mask description indicates, "Hunters of Hunters dress as crows to suggest sky burial." This suggests a reference to the Quran, in which a crow shows Cain where to bury his brother Abel, whom he had just killed. Although crows are often seen as bad omens, they can also symbolize familial love, in Japan in particular. Here, the Crows aim to protect the large family of Hunters from their gruesome fate.

50. First location of *The Old Hunters* DLC, where players face many Hunters condemned to torment. They include the Old Hunters, the numerous, inexperienced recruits of the Healing Church, who assisted in the massacre of the Beastly Scourge.

51. At the end of the game, players face Gehrman, who uses the Burial Blade, the description of which reads: "Gehrman surely saw the hunt as a dirge of farewell, wishing only that his prey might rest in peace, never again to awaken to another harrowing nightmare." The Burial Blade was one of the first, if not the first weapon to be made by the Workshop. It was forged out of a rare mineral, siderite, said to have "fallen from the heavens." These strong characteristics are also found in the Blade of Mercy carried by Eileen, no doubt given by Gehrman to the first of the Crows, and later given to his best disciples.

have eliminated this danger, Eileen grants them a place among the Crows, of which there are few.[52] This gives players access to the "Hunters of Hunters oath," dedicated to hunting other players who have become "addled with blood."[53]

On the other hand, if players don't help Eileen in her quest, she will attack them, on the grounds that they are like the other Hunters, hungry for blood. This leads to a strange scene, where we realize that Eileen has succumbed to the same type of frenzy that affects the Bloody Crow of Cainhurst. Eileen believes all Hunters must die and give her their blood. The roles are therefore reversed: although she claims superiority from the beginning of the game, she ends up succumbing like the other humans if she doesn't receive help at the right time.

This timely help is in the encounter with Henryk, not far from the Tomb of Oedon cemetery. In spite of his murderous rage, Henryk remains a hollow shell. We know nothing about him, except that he formed a duo with Father Gascoigne. The Father's history deserves our attention.

✦ Gascoigne

Although we can choose whether or not to face the Cleric Beast in the game's first location, Father Gascoigne is the first true *Bloodborne* boss: a difficult enemy for this type of fight, signaling an abrupt end to the game's beginning.

By exploring central Yharnam, we can meet some NPCs in their homes, their entryways marked by small lanterns. These NPCs include a young girl who asks the player to find her mother, Viola; this child also gives the player the Tiny Music Box in memory of her parents, and in particular her father who is none other than Gascoigne.[54] Sadly, Viola has already died. We find her body not far from the Tomb of Oedon, where Gascoigne will attack, before losing his life in this bloody duel. Now an orphan, the girl will succumb in turn if the player suggests she seeks shelter in the Oedon Chapel, where the city's refugees have gathered. Finally, we'll add that Gascoigne and Viola had two daughters. However, the elder sister's fate is not so different from the rest of the family: she falls from a ladder not far from her house, thus ending the bleak story of a family not destined to survive the merciless Night of the Hunt.

---

52. "The badge of the Hunter of Hunters is quietly passed down from generation to generation, usually to an outsider from the hinterlands," reads the "Crow" Hunter Badge. It appears that Crow status is handed down by "generation," with one death followed by the birth of a new member.
53. The two quotations come from the Hunter Rune description.
54. When we use the Tiny Music Box during the fight against Gascoigne, he appears highly disturbed by the melody, which gives the player an advantage in the fight.

Apart from this tragic story, the fight with Father Gascoigne is unsettling. In his appearance and movements, this first boss is actually very similar to the player's avatar. Both are Hunters, and both wield a basic hunt weapon (depending on the player's choice at the beginning of the game, both fight using an ax and a blunderbuss), both are dressed in the same types of clothes, and finally, both use the same fighting techniques. This recalls traditional evil twin fights (like the famous Doppelgängers in the *Castlevania* or *Devil May Cry* series), except that this fight, always intense and difficult, usually takes place at the end of the adventure. In *Bloodborne*, it happens right at the beginning of the game! The fight can throw off players, who find themselves locked in battle with one of their fellow hunters, who is addled with blood and driven by an unknown force. The second phase of the battle, in which Father Gascoigne transforms into an uncontrollable beast, heightens the sense of anxiety and gives players an idea of what may await them. Will they also fall prey to beasthood? And if so, when will it strike?

Father Gascoigne is also the player's first contact with Yharnam's religious community—another source of concern. Gascoigne's greeting does not bode well for the mental state of religious men in the area, a feeling of foreboding that is confirmed quickly as the story continues and players discover the Cathedral Ward. Here, however, we should note that "Father" doesn't indicate a connection with the Healing Church; rather, it comes from a land far from Yharnam, but still suggests that Gascoigne once had close ties with religion. Once he moved to Yharnam with his family, he joined the Healing Church, as suggested by the shroud he wears as a scarf around his neck, one of the symbols of Laurence's organization. No one knows Gascoigne's full history, except that he worked with Henryk, with whom it seems that he led missions outside of the Healing Church Hunters.

✤ Hunters of the Healing Church

Those who swapped their lightweight weapons and protections for heavy weapons and armor in order to fight the beasts for the Church were led by the famous Ludwig. Ludwig's reality is in stark contrast with his illustrious legend.[55] As with Knight Artorias from the first *Dark Souls*, the game world only presents Ludwig in a kind light. It is only in *The Old Hunters* DLC that players meet the Healing Church's first hunter... and he's a boss. He proves to be a giant beast, holding nothing back in his attacks, and abandoning himself to a murderous frenzy. The battle initially

---

55. "The radiant sword indicates the heirs to the will of Ludwig. These hunters, also known as Holy Blades, are what remains of an ancient line of heroes that date back to a very early age of honor and chivalry," indicates the Radiant Sword Hunter Badge.

appears formidable, as the creature inflicts savage violence and non-stop attacks. But then, in the middle of the fight, the tone changes entirely. Ludwig, who seems to regain his composure, produces the superb Holy Moonlight Sword,[56] a recurring item in the *King's Field* and *Souls* games. His chaotic barrage of swipes and bites evolves into a sophisticated series of sword hits, serene and precise as ever. The sword is what maintains Ludwig's last shred of sanity. The cutscene in the middle of the fight depicts this perfectly: slumping on the ground, Ludwig glimpses the green light of the Holy Moonlight Sword that appears by his side. The frame is in a close-up on his eyes, which are pale blue, but symbolize the last vestiges of his humanity. He gazes at the sword, as if reassured, and speaks to it: "Aah, you were at my side, all along. My true mentor... My guiding moonlight..." As a character, Ludwig is constantly being pulled by opposing forces. In the past, while hunting for the Healing Church, he was terrified but nevertheless demonstrated courage.[57] After he became a blood-starved beast, he was able to retain an ounce of humanity through his sword, a serendipitous refuge in the darkness of his soul. After his defeat in the DLC, players can speak with him, and even reassure him as they don the Healing Church-related attire. Finally, before he draws his last breath, he displays loyalty to his religion, even though it was ironically the source of his curse and transformation. In spite of the harm done to him by the blood, and his irreversible beastly state, he has mostly remained steadfast in his faith. He is a respectable character of great distinction, with his Holy Moonlight Sword, but as soon as he can no longer see light—symbol of hope—, he falls prey to bouts of savage violence.

Simon the Harrowed was another one of the Healing Church's first hunters. Known for his refusal to use firearms, he asked the Healing Church Workshop to craft him a special weapon called the Bowblade: a large curved blade that could also be used as a bow as soon as he needed a longer-range weapon. He was scoffed by his associates, who didn't think it would hold up for very long against the hostile beasts. However, Simon's critics met the same fate as him, and he also wound up in the Hunter's Nightmare, a place "where hunters end up when drunk with blood," as he says to the player when they meet.

An interesting detail: Simon wears the Harrowed Set. The description of this set indicates that those who wear it "obfuscate their identities" and that in reality, they serve "as the first line of defense against its outbreak," that is, against the Beastly Scourge. Another character besides Simon wears a Harrowed Hood: the Suspicious

---

56. Incidentally, note the reference to Ludwig van Beethoven and his famous *Moonlight Sonata*.
57. "When Ludwig closed his eyes, he saw darkness, or perhaps nothingness, and that is where he discovered the tiny beings of light. Ludwig was certain that these playful dancing sprites offered 'guidance.' They could empty Ludwig of his fears at least in the midst of a hunt," explains the Guidance Rune.

Beggar we meet in the Forbidden Woods. He appears afraid, hands covered in blood, near several dead bodies. If sent to the Oedon Chapel, he will exterminate the chapel's refugees one by one, or transform into the "Abhorrent Beast" when attacked (a traditional beast, very aggravated, with red eyes). The beggar has the Beast Rune etched in his mind. This rune is a "transcription of the roar of a labyrinth beast," and another Abhorrent Beast serves as a boss in the Ailing Loran Chalice Dungeon. "'Beast' is one of the early Caryll Runes, as well as one of the first to be deemed forbidden," says the description. These clues retrace the beggar's backstory. Like Simon, he was a former Healing Church Hunter, who watched the Beastly Scourge unfold before his eyes. To gain strength, he used the Beast Rune, but allowed himself be corrupted by the insatiable desire for blood, which made him a puppet, killing others endlessly to harvest blood. The beggar may have been close to Simon, or at least one of his former comrades, but their destinies would diverge. The first began wandering, committing massacres among the population, but Simon found himself within the Hunter's Nightmare, before dying a tragic death: in the final location of the DLC, the player finds Simon in death's throes, after being attacked by a being known as Brador.

Brador is actually the disguised Healing Church Assassin. But he did not always play that role. Although he came from a foreign land, he was previously an ordinary member of the church—until he slaughtered one of his compatriots who had transformed, like the game's "other" first boss, into a Cleric Beast. Beset by a murderous frenzy following his literal massacre, Brador made a scalp of his compatriot with the horns of the beast, which he would sport proudly for the rest of his days. In response to this barbarous act, he locked himself away in a cell. But the Healing Church gave him a bell, so they could summon him and give him secret assassination assignments. In this way, Brador kept the Church's secrets.[58] The Church held many secrets: from using Kos's Celestial Water stolen from the Fishing Hamlet to the horrible experiments from the Healing Church laboratories, and the secret of the direct link between the Blood Ministration and the beasts—and maybe even the death of Laurence. This has given rise to an intriguing theory about Brador: could he have been close to Laurence? Laurence was the first member of the Church to transform into a Cleric Beast (as we learn from the description of Laurence's Skull), and may have, at that fateful moment, been near Brador. In his stupefaction and terror, Brador may have struck him violently on the head and decapitated him,[59] scalping

58. "Afterward, he wore his ally's own scalp, and hid himself away, deep below in a cell. The Church provided him with a single, soundless bell of death to ensure their secrets would be kept," says the description of his head attire, topped with a beast's horns.
59. Preserved in the Grand Cathedral, Laurence's Skull has a gash in it that could be from Brador's morgenstern, the famous Bloodletter weapon.

him with extraordinary violence.[60] The gesture would have shocked other members of the organization, and given Brador a certain aura—that of an exceptional, bold murderer, but blood-driven and unpredictable, who must be contained and monitored so he could be used discreetly for strategic assassinations.

Although we already discussed the Blood Saints, Adeline, Adella and Maria, who spent much of their existence conducting experiments for the Healing Church, there remains one person in the organization we have not yet seen: Archibald. He is impossible to meet within the game. However, his name appears in many descriptions, since his research proved useful for so many hunters.

Archibald was fascinated by the blue sparks emitted by the hellish, bony Darkbeasts. We meet a Darkbeast, called Paarl, in a secret place between Yahar'gul and Old Yharnam. This type of beast is distinctive in the electricity (the blue sparks) that emanates from their tattered skin. Small lightning bolts accompany every one of their movements, particularly when they attack. Archibald began studying this phenomenon, though it cast him as a bit of an oddball in the eyes of his colleagues. Conducting experiments "in a style of inquiry that, incidentally, closely followed the methodology of Byrgenwerth,"[61] he naturally lost his credibility within the Healing Church. He still managed to artificially reproduce the Darkbeasts' artificial electric arcs, and to develop some objects that would later be used by hunters (at the time, the hunters were a little too wary of Archibald due to his reputation). There are two examples of this technology in the game: the Bolt Paper, which buffs weapons and allows them to shoot off bolts; and the Tonitrus, a delightful instrument of death bedecked with electrical sparks.

❦ The Executioners

Affiliated with the Healing Church, the Executioners were once charged with hunting and executing the clan of the Vilebloods. The Vilebloods are vampires, viewed by the Church as heretics to be eliminated. When the game begins, only one Executioner remains: Alfred, who seeks his master, Logarius, and the final Vileblood, Queen Annalise.

The player meets Alfred relatively early in the adventure. Alfred proves to be rather talkative, revealing some of Yharnam's history. From Byrgenwerth and the discovery

---

60. However, the DLC allows players to fight Laurence, with his head and scalp intact. This fight takes place inside a nightmare, showing once again that the dream plane of existence deviates greatly from that of Yharnam.
61. Quote from the description of the Spark Hunter Badge. Although we don't know exactly what his "style of inquiry" was, it was different from that of the Healing Church, due to the memorable schism with Willem's college. Unfortunately for Archibald, the simple association of his work with the name "Byrgenwerth" did not do much for his reputation.

of the Pthumerian ruins to the Healing Church and Blood Ministration: Alfred is very familiar with the city's past and will be happy to share what he knows with his new listener. This final Executioner appears trustworthy, with his chivalrous manner and luxurious attire. He also tells the story of the Vilebloods, the "inhuman" beings, as he calls them, and his task to eradicate them. This Manichaean dualism, skillfully implemented early in the game, may disturb newcomers, but will not fool players used to the *Souls* series. The *Souls* games are known for their nuances that color the battle of Good versus Evil, particularly in the recent FromSoftware productions. But we will come back to this a bit later on.

In reality, Alfred is looking for his mentor Logarius, formerly head of the Executioners. With many of his group, Logarius went all the way to Cainhurst Castle, home of the Vilebloods, to eliminate all of the residents, starting with Queen Annalise. The battle raged, and both camps were decimated. Finally, only Logarius and Annalise remained, Annalise being the final descendant of the immortal vampires. Faced with the queen's frightening power, Logarius only managed to lock her in the throne room. To do so, he hid the entryway behind an optical illusion, which would only be revealed to anyone who wore the precious Crown of Illusions. Logarius kept this crown tight on his head, and set up outside the door, now invisible to the rest of the world. The lead Executioner literally gave up the rest of his life to make sure no one would enter or leave the throne room. Logarius was now known as "Martyr Logarius." He became part of the legend even though no one understood the meaning of his sacrifice... at least until the player arrives at Cainhurst Castle. Indeed, Logarius is the level's boss, defending the snowy rooftop heart and soul. Once this martyr has been defeated, the illusion remains until the avatar puts on Logarius's crown. Some players likely retrace their steps after the fight. The diadem reveals the path leading to the encounter with Annalise, who has been held captive for an eternity, seated on her throne.

After discovering the vampire queen, players can return to speak with Alfred and tell him where his sworn enemy is located. Back on the Cainhurst Castle rooftop, we will then witness an extremely violent scene. Alfred stands in the throne room. Dressed in an impressive conical golden helmet,[62] he bears an enormous Logarius' Wheel as a weapon. Alfred's attire and equipment is covered in an excessive amount of blood and viscera, and the queen no longer exists, save a few bits of flesh on her throne.[63] Happy with this massacre, Alfred roars with laughter like a madman.

---

62. This is the Gold Ardeo: "The conical gold helmet, symbol of the executioners, represents luminosity, ambition, and an unflagging resolve to face impurity." The shape of the helmet and the violence of its wearer recall the impressive Pyramid Head from *Silent Hill 2*, a blood-covered executioner in his own way.
63. Annalise can be resuscitated by placing her remains on the Altar of Despair, where Ebrietas resides, in the Choir district. This situation is not without irony: one of the Healing Church's greatest enemies can be brought back to life using the organization's own research.

However, the description of Logarius' Wheel leads us to think that the Executioners always derive euphoria from massacring Vilebloods:

"Weapon wielded by martyr Logarius' band of executioners. Used to slaughter the Vilebloods in Cainhurst. Bathed in pools of their blood, and forever steeped in their ire." Members of this bloody branch of the Healing Church are extremely barbaric towards vampires, who have always been their despised enemies. Alfred's enlightened, serene words from our first encounter with him now appear dishonest, with his true nature revealed. Once again, it is worth remaining skeptical of good-and-evil dualities found in any of the *Souls* characters. If the Vilebloods are indeed beasts who worship the forbidden blood, their enemies the Executioners are just as adept in violent massacres and extermination. It's hard to pick a side!

The Vilebloods

Once, long ago, a scholar from Byrgenwerth robbed the college of a sample of forbidden blood, before fleeing to Cainhurst Castle, which became the home of the Vilebloods. The nobility that lived in the castle[64] was no doubt seduced by the impressive and powerful liquid brought to them by this stranger. They took him in, and over the years they turned into vampires, thirsty for this forbidden blood that gave them unnaturally long lives. They refused to depend directly on Yharnam for their blood supply, so they sent their servants to search for it, so they would never go without. But history repeated itself: a curse similar to the Beastly Scourge, although weaker, descended on Cainhurst, and beasts began to appear in the streets. A small army of knights was formed in the castle to fight these creatures. They were equipped with a silver helm, forged to protect them from the harmful effects of the blood harvested for the nobles. Similar to that of the hunters, their mission was to hunt and eliminate the beasts that prowled the area.

Between bloodbaths and power struggles, the manor saw many generations of Vilebloods. Having learned of the existence of these aristocrats with supernatural abilities and extreme life spans, the Healing Church formed the Executioners with the purpose of eliminating them. Following the assault led by Logarius on Cainhurst Castle, the snow of Annalise's kingdom was awash with the blood of both factions. The only surviving Vileblood, Queen Annalise remained prisoner in her throne room.

She is therefore the only Vileblood that the player meets during the adventure. Dressed in a simple, rather dirty dress, her appearance doesn't reflect the traditional rich ornamentation associated with her rank. Rather, the iron mask around her face

---

64. The coats of arms in the Cainhurst throne room depict two golden lions standing back to back. Lions were often present on royal crests in the Middle Ages. The king of the animals embodies courage, strength and majesty. In heraldry, the color gold symbolizes the bravery of nobles.

is what draws the player's eye. It is impossible to see the queen's face, or the features of the final living vampire. Another source of discomfort, she addresses the player in the first-person plural, we. Is this the royal "we," or the inability to accept the loss of her husband, the king? The second throne, by her side, remains markedly empty. Since the king of the Vilebloods no longer exists, this first encounter with Annalise emanates something unnatural and sinister. Annalise is also the guardian of the oath of her covenant. To join this covenant, players must collect blood dregs, produced using Coldblood (amassed Blood Echoes, similar to groups of souls in *Dark Souls*). Of course, brutally assassinating other hunters yields a maximum amount of blood dregs.[65] Annalise requests blood dregs in order to present them as an offering and bear the Child of Blood, the heir to the Vilebloods. Although the game remains vague about the nature of this Child of Blood and its ties to the blood dregs, an interesting theory has posited that Annalise is actually linked to Yharnam, Queen of Pthumeru.

The Child of Blood is also mentioned in the description of the Blood Rapture Rune: "This rune resonates with servants of the Queen, carrier of the Child of Blood, who yearn for their Queen's blood with little hope of requitement." At first glance, this "queen" could have been Annalise, but this is not the case: if Annalise yearns to "bear the Child of Blood," that means that this has not yet happened. In addition, this rune is obtained following the fight with the "Shadows of Yharnam." These bosses have no connection with the old city of Yharnam, because this fight takes place far from the city, in the Forbidden Woods, near the start of the path towards Byrgenwerth College. The three Shadows get their name from the Pthumerian queen. Moreover, we encounter them again in the Nightmare of Mensis, not far from the staircase that leads to the remains of Yharnam, just before the fight with Mergo's Wet Nurse. The Shadows are thus tied to the queen of Pthumeru, along with the Blood Rapture Rune mentioned above. We can conclude that Yharnam was once pregnant with a Child of Blood, and that Annalise aspires to bear a Great One's child. Why does she wish to amass blood dregs for this purpose? Simply to please Formless Oedon, the only superior being known to be tied to blood. The Formless Oedon Rune tells us: "Human or no, the oozing blood is a medium of the highest grade, and the essence of the formless Great One. Both Oedon, and its inadvertent worshippers, surreptitiously seek the precious blood." Annalise believes that by presenting an impressive offering of blood dregs (the precious blood coveted by Oedon), she could be chosen to bear its child.[66] This theory could also answer the question of which Great One formerly impregnated Yharnam. Although it created the Nightmare of Mensis,

---

65. This covenant is more oriented towards PVP.

66. In the game's Storage, the image for blood dregs looks like a blood pouch containing a swarm of cells that resemble sperm. This creepy object is similar to the Yharnam Stone, an item obtained after the fight with the Queen of Pthumeru, within the depths of the Chalice Dungeons. The stone shows an impregnated version of the blood dregs, with an embryo visible in the mass of cells.

it would not have been Mergo's Wet Nurse, but rather Oedon. This would make Mergo a Child of Blood.

With a little more speculation, we can profile the women who seek to bear Great One children. They come from Cainhurst, or their blood has similar characteristics (i.e. it is partly tainted). Yharnam and Annalise aspired to bear a Child of Blood, and Arianna also gives birth, at the end of the game, to Oedon's stillborn baby. Maria has the same destiny, forced by the Moon Presence to give birth. Both come from the region of Cainhurst, and Maria is even a distant relation of Queen Annalise. And although the Orphan of Kos's mother remains unknown, it seems that the Great Ones prefer women from Cainhurst. This supports the hypothesis of the strong tie between the Queen of Yharnam and the Vilebloods covenant,[67] which revolves around (as we've seen) the consumption of the forbidden blood stolen from Byrgenwerth–blood originally discovered among the Pthumerian ruins.

❧ The Powder Kegs

Forerunner of the Powder Kegs, "Oto" was known for the weapons he built in his workshop. Whether the Piercing Rifle or the Molotov Cocktail, Oto's creations are generally popular with hunters. Some of his fans founded the Powder Kegs faction, made up of weapons and explosive enthusiasts. Its members were obsessed with big explosions, and fire in general. The Powder Kegs Workshop was soon built, devoted to the production of new weapons for the covenant, from the Cannon, a heavy piece of artillery both effective and traditional, to the more subtle Stake Driver, with a very descriptive name, along with the Whirligig Saw, a clever weapon combining a mallet and a double circular saw.

Djura set his sights on a very powerful Gatling Gun, which he later carries at the top of a tower in Old Yharnam to dissuade hunters from entering, or to exterminate them if they prove too eager. Players will bear the consequences of this if

---

67. There are also some interesting visual references: the Queen of Yharnam wears a fascinating white dress, similar to the dress worn by Lucy Westenra in Francis Ford Coppola's film adaptation of *Dracula* (1992). During the story, Lucy transforms into a vampire, and the scene in which she wears this singular dress is one of the film's most memorable: in it, she suffers a brutal, bloody death at the hands of her husband and Van Helsing. If we look past the differences in the context and certain details, everything about Yharnam's appearance in the Nightmare of Mensis suggests this movie scene: the white dress, the blood (the agonizing birth for Yharnam, the stake driven through Lucy's heart in the movie), the pale ambiance (both scenes are bathed in moonlight), and finally, the cries of a baby (Mergo, and the child that Lucy is preparing to drain of blood). Upon seeing Yharnam, anyone who is familiar with Coppola's film would think immediately of Lucy—a vampire, like the Vilebloods! It is also worth noting that the Shadows of Yharnam carry katanas, which recall the blade of Chikage, the weapon "wielded by the royal guards who protect Annalise" according to the description. Finally, in the soundtrack, the music for the fights with Martyr Logarius is the same as the fight with Yharnam. It is called "Queen of the Vilebloods" in reference to Annalise.

they try to enter the old city directly. However, if they bypass the entryway by going through the Unseen Village, they will meet Djura in a calmer state. This former member of the Powder Kegs is really protecting the area's beasts! "The things you hunt, they're not beasts. They're people," says Djura to the player. The former Powder Keg took it on himself to protect Yharnam's inhabitants, after a massive use of fire claimed a multitude of victims during the Beastly Scourge. The victims included some of Djura's old acquaintances, whom he could not bear to see killed. The hunter left his covenant, now known for his fascination with fire, which contrasted entirely with his new convictions. He retired in Old Yharnam, determined to protect the beasts that survived the great fire.

The old hunter with the Gatling Gun was formerly associated with three comrades in arms. During our adventure, we meet two of them—they can be identified by the fact that beasts do not attack them. In fact, the beasts cooperate with them, and together attack any curious person who may approach. Djura's first companion became addled with blood, and wound up in the Hunter's Nightmare, in an ethereal version of Yharnam. Armed with a lighter gun, hiding not far from the river of blood that flows through the heart of the nightmare city, the Powder Kegs hunter fights the player. By referring to the gun's description,[68] we learn that he was the youngest of Djura's three companions. It is possible to fight another of these companions in Old Yharnam, at the base of the tower where Djura is perched. The fight is difficult and tense, with the player caught between the attacks of beasts and the very dexterous opposing hunter, and not to forget the incessant barrage of bullets from Djura! No one knows what happened to Djura's third companion: in any case, there is no sign to clearly identify him in the game. However, this mysterious companion could be one of the Powder Keg bodies we discover in one of Old Yharnam's buildings, where we read this inscription on the ground: "The red moon hangs low, and beasts rule the streets. Are we left no other choice, than to burn it all to cinders?" The inscription recalls Djura's own questions, and his current opposition to the possibility of a massacre. Could he have been the one to kill his former associates from the Powder Kegs, including his old comrade?

Although it seems obvious that the Powder Kegs were behind the massacre in Old Yharnam, considering the amount of explosives and Molotov Cocktails used, it's not impossible that the Healing Church Hunters also participated. Indeed, the Church recruited new, poorly prepared hunters from among the population. With no time to train in hunting methods, and lacking the right reactions to the reality and dangers, they

---

68. "This is a highly-customized, portable version of the stationary Gatling Gun operated by the old hunter Djura in Old Yharnam. It was the weapon of choice of the youngest of Djura's three companions."

face the beasts with unrestrained fire.[69] Old Yharnam was purified with brutal, inhumane methods. The old city was engulfed in flames and the weakest Healing Church Hunters succumbed to frenzy: as they consumed excessive amounts of blood to tolerate the horrors, they themselves became beasts, and wound up in the Hunter's Nightmare.

After the old city was ravaged by fire, the Healing Church declared the Powder Kegs heretics, as if to clear their own name and pin the blame on a scapegoat: the flame and explosion fanatics. The covenant went into hiding, before disappearing completely from Yharnam, leaving a bitter taste behind, along with a wide array of impressive heavy weaponry. One of the Powder Kegs's members, named Valtr, would leave and join another group: the League.

The League

Hunters from the League are representatives of the new *Bloodborne* covenant, which we discover in *The Old Hunters*. Their mission is to hunt creatures they collectively refer to as "vermin," invisible, centipede-like creatures that live in the blood of hunters and are described as "the root of man's impurity." Members of the League use the Impurity Rune to see vermin. These members are often not from Yharnam, and they roam the world to find and kill those whose blood has been tainted by these parasites.

The League has two ranks: the Constables are the leaders, while the Confederates[70] are responsible for eradicating vermin. Valtr is one of these Constables, following in the line of many others. His high rank can be identified by his Master's Iron Helm, a strange full helmet with one single hole on the front.[71] Valtr, who despite his position is no longer able to identify vermin, is looking for a successor to be Constable. Players may become Constable if they carry out Valtr's orders and bring him enough vermin: before disappearing Valtr gives the Master's Iron Helm to the player, who was previously a Confederate, but now is a Constable and Master of the League. Before ending up in the Hunter's Nightmare, Valtr hunted a monster with a group from the League. The beast led them to Yharnam, where it took them by surprise, massacring the entire group with the exception of Valtr. Livid with rage, Valtr was able to eliminate the monstrous creature, before devouring it. This is what gave Valtr his epithet, "Beast Eater."

---

69. Some members of the Healing Church used Flamesprayers, the description of which indicates: "Not the most efficient weapon by any stretch, but sometimes a sea of flame is just what the doctor ordered. Besides, the beasts of Yharnam can always use a good cleansing."

70. Strangely, their name and uniforms directly reference the American Civil War, but in a historically inaccurate way. The American "Confederates" fought for the South, while the blue and gold attire worn by the game's Confederates is identical to that worn by Union soldiers, from the northern United States.

71. The helmet is passed down from generation to generation between the Constables, so the first one may have been one-eyed.

As we learn from the description of Khaki Haori's coat, which previously belonged to him, Yanamura the Wanderer from the Orient once pursued a beast "for honorable revenge." The hunt took him all the way to Yharnam. Was this the same creature that hunted Valtr and his compatriots? No one knows. What's certain is that Yanamura eventually joined the League as a Confederate, and hunted vermin. Sadly, he couldn't tolerate the constant scenes of human impurity, and was eventually driven mad. He spent the rest of his life banging his head against the wall, in a cell of the Healing Church.

The Madaras Twins also fell victim to the vermin. Although their past was on the fringes of the League, their story teaches us more about the origins of the vermin. The twins lived in the Forbidden Woods, where they were raised by a snake before they became hunters. They became known as "the Butchers," probably due to their unorthodox methods, learned from their singular upbringing. The description indicates that "both the twins became hunters, and brought back and dissected their beast prey, in order to support the villagers in their forbidden research": a friendly gesture, which nevertheless had catastrophic results. Indeed, the cadaver of this beast was swarming with vermin. Since the vermin are invisible without the Impurity Rune, they contaminated all of the village's inhabitants, along with other lifeforms: the twins' snake was also a victim, which drove the Butchers mad.[72]

The vermin epidemic, which first took root in a village of the Forbidden Woods, recalls the strange illness that struck Yharnam and led to the Beastly Scourge. Could this poison, also known as "Ashen Blood," be related? Could these vermin, invisible without the Impurity Rune, be behind the illness and madness that struck Yharnam (and Loran much earlier, in the Pthumerian era), a situation that quickly got out of hand, with the widespread use of the Blood Ministration? If this is the case, we can understand why fighting the infected hunters was so important to the League, because they were attacking the problem's origins rather than its result. Caryll, who created the runes and therefore made the vermin visible, perhaps hadn't understood the importance of these creatures, and simply settled for transcribing the inhuman sounds of the Great Ones. In spite of their scorn for humans, the Great Ones may have given them what they needed to eliminate their greatest and most insidious threat, which led to the downfall of the Pthumerian civilization. Unfortunately, men do not change: they focus on reaching the level of the gods, and pay no heed to the human condition's existential limitations...

---

72. "When they discovered vermin even in their beloved snake, the younger brother is said to have murdered the older," indicates the Butcher Mask.

Other Human Characters

❦ Iosefka and the Blood Priest

At the beginning of *Bloodborne*, the player wakes up in Iosefka's clinic, located not far from central Yharnam. A Blood Priest administers the Blood Ministration. This strange character, with his disheveled, grizzled beard, wears a large hat that obscures his face. The clinic belongs to the Healing Church, and appears to be a treatment center for invalids, or those who come to receive the Blood Ministration. Iosefka is the doctor responsible for this location, and she gives the player a few precious flasks to help in the challenging Night of the Hunt. These few flasks contain high-quality blood developed by Iosefka–players receive a significant amount of points from the blood. Later on, Iosefka will close her door to hunters–for hygiene reasons, she says–, but she continues to assist them as best she can. The clinic is an oasis of peace in the game, where the player can also send refugees.

Unfortunately, once twilight has passed, the affable doctor will be discreetly replaced by an impostor. Of course, her voice changes,[73] and she gains a new bone-chilling laugh. Since the dialogue continues through the clinic door, it is difficult to know what's really happened to her. Like other characters in the game, Iosefka seems to have lost her mind, but it is unclear why.

A hidden path in the Forbidden Woods leads to the back of Iosefka's clinic. Here, players can learn about the imposter's experiments: Celestials wander through the halls of her clinic! These deformed, bluish creatures recall the Choir's creations, which seems to tie this impostor Iosefka to the Healing Church's faction, or at least indicate that they are related. To fight, the fake doctor uses the exploding star produced by a Call Beyond, described as "one of the secret rites of the Choir." Imposter Iosefka is therefore indeed a Choir member, and she conducts her experiments on the refugees sent to the clinic by the player. The first victim was the real Iosefka, who we find transformed into a Celestial; she holds the final Iosefka blood vial, proof of her identity.

If we wait until the game's final phase, the Blood Moon, we can meet Impostor Iosefka without having to fight her. A strange scene, grotesque even, takes place in front of our eyes. The impostor crouches on all fours on a stretcher, suffering and spouting nonsensical questions: "God I'm nauseous... Have you ever felt this? It's progressing. I can see things... I knew it, I'm different. I'm no beast... I... Oh... God, it feels awful... but, it proves that I'm chosen. Don't you see? How they writhe, writhe inside my head..."

---

73. Two voice actors are cited in the credits.

It just takes one strike to finish her off with a spray of blood, and players receive One Third of Umbilical Cord. There are several possible interpretations for this.

First, we could assume that the fake Iosefka has been impregnated by a Great One, and is even close to giving birth: her stance, the nausea, the term "chosen" that she uses, and finally the One Third of Umbilical Cord, from the child of a Great One, all seem to support this thesis. However, if we look more closely at the scene, there is another tempting explanation: the impostor is not about to give birth, but rather is undergoing the effects of taking in too much Insight. As she says, she "can see things" and she is "different." She speaks of an "awful" feeling, and beings that writhe inside her head: this could be the effect of the "eyes on the inside," which Willem had also used in the past. It is likely that these eyes appear when characters consume One Third of Umbilical Cord, which we find on her body once she has been killed.[74] It seems that this cord is indeed the one Willem found several years earlier. Each piece of cord found by the player has a description of the cord's origins; the one we get from Imposter Iosefka says: "Provost Willem sought the Cord in order to elevate his being and thoughts to those of a Great One, by lining his brain with eyes." From Willem, the One Third of Umbilical Cord went from the Choir to the hands of Impostor Iosefka. It is also interesting to note that as players explore Byrgenwerth College, they meet and fight a Choir member; although he does not explain why he is there, this suggests that the Healing Church's secret organization has always kept an eye on Willem and his disciples. In this scenario, the Choir would have stolen the Cord of the Eye, which Willem previously stole from the Great One Kos. When the Blood Moon appears, fake Iosefka ingests the cord, thinking she is the chosen one to bear the Child of Blood. Unfortunately for her, the Great Ones choose Arianna, whose veins run with a special, tainted blood, as we saw in the section on the Vilebloods. This attribute is clearly more attractive to the Great Ones who are looking to reproduce. "When the red moon hangs low, the line between man and beast is blurred. And when the Great Ones descend, a womb will be blessed with child," says the note we've already seen, which suggests that only one child is conceived for every Blood Moon. This time, the chosen one is Arianna, and not Impostor Iosefka.

---

74. We only obtain this Cord of the Eye following the scene. If the duel with Imposter Iosefka takes place before the Blood Moon, players will not receive the One Third of Umbilical Cord.

⚜ Micolash

Although we already presented Micolash within the context of the story, we will now take a look at how this character relates to his fellow humans. Of course, we already know that men are fascinated by the power of the Great Ones, and crave access to it, using different means to do so. Some use Blood, which arouses their beasthood, while others focus on Insight and covet the possibilities of the power of the Cosmos. In truth, most of the characters and bosses we meet during the game were not necessarily bad to begin with. Whether beasts (Amelia, Ludwig, Laurence), addled with Blood or Insight (Father Gascoigne, the Celestial Emissary), or simply those who defend themselves against the player's intrusion (Maria, Logarius), it's hard to find any true malfeasance. That's not the case for Micolash, though.

The School of Mensis's spiritual guide didn't go for either Blood or Insight. He stayed true to himself–a little crazy, perhaps–, and willing to do anything to contact a Great One. The rituals developed in the School of Mensis spread terror among the residents of Yahar'gul. Stagecoaches crowd the streets, carrying caskets likely sent by the Witches of Hemwick[75] to provide the bodies necessary for the school's experiments.

When Micolash enters in contact with a Great One and becomes the host of the Nightmare of Mensis, the ritual has disastrous effects. The Blood Moon appears, condemning the human race, starting with the inhabitants of the Unseen Village. Thankfully, Willem and Rom, with their raised status, were able to produce a protective barrier to hide the new moon–rather ironic, since Willem was despairing about the human race and its utility. He nevertheless saved humans from Micolash's harmful actions: good against evil, in a way.

In the end, Micolash seems to be the only truly evil character in *Bloodborne*.[76] Driven by a malicious frenzy, he gleefully embraces his bad-guy role–a stance that was often more nuanced in the *Souls* series.

⚜ Gilbert

Gilbert is not from Yharnam originally. He has a bad memory of his arrival, calling the city's inhabitants inhospitable: "Yharnamites don't share much with outsiders,"

---

75. This hypothesis comes from the fact that Yahar'gul is home to "Eye Collector" enemies (their name in the official guide), who look similar to the Witches of Hemwick, except that the latter are covered with repulsive eyes. The two types of creatures still look very similar, with the same stooping posture and crooked staff. Also, Hemwick Charnel Lane, which leads to the witches' lair, is guarded by a patrol of Executioners: colossal, armed beings wielding large axes, who wear the hunter attire of Yahar'gul, where the School of Mensis was founded.
76. Of course, the Great Ones cannot aspire to this role, as they differ so greatly from the humans. These superior beings only feel scorn for the humans, and care little about their trivial happenings.

he says to the player, hidden behind the bars of his window. He set up in a house in Central Yharnam, where he lives like any other city-dweller. This is lucky, since Gilbert seems more talkative than his neighbors, with plenty of anecdotes about the city's past. He is the one to send the player, who has been seeking a vague "Paleblood" since the beginning of the adventure, in search of different types of blood from the Healing Church. He also tells us, between coughing fits, that he caught the Ashen Blood illness: it is incurable, and the Blood Ministration only softens the pain. This provides a clue about his past: Gilbert must have come from Yharnam before or during the Beastly Scourge years before. He does not seem to understand the link between the multiplying number of beasts and the Healing Church's blood therapy, and is simply glad he is "unharmed by the plague of beasts." At the end of the game, we find ourselves outside of Gilbert's house, after he has become a beast. We must kill him, even though he was one of the first to help us in our quest. "When the red moon hangs low, the line between man and beast is blurred": this adage has never rung so true. Even though Gilbert is a foreigner, he embodies the lives and fates of the Yharnamites like no other.

⚜ Oedon Chapel Residents

Unlike Gilbert, who prefers to stay in his own house, the city's few other surviving residents agree to seek shelter in Oedon Chapel. "The Blind Samaritan," as he is known in the official guide, took over the building to house Yharnamites seeking protection, given the great scale of the Night of the Hunt. The incense burning all around the chapel helps repel the beasts.

Several important characters can be found here, with underlying plotlines. For instance, rivalry breaks out between Blood Saint Adella and Arianna, who both offer us some of their blood to help with our quest. Adella provides the "real" blood from the Healing Church, while Arianna's blood is the tainted Cainhurst blood. Accepting favors from one or the other will increase tensions within the Oedon Chapel.

The other true Yharnamites–the old woman and old man–are generally fairly unpleasant with us. When the beggar[77] arrives in this holy place, quiet murders are committed,[78] leading to mistrust and panic in residents, starting with the Samaritan,

---

77. This is the blood-starved beggar that we mentioned in the section on the Healing Church Hunters, a former companion of Simon.

78. This has been a permanent feature in the series since *Demon's Souls*. There has always been a character who sneakily kills other NPCs: Yurt in *Demon's Souls*, on Mephistopheles' orders, perpetrating carnage within the Nexus; Lautrec takes on this role in the first *Dark Souls* by assassinating the Fire Keeper of the Firelink Shrine, before fleeing like a coward; finally, in *Dark Souls II*, Sorcerer Navlaan convinces the player to execute several NPCs in secret. Players familiar with the series eventually learn to be wary of the slightest character, returning to inhabited areas to make sure no NPCs are missing.

host of the shelter, who seems to be the most afraid of the group. This character appears totally benevolent, but there is something off about him. First, he doesn't look human at all. Though he remains mostly hidden behind his tattered attire, his oversize hands and arms are unsettling, along with his grayish skin and his posture, which suggests that he is missing his lower limbs. It doesn't matter that he speaks comforting words: he is naturally frightening. Another strange detail: he has the Formless Oedon Rune—the same Oedon that will impregnate Arianna if she survives until the Blood Moon appears. Was the Samaritan entrusted with the mission of luring a woman who could bear his master's child to the Oedon Chapel? It seems likely that the chosen one would be among the refugees in the Chapel—the few sane people remaining in Yharnam.

Irreverent Izzy

There is little information available about the hunter Izzy, known as the Irreverent. Like Archibald, his name appears in some item descriptions, but the character doesn't appear in the game itself. Like Archibald, Izzy was fascinated with the Darkbeasts, and he created a number of helpful hunting tools and weapons, in particular two of his creations that we find in the game: the Beast Claw (weapon developed using the bones of a Darkbeast) and the Beast Roar (powerful magic also taken from Darkbeasts), which knocks back foes. These are powerful yet dangerous tools, in that they draw from a person's beasthood, and with each use, draw them closer to becoming a beast.

Simple Gratia

A clumsy colossus, Gratia used different hunting methods from her associates. Since she was uncomfortable with guns, she built the Fist of Gratia, a "chunk of iron fitted with finger holes," to stun her adversaries in melee fighting. Players can loot this weapon from the imposing body of its creator. She was locked up in the Healing Church prison (which we explore in the Hunter's Nightmare), no doubt because of her unpredictable character and the danger she poses her peers. Or perhaps they imprisoned her simply because of who she was: Gratia's corpse, in the corner of the cell, suggests prayer and fear rather than signs of frenzied murder. However, her nickname and unusual appearance led to her sad fate.

The Great Ones and Other Cosmic Beings

The Great Ones pose the greatest mystery in *Bloodborne*. There are very few (if any) clues to explain their existence or intentions. Although these inaccessible beings play an important role in the story, it is tempting, and somewhat necessary, to come up with some hypotheses. We have little to draw on, but sometimes all we need is a name, or a simple gesture!

Based on what we have seen about the game's backstory and characters, it is difficult to place all of the Great Ones in the same category. Some, like Ebrietas, are called "inhuman kin of the Cosmos," while others like Oedon don't really have a form. We have to set aside some of our preconceived notions and view each Great One in their own right, rather than just as members of a superior species. We shouldn't forget that humans were the ones to call them "Great Ones" in the first place: the term is rather vague and religious, reflecting man's desire to attain a higher state–that of these beings.

If our own species were to meet extraterrestrial beings superior to us in all ways, would we stick with our current technology and spiritual knowledge? Or would we take the opportunity to advance to their level, or at least try? Based on the history of the human race, the answer seems obvious. This is one of *Bloodborne*'s primary topics. Every Great One exists on their own level, disdaining the inferior beings who unsuccessfully attempt to imitate them.

This narrative exercise follows in the line of the previous FromSoftware games, providing a fascinating and engaging context for the game. The story unfolds like a giant puzzle–emblematic of the *Souls* series–, while taking on a new dimension this time around. With *Bloodborne*, players must uncover the secret of the Great Ones, from the perspective of a simple human hunter. The puzzle is not just a way to tell a story, but a rare and ingenious "narrative design."[79] We must therefore work to understand the Great Ones, to follow a path that leads us to a fight with one of their most mysterious representatives: the Moon Presence.

❦ The Moon Presence

The Moon Presence is intriguing, particularly in how it appears suddenly at the end of the game, like a *deus ex machina*. It is one of the game's most impenetrable characters, and one of the most fascinating. Based on some clues cleverly sprinkled

---

79. Narrative design includes all of the mechanisms and subtle details used in a game to set up and tell a story, while remaining consistent with the other elements, such as level design, game design, ergonomics, the soundtrack, etc. In this way, players are immersed naturally in the game.

throughout the adventure, we have already proposed one interpretation of this mysterious being's intentions. Here, we will continue our thoughts on this character by exploring new hypotheses.

First of all, its name has given rise to a number of theories. The name is not really a proper noun like Ebrietas and Oedon, or a species classification like the Amygdalas. The Moon Presence is a unique, omnipresent entity, since the moon appears in almost every game panorama. The only exception is during the daytime, even though we know that it is never far off. Before appearing to the player as the game's final boss, this Great One is, as its name implies, a personification of the moon's presence, like Diane in Roman mythology, Ixchel for the Mayans, or Tsukuyomi in Shintoism. The examples are endless: men are time and again inclined to use symbols and give proper nouns to phenomena they can't explain. In *Bloodborne*, the name given to the Moon Presence is somewhat of a default, since this creature's true name remains unknown to humans, the inferior beings.

This Great One proves to be one of the more distant; its level of divinity makes it totally inaccessible to common mortals. It even appears to be above the other Great Ones. Oedon is worshipped by some members of the Healing Church, Ebrietas gave an audience to the Choir, the Amygdalas' curiosity seems to have been sparked by the School of Mensis's rituals, and Mergo's Wet Nurse gave Micolash a prominent place in the nightmare, after he was able to enter into contact with it there. Although the Moon Presence formerly approached Gehrman to impose its Hunter's Dream, it remained discreet by delegating everything to the First Hunter, and replacing him as needed (see one of the three conclusions, where the player's avatar, after killing Gehrman, appears seated in Gehrman's wheelchair). However, the Moon Presence continues to fulfill its Great One role, associated with the moon. The *Bloodborne* moon is different from our own. Its true nature seems to be the red moon that we see in the game's final section. The white moon, seen previously, seems to result from the barrier put in place by Rom and Willem. Indeed, when this barrier disappears and the moon takes on its true red form, humans are in grave danger. They turn into beasts, and the women may be "visited" to bear a Great One's child. The Moon Presence lives through this red moon, and its harmful effects on the population–a population scorned by this Great One.

The Moon Presence lives in several planes of existence: in the main world ("real world" doesn't really apply here), and in the Hunter's Dream that it created, where it appears as the final boss, emerging from a blood-red moon for the end fight. A reference to this Moon Presence can be found in the Hunter's Nightmare, at the end of the DLC, during the cutscene featuring the final boss, the Orphan of Kos: when the Orphan gazes at the moon, at this point pale yellow and somewhat hazy, we often hear crying–not a baby this time, but Gehrman. As it happens, this sound is an audio sample from a rare Gehrman dialogue, where he sobs, distraught about his fate as a prisoner in the dream, and begging his old friends Willem and Laurence to help him. In this brief moment facing the moon, when the cry rings out, a connection is drawn with the Hunter's Dream, and therefore the Moon Presence, omnipresent throughout the different planes of existence.

There is another point to examine—the ties drawn between the Paleblood and the Moon Presence—established by Hidetaka Miyazaki himself during an interview in the official guide. The word "Paleblood" is only used four times during the game.

First, by the Blood Priest at the very beginning of the introduction: "Oh, yes... Paleblood..." he says, before producing a strange sound, as if he interrupts his train of thought to rejoin the conversation. He changes the subject, and then gives the player the Blood Ministration. The word appears a second time in a note scrawled in Iosefka's clinic: "Seek Paleblood to transcend the hunt." This is also where the introduction took place: perhaps the man who mentions the Paleblood just took in this information... The term is mentioned a third time on a note we find in Yahar'gul, the Unseen Village. "Behold! a Paleblood sky!" Finally, it appears in a note in the Lecture Building "The nameless moon presence beckoned by Laurence and his associates. Paleblood."

The term seems to be both significant and unintelligible. Significant because it is one of the first words spoken in the game, and because it is associated with elements essential to the story: "transcend the hunt" or "nameless moon presence." Unintelligible because it could refer to anything. Some believe it refers quite simply to the player's avatar, who will "transcend the hunt" to end it; Miyazaki himself relates the Paleblood to the Moon Presence. In the official guide interview, Miyazaki actually puts forth two interpretations. The first is the sky's color when the Blood Moon appears: a very pale blue, "like a body drained of blood," he explains. The search for the Paleblood, he says, refers to the ritual of Mensis, which must be ended to finish the game. Since the Blood Moon is synonymous with the Moon Presence, Miyazaki adds that Paleblood is another name for this Great One. He provides no further explanation, preferring to leave the topic open to people's imagination... including his own!

Before wrapping up our discussion of the Moon Presence, we should bring up a very interesting theory regarding the Great One's intentions—a very different interpretation than the one we presented in the game story section. Per this theory, the Moon Presence is actually a type of predator that aims to eliminate the Great Ones' children. This theory arises from a strange set of notes we find on the second floor of the Lecture Building; "The nameless moon presence beckoned by Laurence and his associates. Paleblood," "Hunt the Great Ones. Hunt the Great Ones," "Master Willem was right. Evolution without courage will be the ruin of our race," and "Three third cords."

The first note refers to Laurence's summoning of the Moon Presence, with Willem and Gehrman as his "associates." The Great One takes the opportunity to defeat them and implement its plan: hunting the Great Ones, as mentioned in the second note. Under the moon's influence, which is omnipresent throughout the Nights of the Hunt, the hunters fulfill this mission to hunt the Great Ones, particularly their children. "Every Great One loses its child," states a One Third of Umbilical Cord description. However, the cause of this death is never explained: the death is not a natural one; they are hunted. "When the red moon hangs low, the line between man and beast is blurred. And when the Great Ones descend, a womb will be blessed with a child." We've cited this note several times: here, we see a reference to the method of hunting used by the Moon Presence. By appearing as the Blood Moon, it attracts the other Great Ones, motivating them to procreate. The hunters then hunt the newborn and eliminate it. If this is the case, the hunters are simply the Moon Presence's minions.

From this perspective, Kos was deprived of its child in the Fishing Hamlet following the mission led by Willem and other hunters. Then came the Moon Presence's own child, who was no doubt assassinated by Gehrman or the child's own mother, Maria, who was also a hunter, and under the moon's power. Arianna and Oedon's deformed infant was also killed, by the player this time. One anomaly remains: Mergo. No doubt eliminated at the time of the Pthumerians, perhaps following the same methods, Queen Yharnam's son is still alive within the Nightmare of Mensis. The player's final task will be to eliminate this anomaly.

The third and fourth note from the Lecture Building show how Willem discovers the formidable danger posed by the Moon Presence, and that the Moon Presence's hunters were already primarily on this creature's side. No doubt the help from Kos (who gave him and Rom enough eyes and Insight) that allowed him to take stock of the situation.[80] His power remained limited, however, and he could only appeal to Rom to contain the power and influence of the Moon Presence for a certain time. This means that Willem would have scribbled these notes for the next hero (in the mythical sense), who could reverse the situation. The word "courage" in the third note refers to the final battle with the Moon Presence, which becomes possible once the player has taken in the three Thirds of Umbilical Cord. When we, the hero, triumph over this god, we're reincarnated as a Great One, living free of the threat posed by the predatory Moon Presence. The symbol of rebirth is strong, because it represents the evolution of mankind. It is a new beginning, and one of which Master Willem would have been proud.

80. Micolash's words take on a new meaning: "Ahh, Kos, or some say Kosm… As you once did for the vacuous Rom, grant us eyes, grant us eyes. Plant eyes on our brains, to cleanse our beastly idiocy." Kos would thus help Byrgenwerth counter the Moon Presence's destructive plans.

⚜ Formless Oedon

Unlike the Moon Presence, Formless Oedon is a Great One known to humans. The members of the Healing Church worshipped it and its blood, "the essence of the formless Great One," as we learn from the Formless Oedon Rune, which also indicates that Oedon "surreptitiously seeks the precious blood."[81] The rune's maker, Caryll, was able to write down the sounds Oedon made, and even its voice. Seeking prodigious blood, the priests attempted to grow closer to the Great One. For this reason, a number of locations in Yharnam were named after it, such as Oedon Chapel or Tomb. One theory posits how this Great One died, based on this location. It seems that Oedon changed form to become "Formless." "The Great One Oedon, lacking form, exists only in voice, and is symbolized by this rune," explains the rest of its rune. Like the Moon Presence, which lives through the moons (in the main world, as well as in dreams and nightmares), Oedon affirms its presence through its voice. No one knows what this voice sounds like, but the Formless Great One does exist in the world of humans. Oedon, or its presence, comes to impregnate Arianna at the end of the game, as we've seen. Although it is possible for it to live within several planes of existence, the theory of this Great One's death is not the most convincing. The Tomb of Oedon (a simple cemetery) seems to be a mere homage to the formless being. The cemetery that borders the Oedon Chapel seems to be a religious architectural grouping–a place of worship. The description with the Tomb of Oedon Key clearly mentions "the residents of Oedon" to refer to those who live in this location, in the heart of the Cathedral Ward in Yharnam.

The name "Oedon" could come from the odeons of Ancient Rome and Greece. These buildings, smaller than the theaters, were generally used to host singing exercises or poetry competitions: the buildings were dedicated to the voice, a connection to this Great One, perhaps.

⚜ Mergo's Wet Nurse and the Brain of Mensis

It's strange: there are two Great Ones in the Nightmare of Mensis. One is Mergo's Wet Nurse (creator of the nightmare and very aggressive final level boss) and the other is the Brain of Mensis, inert, hidden in the shadowy recesses of the nightmare's castle. What made this cohabitation possible?

Mergo's Wet Nurse is a large creature with two legs, black and winged like a crow. With six arms, each bearing a dark blade that reflects moonlight depending on

---

81. Oedon's precious blood is the blood dregs, or more generally the blood of the clan of Cainhurst, according to the interpretation we presented in the Vilebloods section.

the attack angle, it is dressed (so to speak) in a few tatters. Its face remains hidden behind the black shreds of clothing or flesh, all camouflaged by the dark night. The fight takes place at the top of the nightmare's castle, in a circular, dilapidated room missing its ceiling, open to the starless sky, bathed only in the pale light of the immense full moon. In the center of the room, baby Mergo cries in a cradle. The cradle appears empty, but is difficult to see. Only the groans indicate a presence, before becoming silent when the Wet Nurse dies. Like in the fight with Gascoigne, it is possible to use the Tiny Music Box against Mergo's Wet Nurse, which becomes disturbed. The boss theme also plays a few notes from the music box, suggesting a connection between the Great One and the melody. Since nothing else suggests a connection between Mergo's Wet Nurse and the Gascoigne family, we can assume that this is a traditional Yharnam lullaby, which could go as far back as the Pthumeru civilization, or that the music box was found in the remains of the ancient civilization, restored by Gascoigne and given to his daughters, carrying on the calming melody through ages and civilizations.

Mergo's Wet Nurse has its fair share of mysteries, but they're nothing compared to the enigmas surrounding the existence of the Brain of Mensis. The Living String relic calls the Brain of Mensis "a legitimate Great One," but it seems that the brain was created using members of the School of Mensis, according to Mergo's One Third of Umbilical Cord: "This Cord granted Mensis audience with Mergo, but resulted in the stillbirth of their brains." It seems that this creature, a gigantic mass covered in eyes, resulted from the amalgamation of the brains of Micolash's associates. The Brain of Mensis would then have been charged with defending the castle against invaders. As a consequence, on the outskirts of the fortress, players are stabbed by almost invisible needles, which inflict massive Frenzy damage—this detail recalls the "Winter Lantern" creatures, as they're named in the official guide, frightening monsters with visible brains and a number of protruding eyes, inflicting Frenzy with daunting speed. There are many guardians of this type, located on the path leading to the Brain of Mensis. When players pull the right lever, this creature falls into the murky depths of the castle, recalling the Abyss from *Dark Souls*. The Brain of Mensis will no longer attack, and can be approached safely. The Brain will drop the Moon Rune if players make contact with it, using a gesture with their arms in the shape of a crescent moon. Could its power have come from the moonlight on the castle, which explains its powerlessness in the dark depths? A few strikes will kill it.

⚜ Amygdalas and Patches

Many Amygdala Great Ones inhabit the *Bloodborne* world, and players meet several of them throughout the adventure. The first time is when exiting Oedon Chapel, in a small space with a well at the center: a hunter's corpse lies in a corner, and if you approach it, a portal will appear to a different dimension, and an Amygdala arm stretches out. If the arm catches you, you instantly become frenzied and die. Of course, if players have over forty Insight points, they can see the Amygdala perched on the chapel's facade waiting for its next victim. Using the "Eye of a Blood-Drunk Hunter," from the Hunter's Dream messengers, the same Amygdala will transport the player to the Hunter's Nightmare, where the DLC begins. Many other Amygdalas live on the roofs of Yharnam, in a dimension invisible to humans. Most can be found in Yahar'gul, where the ancient Mensis rituals draw them in. On the path that connects the Cathedral Ward to the Unseen Village, another Amygdala captures players[82] in the same way as in the well area. This time, we are taken to the Lecture Building, where we meet the spider Patches. The Lecture Building is a separate location, an ethereal representation of a university center, like an echo of Byrgenwerth College. From there, we can reach the Nightmare Frontier, an otherworldly area where players fight one of the Amygdalas. This Amygdala is giant and aggressive, appearing larger than its peers, as if there exists a hierarchy between the Amygdalas and we have to fight their queen. Do they act with a collective mind, like a colony of ants? Indeed, their behavior doesn't seem specific to any one individual. These Great Ones remain shrouded in mystery.

Physically, the Amygdalas resemble large, biped spiders. In addition to their two legs, they have eight long arms[83] spread out like a spider's legs along their skeletal body.[84] Higher up, their oval head[85] draws the eye, with its thick hairs protruding from between their many cavities. Most Amygdalas have tentacles, the one exception being the "queen" who lives in the Nightmare Frontier. It can also cast some occult spells; when it uses magic during the fight, previously invisible eyes jut out of the cavities in its head. It also has the Ailing Loran Chalice. It's possible that Amygdalas were worshipped in Loran as they would be later in Yahar'gul, telling by the number of statues in their likeness (often poorly constructed and small, with only two arms). These Great Ones may be any size: from the giant queen in the Nightmare Frontier, to the medium-sized ones from Yahar'gul, to the much more modest Amygdalas located elsewhere. Amygdalan Arms, for instance, are small enough for hunters to use as weapons, as their description indicates: "The arm of a small Amygdala Great One."

In the official guide, the Amygdalas are called "giant false Gods." Although the Great Ones are not true "gods" in the mythological sense, but rather are superior

---

82. Players are captured only if they have a Tonsil Stone, an item that resembles a smaller version of an Amygdala head. However, at this time during the adventure, players have no idea what this Great One looks like, or what purpose the Tonsil Stone serves—the item is simply described as "a latticed, deformed rock, or perhaps a meteorite."

83. Amygdalas have ten limbs, which technically distinguishes them from spiders, with their four pairs of legs. It is amusing to note that the true "spiders" in *Bloodborne*, at the castle's entryway in the Nightmare of Mensis, have no fewer than twelve legs. Not a very attractive quality!

84. If we are to believe the Amygdalan Arm description, their bones are quite tough.

85. The Latin word "*amygdala*," derived from the ancient Greek ἀμυγδάλη (*amugdálē*), means almond: the Great One's elliptical, cracked head certainly recalls this shape.

beings that exist in other dimensions, they are still considered as such by humans. However, the official guide doesn't refer to the other Great Ones as "false Gods," which could imply that the Amygdalas we meet in the game aren't actually related to the Great One named Amygdala. The latter may exist in a different dimension—for instance, in a dream it created—, or it could actually be a collective mind shared between the different creatures of this type, and this common mind forms the one true Amygdala.

The term "*amygdala*" refers to two parts of the human body: medically, "amygdale" refers to the tonsils (from Latin, in addition to "almonds"), and more commonly, amygdalae are bodies found in the human brain. The first, tonsils,[86] play a role in the immune response. Since the Amygdala boss is located in an area known as the Nightmare Frontier, its goal could be to prevent parasites (hunters) from reaching the other Great Ones' dreams and nightmares! The Amygdalas may therefore be protectors, a first level of defense placed at the border of the dreamlike worlds where the Great Ones live. Our brain's amygdalae, on the other hand, serves to detect threats: they can trigger anxiety and fear, so that our bodies react correctly even to the slightest risk. This reference may tie into the last one, in that the Amygdalas are responsible for protecting the Great Ones, acting as sentinels.

Some humans worship the Amygdalas. Patches the Spider falls into this category (his name clearly referencing Patches the Hyena and Mild-Mannered Pate from the *Souls* games). It comes as no surprise, therefore, that this evil character pushes the player into a poisoned river in the Nightmare Frontier the first chance he gets. For much of the game, we can't see Patches: he speaks to us through closed doors. But his characteristically sneaky voice allows us to identify him. The first encounter takes place in the Forbidden Woods: Patches moves from house to house, in an attempt to speak with the player; here, he gives players the aforementioned Tonsil Stone, allowing them to meet his god, Amygdala.

However, it is difficult to pin down Patches' role. Obviously, his primary intention is to give players as an offering to satisfy his god, without thinking for an instant that this hunter could possibly defeat the Great One and kill Amygdala. Patches is thus responsible for the destruction of the god that he worships. He appears to be somewhat simple-minded and behind his manipulative words, he lacks self-confidence. After Amygdala dies, he tries to rally us to his side by begging for our friendship, before heading off in search of a new god to worship.

---

86. The object used to reach the Lecture Building is called the "Tonsil Stone." In the French translation, it is called a "*caséum*": this refers specifically to the "tonsilloliths" formed by some people's tonsils that cause bad breath: this may be a humorous, cryptic reference in the French translation, which makes more sense once the Great One is revealed.

Patches the Spider has a human head and (no surprise) a spider-like body. This physical trait confirms one detail about the *Bloodborne* universe: those who worship the Great Ones eventually go through corporeal changes that reflect the "divinity" they worship. For instance, the fishermen who worship Kos are deformed and pale, slumping under the weight of clusters of shells,[87] and partially transformed into gastropods, like the "Snail Woman" monster. These transformations relate to Kos's intimate relationship with the ocean. Amygdala resembles a spider, so it is not surprising that its devotees all take on this characteristic as well: Patches retained his human head, but gained a large spider body. This metamorphosis allows Patches to move more quickly between the different planes of existence. From the Forbidden Woods, he easily moves to the Lecture Building, then to the Nightmare Frontier, tracking the player's every move.

⚜ Kos

All signs indicate that the giant white body washed up on the shore at the end of *The Old Hunters* is the Great One Kos. The village fishermen continue to worship "Mother Kos," whom they associate with the ocean. In the same way that the Moon Presence is related to the moon, Kos's identity seems to be bound to the sea.[88] The symbolism of the primeval waters, the source for the creation of the world in many myths, resonates here. The Great Ones are not supposed to give birth, yet the Orphan of Kos is born right in front of our eyes, emerging from the abdomen of this strange white creature. The scene takes place within the nightmare created by Kos, which allows it to take on different forms, like the Moon Presence at the end of the game. The creature is therefore one incarnation of Kos, constantly reliving, deadly birth. "Every Great One loses its child, and then yearns for a surrogate," indicates the description for One Third of Umbilical Cord. The Great One that lost Mergo created the Nightmare of Mensis, a home for the still-living child; Kos did the same thing in the Hunter's Nightmare, to relive this terrible moment. The dreams seem to act as surrogates for these Great Ones.

In our presentation of the game's history, we saw that Willem stole the Cord of the Eye from Kos. The deeds perpetrated by the members of Byrgenwerth College in the Fishing Hamlet went much farther than petty theft, however. When the Fishing Hamlet's priest gives the player's avatar the Accursed Brew, we find the following

---

87. Their monstrous appearance recalls the hideous pirates from the ghost ship the *Flying Dutchman*, in the movie *Pirates of the Caribbean: Dead Man's Chest*, a clever blend of human features and sea creature oddities.
88. A revealing detail: before opening the path towards the Fishing Hamlet, the hands of the Astral Clocktower stop on the same symbol as that of the Deep Sea Rune, a direct reference to the sea.

description: "Skull of a local from the violated fishing hamlet. The inside of the skull was forcibly searched for eyes, as evidenced by innumerable scratches and indentations." This skull is proof of the barbarous experiments and dissections conducted by Byrgenwerth. Willem, of course, was obsessed with eyes, focusing his research on this study. It is also likely that hunters participated in the massacre while protecting the scholars, helping them capture fishermen for their studies.

These hunters probably included Maria and Gehrman. Disgusted by the carnage, Maria threw her weapon down to the bottom of a village well: the famous Rakuyo sword. The first words that Maria hurls at the player contain an amusing play on words: "A corpse should be left well alone." No doubt, the main "corpse" she is referring to here is none other than her own, which the player just "inspected" using the very common *Bloodborne* and *Souls* action. This warning could also be applied to the corpses of Kos and Kos's child, and even to the fishermen's bodies. Increasing the ambiguity of these words, Maria adds: "Oh, I know very well how the secrets beckon so sweetly."

No one knows the scope of Gehrman's involvement, but one detail suggests that he was profoundly traumatized by these events. When presenting the Moon Presence, we mentioned the scene where the Orphan of Kos stares at the moon and we hear Gehrman sobbing. This crying could have a simple interpretation–that the First Hunter is suffering for Kos, echoing through the different planes of existence[89]; however, these tears could also be tied to the massacre perpetrated by Byrgenwerth, in which he participated. This could explain why, once the Orphan of Kos has been defeated, the Doll from the Hunter's Dream shows the player that the First Hunter is sleeping peacefully, finally at peace. It's almost as though the Hunter's Nightmare has ended one of his worst memories, tied to the rampage in the Fishing Hamlet. Or is he simply relieved to see the end of a terrible period, where his "children" hunters were abandoned in this nightmare, with no escape?

The Hunter's Nightmare is a curse, a damned place for troubled hunters–those in the grips of frenzy, or even in the throes of death. "Curse the fiends, their children too. And their children, forever, true." This is spoken by a female voice[90] when players are trapped by the Amygdala that transports them to the Hunter's Nightmare. Farther on, the priest at the entry to the Fishing Hamlet echoes her words: "Let the pungence of Kos cling, like a mother's devotion...," but also: "Lay the curse of blood upon them, and their children, and their children's children, for evermore," and: "Each wretched birth will plunge each child into a lifetime of misery." Finally, Simon of the Healing Church, about to die at the end of the DLC, confesses: "This village is the true secret. Testament to the old sins... It feeds this Hunter's Nightmare... Please, bring to an end

89. Is there anything worse than losing a child? The *Bloodborne* "gods" tell the world that there is not.
90. Could this anonymous voice be from "Mother Kos"?

to the horror... So our forefathers sinned?...We hunters cannot bear their weight forever..." These three characters all touch on the same idea: due to the "profanation" (a tame euphemism) committed by the hunters in the Fishing Hamlet, and the subsequent affront to Kos, the latter put a curse on all of the hunters and their successors, throwing them into its world, the Hunter's Nightmare, where they would be tortured for eternity. Gehrman understood the consequences of their actions in the Fishing Hamlet far too late. The damage was done, and an angry Kos had already enacted the curse. However, as we've seen, the First Hunter formed the Crows in an attempt to limit the damage by saving some of his fellow hunters. It is not by chance that the Hunter's Dream and Nightmare are opposites: they directly recall heaven and hell, created following the crimes committed by the first hunters.

The tie between the Moon Presence's dream and Kos is the subject of an interesting theory, particularly with regard to Gehrman. Insofar as he participated in the massacres committed by Byrgenwerth, it's possible he was the one to steal the One Third of Umbilical Cord from the entrails of Kos. In this case, he would have been the first target of the curse that struck present and future hunters. Per this same theory, Gehrman from the Hunter's Dream would also live through the Orphan of Kos in the Hunter's Nightmare: this would give him a ringside seat to Kos's fury by continually experiencing the Great One's birth, aggression, and immense pain. The shift from one dream to another would be made as Gehrman sleeps.[91] Then, he would awake in the mind of the Orphan of Kos. Like many hunters, the Orphan of Kos wears a cape, and brandishes a weapon created from the placenta of Kos, the shape of which recalls Gehrman's famous scythe. As we've seen many times, there is nothing random about any of these details in *Bloodborne*. The anxious, unsettled words Gehrman stammers in his sleep, begging Laurence or even Willem to free him, later become clear when the Plain Doll shows the player that her master seems peaceful after the defeat of the Orphan of Kos, marking the end of the Hunter's Nightmare, and thus Gehrman's ordeal.

Finally, we can look at another aspect of Kos, the being found washed up on the bank in the nightmare. It seems to have died long ago, of a mysterious cause. "When the carcass of Kos washed up on the coast, its insides were teeming with tiny parasites, unlike any found in humans." This is the description of the Kos Parasite weapon, dropped by the defeated Orphan of Kos. In the real world, in the past, the fishermen found the Great One washed up on the shore. In their culture, they venerated the ocean, a source of abundance and nourishment. This new creature strengthened their beliefs in another spiritual dimension. Like the Irish gods (the Tuatha Dé

---

91. Once the initial game stages and levels have been completed, the old man proves less helpful than the Doll, since he sleeps most of the time when the player is in the Hunter's Dream. This phenomenon was already apparent in the main game, and makes more sense within the DLC.

Danann) who arrived from the sea, according to Celtic legend, this mysterious and divine white creature abruptly brought these fishermen into contact with the Great Ones. In the wake of this event, they discovered the "Celestial Water," taken from the ocean, which they began consuming as part of a religion devoted to "Mother Kos." Then the physical changes began, drawing closer ties between these fishermen and the ocean. No one knows anything about the parasites found on the washed-up white creature, except that they proved less harmful to humans than to the celestial Great One. In the beginning, the parasites must have been in the Celestial Water that the fishermen drank, and then the test subjects in the Healing Church's laboratories. In spite of the vile deformities it caused, they took to this water due to the new abilities it gave them, including discovering the Cosmos, like the Lumenwood later. Kos—with its Cosmos-derived name[92]—seems to draw its power from the Cosmos. The pale color of the creature is also found in the Celestials, who have an obvious connection to the Cosmos, and also in Ebrietas, simply known as "Daughter of the Cosmos."

☙ Ebrietas, Daughter of the Cosmos

Ebrietas, Daughter of the Cosmos, formerly known as the "left behind Great One," was found one day in the Pthumerian crypts by members of the Choir. Ebrietas granted the Choir an audience, which allowed them to conduct experiments on the eldritch Truth, and eventually led to the creation of the Celestials, as we've seen.

Ebrietas's monstrous appearance is tricky to describe. Heaps of tentacles, alongside scraggy wings, which all meet at the center of the pale creature, on a deformed, repugnant body as large as it is repulsive. The head is split into two parts, opening onto a cluster of pale, slimy tubes. At the creature's core, a giant brain regularly appears, covered in red and green eyes. Not only is this one of the game's most frightening monsters, the fight against Ebrietas is no picnic, either. It uses many curses, calling on the Cosmos. One of these curses is a Call Beyond, a powerful exploding star once studied by the Choir (which developed a ritual popular with the Choir's members). The Choir eventually produced a hunter's tool, which the player can use during the adventure.

Ebrietas is the only Great One that has no connection with a dream or nightmare. This Great One was indeed left behind, abandoned in the world of humans—the Pthumerians at the time. From that point forward, Ebrietas lived in the Choir's area, more specifically in a location called the Altar of Despair. Although the Daughter of the Cosmos initially seems all-powerful, it eventually looks rather pathetic.

---

92. "Ahh, Kos, or some say Kosm…" and "The Cosmos, of course!" are two noteworthy quotes from Micolash, who draws the connection between the Great One and the Cosmos in his fight with the player.

⚜ Rom, the Vacuous Spider

Rom was formerly a student at Byrgenwerth. Thanks to Willem's research, it accessed the eldritch Truth, undergoing mental and physical metamorphosis. It transformed into a large "spider," with small legs and a giant body, similar to the Amygdala, particularly in its lumpy, eye-covered head. After becoming an inhuman kin of the Cosmos, nothing about Rom was mortal. It was no doubt one of the first to reach the Cosmos, but it lost his mind and the memory of its origins and beliefs. Thankfully, Willem was able to channel this new strength to stave off the Mensis ritual, as we explained in the section on the game's story.

Rom's precise identity remains a mystery. However, the creature's identity is less important than its role and its past. It will be more interesting to look at where Willem placed Rom to protect humanity: the Moonside Lake. Ancient beliefs hold that lakes are the eyes of the earth–specifically, eyes through which lower beings, which live below ground, watch the divinities on the surface. Although the lower *Bloodborne* entities, the humans, obviously don't live underground, they still wish to access the knowledge of the superior beings, the Great Ones. The Great Ones exist in higher dimensions, such as the Cosmos or the Amygdalas' plane of existence. The lake as the "eye of the earth" is an apt symbol here: Rom, within Moonside Lake, places a barrier to hide the red moon, and consequently, some of the dimensions where the Great Ones live. By solving the riddle of Rom and the lake, we look through the "eye of the earth": the human player, an inferior being, can observe the Great Ones, superior beings.

Another element of symbolism in the game is the Lake runes, which describe such an expanse of water as a powerful defense, a type of fortification. Rom lives in the Moonside Lake, translated in the French version by "Lac Sélène", a name which holds its own meaning. The connection here with the moon recalls Greek mythology, and the goddess of the moon, Selene. If we take this farther, we can compare Rom with Endymion, the moon goddess's lover. The goddess puts him to sleep to grant him eternal life. As in the *Souls* games, time feels intangible, and Rom seems to be capable of maintaining the barrier in place for all of eternity if necessary. Slowly, as if asleep, but surely. To conclude this parallel, the moon goddess had fifty daughters, the Menae: a large number of children which recalls the many spiders that "help" Rom fight the player, and consequently defend the full moon, Selene.

DARK SOULS

ダークソウル

BEYOND THE GRAVE

CHAPTER THREE
THEMES

Cosmic horror – Lovecraft's shadow

It's impossible to cover *Bloodborne*'s themes without first looking at the DNA this work shares with the tales of Howard Phillips Lovecraft. This famous twentieth-century writer, now known as one of the most influential and essential authors of horror, produced a wealth of terrifying short stories. These stories depict characters who, by chance, or due to their own research, find themselves faced with indescribably abominable apparitions, as they become aware of a supernatural reality that often drives them to madness—a visceral fear and a form of paranoia that haunted Lovecraft in his own life.

A Sick Mind Inside a Sick Body

H. P. Lovecraft was born on August 20, 1890 in Providence, Rhode Island, to a family descended from wealthy British colonists.[93] Early on, a major event marked Lovecraft's childhood: when he was only three, his father, Winfield Scott Lovecraft, began to experience psychotic episodes. A victim of severe hallucinations, he was committed to Butler Hospital, where he died five years later.

Lovecraft was raised by his mother (Sarah Susan Phillips Lovecraft), his grandmother, and his two maternal aunts. Obsessed with reading, he soon showed talent for memorizing poetry, and then for writing—he wrote his first poems at the age of six. His grandfather, who strongly encouraged this passion, would tell him horror stories of his own invention. The seeds were thus planted in his brain.

The boy's schooling was irregular, due to his delicate and sickly constitution. He plunged even deeper into his reading, devouring books from his grandfather's library in the attic. He suffered from parasomnia (a sleep disorder), and more specifically night terrors: his nightmares were haunted by frightening creatures. In two

93. His family tree goes back to seventeenth-century New England.

of his short stories, these creatures are called "nightgaunts," described as vaguely human-shaped, faceless monsters that are all-black, with horns, a tail and bat wings.

His grandfather's death in 1904 affected him greatly, and the poor management of the family's estate placed his surviving family in a difficult financial situation. The house was sold, and Lovecraft and his mother were forced to move to a smaller house. He lived secluded with her[94] for several years. At first, he dreamed of becoming an astronaut, but had to give this up due to his shortcomings in math.[95] He then devoted himself fully to reading and writing.

In 1913, he wrote to a pulp magazine,[96] *The Argosy*, to criticize the sappy love stories written by Frederick Jackson. This would kick off a lively debate in the magazine's letters to the editor, which drew the attention of the United Amateur Press Association. The latter soon contacted Lovecraft to join their ranks. The budding author accepted, and produced a number of poems and short stories. He was published for the first time in 1916 in the association's review, with a story entitled *The Alchemist*. At the same time, between 1915 and 1923, he also published his own journal, *The Conservative*, in which he and other amateur journalists wrote articles about politics,[97] the social climate and literature, along with some poems and short stories.

From Amateur to Author

When she experienced serious depression and bouts of hysteria, his mother was committed in 1919 to Butler Hospital—the same psychiatric hospital where her husband spent the final years of his life. She died here in 1921 following a postoperative complication. This event threw a darker cloud over Lovecraft, who still managed to get published in 1919.[98]

94. Lovecraft later said that his mother's constant presence and the strange love-hate relationship she had maintained with him since her husband's death had a negative impact on him. For instance, when he was still a child, she would openly tell the neighbours he was an ugly boy. This likely increased his desire for reclusion. Regarding his emotional and psychological development, his wife Sonia later said that as a spouse, although he was an attentive lover, he took no initiative, no matter the field.
95. He later revealed that he suffered a "nervous breakdown" (in his words).
96. These inexpensive publications flourished in the United States during the first half of the twentieth century. They covered a wide variety of popular genres and helped jumpstart the careers of many fantasy and science fiction authors (including Philip K. Dick, Isaac Asimov, Ray Bradbury and Edgar Rice Burroughs).
97. Lovecraft's xenophobia is still a topic of debate. His racism subsided somewhat during the later years of his life.
98. Among his first texts, the *Dagon* novel was published by the magazine *The Vagrant* in 1919. The work contains his characteristic style, particularly his first-person narration and descriptions rife with adjectives and comparisons.

His early works draw clear influence from Edgar Allan Poe.[99] However, the money he made from these publications and his meager inheritance were not sufficient for his lifestyle. Being a "gentleman" (in the British sense of the term) was important to him, and his pride prevented him from taking on a variety of small jobs in order to earn money—a situation he felt was beneath an author like him.

Around this time, he met Sonia Greene at an amateur press convention. They fell in love and were married in 1924, before moving together to Brooklyn, New York.

Unfortunately, Sonia came up against financial problems that forced her to close her hat shop. To make matters worse, she fell ill, and Lovecraft's income was insufficient for the two of them. Sonia had to take on odd jobs, and subsequently moved to be closer to her work, leaving Lovecraft alone in their apartment. They separated a few years later.

Though he was initially happy to move to New York, Lovecraft began to regret this decision over time. He remained poor, and continued to lose weight at an alarming rate. He continued to write for a pulp magazine, *Weird Tales*. However, he was robbed, which was the straw that broke the camel's back. He left New York to return to Providence, where he spent the last decade of his life—the most prolific in terms of his literary production.[100]

He also maintained long, passionate correspondence with authors and future writers, such as two of his fellow *Weird Tales* writers, Clark Ashton Smith (with over one hundred horror and science fiction short stories to his name) and Robert E. Howard (the famous creator of *Conan*), along with Robert Bloch (*Psycho*) and, later, August Derleth. This group of friends would be dubbed the "Lovecraft Circle," referring the reciprocal influences of the various members, who didn't hesitate to borrow concepts and elements from Lovecraft's mythological outlines and stories, with Lovecraft's blessing (and he did the same with their works).

Although he had gained a respectable following, and *Weird Tales* sold well, Lovecraft still struggled to make ends meet. Too sensitive to criticism, with very low self-confidence,[101] he refused offers from interested publishers, and didn't bother sharing some

---

99. This 19th-century author, famous for his many short stories such as *The Fall of the House of Usher* and *The Purloined Letter*, or the poem *The Raven*, was one of the most important American authors of the Romantic era. His works are often considered precursors to the fantasy genre and the macabre. His impact can be felt in many artistic fields.

100. His style became richer, and he drew influence from another writer, Lord Dunsany. Dunsany was an Irish writer and contemporary of Lovecraft (1878–1957) who specialized in fantasy works (*The King of Elfland's Daughter*), prefiguring many works from the 20th century. Lovecraft drew inspiration from the latter to conceive his imaginary world "Dreamlands."

101. At the beginning of his career, it seems that he destroyed many of his short stories. He was very critical of his own work. He felt that he didn't have his own style, and remained in the shadow of Poe and Lord Dunsany—in his final years this fear pushed him to refine his writing and produce more contemporary stories.

works which would likely have been quite successful.[102] He continued to live in poverty, consumed by anxiety. The tide began to turn in 1936 when a young publisher, Julius Schwartz, agreed to publish *At the Mountains of Madness*[103] as a three-part series, in *Astounding Stories* (another pulp magazine), followed in June by the short story *The Shadow Out of Time*. These two publications brought the author a decent sum of money—the greatest amount of his career.

However, Lovecraft's friend Robert E. Howard committed suicide that same month, which greatly upset him. He began experiencing terrible stomach pain, and at the beginning of 1937, he was diagnosed with cancer of the small intestine. He died on March 15, without any idea of how great his fame would grow.

Posterity and Influence

Lovecraft's legacy is in large part due to one of his former correspondents, August Derleth, who was only twenty-five years old in 1937. With the help of his friend Donald Wandrei (who had been instrumental in publishing *The Shadow Out of Time*), Derleth tried to publish Lovecraft's short stories still in manuscript form, with no success. To this end, in 1939 the two writers decided to found their own publishing house, called Arkham House.[104] Derleth and Wandrei played an important role in Lovecraft's posthumous renaissance, and Derleth even worked to complete the unfinished pieces, or write new stories based on stories the author had just started to sketch out. Though it led to a number of controversies and negative reactions, August Derleth expanded Lovecraft's cryptic cosmogony, which he grouped under the (misleading) name "the Cthulhu Mythos."[105] Cthulhu wasn't the most significant being in the Lovecraft pantheon (if, in fact, there ever was a real hierarchy in his works).

Several critics, such as Dirk Mosig and Richard Louis Tierney, criticize August Derleth for warping Lovecraft's universe by imposing a moral, even binary vision[106]

---

102. This is particularly the case for *The Shadow over Innsmouth*, written in 1931. August Derleth was fascinated by this story, and submitted it in secret to *Weird Tales* in 1933, but it was rejected. In 1936, Visionary Publishing Company published *The Shadow over Innsmouth* as a book—the only book of Lovecraft's to be published in his lifetime. *The Shadow over Innsmouth* only sold a few hundred copies: a failure for Visionary Publishing, which didn't come back knocking on his door.
103. Written in 1931, the manuscript had been previously rejected by *Weird Tales*.
104. Arkham is a fictional Massachusetts town developed by Lovecraft, serving as the backdrop for some of his short stories. Arkham Asylum in *Batman*, for instance, is a direct reference to Lovecraft (the city of Arkham was also home to a mental asylum).
105. Lovecraft favored the term "Yog Sothothery" in reference to Yog Sothoth, one of the major cosmic entities in his work.
106. Derleth was Protestant, while Lovecraft was an atheist. It is also worth noting that he associated some of the Great Old Ones with the four elements.

to a universe that freed itself of human considerations, and didn't aim to be perfectly comprehensible.[107]

Either way, this visibility from Arkham House has ensured that Lovecraft's influence will continue to live on. Several famous writers have directly claimed him as an influence, such as the authors Stephen King (*The Shining*, *The Mist*, *Bag of Bones*) and Clive Barker (*Everville*, *Hellraiser*), along with directors John Carpenter (*The Thing*, *In the Mouth of Madness*) and Guillermo del Toro[108] (*The Devil's Backbone*, *Pan's Labyrinth*, *Hellboy*).

Little by little, Lovecraft's work began to resonate with horror fans, with its powerful imaginary world. In 1981, a new tabletop RPG was developed by Sandy Petersen based on *Call of Cthulhu*, with great success. Countless board games, tabletop RPGs and video games[109] use Lovecraft's cosmogony directly, draw inspiration from it, or subtly reference it. Tentacled horrors have become a Lovecraft stereotype, and his opus is an integral part of pop culture. However, considering his work based on this imagery alone is reductive: it doesn't reflect the rich character of his work, which drew from humanity's weaknesses and flaws, and pushed the envelope on playing on people's fears.

The Otherworldly

"The oldest and strongest emotion of mankind is fear, and the oldest and strongest kind of fear is fear of the unknown."

This Lovecraft quote perfectly sums up his work. However, in his work, the "unknown" doesn't refer to the unfamiliar or a lack of knowledge of precise facts. Lovecraft's unknown is that of the Cosmos, of transcendental reality: humans are but a speck of dust in the vast universe, which was once governed by indescribable cosmic beings, who still maintain influence and control over humanity, though most humans remain blissfully unaware of this. These superior beings from other stellar dimensions are known as the Great Old Ones. The vestiges they left behind are buried or sunken in ruins from thousand-year-old Cyclopean cities. Their influence reverberates through the most lucid of nightmares. In *The Call of Cthulhu*, we can read: "Even now They talked in Their tombs. When, after infinities of chaos, the first men

---

107. However, Lovecraft encouraged his writer friends to borrow from the "myth" and expand and adapt it in their own style.
108. Del Toro has worked unsuccessfully since 2002 to produce a movie version of *At the Mountains of Madness*.
109. One example is the official adaptation of *Call of Cthulhu: Dark Corners of the Earth*, or other games that drew inspiration from Lovecraft such as *Alone in the Dark*, *Amnesia: The Dark Descent*, *Eternal Darkness*, along with *Souls* and *Bloodborne*.

came, the Great Old Ones spoke to the sensitive among them by molding their dreams; for only thus could Their language reach the fleshly minds of mammals."

Lovecraft unfolds his themes in this way, exposing humanity's insignificance within the cosmic reality, while depicting ineffable superior beings, which have exerted mysterious control over humanity since the dawn of time. Cthulhu is one of these Great Old Ones, and its true form is too vile to apprehend. Lovecraft describes this creature as a monster several hundred meters tall, with an octopus head covered in numerous tentacles and immense dragon wings. However, every Great Old One has its own specific appearance, generally chaotic, and beyond human comprehension: "These Great Old Ones [...] were not composed altogether of flesh and blood. They had shape—for did not this star-fashioned image prove it?—but that shape was not made of matter."[110]

Bloodborne pays direct homage to Lovecraft in its own mythology, just as obscure as that of the American author. The gods (or equivalent) in *Bloodborne* are called Great Ones, a close reference to Lovecraft's "Great Old Ones." The tentacle-covered, hideous appearance of the Amygdalas, Ebrietas and the Moon Presence[111] all directly evoke Lovecraft's imagery, as it has spread through pop culture.

In its very form, *Bloodborne* continually echoes Lovecraft. The Brain of Mensis, shapeless mush dotted with eyes, resembles common depictions of the shoggoths, a type of monster created by the Great Old Ones to serve as slaves.[112] Rom the Vacuous Spider and Moonside Lake also recall Lovecraft, particularly in a few lines from *The Call of Cthulhu*: "The region now entered by the police was one of traditionally evil repute, substantially unknown and untraversed by white men. There were legends of a hidden lake unglimpsed by mortal sight, in which dwelt a huge, formless white polypous thing with luminous eyes."

When reading the passage from *The Nameless City*, as the character crosses the ruins of a secret city built by the Great Old Ones, *Bloodborne* players are likely to recall the numerous statues of Amygdalas found throughout the sacred spaces in *Bloodborne*: "[...] and contained the mummified forms of creatures outreaching in grotesqueness the most chaotic dreams of man. To convey any idea of these monstrosities is impossible. They were of the reptile kind, with body lines suggesting sometimes the crocodile, sometimes the seal, but more often nothing of which either the naturalist or the palaeontologist ever heard."

An especially uncanny resemblance can be found in the short story *The Shadow over Innsmouth*, in which Innsmouth is a small fishing town, where the fishermen appear abnormal and repugnant (midway between fish and men), and they worship an entity

---

110. *The Call of Cthulhu*.
111. In *The Dream-Quest of Unknown Kadath*, the moon in Dreamlands is home to monstrous beasts.
112. The story is found in *At the Mountains of Madness*, which ventures into the genre of science fiction.

from the ocean, Dagon. Of course, this village closely resembles the cursed Fishing Hamlet from *The Old Hunters*.

However, *Bloodborne*'s visual references to Lovecraft are just the beginning.

Beyond Good and Evil

As we saw throughout the "Universe" chapter, the Great Ones are governed by unknown laws, and they transcend human morals and emotions. This is also the case for Lovecraft's Great Old Ones: the author posits that the human mind is fundamentally limited, and that there are concepts we can only imagine but never fully comprehend, such as nothingness or the infinite. In the same way, only a small part of the visual spectrum and sound frequencies are accessible to our senses, not to mention the phenomena that totally escape human perception: much of what is "real" remains unknowable to us. This is why these superior entities are impossible to describe, as we read in *The Unnamable*: "It was everywhere—a gelatin—a slime—yet it had shapes, a thousand shapes of horror beyond all memory. There were eyes—and a blemish. It was the pit—the maelstrom—the ultimate abomination."

Lovecraft pushed the concept even farther with the short story *The Colour Out of Space*, in which a strange meteorite crashes into Earth, bringing with it a cosmic being, and causing the slow decomposition of all living things in the region. This life form uses a color outside of the visible spectrum, intolerable to the human eye and thought: "For the terror had not faded with the silhouette, and in a fearsome instant of deeper darkness the watchers saw wriggling at that treetop height a thousand tiny points of faint and unhallowed radiance [...]. It was a monstrous constellation of unnatural light, like a glutted swarm of corpse-fed fireflies dancing hellish sarabands over an accursed marsh; and its colour was that same nameless intrusion which Ammi had come to recognise and dread." There's another comparison here with *Bloodborne*: the Great One Oedon is formless and can only communicate using supernatural sounds, transcribed in the Caryll runes. Lovecraft also gave his entities difficult-to-pronounce names: *Nyarlathotep, Tsathoggua, Azathoth, Cthulhu*.[113] The language of the Great Old Ones is not intended to be understandable; *Bloodborne* also uses complex spellings: *Pthumeru, Byrgenwerth, Yahar'gul...* Lovecraft also had a tendency to use archaic English words such as "gibbous" (referring to an almost-full moon) or "eldritch" (ghostly, supernatural, etc.). *Bloodborne* references the second term directly with the "eldritch Truth."

---

113. Now, Lovecraft's cosmic pantheon (with the many additions from August Derleth and later authors, including those who designed the tabletop game) includes over one hundred divinities.

However, this "Truth" is nothing but an illusion. The Great Ones' purpose, like the Great Old Ones', is beyond human comprehension. The game also uses this idea of control exerted by superior forces, through the Moon Presence, who influences the path of the main character and holds Gehrman under its power. *Bloodborne* and Lovecraft's world both use a dreamland as a specific dimension, through which the Great Ones or Great Old Ones may enter into contact with humans. In the short story *Beyond the Wall of Sleep*, the protagonist is able to communicate with one of these entities after exploring the Dreamlands, a dimension in which the mind leaves the body behind.

Human curiosity eventually unearths what should remain hidden, as in *The Nameless City*: "When I drew nigh the nameless city I knew it was accursed. I was travelling in a parched and terrible valley under the moon, and afar I saw it protruding uncannily above the sands as parts of a corpse may protrude from an ill-made grave. Fear spoke from the age-worn stones of this hoary survivor of the deluge, this great-grandmother of the eldest pyramid; and a viewless aura repelled me and bade me retreat from antique and sinister secrets that no man should see, and no man else had ever dared to see."

In *Bloodborne*, Byrgenwerth College seeks to unravel these occult secrets, and take the human mind to new heights. In Lovecraft's fictional world, Miskatonic University conducts this type of research and houses a library full of occult books, such as the mysterious *Necronomicon* written by Abdul al-Hazred, found later in many works of popular culture.

But contact with this dimension generally leads to madness, as in the short story *Dagon*: "Then suddenly I saw it. With only a slight churning to mark its rise to the surface, the thing slid into view above the dark waters. Vast, Polyphemus-like, and loathsome, it darted like a stupendous monster of nightmares to the monolith, about which it flung its gigantic scaly arms, the while it bowed its hideous head and gave vent to certain measured sounds. I think I went mad then." *Bloodborne* integrated this concept into the very game mechanics—even just standing in the field of vision of some monsters such as the Brain of Mensis can inflict "frenzy."

This senseless quest for the eldritch Truth drives humans to conduct abominable experiments. This is the case for the laboratories supervised by Lady Maria, where patients are injected with old blood combined with water from the ocean of Kos. In the end, all that remains of them is a formless, still-conscious mass that regenerates each time it is struck. The main character of the short story *The Whisperer in Darkness* has a similar experience when he discovers that folklorist Henry Wentworth Akeley had his brain removed by the Great Old Ones, to allow his mind to be free of his body and become aware of the cosmic dimension. His brain was placed into a cylinder, in which he can live forever.

In many respects, *Bloodborne* has a number of clear visual and thematic elements that resonate with Lovecraft's universe. Humanity's insignificance, an indescribable reality, dominant forces, ineluctability, fear of the absolute: Hidetaka Miyazaki incorporated all of these concepts into his work, with a significant twist, of course, allowing him to introduce his own perspective.[114] With its own story, *Bloodborne* also moves away from Lovecraft's model to explore other facets of anguish and of the human psyche.

Borne by Blood

As we saw in the "Universe" chapter, the title "Bloodborne" is a significant term in the game. Blood is reflected in the game's appearance, storyline and gameplay. From a symbolic standpoint, blood is ambivalent, and loaded with contradictions that provide fertile ground for *Bloodborne*'s themes.

"Blood is Life"

A vital fluid that nourishes the heart and brain, transports oxygen and nutrients, protects us from infections via the immune system, and circulates hormones throughout the body, blood is the "essence" of human beings. Although its primary functions were only fully understood recently,[115] blood was long ago associated with life through the simple observation that anyone who loses too much blood will die. People and religions from the world over have given it a particular status, associating it with fertility or vital force.

In Greek mythology, Adonis is mortally wounded by a boar on a hunting trip. A drop of blood fell to the ground, and his lover Aphrodite (goddess of love) shed a tear on it, creating an anemone flower. Deities of vengeance,[116] the Erinyes were born of the blood of Uranus, which fell on Gaia, Mother Earth. In Norse mythology, Odin slays the giant primordial creature Ymir. He then uses the body to form the Earth, and the blood from the giant creates the rivers, lakes and seas. The Aztecs considered blood a precious liquid necessary to the sun god Tonatiuh. During ritual sacrifices, they would offer up blood to this god so that he would continue his course through the sky.

114. See the section on "Killing the Nightmare" in the "Decryption" chapter.
115. Blood circulation was theorized by the Englishman William Harvey at the beginning of the 17th century, but it was still impossible to know what exactly it was transporting.
116. The Romans knew them as the "Furies."

Blood is also considered sacred, an idea found in both Judaism and Christianity. The Bible draws a direct link between blood and life, or the soul. In Deuteronomy: "Only be sure that thou eat not the blood: for the blood is the life[117]; and thou mayest not eat the life with the flesh." Further, in Leviticus: "for [the blood] is the life of all flesh." This ban, forbidding humans from consuming blood, was primarily aimed at cannibalism; ironically, the myth of vampires draws from the same source. In Bram Stoker's *Dracula*, and in Francis Ford Coppola's film adaptation, "the blood is the life" mantra is taken directly from the Bible. On the other hand, Christ's blood promises to atone for sins. Throughout the Middle Ages, particularly as written by Chrétien de Troyes, the myth of the Grail became a mystical quest in search of the goblet holding Christ's blood which would grant immortality.

To drink blood is to literally draw vital force from one's enemy or victim. When the hero Sigurd finally vanquishes the dragon Fafnir in Norse mythology, he devours its heart and bathes in its blood, which hardens his skin and makes him invincible. In hunting tradition, up until the 18th century, it wasn't uncommon for some hunters to taste the blood of their slaughtered prey.

Bloodborne borrows this concept: the blood of victims ("Blood Echoes") allows players to level up and gain energy. Like vampires, players feed on the blood of their enemies. The Blood Vials restore health to varying degrees, sometimes giving players additional abilities. This is the case with the Blood of Adella, which gradually restores health points for twenty seconds. The Blood Ministration developed by the Healing Church relies on the beneficial properties of this precious fluid.

Its bright and strong ruby color has always been visually impressive: prehistoric men used animal blood in their cave paintings. *Bloodborne*'s backdrops use many different tones of red, along with the sprays of blood that punctuate fights. The game's violence is primarily sensory, since the image of spilling blood echoes the physical, material dimension of life, and our own vulnerability.

Blood appears in a wide variety of expressions, which emphasize the multiple associations we have with it: a line of descent ("his blood runs through my veins"), nobility,[118] emotions ("in cold blood," "make someone's blood run cold"), etc. However, although blood is unequivocally associated with life, it is also synonymous with fear.

---

117. The Latin term *anima* used in the Vulgate (Latin translation of the Bible from the end of the 4th century) has a number of meanings: the primary meaning is "air" or "breath." As such, it also means "vital principle" or "soul" (in contrast to the body). Most English versions of the Bible use the term "life."

118. The expression "blue blooded" has long been used to refer to nobility, with the contemptible notion that theirs was a "pure" blood that could not be mixed with that of the people. The Vileblood covenant in *Bloodborne* recalls this idea. For the naturalist writers of the 19th century—Émile Zola, in particular—blood also carried genetic deficiencies. Zola, the author of the Rougon-Macquart family cycle, juxtaposed these deficiencies with social determinism (by which society and social interactions determine an individual's behavior) in his various characters.

Impure Blood

Both a "vital principle" and a reminder of our own mortality, blood is fascinatingly ambiguous. For a long time, it has both impressed and terrified humans. Abundant in our bodies (the average adult has around 1.5 gallons), it can gush out in large quantities depending on an injury's severity, until death follows. A person who loses blood becomes pallid, an unsettling color associated with weakness and disease.

But menstruation has been subject to the most taboo and prejudice. This natural physiological phenomenon was misunderstood for centuries, and has been decreed noxious in both Judaism and Islam. These religions forbid sexual relations during a woman's period, a time during which the woman and her menstrual blood are considered impure.[119] The same thing applies to the blood lost during childbirth. Here, we can recall Queen Yharnam with her bloody abdomen, a reminder of her loss of Mergo: the ruby red clashes with the virginal white of her dress, in an indelible stain.

Based on its origins, blood can therefore be viewed as sacred or impure, a duality we can also see in *Bloodborne*. Initially, the Old Blood was seen as invaluable, giving access to new knowledge that could lift humans to a higher plane of existence. But for Willem and Byrgenwerth College, this blood also caused people to turn into beasts, and they felt it must be forbidden. "Fear the old blood" became the College's motto. Even Laurence eventually heeded this warning, while developing his Blood Ministration with the Healing Church.

The Old Blood recalls the "*ichor*" of Greek mythology—it was the name given to the blood of the gods, which was toxic to humans. This also recalls the notion of sacredness and taboo. Ashen Blood, the cause of the Beastly Scourge, serves as a punishment to mankind for administering the Great Ones' vital fluid to humans. In response, people flocked to the Healing Church for the Blood Ministration, without realizing that this treatment was responsible for spreading the poison.

---

119. In the Quran, sura 2, verse 222: "It is harm, so keep away from wives during menstruation. And do not approach them until they are pure. And when they have purified themselves, then come to them from where Allah has ordained for you. Indeed, Allah loves those who are constantly repentant and loves those who purify themselves." In Leviticus (15:19): "And if a woman have an issue, and her issue in her flesh be blood, she shall be put apart seven days: and whosoever toucheth her shall be unclean until the even." (King James Bible)

Blood Transfusion

At the beginning of *Bloodborne*, the Hunter (the player's avatar) receives the Blood Ministration through a transfusion, viewed in first-person perspective to heighten the player's identification with the avatar. The surroundings are insalubrious, the old man doesn't inspire confidence, and the tools used certainly don't look sterilized. Players also remain unaware of the type of blood that is being transfused. These unknowns spawn anxiety, reinforced by the impression we are entering into a Faustian bargain,[120] and by the nightmarish visions that follow—the beast who dies in the flames, and then the monstrous, skeletal children who serve as messengers.

The Beastly Scourge and Blood Ministration also echo our modern fears about blood-borne illnesses such as AIDS.

For a long time, doctors would perform bloodletting to empty patients of their "contaminated" blood in the hope of healing them. It wasn't until the 17th century, in 1667, that the first blood transfusion was performed by physician Jean Baptiste Denis on a feverish adolescent who had already been bled by leeches twenty times. However, the (effective) transfusion was conducted using sheep's blood: the idea of using human blood didn't even occur to the doctor.

It wasn't until 1818 that British physician James Blundell performed the first human blood transfusion, before the idea of blood types had been discovered, which explained the complications between incompatible donors and patients. The first blood types were discovered in 1900 by Austrian biologist Karl Landsteiner, who created the ABO classification. Ten years later, researchers first discovered a transmissible disease through transfusion: a New Yorker who contracted malaria. Towards the end of the twentieth century, transfusion had saved countless lives,[121] all while the fear of AIDS transmission also grew.[122]

In *Bloodborne*, blood is taken using thick needles—a source of dread for some–, in rather dubious hygienic conditions. The game plays with this seedy aesthetic, which brings to mind the somber times of the Great Plague.[123] In F. W. Murnau's film *Nosferatu*, a loose interpretation of Bram Stoker's *Dracula*, the vampire spreads the plague through the village. In *Bloodborne*, the prostitute Arianna says that she

---

120. When starting *Bloodborne*, players must sign a contract. In the legend of Faust, popularized by Goethe's novel, the eponymous character makes a pact with the devil by signing a contract with his blood, selling his soul in exchange for the satisfaction of his desires. In the Faust legend, the devil appears as Mephistopheles, one of the seven princes of hell. Mephistopheles is also a Machiavellian character in *Demon's Souls*. The hunters in *Bloodborne* are known as "echo fiends" according to the description of blood dregs.
121. The Jehovah's Witness religious denomination refuses blood transfusions, citing the Bible's sacred view of blood.
122. Of course, blood is now tested for HIV prior to every transfusion.
123. The black and white Church attire recalls the plague physicians of the Middle Ages, who would wear a mask in the form of a bird's beak, similar to that of Eileen in the game.

understands if the player doesn't want to take her blood, a clear allusion to sexually transmitted diseases.

The game espouses all of the contradictions surrounding blood, its meaning and symbolism. Both a vector for disease and death, or vital energy and healing, blood represents a physical part of human existence, and our earthly, biological dimension: a sign of our mortality, and of our ability to give life.

Procreation

In the *Bloodborne* universe, the Great Ones are never able to have children, for mysterious reasons subject to interpretation. Giving life is viewed as one of the most beautiful and sacred acts that exists, with a multitude of meanings and consequences. Selflessness, hope for the future, continuation of the species, a gift of nature, or a mirror of oneself, newborns mirror their parents' aspirations and are a symbol of life, but also a testament to the past, and a heritage. Perhaps the true core of *Bloodborne* lies in this theme of procreation, first embodied by the pain of losing a child.

Menstruation and Childbirth

Halfway through *Bloodborne*, during the fight with Rom, a change occurs. The game moves away from traditional Gothic horror and towards a more mystical, metaphorical domain. Visually, the scene following the fight is very evocative. The red moon appears, massive against an opaline backdrop, mirroring Yharnam's sullied dress and Mergo's cries. Miyazaki has said that the "Paleblood" refers to the color of the sky after the blood moon. He refers to a "body drained of blood."

The events taking place here may appear especially strange during a player's first game, but they become clear later on. Yharnam cries for Mergo, and a Great One has just impregnated a human. The procreation is doomed to fail, since "every Great One loses its child." This implacable truth directly parallels our taboos about reproduction: sterility, miscarriages, abortion, stillborn children, death during childbirth, etc. *Bloodborne* goes so far as to place players face to face with one of the Great Ones' children—Arianna's monstrous yet vulnerable baby—which they can kill to obtain a One Third of Umbilical Cord: an atrocious vision that plays on our fears and pain of childbirth.

Besides Oedon, who is formless, all of the other Great Ones seen in Bloodborne are of a "feminine" nature (if we can actually assign them a gender): Ebrietas (Daughter of the Cosmos), the Moon Presence, Kos (Mother Kos), Mergo's Wet Nurse, and even the Amygdalas. This hearkens back to the theme of maternity, emphasized by the presence of a "wet nurse," whose role is to take care of an infant, and to feed it with breast milk when the mother is not able to. An amusing detail: breast milk has historically been called "white blood": could this be a connection to the Paleblood, shedding some light on this cryptic term?

The game revolves around essential elements tied to menstruation: blood and the moon. The word "menstruation" comes from the Latin *menstrua*, whose root (*men-sis*) means "month"[124] and was used during Antiquity to define the lunar cycle, whose duration was between twenty-nine and thirty days. The lunar cycle and menstrual cycle (the latter of which lasts twenty-eight days on average) are associated due to their length and four symmetrical phases: preovulation and the waxing moon, ovulation for the full moon, the premenstrual phase for the waning moon, and menstruation for the new moon.

Clearly, it's no coincidence that one of *Bloodborne*'s major organizations is named Mensis. Mythology has often associated the moon and menstruation. For the Incas, Mama Quilla was goddess of the moon and of the menstrual cycle. Associating blood red with the moon in *Bloodborne* follows in the same logic. Often, the moon symbolizes femininity or fertility, and has been personified in a number of mythologies—Greek, Sumerian, Japanese, etc.

The idea of a "moon presence" also suggests the mystical dimension of this celestial body, which plays an essential role in the geology of our planet, whether through the tides or seismic activity, and by affecting farm crops. The name "Rom" could also be a reference to the acronym ROM (rupture of membranes) which refers to the waters breaking before birth.

Bloodborne's story can also be seen as an extended metaphor for the anxieties and pain of having a child, from menstruation to birth.[125] Such is the case for Queen Yharnam, whose ghostly, bloodstained silhouette appears during major moments of the game. However, this also applies to Kos, whose carcass gives birth to a child within an ever-repeating nightmare. An orphan, left behind by its own kind, with its eyes steadily riveted on the moon and the Cosmos.

---

124. "Moon" and "month" are associated in many languages: in Greek, μήνη (*mene*) means moon, and μήν (*men*) means month. In Sanskrit, मास (*mâsa*) refers to both moon and month. Of course, in English "moon" also pairs with "month," like the German *Mond* and *Monat*, which have Indo-European roots—the word mḗh₁n̥s, which means both moon and month.
125. The blood dregs (obtained by killing hunters for the Vileblood oath) look like sperm mixed with blood. The associated description suggests this idea of fecundity: "They often appear in the blood of echo fiends, that is to say, the blood of hunters. Queen Annalise partakes in these blood dregs offerings, so that she may one day bear the Child of Blood, the next Vileblood heir."

Creator and Creature

"Hunters have told me about the church. About the gods, and their love. But, do the gods love their creations? I am a doll, created by you humans. Would you ever think to love me? Of course, I do love you. Isn't that is how you've made me?"

Do we give life to love or be loved? Can the action of giving life be selfless? In this speech, the Doll in the Hunter's Dream puts her finger on one of humanity's oldest questions, and a question often pondered in the first religions: do gods love their creations?

In the Greek pantheon, the Titan Cronos, perturbed by a prophecy which said he would be overthrown by his son,[126] devours his children one by one: the gods Hestia, Hera, Demeter, Hades and Poseidon. The sixth god, Zeus, fulfilled the prophecy and forced Cronos to disgorge his brothers and sisters. In monotheist religions, God watches over his people, but his presence is still questioned in moments of doubt (catastrophes, personal tragedies, etc.). Implicit in this is a fear of abandonment and dereliction.

The proven existence of superior beings or creators could give meaning to human existence, justify it, and explain its chaotic nature. In the vast span of the universe, it may be comforting to know that our world is not totally random, and that it is guided by a benevolent, unintelligible purpose. The indifference, and even scorn, of the Great Ones with respect to humanity is all the more difficult to swallow. For the church in *Bloodborne*, the "gods"[127] are full of love, if we're to believe the Doll. The humans take comfort in this certainty, which willingly disregards the terrifying truth: that humanity is insignificant in relation to the Cosmos.

But man is not just creature: he is also creator. Unlike the Great Ones, humans can give life, which casts doubt on the balance of power between these two types of beings. The renewed attempts of the Great Ones to impregnate a human seem to indicate that they are actually jealous of these inferior creatures who can reproduce and therefore perpetuate their species. Unable to reproduce, these beings seek surrogates.

From this angle, a connection between Gehrman and the Moon Presence is interesting: the Old Hunter is more like a puppet than a child. The Great One who made him its prisoner, to seduce or console him, brought to life a Doll that Gehrman had lovingly made in memory of Lady Maria. The story echoes the Greek myth *Pygmalion*. Scandalized by the practices of women in Cyprus (the Propoetides, seen as prostitutes and witches), the sculptor Pygmalion took a vow of celibacy, until he fell in love with an ivory statue of his own creation, Galatea. Aphrodite, goddess of love, agreed to bring this statue to life. Pygmalion had children with her, and the Propoetides were changed into ivory.

---

126. He had already overthrown his father, Ouranos.
127. Nothing indicates that the Great Ones are behind the creation of humanity.

In *Bloodborne*, when the Doll ponders the love of her creator, it is with evident respect and a feeling of inferiority towards her progenitor. She is its object. However, her speech also emphasizes that all intelligent creatures look for themselves in their creator or the person who raises them. A doll may accept that her existence is entirely determined by her role, but humans are not satisfied by such a limited role.[128]

Once we have defined ourselves, become aware of ourselves and freed ourselves, what remains? Transmission: the key to evolution. Superior beings who obey incomprehensible and inaccessible laws, the Great Ones are no less limited by their inability to successfully bear life. They have no direct inheritance, and their attempts to use human bodies as surrogates have not been fruitful. Humans, for their part, aim to do the opposite, by reaching the level of their "gods": a hubris for which they will pay the price.

Hubris and Knowledge

What secrets hide within this universe? All of *Bloodborne* revolves around this attempt to learn a higher, cosmic truth, which is above all spiritual in nature. The moon is not just a symbol of fertility—it also represents the night and dreams. The different dream-like layers of *Bloodborne* and the insidious nature of the Moon Presence invite this more intimate understanding of the adventure, which is experienced as a metaphorical progression towards the monstrosities that strike the human unconscious—an inverted awakening. In Buddhism, Buddha is said to have meditated for twenty-eight days under a fig tree before reaching nirvana, the same length of time as a moon cycle.

In *Bloodborne*, Byrgenwerth College sought the "eyes on the inside," symbols of spiritual enlightenment, but also a literal monstrosity of the mind. This quest for the eldritch Truth brought man too close to the "divine," the Beastly Scourge.

Pride: Wisdom's Foe

One of the most influential humanists of the Renaissance, writer François Rabelais (*Pantagruel*, *Gargantua*), wrote: "wisdom enters not into a malicious mind, and science without conscience is but the ruin of the soul." This famous saying opposes two etymologically connected words, *science* and *conscience*, derived from the Latin words

---

128. Many religions evoke the idea that we will eventually attain a superior or divine reality—such as the promise to be freed from the bounds of material existence, and thus mortality.

scientia (knowledge) and *conscientia* (originally referring to shared knowledge, but also with the modern English meaning).

Conscience is humanity's distinctive feature, the proof of our existence, and our quest for knowledge is what allows us to evolve. Since ancient times, wise men, sages, philosophers[129] and scientists have worked to push the boundaries of human knowledge, with the aim of understanding the universe, and identifying some sort of logic, a meaning to explain our existence.

However, as we see in the Rabelais quote, and in myths and religions, we must be careful what we do with this knowledge. The desire for grandeur and power can take over and distract from essential values.

The Biblical myth of the tower of Babel is a well-known metaphor for the punishment of arrogant humans who try to reach the heavens, and the divine. After the flood, humans settled in Mesopotamia and worked to build a city and then a tower, the top of which would touch the sky. God punished them by dispersing them throughout the Earth and by making them speak a variety of languages (previously, there was only one) so they could no longer understand one another. This led to the different languages for each people.

Although the Greeks didn't have the concept of "sin" as developed in monotheist religions, they had their own conception of moral crime, called *hubris* (or *hybris*), associated with the idea of excess. Hubris is an impassioned feeling, arising particularly from pride, that in its extreme form pushes us to oppose the divine, to attempt to transcend the human condition and become equal to a god. Many Greek myths invoke hubris: they include the myth of Icarus, who used wings made by his father Daedalus to fly towards the sun, but the wax of his wings melted, and he perished in the sea; another story is that of Tantalus, son of Zeus and the nymph Plouto, who is said to have been punished[130] for sharing divine secrets with humans, or sharing the nectar of the gods with his mortal friends.

This same hubris ate away at Micolash[131] and Willem, the latter of whom went so far as to create his own Great One with Rom, intending to place himself on the same level as these superior beings. It was only at the last moment that he realized the reach of the catastrophe and the consequences of his and humanity's pride. In reality, even though he used Rom to hide the ritual of Mensis, it was already too late.

The many experiments conducted on blood, particularly in the laboratory or in Iosefka's clinic, perfectly echo Rabelais's quote: humans, or even children (for the Choir), are used as guinea pigs with no moral consideration or consent from

129. Ancient philosophers were also the "scientists" of the era, studying astronomy, arithmetic, etc.
130. Although different versions of his punishment exist, the torment of Tantalus today refers to the act of bringing food to a famished victim, and then snatching it away before they can eat.
131. The bizarre cages worn by the School of Mensis to communicate with the Cosmos are in the shape of a tower.

their subjects,[132] with the sole purpose of understanding a truth that doesn't exist. Clumsy and pathetic, the resulting creatures in no way suggest spiritual elevation, like the living failures or Rom, who is given a revealing nickname: the Vacuous Spider. Micolash suggests that Kos is the one who gave Rom eyes on the inside, but this divine gift seems to have instead withered his mind. Is experiencing the profound nature of the Cosmos beyond human reach? Any attempt seems to result in madness, stupefaction or death.

Rise and Fall

The Greek myth of Prometheus revolves around human access to knowledge. The Titan Prometheus fashioned man out of clay, and the goddess Athena gave him the breath of life. Following the victory of the gods in the Titanomachy (war between Zeus and the Olympians against Cronos and most of the other Titans), Zeus exiled his enemies in Tartarus.[133] Prometheus took advantage of this to steal the divine fire on the Sun Chariot and give it to his creations, humans, before teaching them metalworking. Furious, Zeus punished Prometheus, tying him to a rock on Mount Caucasus, where every day an eagle would come to eat his liver, which would regrow each night: a torture that would continue until the demigod Heracles came to free him.

Access to fire—symbolically, knowledge—brought humanity closer to the divine. A number of myths incorporate this theme. In Genesis, the snake (later equated with Satan) coaxed Adam and Eve into eating the forbidden fruit (knowledge of good and evil), which caused them to be expelled from the Garden of Eden. In the sacred poems of Rigveda (one of the four canonical texts of Hinduism), the hero Mātariśvan[134] succeeds in capturing fire, previously hidden from humans, and gives it to them. In the Book of Enoch,[135] the fallen angel Azazel brings fire to men and teaches them to make weapons, as well as ornaments and makeup, inciting humanity to debauchery. The text specifies: "Thou seest what Azazel hath done, who hath taught all unrighteousness on earth and revealed the eternal secrets which were in heaven, which men were striving to learn."

Bloodborne presents a parallel with this story, as Ebrietas grants the Choir an audience. This allows its members to glimpse a fragment of the eldritch Truth and leads them to conduct experiments with the goal of lifting humanity to the level of the Great Ones, such as the Celestials and the Celestial Emissary. We can also imagine that

---

132. This is true for Impostor Iosefka, who conducted experiments on the true Iosefka and on other characters the player can choose to send her.
133. A place of atonement and suffering, similar to the future Christian hell.
134. Perhaps an incarnation of Agni, god of fire and divine knowledge.
135. An apocryphal (non-canonical) book of the Bible.

Ebrietas once held a similar audience with the Pthumerians. Perhaps this was the reason Ebrietas is known as "abandoned Ebrietas"–the Great Ones abandoned Ebrietas after this contact with the Pthumerian civilization, perhaps as punishment for having given away a fraction of their cosmic superiority to these inferior beings. This theory strengthens the ties with the Prometheus myth of gaining knowledge.

It also works well with one of the themes in *Bloodborne* and all of the *Souls* games: the cyclical rise and fall of civilization. The centuries have seen great empires, dynasties, and cultures built from the ground up, and then crumble into dust. From the Mesopotamian empires (Assyrian, neo-Assyrian, Sumerian, etc.) to the Mayans, along with the Roman Empire, Greece and Ancient Egypt, and the Ottoman Empire: numerous are the empires that have declined or disappeared completely. Decline can be caused by many different factors, both internal (crises, wars) and external (epidemics, natural disasters). Historians have often pondered the seemingly inevitable cycle of rise and fall. Although the circumstances are never exactly the same, history seems to repeat itself, as if peoples must continually rebuild on the ruins after reaching the highest point they can attain, without necessarily learning from the errors of the past. In any case, this is what happens in *Bloodborne*. Fascinated by their discovery of the Pthumerian civilization and the Great Ones, humans were naturally driven by their curiosity and the unprecedented opportunity to transcend their condition, to learn more about the mysteries of the universe. Focusing solely on the greatness of the Pthumerian civilization, they didn't stop to consider what had caused its disappearance, and eventually make the same mistakes, with the Blood Ministration and appearance of the Beastly Scourge, which previously led to the fall of this ancient people. History seems to eternally start from scratch.

If knowledge is a treasure, it must be treated with moderation and patience, which are the true keys to wisdom. When insight is acquired too quickly, madness often follows. This may be one moral to take away from *Bloodborne*, the objective of which seems to reveal the two most meaningful, extreme ends of the human condition: the potential of our mind and our bestiality. From this perspective, the body becomes a monstrous entity.

The Monster Within

No matter how much spiritual and cognitive advancement humans gain over time, the human body is what ties us to the sensory world and to our animal roots. This source of fascination is analyzed, dissected, deified and presented in its basest aspect, depending on the approach. *Bloodborne* tells us this story of flesh and blood.

Beast Folklore

Gothic horror buffs won't feel disoriented by *Bloodborne*'s bestiary, full of ly-canthropes (Yharnam's aggressive werewolves, the Cleric Beast, Amelia, Ludwig, Laurence, etc.) and vampires (the Vileblood covenant). The game doesn't just stick to this symbolic imagery: it presents the contrasts of human existence. The scholars of Byrgenwerth who seek spiritual enlightenment find their alter egos in the victims of the Old Blood and the Beastly Scourge, who have lost their mind and become violent, transformed into monstrous beings: two sides of humanity that are more two sides of the same coin than in opposition.

In the collective psyche, the werewolves[136] recall a number of ideas such as the an-cestral fear of being eaten by wolves, budding sexuality, and the expression of ag-gressive instincts. From a psychoanalytical perspective, it is the fear of our true nature. However, wolves have not always had negative connotations. Ancient myths and legends viewed the wolf as a positive animal: the she-wolf who feeds Romulus and Remus, the wolves that guide the supreme gods Odin (Norse mythology) and Lug (Celtic mythology). Shamans from certain American Indian tribes sometimes use wolf pelts during ceremonies to summon animal spirits. Sometimes, wolves have ambivalent associations: in Norse mythology, Fenrir is a monstrous wolf who partici-pates in destroying the world in Ragnarok, the battle of the end of time during which the animal kills Odin. For the Greeks, transforming into a wolf was a divine punish-ment for those who (like King Lycaon) had offended the Olympians.

It wasn't until the Middle Ages that the wolf became a feared, demonized animal, as the Christians made it a symbol of the devil in their attempts to dismantle pagan myths and beliefs. Werewolf legends have nevertheless existed for millennia, and de-veloped in Russia, Europe and the Americas. Recently, horror films have used this myth in many ways.[137]

Werewolves are frightening, violent and capable of devouring humans. Generally large and muscular, they may appear fully wolf-like or have some anthropomorphic attributes. *Bloodborne* has emphasized their most terrifying features, particularly in the werewolf bosses, which are much larger than the player's avatar. The fact that *Bloodborne*'s pri-mary activity is hunting recalls werewolf hunts during the Middle Ages, as well as du-ring the "modern" era, with the affair of the Beast of Gévaudan in 18th-century France. However, the *Bloodborne* protagonist isn't fighting to kill an animal, but rather a fellow man who regressed and became overwhelmed by his primitive survival instincts.

---

136. From the Greek λυκάνθρωπος (lukanthropos), from λύκος (lukos), wolf, and ἄνθρωπος (anthropos), man.
137. In particular, we recommend *An American Werewolf in London* (John Landis, 1981), *The Howling* (Joe Dante, 1981), and *The Company of Wolves* (Neil Jordan, 1984).

There's an interesting parallel with the symbolism of the hunt, an ancestral activity found throughout humanity's evolution. Depending on the peoples and customs, hunting didn't consist solely in killing game for food. It adhered to precise rituals, respecting the fauna, to make sure it wouldn't threaten species renewal. Sometimes, prey was a gift from the gods. Gods such as the goddess Artemis had a twofold role when it came to animals: both as a guardian and as a hunter. For Native Americans, hunting had a spiritual dimension: animals were sacred and symbolic, as seen in totems, for instance.[138]

The hunt was also a question of life or death, setting up an interesting dynamic between hunter and hunted. Finally, the killing can be seen as a rejection of our animal side, and our ignorance. *Bloodborne* also presents an analogy: the character's quest leads him to transcend his beastly nature. Werewolves are, in appearance, a manifestation of physical aggression, a reflection of the violent instincts that the game glorifies, since all of *Bloodborne* takes place within this maelstrom of dust, blood and slashed flesh. Critical hits are called "visceral attacks," as we plunge our blade directly into the viscera of our opponents. The danger here is if we surrender ourselves to these destructive impulses and lose sight of spiritual awakening. This has happened to some hunters, who Eileen wishes to "free" by killing them, at the risk of becoming mad herself if the player doesn't help her. Evil is often more insidious than it appears.

The Noble Monster

Even sneakier is the beast hiding behind nobility. In *Bloodborne*, the Vileblood clan directly references the vampire myth. These blood-drinkers can be found in stories throughout the ages, in beliefs and traditions held by the Persians, Babylonians, Greeks, Egyptians, through to the vampire figure from Slavic folklore in the 17th and 18th centuries. The historical figure of Vlad III Basarab, prince of Wallachia in the 15th century, was nicknamed "the Impaler" (*Țepeș*, in Romanian) after supposedly impaling over twenty thousand Turks on stakes[139]. His legend and other nickname, "Drăculea,"[140] served as a basis for Bram Stoker's novel *Dracula*: bloody origins for this vampire,[141] who thus cast this monster as a reflection of the worst side of humanity, with his propensity to kill his fellow men and taste for murder and domination.

---

138. All tribe members had a totem animal (bear, bison, wolf, coyote, turtle, etc.), seen in a vision or attributed by a shaman. This totem animal would spiritually guide people throughout their lives. The crow, Eileen's symbol in *Bloodborne*, was both a bearer of magic and messenger of death.
139. In reality, he probably only impaled a few people of high rank. However, his acts were gruesome enough to leave quite the impression.
140. "Son of Dragon," in reference to his father, Vlad II, a member of the Order of the Dragon.
141. Dracula wasn't the first vampire to appear in literature—the short story *The Vampyre* was written in 1819 by John William Polidori, who popularized this creature.

But as we've seen in "Borne by Blood," the essential characteristic of vampires is that they literally feed on the vital force of their victims. Although vampires are symbolically tied to the fear of death and contamination (beliefs suggest that vampirism is transmitted through the teeth), to the mysteries of blood, or even to sexuality,[142] the vampire is sometimes also interpreted as an allegory of power and control over the oppressed.[143]

After making the people of Yharnam reliant on the Blood Ministration, the Healing Church enslaved them, eventually going off the rails—the Choir's experiments on children recall the scandals that sometimes rattle the Catholic Church. The body turns into an object of manipulation, subject to needs that can be controlled or even created.

Bloodborne has touches of delicious irony: the important figures of the Healing Church eventually also succumb to the scourge, starting with Laurence, the First Vicar. The bestial instinct is hidden well away, here in the church's cathedral, where Laurence's skull lies on an altar. This scene serves as a metaphor for the true face of this institution, which has no compunction in training hunters to massacre the victims of a scourge caused—and encouraged—by its own negligence.

The human body is a testament to human frailty, with its core animal instinct, easily succumbing to its elementary needs and addictions. This is what leads some to free themselves of it.

Is the Body the Pawn of the Soul, or Vice-Versa?

The Choir, Byrgenwerth and the laboratories of the School of Mensis all work to raise the human mind to unexplored cosmic realms. A quest for transcendence akin to the ultimate philosophical exploration, far from material reality. Many intellectual movements, particularly of the religious variety, have argued for the spiritual over the material, as if the body and spirit could only be in conflict, with the soul prisoner to the body.

"Man is neither angel nor beast, and unhappily whoever wants to act the angel, acts the beast": could the *Bloodborne* creators have had this quote from Blaise Pascal in mind? The game seems to provide a literal illustration of this quote, through its presentation of the physical consequences of the attempts at spiritual elevation, towards a Cosmos inhabited by monstrous entities. The skulls of the Blood Saints who

---

142. This eroticism is absent from *Bloodborne*, however.
143. A theme we find in various films such as Tim Burton's *Batman Returns*, in which Max Shreck (whose name is a nod to actor Max Schreck, who played the vampire *Nosferatu* in Murnau's film) drains Gotham of its lifeblood by siphoning off its natural resources, or the Wachowskis' *Jupiter Ascending*, in which humanity descends from ancient, royal extraterrestrials capable of regenerating indefinitely by harvesting humans for their vital energy.

received the mix of blood and water became warped and swollen, before their whole bodies turned into a gelatinous mass: a hideous contrast with the intended result. The Celestials, with their appearance that mimics stereotyped visions of extraterrestrials, are human caricatures with a prominent skull and florescent blue skin. Members of the School of Mensis have died with their heads imprisoned in absurd cage-antennas—the grotesque proportions reflect the game's commentary. The disgusting Brain of Mensis also makes more sense from this perspective: this messy array of eyes and flesh may symbolize the true nature of the church's mind and its senseless crusade. Micolash now (literally) lives within a nightmare.

And when players select the way of "insight" and raise themselves to the level of the Great Ones, they are reborn as a strange inhuman larva, far from the majesty we would expect from a being graced by divinity.

Of course, *Bloodborne* doesn't provide a true conclusion—the final sentence of the game (spoken by the Doll) ends with a comma—and refrains from pronouncing a final judgment. Everyone will have their own interpretations, of course, but it's important to consider the game's nuances. Bestial or spiritual instincts? This dichotomy, found in the schism between the different factions and in the game's very mechanics, is only an illusion. The dichotomy is really two sides of the same coin: that of the violence that lies within human beings. On one side, violence is portrayed in its more direct manifestation, physical, brutal and animal. On the other side, psychological violence leads to madness, and what one can contemplate with eyes on the inside, mirrors of the soul.

By presenting these two extremes, *Bloodborne* may be asking us to land somewhere in the middle, where humanity's salvation lies.

DARK SOULS

ダークソウル

BEYOND THE GRAVE

CHAPTER FOUR
MUSIC

B loodborne's musical adventure began early in the game's design stages. The *Souls* compositions were very impressive in their own right, but *Bloodborne* conjures up a new sound. Working with Keiichi Kitahara, lead sound designer for Sony Japan Studio, Hidetaka Miyazaki felt that the soundtrack needed a new approach, one that would draw inspiration from the West this time around. Miyazaki was enamored by the *Dark Souls* video montages he had seen online: they were accompanied by a piece from the album *Divinus*, from a studio specializing in trailer music called City of the Fallen, founded by soundtrack composer Ryan Amon (*Elysium*).

With this first source of inspiration, Kitahara reached out to the American branch of Sony. Chuck Doud was hired as musical director, a position he had already filled for large games such as the *Uncharted* and *God of War* series. Peter Scaturro and Keith Leary were chosen to produce the original soundtrack. Taking Miyazaki's recommendation, they contacted Ryan Amon, who agreed to work on the project. His work would set the tone for the rest of the score.

A Sound Emerges

Bloodborne received a generous music budget, and the composers' music would eventually be performed by both an orchestra and a choir. To this end, composer Penka Kouneva joined the project to produce the orchestrations. She had previously worked with Amon on the movie *Elysium*, and had made a name for herself by producing the orchestrations for several films and games by Steve Jablonsky (*Transformers*, *The Last Witch Hunter*, *Gears of War 2* and *3*) as well as some Blizzard games (*Starcraft II*, *Diablo III*, *World of Warcraft*).

First, the music designers worked to define the game's "Victorian and Gothic" sound, while providing Miyazaki with a variety of options: they sent him over twenty different soundtracks to illustrate their approach. Their primary source of inspiration was music from Coppola's *Dracula*, composed by Wojciech Kilar.[144]

---

144. This prolific composer, who drew fame from other films such as Paul Grimault's *The King and the Mockingbird* and Roman Polanski's *The Ninth Gate*, had recently died, on December 29, 2013. Amon thus paid him tribute by drawing inspiration from his work.

Generally, they avoided use of the organ,[145] flutes and certain brass instruments. The music revolves around the strings and the choirs, with some brass, piano, celesta and percussion. The focus is on the string and vocal solos. Ryan Amon's main theme weaves together these various elements, with a dirge-like motif on the cello, the regular beat of a *berimbau* (a Brazilian instrument from the percussion family), a soprano, strings and percussion. To intensify the feeling of horror in the audio environment, the composer and orchestrator used a variety of techniques from formal contemporary classical music[146]: dissonant harmonies, aleatoric music,[147] tone clusters,[148] etc. With this main theme designed around the keywords "melancholy" and "desolation," *Bloodborne*'s sound was born.

From Composing to Recording

Over the next few months, a team of composers was assembled. Three musicians from FromSoftware were summoned on the Japanese side. Tsukasa Saitô was already the lead sound designer within the game's sound division; he had previously worked on *King's Field IV*[149] and the *Armored Core* series. Yuka Kitamura was known for her work on *Armored Core: Verdict Day* and especially *Dark Souls II*, for which she had composed around ten pieces (including the famous Sir Alonne from the *Crown of the Old Iron King* DLC), working alongside Motoi Sakuraba. Nobuyoshi Suzuki was a newcomer.

Composer Michael Wandmacher also joined the team (*My Bloody Valentine 3D*, *Piranha 3D*, and the games *Twisted Metal* and *Singularity*), followed a few months later by Cris Velasco (*God of War, Mass Effect 3*). When Velasco joined the team, the project was nearing its end and the other composers were almost finished. Velasco was called in to help write the music for the boss fights in the Chalice Dungeon (*Terror*) and the fight against Amygdala in the Nightmare Frontier. Before beginning the compositions,

---

145. However, an organ was indeed used during the fight against Laurence in *The Old Hunters*.
146. Formal contemporary classical music refers to certain works from the 1950s onward. This type of music abandons many of the forms and rules of classical composition with the aim of refreshing or deconstructing traditional composition—for instance, it's often free of melody and tonality. For *Bloodborne*'s orchestrations, Penka Kouneva says she drew inspiration from György Ligeti (popularized by his works used in Stanley Kubrick's movies—particularly his sinister *Requiem* from the blockbuster *2001: a Space Odyssey*) and Alban Berg (a composer from the early 20th century, and student of Arnold Schoenberg, who ventured into the world of atonality).
147. This means allowing randomness within the composition and in the players' interpretation: an ideal technique when creating a chaotic, terrifying sound.
148. A tone cluster is a chord containing at least three adjacent tones. On the page, it indeed resembles a cluster of grapes.
149. The *King's Field* games were the predecessors of the *Souls* games. See the first volume of this book, *Dark Souls: Beyond the Grave*.

he immersed himself in the other composers' work to learn their style. He used their completed music for *Bloodborne* as a base.

Throughout the project, which began over two years before the game was released, each composer worked individually using Ryan Amon's main theme, the concept art, directions from Miyazaki and the American producers along with the instrumental constraints[150] imposed by orchestrator Penka Kouneva, to harmonize the compositions.

The recording sessions, which allowed the team of composers to meet in person for the first time, took place in England, at London's AIR Studios and Abbey Road Studios, with an orchestra and a choir of thirty-two singers. To help integrate the music into the game, and in particular the transition that takes place halfway during boss fights, the different sections were recorded separately. In total, *Bloodborne*'s soundtrack was produced during five orchestra recording sessions, lasting a total of eighteen hours, and three choral recording sessions spread out over nine hours. The five additional pieces for the DLC[151] were orchestrated solely by Jim Fowler (who had already worked on the main game as an assistant orchestrator). They were recorded in four hours with an orchestra, and two hours with the choir. For practical reasons, the dissonant orchestral effects were added in postproduction using the Symphobia sound library.

In total, *Bloodborne*'s soundtrack contains over an hour and a half of music, made by six composers from around the globe, with an orchestra and a choir, two orchestrators, and three different countries involved. Clearly, expectations were high, and the result lives up to these ambitions.

The Night Unfurls

Bloodborne's primary musical success lies in its surprising coherence. After many playthroughs, attentive music lovers may be able to detect the traits and sensibilities of each composer, but the approach is nevertheless remarkably uniform. Kilar's *Dracula* can indeed be felt throughout the soundtrack: string solos with spectral vocals, nightmarish choirs, and ostinatos evoking a slow death march: the musical tone of Coppola's film was recycled by *Bloodborne*'s composers, who applied their own sensibilities to it with more violent and less romantic touches, in line with the game.[152] The subject seems to have significantly inspired them, especially if we compare

---

150. The score uses the following basic list of instruments: twenty-two violins, eight violas, eight cellos, six double basses, six horns, four trombones, one cimbasso; percussion included kettledrums and chimes.
151. They were composed by the three FromSoftware musicians: Tsukasa Saitô, Yuka Kitamura and Nobuyoshi Suzuki.
152. A piece such as *The Storm* from *Dracula*'s soundtrack, with its rhythmic drumming and terrifying crescendo, contains the seeds for *Bloodborne*'s action tracks.

the results with what Ryan Amon produced for films such as *Elysium*: its aggressive approach is night and day from the subtle compositions of *Bloodborne*.

As in the *Souls* games, *Bloodborne* is sparing with its musical accompaniments: they are generally reserved for boss fights or crucial locations, after the introduction clip and title screen. Most exploration therefore takes place without music, with only sounds from the environment. This plunges players into a rich environment: axes scraping on the ground, delirious cries and laughter, and supernatural whispers. The sound environment was painstakingly designed, producing a highly oppressive feeling.

The game's title screen is our first contact with the music: Ryan Amon's "The Night Unfurls" welcomes players with unsettling, quavering strings woven together with soloist Melissa Reese's icy voice, as her vocals soar eerily above the violins' melancholic melody. Interviewed by *PlayStation Blog* in 2015, Amon explained the intentions of all of the composers: "There was a great emphasis on capturing the small intuitive details of the world, especially the loneliness and forlorn beauty of it."

Dreams and Nightmares

In spite of its horror elements, the *Bloodborne* universe is permeated by a sadness found throughout the soundtrack. "Hunter's Dream" has a dreamlike quality to it, with its long-held strings, on top of which a viola plays a fragmented melody with scattered motifs, broken up by delicate silences from the solo instrument. The delicate foundation of held strings contributes to the feeling of a waking dream, reinforced when the female voice enters. The creamy smoothness of this music is hiding a bitter note, revealed in the second version of the theme, "Moonlit Melody," a variation that mirrors "Hunter's Dream"[153] starting with a vocal sigh, before the viola takes over, blending together voice and instrument. The tone is darker, reflecting Gehrman's tragic destiny while announcing the imminent arrival of the Moon Presence.[154] In many ways, the "hub" music is similar to that found in the *Souls* games, which uses the same melancholic approach and held notes, as if to indicate a hazy, uncertain temporality.

The genius of these games lies in part in the way they break with habitual, fixed models. Thus, while maintaining coherence between exploration and boss fights, *Bloodborne* still manages to toss in some surprises, like the first *Dark Souls* did with the majestic choirs at Ash Lake. A choir greets players when they first visit Yahar'gul, the Unseen Village. A solemn, bass voice seems to recite an incantation,

153. These two pieces were composed by Amon.
154. This change in the music (as well as the backdrop) in the Hunter's Dream coincides with the final third of the game and the appearance of the Blood Moon. This new music can also be heard before the victory against Rom, when players have over fifty Insight points.

and a dissonant choir of women's voices responds, until a mixed choir comes in to establish a disturbing, funereal ambiance. This disturbing chant fades away when the player returns to the village during the game's second half, after defeating Rom. This is because the Mensis ritual is over,[155] suggesting that the voices were a direct part of the game's universe. A constant, chilling presence.

Finally, exploration of the Upper Cathedral Ward is also accompanied by nerve-racking music, with grating, atonal violins, and spectral choirs, evoking an unspeakable, horrific reality.[156] Whispers in the background reinforce the unease that washes over players, echoing the terrible experiments conducted by the Choir.

Infernal Beasts

In the first part of *Bloodborne*, players lay waste to frenzied humans and hideous beasts. Boss fights in this stage are particularly violent and bloody. Unlike clashes in the *Souls* games, most of *Bloodborne*'s major fights are divided into two phases: the enemy generally becomes tougher and more aggressive during the second half. The music follows in the same vein, transitioning in real time to underscore the fight's increasing intensity.

The first big fight takes place against the Cleric Beast, with music by Tsukasa Saitô. The boss's strident cries are paired with a mixed choir that is both majestic and morose, intoning words of Latin—a religious approach that recalls the beast's true nature, formerly a member of the Healing Church. With its dissonance and heady, rhythmic string-based ostinato, this piece conveys the creature's intimidating power. Miyazaki employed this same approach in the *Souls* games, having the surging music reflect the boss's appearance to awe players and make them feel bereft and powerless, before they gather up their courage to face the boss. The piece "Cleric Beast" fills this role perfectly, as players face the Cleric Beast and Vicar Amelia.

The First Vicar Laurence, now transformed into a monster, gets another Latin choir, like an echo of the first, joined by an organ to supplement the religious associations. Supported by brass, the first part of the music is epic in flavor, not

---

155. It isn't clear exactly what purpose this ceremony serves. Since the context changes and the music goes away during the second half of the game, after Rom's death, this ritual may have aimed to summon the Blood Moon. This would explain why we see a message on the ground: "Behold! a Paleblood sky!," and then during our second visit to Yahar'gul, we can observe sacrificed, kneeling cadavers, surrounded by an aura of light and turned towards the moon. The ritual may also serve as preparation for the coming of the One Reborn. Or perhaps it is simply in remembrance of Micolash's ritual. The Latin words in "Hail the Nightmare," heard when we first visit Yahar'gul, refer to this ritual, referring to the Beastly Scourge and imploring a mother (Probably Mother Kos—Micolash refers to Kos in the Nightmare of Mensis) while alluding to a lake with silver reflections (Rom's lake, or the ocean where Kos lived).
156. The choir passage recalls Ligeti's *Requiem*, used by Kubrick in *2001: A Space Odyssey* to evoke a similar, unknowable reality.

dissimilar from Carl Orff's *Carmina Burana*, before recalling Laurence's tragic end with a heart-rending melody on the violin, then taken back up by the full orchestra in a final, desperate ballet.

Without always using a choir, the music paired with the other boss fights strives to instill a feeling of terror. One example is "Blood-Starved Beast" and its strident strings, driving percussion and bright brass.

Another is "Darkbeast" (for Darkbeast Paarl), which uses strings, brass and the choir to produce a motif of seven repeated notes that build over a long crescendo, creating an increasingly crushing atmosphere.

Man is Wolf to Man

However, the most fearsome enemies in *Bloodborne* are not necessarily beasts. Some, like Father Gascoigne, are driven by their instincts—Ryan Amon's music conveys an inner simmering that breaks out into turbulent violence, paced by ferocious percussive hammering and an aggressive choir. Others try to fight this return to beasthood, like Ludwig. The musical transition midway through the fight with the cursed hunter is one of the most characteristic of the game. During the first phase, cello and choir create a dark atmosphere, echoing Ludwig's condition. Then, when Ludwig recovers his Holy Moonlight Sword, he regains a fraction of his conscience, and Nobuyoshi Suzuki's music takes a turn for the lyrical and hyperbolic: the choir floats up into higher pitches, the brass breaks into a heroic motif, and the full orchestra joins in with explosions of fury, and suffused with tragedy.[157]

Hunters generally meet a grim fate in *Bloodborne*. They are often destined for death, frenzy or eternal wandering. Tsukasa Saitô understood this well when composing Gehrman's very melancholic theme: the strings feature prominently until the final third, when voices come in to reinforce the plaintive despair exuded by the piece. Unquestionably one of the most moving and expressive pieces of the game, it serves as a nice contrast for one of the final fights.

In a more frenzied register, but just as dramatic, Lady Maria's music blends bells, violin ostinatos and harsh percussion to convey the character's already sealed fate. Her theme is infused with sadness—composer Yuka Kitamura continually builds the intensity with brass and the choir, until reaching an intense, fatalistic climax.

---

157. It's likely just a coincidence, but one of the violin parts recalls the music of the Great Grey Wolf Sif from the first *Dark Souls*. This wouldn't be the first time that a motif is echoed throughout Hidetaka Miyazaki's games.

Other humans have tried to overstep their condition, like the Witch of Hemwick, introduced by a gypsy violin, unsettling, trembling strings, ghostly choirs and a spectral, high voice. This sinister piece was composed by Michael Wandmacher, who also created one of the most breathtaking pieces of *Bloodborne*: the fight against Micolash. The theme builds in a crescendo, revolving around a heady piano accompaniment, a flood of oft-discordant notes responding to a dissonant choir. The orchestration intentionally superimposes partially independent instrumental and vocal parts to convey the character's madness and his quest for transcendence.

Cosmic Terror

Bloodborne's story really comes into its own when players realize they're dealing with powers beyond their comprehension. Fights with these disgusting divinities covered in tentacles are given music to reflect their immoderation and horror. Composer Nobuyoshi Suzuki described his approach for the fight with the abominable One Reborn: "The feeling of horror and of something disgusting was the underlying premise, with greater themes of adornment and royalty." With its grating sounds, dissonant effects and sepulchral choir, the piece entitled "The One Reborn" evokes strong nightmarish imagery, culminating in an apocalyptic finale.

The composer uses this grandiloquence for the Living Failures, while the rhythm ostensibly borrows from "Mars," from Gustav Holst's *The Planets*.[158] In Ebrietas's theme, Yuka Kitamura takes the blend of darkness and excess to new heights: "I sensed themes of the universe, of finality, of something godly, and I was filled with visions of the end of the world as I worked on that song." In constant evolution and peppered with climaxes, "Ebrietas" is perhaps the best reflection of the game's Lovecraftian terror. The piece gets at its very core—a mix of fascination, pure terror and magnificence.

For the fight against Rom the Vacuous Spider, Kitamura preferred a more contained, contemplative piece, oscillating between the dreamlike choir and crystalline tones on one hand, and spine-chilling, grating violins on the other. In the fight's second phase, the choir enters a more frightening register, reinforced by oppressive whispers.

While the rest of the Great One themes are also quite expressive, many of them play more openly with a bitter, aggressive tone.[159] This is true for "Amygdala," composed by Cris Velasco, who echoes the epic surges of his *God of War* compositions, darkened by his abundant dissonance. Tsukasa Saitô's, "Orphan of Kos" first opens

---

158. Composed between 1914 and 1916, Holst's orchestral suite is regularly named as a major source of inspiration for film score composers, from John Williams to Hans Zimmer.
159. Except for the fight with Mergo's Wet Nurse, in which the contrast provided by the sinister music box provides a distinctive tone.

with a melancholic, creepy first half supported by a celestial choir, before the second half ventures into darker territory, with a violent ostinato from the violins. The Moon Presence's music, whose melody sung by the soprano is taken from the game's main theme, proves more stressful than contemplative: soon, dissonance takes over, with percussion and alarming entrances from the choir, cycling through the same two chords in a reflection of the unnameable terror that must now be defeated.

This provides a logical conclusion for the adventure, cadenced by Miyazaki's characteristic quest for accomplishment, in which we are put face to face with our fears and flaws, and eventually overcome them. Drawing on the talent and inspiration of six composers, *Bloodborne*'s soundtrack is awe-inspiring in the way it translates FromSoftware's themes and rich universe into captivating music. It provides a subtle and exciting blend of darkness and beauty, horror and fascination, as the violence conceals a delicate lyricism.

DARK SOULS

ダークソウル

BEYOND THE GRAVE

BOOK II
DARK SOULS III

DARK SOULS

ダークソウル

BEYOND THE GRAVE

CHAPTER ONE
CREATION

I N MID-2013, developers were just finishing off *Darks Souls II*, and *Bloodborne* had gotten off to a solid start. FromSoftware's president of the time, Naotoshi Zin, decided to get the ball rolling on a third episode of *Dark Souls*, also for PS3/Xbox 360. The team working on *DS II* would transition into this new project as soon as they were done with development. If worst came to worst, and *Bloodborne* was a flop, *Dark Souls III* could at least be FromSoftware back-up plan.

Miyazaki's Return

One of *Dark Souls II*'s co-directors, Yui Tanimura, was enlisted to lead the project alongside Isamu Okano, the creative director behind *Steel Battalion: Heavy Armor*, a *mecha* simulator created by FromSoftware in 2012. However, the prototype phase for this future *Dark Souls* proved onerous, and the project had trouble identifying the path it would take. Naotoshi Zin asked Miyazaki to rejoin the team and return to his former role of creative director. Although he was busy with *Bloodborne* development, he accepted, and saw this as an opportunity to go back to one of his first loves, as he explained to *GamesMaster* in 2015: "Because of the character of *Bloodborne*'s gameplay, its battle style, as well as the role-playing elements, it's limited compared to the *Dark Souls* franchise. It doesn't necessarily mean *Bloodborne* was bad. However, while working on [it], I realized I wanted to [create] something which had a wide range of battle styles, or featured magic, or those things which allow players to wear awesome armor. Those elements are what actually made me come [back] to the *Dark Souls* franchise." He also cited his avid interest in dark fantasy.

Though he took the helm once more for the third episode, Miyazaki was still assisted in the game's management by Tanimura and Okano, which allowed him to focus on the elements most important to him, such as the story, artistic direction, and fight design, while the two other directors concentrated on online functionality, if we are to believe what he told *Gamespot* in 2016: "This was the first time I decided to work in tandem with other directors. [...] This allowed me to have them control a number of duties, such as working on the game's networking and balancing of the multiplayer."

Development shifted to a higher gear after *Dark Souls II* was released for the new generation of consoles. The project's team comprised more than one hundred and fifty internal employees: around forty programmers, thirty designers (fights, levels, system) and fifty graphic designers and animators, with an impressive list of nearly thirty concept artists, six audio engineers and four composers.[160] With the exception of a few concept artists who were still overseen by Daisuke Satake, and some others who lent a hand after *Bloodborne* was completed, such as lead programmer Jun Itô, most of the team was totally independent from the *Bloodborne* team, and had come straight from working on *Dark Souls II*. Some of this team's notable members included gameplay designers Hiroshi Yoshida, Shigeto Hirai and Atsushi Uchikawa. In addition, as in *Bloodborne*, *Dark Souls III* also subcontracted around ten other studios to help with development, which required the creative directors to juggle communication between internal and external teams to ensure that the project went smoothly.[161] But more than ever, the video game was a collaborative project, as Miyazaki recalled during an interview with *Kotaku*: "If anything, my vision of a game is something that is formed, honed, and polished by working with those around me, especially with the great folks on the development team. This, to me, is something integral to the way I develop games, and the game so created is, without doubt, 'our' game."

Change Within Continuity

Although he was starting afresh with the project, Miyazaki kept some of the same elements selected by Tanimura and Okano, in keeping with *Dark Souls II*, as he explained to *Famitsu* in 2015: "*Dark Souls III*'s design was similar to the second. We kept the practical elements." Changes, such as the use of two weapons, were used once again and refined. Critics of *DS II* had made themselves heard, and the idea was to design an adventure with fewer, but larger locations, giving players more freedom to observe the areas and make strategic choices.

Almost as soon as *Bloodborne* was released, neophytes griped about its considerable difficulty: "Indeed, we've received feedback that the *Bloodborne* early game was too difficult and many inexperienced players were frustrated. Therefore *Dark Souls III* early game difficulty was toned down to guide players into the game," explained Miyazaki to *GNN* in 2016. His vision hadn't changed—difficulty was not the game's primary aim, but rather a way to give players a sense of achievement for having overcome all of the obstacles. A little tongue in cheek, he told *Le Monde*: "I have to say—my goal isn't to kill players. What I want them to feel is love."

160. See "The Music of Dark Souls III."
161. See "Sub-Contracting and the Creator's Vision" in Book III: Decryption.

As before, this strategy was at the core of the development team's reflections about the combat system. This led the team to introduce the Battle Arts, as Miyazaki explained to *Polygon* in 2015: "It will drastically change the gameplay; it's not a minor thing. Battle Arts allow a player to have a wide range of tactical options." More specifically, he wanted these abilities to give players a new perspective, with a greater risk leading to a greater reward.

For Miyazaki, it was important to not infringe upon the role-playing nature of the game, while still allowing a wide choice of weapons: "We're trying to keep it so that whatever type of character you create initially, it doesn't really matter in terms of what weapons you wish to use later on. However we're also trying to ensure that the classes and the character you create at the very beginning are still important and have an impact on you at the end of gameplay, too–so those are the two things we're trying to balance, and the new weapon skill system adds to that," he told *VG247* in 2015.

Dark Souls III also draws some influence from *Bloodborne*, which was being developed at the same time: the torch,[162] the two-phased boss fights (one build-up phase, and a second phase where the boss changes its types of hits), along with greater fluidity in the fights. Rolls are much quicker, equipment weight matters less–even knights can dodge relatively quickly.[163]

The Firelink Shrine became a closed-off hub, similar to the Hunter's Dream from *Bloodborne*, and even more so to the Nexus of *Demon's Souls*. The reference is made stronger by the character of the Fire Keeper, also blind like the Maiden in Black and with similar dialogue when the player wishes to level up: "Then touch the darkness with-in me" for the Fire Keeper, and "Then touch the Demon inside me" for the Maiden in Black. A magic meter was used once again, similar to that in *Demon's Souls*. It allows players to replenish their energy using a special Estus Flask, known as the Ashen Estus Flask. Like the first *Dark Souls*, and unlike the second, which allowed players to collect additional healing items, the Estus Flasks are limited in number and can only be totally refilled at a bonfire.

There's no doubt that the designers wanted to take the best from every previous *Souls* episode while adding new elements, such as *Bloodborne*'s more dynamic fights. This can also be felt in the game's overall structure, as Miyazaki explained to *VG247*: "In terms of the world design, and other elements, my preference is to return to something structurally a little more like the first game, and *Bloodborne*, with the world a little more connected."

---

162. This element was supposed to play a significant role in *Dark Souls II* until alterations to the game engine changed this approach.
163. Miyazaki says he drew inspiration from Legolas in *Lord of the Rings*, and increased the bow's shot frequency to give fights a new, more dynamic feel.

However, after the game came out, some critics pointed to the greater linearity of the third episode, which Miyazaki came to regret. He admitted as much to *Gamespot* in 2016: "I think there was room for improvement, such as with the map design. I believe the maps we prepared are well-suited for exploration considering that the size of the map is much larger and dimensional than before. But, I also feel that the way the maps connected to each other was a bit weak."

A Withered Beauty

Miyazaki's return to the *Dark Souls* world allowed him to link back up with the first game's story. As he said to *Kotaku* in 2016: "*Dark Souls III* was designed to be a sequel, so the story, in like manner, is made as a sequel, too. The story for this game is built upon the story of the fire keepers from *Dark Souls I* and *II*." There are many more references to the first *Dark Souls* than in the second episode, even if they have to be interpreted in item descriptions to identify allusions to Gwynevere, for instance. Although the player's objective–to find the Lords of Cinder–is expressed more clearly at the beginning of the adventure, the narration remains faithful to the creator's design, according great importance to the player's imagination and freedom of interpretation. Miyazaki nevertheless told GNN that he had come up with the third volume's story from the beginning: "Actually one of my hobbies is to design settings and lore. When I was making the first game I already had the whole picture in my mind."[164]

To create Lothric and its surroundings, FromSoftware's artistic and technical teams worked even harder, following Miyazaki's precise vision blending horror and splendor. In interviews, he has claimed that he is most interested in the inherent beauty of things that may first appear ugly.

Visually, the game tends to intensify the disturbing elegance found in the previous episodes. Miyazaki explained it thus to *Vice*: "We have also changed the game's palette to fit into this concept of withering beauty. The colours are more muted and sublime. The levels, dragons, enemies, monsters, even NPCs still have that sense of dignity." His comments to Polygon in 2015 show his desire to play on subtlety and ambiguity: "One of the elements I want to bring to boss character design is contradiction. We have the Dancer of the Frigid Valley; she is definitely a formidable enemy, but at the same time players sense not only that it's scary, but [that] there's a sense of sadness. Contradicting elements–that's something I want to bring to boss character design, not just fearful enemies but something more that can be sensed from each boss character."

---

164. Readers can interpret this as they wish. As far as creation goes, nothing is ever set in stone; since he declared earlier that he wasn't a fan of the idea of sequels, it's difficult to know if he really planned everything out from the beginning.

The game's atmosphere also reflects this intention. Miyazaki recognizes that the game's early environments have a similar feel to the other *Souls* games, but this only serves to better surprise players when they reach locations in the second part of the game, such as the city of Irithyll covered in snow,[165] or Archdragon Peak, sunny as a summer's day.

Miyazaki's goal is to gradually immerse players in a dark, melancholic universe: "As you progress through the game, players will see the development of an 'end of days.' This is evoked through the sadness and melancholy of enemies in the world. [...] we emphasise sadness and loneliness, too, which can be seen in both the environments and life forms within the game."

Dozens of artists worked to concoct the many nuanced atmospheres and creatures, which were all powered by the same game engine as *Bloodborne*. This step was fun for Miyazaki: "I always get excited when I see something come to life beyond my expectations during the course of working with the art designer," he told *Gamespot* in 2016. The game's modelers put a great deal of attention into creating dynamic lighting, ash, and the animation of characters' attire.

The visual detail fulfills Miyazaki's objective, by rounding off the thematic focus from the first *Dark Souls*, with the metaphor of fire once again at the heart of the game: "Fire, compared to light, gives people an unreal and wavering impression. Fire also represents dual properties like hot and cold, light and dark, life and death. The uncertainty of Fire is more suited to the world of *Dark Souls* in my mind." As he said to *VG247*: "All of *Dark Souls III*'s design is basically based on my own personal preference."

This also led Miyazaki to come up with Embers, which replace the Body Form from the previous *Souls* games. This choice was in response to players' feedback, as he explained to *Wired* in 2016: "One of the complaints I hear from fans is that they don't want to be 'ugly' when they're Hollow [a degenerative, almost cadaverous character state in previous games, reached after dying and limiting certain game features]. They're playing a character they've spent so much time creating, down to facial detail, and they don't want to lose that. So I decided to add a new state instead."[166]

A FromSoftware Blockbuster

In October 2015, FromSoftware launched a beta test for *Dark Souls III*, in order to make adjustments to the online game. The final version was released in Japan on

---

165. The Painted World of Ariamis in the first *Dark Souls* also provides a wintery atmosphere, though it is less dream-like.
166. The Untrue Dark Ring also allows players to keep their human appearance when Undead.

March 24, 2016 for PS4 and Xbox One, and then for the rest of the world on April 12, for all platforms, including Microsoft Windows.

With a huge marketing push, *Dark Souls III* benefited from fans' continued excitement and devotion to the series, as well as new players who had been won over by *Bloodborne* the previous year: it sold over two million copies. Without citing exact numbers, Namco Bandai announced that opening day sales in the United States shattered the publisher's record.

Though *Dark Souls III* didn't achieve the same unexpected, spectacular success as *Bloodborne*, considering its niche audience, it still confirmed the series was as strong as ever. But Miyazaki confirmed that it was really time for FromSoftware to move on to something else. *Dark Souls III* was the last game to be started before he became president of FromSoftware, in May of 2014. He feels that it's important to take what they have learned from one series to come up with new, exciting games for players. He explained this to *Gamespot* in 2015: "I don't think it'd be the right choice to continue indefinitely creating *Souls* and *Bloodborne* games. I'm considering *Dark Souls III* to be the big closure on the series." He also echoed this thought in 2016: "We will strive in continuing to create special games of value, so that when people look back to the *Dark Souls* series, they will distinguish it as the beginning of a new stage for From Software." And finally, he told *Rolling Stone* the next year, when describing his role as president: "A very recent and straightforward example was the decision to define *Dark Souls III* as a major milestone, allowing us to move on and challenge ourselves with a completely new project."

His intentions are pretty clear here: *Dark Souls III* marks the end of an era. At the same time, the farewell is a bit too long in coming.

Ꭲhe Quest for the Dark Soul

On April 13, 2016, the day after the game was released outside of Japan, FromSoftware announced that the game's first expansion would be available in the fall. This had been a bit of a tradition for the series since *Artorias of the Abyss*, and now almost an obligation. A few days later, some specifics were also released: two DLCs were planned, and the second would appear in early 2017.

With *Dark Souls III* hot off the press, Miyazaki's team began working on two additional adventures that would form one full narrative, each with different atmospheres. The first additional DLC, *Ashes of Ariandel*, takes place in a snowy, painted world, similar to that of Ariamis in the first *Dark Souls*.

"There are some connections between this Painted World and the one from the original *Dark Souls*. The reason I decided to return to the Painted World is because it matches with the theme I'm trying to describe in the first DLC," the creative director explained to *Polygon*. By playing around with the map-building for *Dark Souls III*, Miyazaki wanted to immerse players in a vast, open world with no safe areas, where they could be attacked by vicious creatures, including packs of wolves. Bands of enemies give the game's fights a new feel. For players interested in PvP,[167] the team added an arena that can be accessed after defeating the optional boss.

The second DLC, *The Ringed City*, has a totally different feel to it, even though it continues one of the narrative arcs from *Ashes of Ariandel*. Miyazaki explained this deliberate choice to *IGN Japan*: "Each DLC has its different game composition, map, situations and concepts, so DLC2 will not feature another snowy map. DLC1's theme is Gothic Horror, and DLC2's theme is digging deeper into the *Dark Souls III* universe." However, although *The Ringed City* marks the (temporary?) end of the series, Hidetaka Miyazaki tends to emphasize that we shouldn't view the DLC as the game's conclusion. For him, the end of *Dark Souls III* is complete, and the two DLCs should be seen as independent, even though they reveal important elements of the game's universe, particularly with regard to Pontiff Sulyvahn or the Pygmies. He expressed his objective to *DualShockers*: "What we're trying to do is approaching the big theme from the main games from a different perspective. With a 'different perspective' I mean that we've been using the Painted World as a different perspective in order to describe the main game's theme symbolically."

Ashes of Ariandel was released on October 24, 2016, followed by *The Ringed City* on March 28, 2017. This additional story was greeted with enthusiasm, and *The Ringed City* in particular, which offered more content than the first DLC. It was a fitting swan song for the series—in an interview with Famitsu[168] for the release of *The Ringed City*, Miyazaki confirmed again that there was no new *Dark Souls* in the works, and that nothing was planned for the moment. A slightly risky position for FromSoftware to take, considering the impact of the series, but the creative director and president remains confident: "If we avoided risks, we wouldn't have positioned [*Dark Souls III*] to be a turning point in the series and an end to the current storyline. I believe the new projects we will be announcing will show our stance and direction we're headed to," he said in an interview with *Kotaku*.

In conclusion, and as was customary, a "Game of the Year" edition was released on April 21, 2017 with the basic game and its DLCs, called *The Fire Fades Edition*. Thus was the final stone placed in the *Dark Souls* edifice.

---

167. The *Dark Souls* community has always been very important to Miyazaki. As he told *Wired* in 2016: "Some of the stuff the community has done, collaborating on *Twitch*, or playing with *Guitar Hero* controllers, is incredible though. I've been very happy to see that kind of creativity."
168. Translated by user Black Kite on Twitter (@bk2128).

DARK SOULS

ダークソウル

BEYOND THE GRAVE

CHAPTER TWO
UNIVERSE

A LTHOUGH players could explore *Dark Souls II* without knowing anything about the first episode's universe, *Dark Souls III* is a true sequel. It isn't uncommon to find a name or face from the previous episodes, starting with the first. Before we cover the *Dark Souls III* story, it's important to be familiar with the main elements of the previous narratives. We'll do a "Previously on..." recap sequence to refresh our memory on the essential *Dark Souls* mythology.[169] Then, we'll look at what happened during the gap between the two first episodes and *Dark Souls III*, before we get into the game's core components, and describe the player's adventure.

What You Need to Know About Dark Souls I and II

The Age of Ancients

Information about the *Dark Souls* world goes all the way back to the Age of Ancients, also called the Age of Dragons. The powerful fire breathers ruled over the world, conquering weaker creatures, who would eventually seek refuge underground. Below the surface, the exiled creatures made a discovery that would drastically change the course of future events: Fire. Four fortunate beings drew powerful souls from this Fire: they would later become the Lords. Nito received the Soul of the dead; the Witch of Izalith the Soul of life; Gwyn the Soul of light; and the Pygmy the Dark Soul. The dark, hopeless world, frozen in time under the dominion of the dragons, began to shift. The spark of Fire caused these underground beings to diversify: among them now were giants, witches, humans, and even gods. After being frozen for eons, time slowly began its course once more, announcing the end of the seemingly immutable Age of Ancients. With the power of Fire at his disposal, Gwyn led the battle against

169. For a comprehensive explanation of the story and characters, see the first volume, *Dark Souls: Beyond the Grave*.

the dragons. Assisted by Nito and the Witch of Izalith, he led the rebels to victory. He had help from the outcast Seath the Scaleless, an albino dragon who turned against his fellow dragons. The fourth Lord, the Pygmy, who could have helped in Gwyn's fight against the dragons, preferred to stay away until he was totally forgotten. After his victory, Gwyn declared the end of the Age of Ancients and the beginning of the Age of Fire.

The Reign of the Gods During the Age of Fire

The Age of Fire was the age of the gods. The gods, including Gwyn and his entourage, were created along with the Fire. They founded the city of Anor Londo, in the vast, splendid region of Lordran. Humans, giants and witches lived together and prospered under the rule of the gods.[170]

During this period of prosperity, Gwyn, Lord of Sunlight, fathered three children.[171] The firstborn became a god of war, but his father would eventually reject him, and his name was expunged from all of the kingdom's archives.[172] Gwyn then had a daughter, Gwynevere, known as the "Princess of Sunlight," and a son, Gwyndolin, "the Dark Sun." At that time, all of the gods lived in Anor Londo, Lordran's tallest and most beautiful city. From their ivory tower, they still noticed that Fire, as represented by the First Flame, was not eternal. It began to show signs of diminishing. The concept of time (still very loose within the *Souls* series), began with the discovery of Fire, and took on a new, unexpected importance. Gwyn and his fellow gods decided that the Fire must never go out, to ensure the permanence of the age of the gods.

They soon understood that humans were good fuel to supply the Fire. Gwyn and his uncle Lloyd founded the Way of White covenant, a religious order to recruit humans and get them to practice the Rite of Kindling–that is, to sacrifice their humanity[173] (or that of other humans) in order to feed the Fire and rekindle it. Luckily for them, there were many humans to be found throughout Lordran, and their numbers only continued to grow. This meant that kindling was never in short supply.

Hailed by Gwyn as the solution to preserve the Age of Fire, humanity would also be the source of this era's downfall.

---

170. The description of the Lightning Bolt from *Dark Souls III* references this time of peace: "Bolts imbued with lightning created by the giant blacksmith of the gods. [...] These bolts are likely artifacts of the dragonless era, when the pact between gods and humans was upheld."
171. According to information culled from *Dark Souls III* and in particular the second DLC, *The Ringed City*, Gwyn had at least five children: the three mentioned in the first episode, and then Yorshka and Filianore.
172. The description of the Ring of the Sun's First Born tells this story: "The Sun's first born was once a god of war, until he was stripped of his stature as punishment for his foolishness. No wonder his very name has slipped from the annals of history."
173. Humanity is a recurring item in the first two *Dark Souls*, which can be taken from the dead bodies of other humans.

The Pygmy and the Dark Soul

A part of every human, humanity originated from the Dark Soul, which the Pygmy had inherited from the Fire. The furtive Pygmy, who hid away during the battle with the dragons and who saw the beginning of the Age of Fire, was none other than the first human.[174] His schemes were more underhand than those of the gods. Each humanity contained a fragment of Dark; the Pygmy, using his Lord Soul, placed the "Darksign" upon each of his descendants, thereby preventing their death. If they lose their lives, they enter an undead state: they can be "revived" by humanity. Once undead, humans eventually go mad and sink into a murderous frenzy in which they cannot regain their humanity: beings in this sad state are known as "hollows." The Darksign nevertheless made humans rather strong.

Increasing in number, each with a fragment of Dark to contrast with the light of the Fire, humans began to inspire fear within the gods. Undeads and hollows were imprisoned by the Way of White,[175] but it was already too late: the gathering of Dark in Lordran marked the true decline of the Fire.

The Appearance of Chaos and the Abyss

To strengthen the Fire, the Witch of Izalith, who had previously helped Gwyn in the uprising against the dragons, tapped into her Lord Soul and drew out an enormous amount of energy. This attempt to rekindle the First Flame failed, and also resulted in the unintended creation of an entity called "Chaos." The infernal flames of Chaos ravaged the underground city of Izalith and devoured the witch's soul. The witch was transformed into a being called the Bed of Chaos, which formed the first demons. Most of the demons remained underground, but the ones who managed to reach the surface were subjugated by the gods.

Far from there, in the region of Oolacile, the Abyss appeared. Although the reasons for its apparition are unclear, the first appearance of the Abyss was recorded in the annals of Oolacile: the region was invaded by a deep, dense and indestructible darkness. It is likely that it appeared when the Pygmy drew upon his Lord Soul to affix the Darksign on humans. It would appear that Chaos and the Abyss were created in a similar way—from the good intentions of those using their Lord Souls. In this way, they can be seen as a corruption of Fire and the Dark, respectively.

---

174. In *The Ringed City*, we learn that the mythical Pygmy is more than one person—the "Pygmy" was instead a full-blown species, and the very first human. We'll come back to this during our discussion of the DLC.
175. When they weren't sacrificed in the Fire as part of the Rite of Kindling, the Undead Bone Shard description says that "The bonfire's cinders are the bones of Undead, and a bone that still burns is a fresh cinder indeed."

The First Lord of Cinder and the Decision of the Chosen Undead

Following the Witch of Izalith's failure, the First Flame grew too weak to continue burning. Gwyn decided to "link" the Fire, a process that would slow its disappearance, but would require the sacrifice of a hero. He went to the Kiln of the First Flame, a sacred place where the First Flame was kept, in order to offer up his soul to the precious Fire. The Lord of Sunlight thus became the first Lord of Cinder.

Many centuries later, however, the effects of Gwyn's sacrifice began to decline. The Fire was once again on the verge of going out. But the land of Lordran had changed dramatically. The gods had withdrawn from Anor Londo, and the number of hollows continued to grow—they were locked up in prisons or wandered desperately throughout the kingdom. This is when the Primordial Serpent Frampt,[176] known as the "Kingseeker," teamed up with one of Gwyn's sons, Gwyndolin, the only god who chose not to leave Anor Londo. Together, they devised the prophecy of the Chosen Undead, referring to a "chosen one" who would be manipulated into linking the Fire and thus perpetuating the Age of Fire.

Players of the first *Dark Souls* are this chosen one. They complete the tasks set out by Frampt and Gwyndolin. However, during the adventure, the Chosen Undead meets Darkstalker Kaathe. This is another Primordial Serpent, pursuing a different objective from Frampt. Kaathe aspires to end the Age of Fire, and to bring on the Age of Dark. He is the one to explain the origins of the Dark to the Chosen Undead, and reveals the existence of the Pygmy. He proposes the idea of ending the Age of Fire (the age of the gods) by refusing to link the Fire, in order to usher in the Age of Dark (the age of humans).

This decision falls to the player at the end of the adventure, after taking down the final boss: Gwyn himself.[177] After the fight, the player can choose to either rekindle the Age of Fire once more, and become the new Lord of Cinder, or end the sacrificial cycle to become the Dark Lord. The second choice would thus mark the beginning of the age of humans...

---

176. Little information is known about the Primordial Serpents. No one knows how many there were, or their true intentions, but the adjective "primordial," their giant size, and their influence throughout the first *Dark Souls* gives them an almost divine status. They are very important, yet also troubling and enigmatic creatures.
177. Even though the final boss of *Dark Souls* is called "Gwyn, Lord of Cinder," he could actually be any other Chosen Undead who linked the Fire before the player along the chain of sacrifices.

The Eternal Cycle of Fire and Dark

The context of *Dark Souls II* is radically different, but we're back once again in the Age of Fire, as the game abandons the mythological legacy of the first episode. However, we meet a character who shares some very surprising information: Straid of Olaphis. In a conversation, Straid mentions his vision of a cycle of Fire and Dark. He believes that the Fire has a limited duration (maintained only by the sacrifices of the successive Lords of Cinder), and will eventually be snuffed out, making way for the Dark. Much later on, however, the embers of the old Fire eventually rekindle and the Dark makes way for the new Flame, and thus a new cycle. Straid once lived in the former kingdom of Olaphis, already prey to the cycle of Fire and Dark, well before King Vendrick ruled the land of Drangleic, the kingdom where *Dark Souls II* takes place. The strange character of Straid was turned into stone long ago, until he is awoken by the player, to whom he explains his point of view.

Through this, we understand that the struggle between Fire and Dark exists on a much broader scale than we may have understood in our time in Lordran (the first struggle in a long chain). Fire and Dark follow one after the other in time, but also in space: *Dark Souls II* takes place in a new location, but it revolves around similar issues.

Dark Souls III, which takes place much later, also introduces new kingdoms. Although it presents some original features, its story abounds with references to the first *Dark Souls*.

Between Dark Souls I and III

Chronology

Throughout the cycles, the Lords of Cinder follow one after the other. The story of *Dark Souls III* presents four of them[178]: Ludleth, Aldrich, the Abyss Watchers and Yhorm. A fifth, Prince Lothric, rejects his fate of becoming Lord of Cinder by refusing to link the Fire. There's no use trying to figure out the chronology of the four sacrifices. Each Lord of Cinder fulfilled this duty willingly or not, within their own kingdom or region, prolonging the Fire's power for a time. However, when the fifth sacrifice is rejected, the bell tolls to signal the Fire's danger. From this crucial moment onward, events follow a certain chronology, which we will return to. Before we look at the sequence of events, let's focus on the background of these five chosen ones.

The Lords of Cinder

Originally from the land of Courland, Ludleth sacrificed himself for the Fire, believing it was for the greater good. However, this did not prevent the downfall of his kingdom.

Far from Courland, in the region of Farron, several undeads had grouped together in the Watchdogs of Farron covenant, with strength and a strong will to hunt the monstrosities caused by the Abyss. They fought in memory of the Wolf Knight. The Wolf Knight was none other than Artorias the Abysswalker, who fought the Abyss beside his faithful gray wolf, Sif, within the ancient lands of Oolacile. Farron's Legion, acting as a lone man representing the soul of the Wolf's Blood, decided to link the Fire.

---

178. No doubt the four final beings to link the Fire.

Together, they became the new Lord of Cinder. The region of Farron would neverthe-less fall into ruin, overtaken and tainted by the Abyss.[179]

In the Cathedral of the Deep, a being named Aldrich would devour those around him–adults and children alike.[180] Formerly known as the "Saint of the Deep," he even-tually changed into an enormous, insatiable mass of sludge. Aldrich was then forced to link the Fire to become the Lord of Cinder, thereby sacrificing all of the souls he had absorbed during his abominable existence. After his immolation, his dead body was buried in a giant, superbly decorated black coffin, located at the heart of the Cathedral of the Deep.

The story of the Profaned Capital and Yhorm the Giant, who also linked the Fire, is particularly unclear. Yhorm was "the descendant of an ancient conqueror"[181] and through his exceptional strength, he subjugated the people of the Profaned Capital. Among these oppressed, a powerful pyromancy appeared: the Profaned Flame, an eternal, forbidden fire that drew interest among the populace. Its true origins are unknown: the legend simply indicates that the Profaned Flame was "triggered by the curse of those women, relatives of a certain oracle."[182] However, if we're to believe

179. This is the explanation found with the Exile Mask: "After the Legion's Watchers became Lords of Cinder, the wolf's blood dried up, and Farron was consumed by a festering wood." The "wood" here is none other than the Darkroot Wood from the first episode. The wood was located in the ruins of Oolacile, the region that had fallen prey to the Abyss long ago, and where Artorias had written his legend. Indeed, in the Farron Keep area, we find numerous elements with ties to Oolacile.
180. Hawkwood describes Aldrich's life quite well before his sacrifice in the Fire: "A right and proper cleric, only, he developed a habit of devouring men. He ate so many that he bloated like a drowned pig, then softened into sludge, so they stuck him in the Cathedral of the Deep. And they made him a Lord of Cinder. Not for virtue, but for might."
181. From the description of the Soul of Yhorm the Giant.
182. From the description of the Eleonora weapon, found in the depths of the Profaned Capital on one of the enormous creatures asleep underground. These creatures are malformed beings, with giant, eight-fingered hands in place of their heads and heaps of slimy bulbs on their stomachs—no doubt a result of the curse that struck the city's inhabitants. In the official guide's bestiary, this monster is known as the "Monstrosity of Sin." This is not the first time the notion of sin has appeared in the *Dark Souls* universe. Sin is reflected in the Lost Sinner in *Dark Souls II*, who attempted to light the First Flame like the Witch of Izalith. It can also be seen in Aldia, the Scholar of the First Sin, a character from the same game whose role takes an unexpected turn in the *Scholar of the First Sin* edition: he echoes Kaathe in the first *Dark Souls*, reminding players of the origins of humanity and the existence of the struggle between Fire and Dark. In this context, the original sin would be the Pygmy's act of placing the Darksign on humans by drawing into his Dark Soul to make them strong enough to hasten the end of the Age of Fire and bring on the Age of Dark.

the clues left throughout the game,[183] it seems likely that the Profaned Flame was actually created using the Dark, or even the Abyss—a detail that will be important later on. In spite of the defiance he inspired in his subjects, Yhorm wanted to get closer to the humans. He became friends with a man called Siegward of Catarina, an obliging knight who enjoyed life. Before becoming a Lord of Cinder, Yhorm asked a favor of Siegward: if he came back to life after his sacrifice for the Fire, Siegward should return and kill him for good. For this purpose, he gave him the Storm Ruler sword, the only weapon that could kill a Giant.[184] Then, Yhorm linked the Fire, and became Lord of Cinder, as the Profaned Flame also continued to grow day after day.[185] It was one way to fight the Dark or the Abyss that began to invade the depths of the Profaned Capital. With this mix of Dark and Fire, revived vigorously by Yhorm, the Profaned Capital was set ablaze in a giant explosion, slaughtering the inhabitants.

In the meantime, a young wandering sorcerer named Sulyvahn reached the Profaned Capital, where he discovered the Profaned Flame and its fascinating power. This would change the course of his life,[186] and soon, the course of the entire world.

But as is always the case, in spite of all these sacrifices, the Fire eventually began to show signs of decline.

Lothric

In the first *Dark Souls*, we learn of the exile of the gods. After leaving the city of Anor Londo, Gwynevere, Princess of Sunlight settled in the kingdom of Lothric,

---

183. In addition to the information from the previous note, we'll also add that the Monstrosities of Sin are vulnerable to the Wolf Knight's Greatsword and the Farron Greatsword, effective weapons against creatures of the Abyss. Eleonora can also be traded for a Hollow Gem with Pickle Pee, Pump-a-Rum Crow ("Snuggly"). This item can be used to infuse a weapon to make a Hollow weapon. To forge these Hollow weapons, you must first find Profaned Coal within the Profaned Capital, with the following description: "Remnants of the fire that burned down the Profaned Capital." This coal can be used to create Hollow weapons, along with Dark weapons. Finally, when we give it to Blacksmith Andre, he will declare, "This is much too dark. I see the Abyss in it… Your fight is for the flame, and for y' fellow kin. Just like mine. A cursed fate this may be, but hope remains, does it not?"
184. The description of the Storm Ruler weapon depicts this episode: "Yhorm the Giant once held two of these, but gave one to the humans that doubted him, and left the other to a dear friend before facing his fate as a Lord of Cinder." This sword has the same name and attributes as the one used to fight the Storm King in *Demon's Souls*.
185. "Lonely Yhorm became a Lord of Cinder to put the Profaned Flame to rest, knowing full well that those who spoke of him as lord were quite insincere," reads the description of the Cinders of a Lord, retrieved after the fight with Yhorm.
186. "Long ago, when Sulyvahn was yet a young sorcerer, he discovered the Profaned Capital and an unfading flame below a distant tundra of Irithyll, and a burning ambition took root within him," says the description of the Profaned Greatsword, one of Sulyvahn's favorite weapons.

where she married King Oceiros.[187] With him, she would have several children, all daughters to begin with,[188] leaving the king without an heir. Finally, likely using fairly dubious methods,[189] Gwynevere gave birth to twin boys. She raised the younger prince, Lothric, with the goal of making him a powerful Lord of Cinder: as daughter and heir of Gwyn, it was her duty to continue this honorable line of Fire with her long-awaited son.

Royal power rested on three distinct pillars: the high priestess, the group of scholars, and the knights symbolizing faith, intelligence and strength, respectively. High Priestess Emma served as wet nurse to Prince Lothric, the scholars were in charge of teaching, and the knights protected the kingdom. The First of the Scholars was the prince's mentor; unfortunately for the royal family and their hopes, the mentor questioned the role of Fire and influenced Lothric,[190] who refused to become Lord of Cinder.

The identity of the First of the Scholars remains one of the story's greatest question marks. It's possible that he is actually Sulyvahn, the young sorcerer who took possession of the Profaned Flame (which arose from the Dark). Following his extensive experience from his journeys across the globe, he may have helped found the Grand Archives of Lothric, in order to further the studies on magic and crystals previously initiated by Seath the Scaleless and Big Hat Logan (significant characters from the first episode). There are only a few clues to support this hypothesis, but they are rather convincing. The most compelling is the statue near the High Wall of Lothric, not far from the cathedral. It depicts the young prince in prayer attire holding the Profaned Greatsword in his right hand, which is adorned with a double bracelet: both of these items belong to Sulyvahn, as we can see in our fight with him. Another clothing detail is also noteworthy: Sulyvahn's attire is identical to the robes worn by all of the scholars in the Grand Archives—a chasuble finely embroidered with gold thread. Sulyvahn also uses an altered, violet version of the Soul Spear, the origins of which go all the way back to the research of Big Hat Logan, which confirms his ties with the Grand Archives. The only other sorcerers to use this type of violet magic are the two Crystal Sages, twins and "successors to the great sage Logan"[191] who

---

187. Nothing suggests that Oceiros was the same person as Flame God Flann, Gwynevere's husband mentioned in the description of the Ring of the Sun Princess from the first episode. The same ring (called the "Sun Princess Ring") in *Dark Souls III* has a vaguer description, removing the reference to Flann: "Gwynevere left her home with a great many other deities, and became a wife and mother, raising several heavenly children."

188. The game confirms the identity of two of these daughters. The first was named Gertrude, the Heavenly Daughter. "The Heavenly Daughter is said to be the Queen's child," explains the Bountiful Light miracle. The second is known as "The Dancer": we'll come back to her.

189. "The Lothric bloodline," according to the description of Lothric's Cinders of a Lord, "was obsessed with creating a worthy heir, and when this proved impossible, resorted to unspeakable means."

190. According to the description of the Soul Stream: "The first of the Scholars doubted the linking of the fire."

191. From the description of Sage's Big Hat.

"once served as spiritual guides to the scholars of the Grand Archives."[192] Sulyvahn and the Crystal Sages are therefore related, which strengthens the hypothesis that Sulyvahn helped create the Grand Archives. Finally, Sulyvahn's connection with the Dark through the Profaned Flame seems to make him the ideal candidate to be the First of the Scholars, manipulating the mind of the royal line's final hope, born and raised to be sacrificed to the Fire.

Of course, Lothric's refusal to become Lord of Cinder had repercussions. The Three Pillars of the kingdom split apart and weakened. The knights joined High Priestess Emma to serve the Fire and declared the scholars heretics. The doors of the Grand Archives were thus condemned.[193] However, King Oceiros had developed a penchant for studying crystals and magic, and he decided to join the "heretics of the Grand Archives, where he discovered the twisted worship of Seath the paledrake."[194] Oceiros was fascinated with dragons and their scales, along with the rest of the knights of Lothric. These knights diverged from the other Pillars, which would weaken the kingdom even further. During this dark period, Oceiros and Gwynevere had a final child, no doubt a result of his father's experiments. He was even named "Ocelotte, child of dragons."[195]

Gwynevere mysteriously disappears "after giving birth to Ocelotte,"[196] as her husband's mind was slipping away. Now known as "Oceiros the Consumed King," he went into exile as well, taking with him his son Ocelotte (the result of his experiments), whom he eventually lost. Numerous assassins went off in search of the former king, but none fulfilled this mission. Oceiros was declared dead.[197]

On a greater scale, Prince Lothric's refusal to link the Fire led to an unprecedented phenomenon: the bell tolled and "the ash seeketh embers." It was almost as though the Fire sent out a cry for help, making Lothric's kingdom a point of convergence, a focal point for other kingdoms and a crucial location for the fate of the Age of Fire.

---

192. From the description of the Soul of a Crystal Sage.
193. The text associated with the Grand Archives Key explains: "With the fire fading, and the spreading pus of man tainting the castle, the Grand Archives closed its doors for good."
194. From the description of the Soul of Consumed Oceiros.
195. Dialogue from Oceiros, during his fight with the player.
196. From the item description for the "Divine Blessing."
197. The Shadow Mask describes the king's exile: "The late King Oceiros was obsessed by dragons, to the extent that he would later be known as the Consumed King. Countless assassins were sent to end his reign, but none returned." The adjective "late" is of course incorrect, because players confront this king in the hidden area of the Consumed King's Garden. At this point, he has partially transformed into Seath the Scaleless, an albino dragon without scales, using the magic of crystals.

The Convergence of Worlds and the Ash Seeketh Embers

As in the other *Souls* games, the introduction supplies essential information for understanding the game's context. We've transcribed it for you here:

> Yes, indeed.
> It is called Lothric,
> where the transitory lands of the Lords of Cinder
> converge.
> In venturing north, the pilgrims discover the truth
> of the old words.
> "The fire fades, and the Lords go without thrones."
> When the link of Fire is threatened, the bell tolls,
> unearthing the old Lords of Cinder from their
> graves.
> Aldrich, Saint of the Deep.
> Farron's Undead Legion,
> the Abyss Watchers.
> And the reclusive lord of the Profaned Capital.
> Yhorm the Giant.
> Only, in truth...
> The Lords will abandon their thrones, and
> the Unkindled will rise.
> Nameless, accursed Undead, unfit even to be cinder.
> And so it is, that ash seeketh embers.

Though the timeline is hazy, we know that many events took place after Prince Lothric's refusal to link the Fire. The most important relates to the convergence between "the transitory lands of the Lords of Cinder," which led to the game's singular geography. We can see that the kingdoms came physically nearer Lothric Castle, where Prince Lothric still resides along with his twin brother and protector, Lorian: Irithyll of the Boreal Valley, the Profaned Capital, the Cathedral of the Deep,

Farron Keep, and even the old city of the gods, Anor Londo, are located at the foot of this illustrious castle, in a jumbled cluster of regions with their vastly different cultures and legends.[198]

The introduction also mentions the "pilgrims," strange creatures clothed in rags, propped up on fragile canes almost as feeble as they seem to be. On their backs, they carry a shell, or rather a cocoon (as we'll see later). Laden with chains, these pilgrims move together in groups towards the kingdom of Lothric from Londor, the land of hollows, a place known for its Sable Church, an organization founded by three sisters[199] following instructions from Darkstalker Kaathe from the first episode. The pilgrims have close ties with the Dark, and the decline of the Fire draws them towards the point of convergence, in accordance with a prophecy they call "the old words." These words remain unknown, but we can infer that they announce the imminent arrival of a new Age of Dark.

The Fire's bell tolls, unearthing the corpses of the ancient Lords of Cinder: Yhorm, Ludleth, the Abyss Watchers and Aldrich rise from their graves, called to fill the vacant thrones of the Firelink Shrine, a symbolic location for preserving the Fire. Only trusty Ludleth answers the call and proudly takes his place on his throne. The other Lords of Cinder decline the invitation and set off to attend to more personal occupations. The Lords therefore go without thrones.[200]

The Abyss Watchers went to Farron Keep. In a twist of fate, their former lands were corrupted by the Abyss, which soon reached and tainted the members of this former Lord of Cinder. They thus followed in the footsteps of their hero, Wolf Knight Artorias, who left to fight the Abyss only to lose himself to its corruption.

No one knows why Yhorm didn't return to the Firelink Shrine. Back in the Profaned Capital, the Giant witnessed the destruction that struck his city after he sacrificed himself to the Fire. He nevertheless returned to the throne where he had reigned authoritatively over the Profaned Capital. Here, he would sink into despair, surrounded only by a few servants and what remained of the city's treasure—thousands of valuable objects, chalices, goblets, dishes and various ornaments.

198. The Stone-Humped Hag, a merchant we meet at the beginning of the second DLC, *The Ringed City*, describes this phenomenon: "At the close of the Age of Fire, all lands meet at the end of the earth."
199. Long unknown, the name of the eldest sister is revealed in the first DLC, *Ashes of Ariandel*: Elfriede is the oldest of the sisters, followed by Yuria, and then by the youngest, Liliane. Three item descriptions provide information on the sisters: according to the Onyx Blade, Elfriede is "the eldest amongst her sisters and leader of the Sable Church"; the Beak Mask says that it "belongs to Yuria, the second eldest," one of the "three mentors of the Sable Church of Londor"; finally, the Dark Blade miracle description says that "the third daughter, Liliane," was "one of the founders of the Sable Church." We should note that Liliane doesn't physically appear during the game, unlike Yuria (merchant NPC) and Elfriede, a difficult boss at the end of the first DLC.
200. The French translation for the game speaks of an "age of throneless Lords," instead of sticking to the English original, recalling the Age of Ancients, Fire, or Dark. This is an interesting difference, since the French version seems to highlight the importance of this new "age."

Aldrich left his tomb in the Cathedral of the Deep, and "when Aldrich ruminated on the fading of the fire, it inspired visions of a coming age of the deep sea. He knew the path would be arduous, but he had no fear. He would devour the gods himself."[201] A great mystery surrounds this "coming age of the deep sea." In any case, Aldrich's desire eventually gave his soul a dark blue color, along with the deacons and three archdeacons—McDonnell, Royce and Klimt—who watched over him. Hungry for power and for gods, Aldrich was nicknamed the "Devourer of Gods."

On his end, Sulyvahn had abandoned his young prince. He was no doubt banished by the High Priestess Emma and the order of the knights, after his dark schemes were exposed. No matter! His path led him to Irithyll, which he successfully conquered. Now known as the "Pontiff," and wielding unprecedented power and control, he began to build a protection system to stop those who wished to lead the Lords of Cinder back to their throne and continue the Age of Fire. He sent a Crystal Sage to the region of Farron, both to "train the sorcerers of Farron"[202] to defend their bastion, and to protect the path that (since the convergence of the worlds) had led to the Cathedral of the Deep, and thus to the tomb of Aldrich. At the same time, Sulyvahn took Aldrich under his wing and hid him in the heights of Anor Londo, whose immense buildings remained hidden within the fog beyond Irithyll. The Pontiff captured Gwyn's unloved son, Gwyndolin, to serve him up as an offering to the Devourer of Gods. His new retreat was located at the foot of Gwynevere's old throne room, where players fought Ornstein and Smough in the first *Dark Souls*. Archdeacon McDonnell, also charged with protecting Aldrich, joined Sulyvahn to found the Aldrich Faithful covenant. "The faithful ensure that Aldrich, Devourer of Gods, remains undisturbed, by taking the form of loyal spirits and hunting down those who would trespass the ruined cathedral."[203] Yhorm the Giant was harder to sway, but Sulyvahn called upon some of the best sorcerers from within the depths of the Profaned Capital, sorcerers from Big Hat Logan's school of magic. In addition to their undeniable affinity for Dark, their exceptional training had given them very dissuasive powers. In an act of foresight, Sulyvahn also needed to block off access to Lothric Castle. He sent some outrider knights, accompanied by two of his faithful servants: Vordt and the Dancer. The Dancer is said to be "a distant daughter of the formal royal family,"[204] namely, one of Gwynevere's daughters, possibly kidnapped by Sulyvahn when he was banished from the court. Then

201. From the description of the Soul of Aldrich.
202. From the description of the Crystal Hail spell.
203. From description of the Aldrich Faithful covenant item.
204. From the description of the Soul of the Dancer. This soul allows players to create the Soothing Sunlight, one of the "miracles of Gwynevere."

he transformed her into a "beastly creature"[205] using evil black orbs for eyes.[206] Vordt and the Dancer ventured until they reached the High Wall of Lothric, where they met the High Priestess Emma, whom they imprisoned. Then, they stood watch at strategic locations to block anyone from entering or exiting.

Sulyvahn therefore made sure that no one could lead the Lords of Cinder back to their throne. The enemies who rose up against him were known as the Unkindled, or Ashen Ones: "Nameless, accursed Undead, unfit even to be cinder," to recall the description from the introductory cutscene. Since the tolling of the bell, they have appeared throughout the world, solely focused on ending the age of throneless lords. One of these Unkindled is embodied by players—years, or even centuries later, when the *Dark Souls III* adventure begins.

205. This phrasing comes from the description of the Dancer's Armor: "The black eyes of the Pontiff eventually transformed the Dancer into a beastly creature."
206. The descriptions of the Pontiff's Right Eye and Left Eye reveal Sulyvahn's cruelty: "Knights who peer into the black orb are lured into battles of death, transformed into frenzied beasts. No wonder the Pontiff only provides these rings to those dispatched to foreign lands."

Dark Souls III

The Unkindled

Players awake in a coffin—no doubt their own. In the Cemetery of Ash, where the coffin is located, the Unkindled await summoning by the Fire to reestablish order. These Unkindled were once humans or hollows, sacrificed to the fire through the Rite of Kindling, a sacrificial ritual to feed the Fire between two Lords of Cinder. The Unkindled thus lost their humanity, the fragment of Dark inherited from the Pygmy, lost in the ritual. However, they can carry "embers,"[207] from which they draw power. Seen as nobodies, merely fuel to feed the Fire, they are unlikely candidates as the final hope to bring back the true heroes of the Fire: the ancient Lords of Cinder, now all fallen or corrupt. This is nevertheless their mission.

Though lacking humanity, the Unkindled retained their Darksign, which makes them rather hardy. However, they can't transform into a hollow: when an Unkindled dies, they leave nothing but ash behind.[208] Later in the adventure, we find out that getting a Dark Sigil exposes the Unkindled to the hollow curse, an important topic we'll cover in the "Marriage and Dark Sigils" section.

Once they've settled into their role as an Unkindled, players must complete a first challenge when attempting to leave the Cemetery of Ash. The Judge of Fire, Iudex Gundyr, tests their strength and perseverance, before letting them pass and reach the Firelink Shrine. The sacred space juts out from the horizon, as the proud belfry where the bell that once tolled reaches up skyward.

---

207. Embers are used in the same way as humanities from the previous episodes: by consuming embers, players regain all of their health points and can use the online game system to summon or invade other players.
208. By bringing collected ash to the Firelink Shrine Handmaid (who serves as the game's primary merchant), we can gain access to new items.

Exploring the Firelink Shrine

Only the calming atmosphere of the Firelink Shrine from the first *Dark Souls* was kept for this third episode. The new Firelink Shrine is more akin to the isolated Nexus from *Demon's Souls* than the open-air haven of peace from the first episode, amid the hostile vastness of Lordran. First off, players can warp from this area to anywhere in the kingdom of Lothric or its surroundings, as with the Archstones in the Nexus. The Fire Keeper is also very reminiscent of the Maiden in Black, even down to her dialogue. Finally, most NPCs we meet along our adventure come here to provide aid, like the allies in *Demon's Souls* located in the Nexus. The steles and archstones have made way for the thrones of the Lords of Cinder, arranged in the same way around the center of the room. Only Ludleth sits on his throne—the others remain absent, waiting for players to bring back the Cinder of a Lord: "If the lords will not return to their thrones themselves, let them return as cinders."[209]

The characters living within the Firelink Shrine each provide players with a specific type of help. Blacksmith Andre of Astora, who also appeared in the first episode, is charged with forging and infusing weapons. The Shrine Handmaid acts as a (somewhat crabby) merchant. The ever-present Crestfallen Warrior, hunched over in despondency, is here once again: he's called Hawkwood, and is privy to information on Lothric and the former Lords of Cinder, which he shares with us. Finally, the Fire Keeper allows players to level up, but provides no answers to questions players might have along the way. Soon, new faces appear in the shrine: several characters who agree to help us warp to Firelink.[210] They provide for a wide variety of encounters and support, making the Firelink Shrine an essential location, a peaceful haven in an increasingly hostile world.

The Unkindled Quest

When we receive the Coiled Sword after fighting Iudex Gundyr, we can finally set out on the Unkindled quest by lighting the bonfire at the center of the Firelink Shrine. Then, we warp to the High Wall of Lothric, where the real adventure begins.

---

209. From the description of the Cinders of a Lord.
210. Irina of Carim, performer of miracles; Cornyx of the Great Swamp, a pyromancer ecstatic to have a new student; Greirat, part-thief, part-merchant; Karla, fan of Dark black magic; the mysterious Ringfinger Leonhard, fond of invading others; Sirris of the Sunless Realms, a righter of wrongs, and therefore Leonhard's enemy; Yoel the Pilgrim and Yuria of Londor, strange travelers from the dark lands of hollows; Unbreakable Patches, regrettably well-known to *Souls* players; and finally, Orbeck of Vinheim, fallen sorcerer from the Vinheim Dragon School, who will condescend to teach players new spells in exchange for rare scrolls.

The first Lord of Cinder we meet is that of Wolf's Blood, an entity collectively formed by the Abyss Watchers. Before that, in Farron Keep, there are three fires to put out. Hawkwood explains to players that "gaining admission to the Legion is a matter of some ceremony. Inside their keep, snuffing out the flames of three altars opens the door to the wolf's blood." The three altars are a nod to the first game, since their engravings represent Nito, the Witch of Izalith in her Bed of Chaos form, and the Four Kings of the city of New Londo, who have become Darkwraiths. The mission of the first *Dark Souls* is to collect their four souls to eventually fight Gwyn, the first Lord of Cinder and final boss of the game. The altars, placed just before the fight with the Abyss Watchers, foreshadow the third game's objective: we must fight this first Lord of Cinder out of a total of four, not counting the game's final boss.

A bit further on, beyond the Crucifixion Woods, Aldrich was supposed to be found in the Cathedral of the Deep. Players only encounter Archdeacon Royce, accompanied by a number of highly aggressive deacons, and a scheming doll next to Aldrich's tomb. Both the description of the Soul of the Deacons of the Deep[211] and that of the Small Doll[212] suggest that Aldrich allied with Pontiff Sulyvahn before going to Irithyll of the Boreal Valley. Once in this new destination, players discover a captivating city bathed in moonlight and the northern lights. Here, players fight Sulyvahn, before reaching another city obscured by fog: Anor Londo. With nostalgic memories of the first *Dark Souls*, they come upon Aldrich. He wears Gwyndolin's Crown of the Dark Sun, after having gradually devoured this god. Following a remarkable fight, players obtain the Cinders of a second Lord.

After climbing up to Anor Londo from Irithyll, players must descend to the Profaned Capital to hunt Yhorm the Giant.[213] With the help of a so-called Siegward of Catarina, an old friend of the Giant whom he promised he would kill if he came back to life, the player's Unkindled avatar triumphs over the impressive Yhorm. Once the third Lord of Cinder has been defeated, players are called to rejoin High Priestess Emma in the cathedral of the High Wall of Lothric, the game's first area. "Ahh, Unkindled One. Fire fades and awaits its one last Lord. Prince Lothric is in your hands... Please save his soul. Tell him what he must be... a Lord." These are her final words, begging the player to convince Prince Lothric to become Lord of Cinder. Then, she dies, leaving behind her the Basin of Vows. Players then place the "basin at a statue of a beheading knight," located at the base of the cathedral, to open up access to Lothric Castle.

---

211. "After Aldrich left for the Boreal valley, Archdeacon Royce remained in the cathedral with the high priests, to keep eternal watch over their master's coffin."
212. "In the legendary old city of Irithyll situated in the Boreal Valley, the Pontiff Sulyvahn gave this doll to valued subjects, so that they might use it to cross the barrier when they return home. Listen carefully, and you can hear it say, 'Wherever you go, the moon still sets in Irithyll. Wherever you may be, Irithyll is your home.'"
213. We may have to start out by fighting the Abyss Watchers, but we can still decide to continue to Yhorm instead of Aldrich. One is simply located above Irithyll, and the other is in its depths.

The final protective measure put in place by Sulyvahn, the Dancer of the Boreal Valley suddenly attacks our hero, making for an unforgettable fight.

After this fight, we can finally enter Lothric Castle. The area is bathed in a strange light. It appears the sun has been eclipsed, giving the location a gloomy yet beautiful atmosphere. This eclipse is in the same shape as the Darksign on humans, contained in the player's inventory since the first *Dark Souls*. Its shape is that of a black disk encircled with a border of orangey flames: an eloquent symbol for the final stage of the adventure, watched closely by all those who fear the Fire will go out. When Prince Lothric refuses to link the Fire, this Darksign appears in the sky, a symbol of humanity, symbol of Dark. Mysterious beings from Londor, the land of hollows, the pilgrims are now transformed into "butterflies"[214]: spindly, winged creatures who roam around the castle where the twin princes have hidden away. Even these strange beings, closely associated with Dark, are now converging on this location, the center of the world. Everything announces the decline of Fire and rise of Dark. The castle exudes a palpable despair, which must be overcome by the Unkindled on the quest for the Cinders of the final Lord.

"Oh, dear, another dogged contender. Welcome, Unkindled One, purloiner of Cinders. Mind you, the mantle of Lord interests me none. The fire linking curse, the legacy of lords, let it all fade into nothing," says Lothric to players as they arrive in the immense foyer. Thus begins the fight with the twin princes. The first part of the fight focuses on Lorian, skillful and powerful protector of his brother. When the elder prince dies, his younger brother Lothric joins the fight and begins by reviving Lorian, who carries him on his back for the rest of the fight. Skinny and stooped, Lothric is indeed more puny than his brother, and we wonder why Gwynevere's and the kingdom's hopes rested on him rather than his brother Lorian. The fight becomes pathetic when Lothric drags himself along the ground to revive his brother, and when we hear him speak of a "curse," and conclude that "this spot marks our grave." It seems as though he's fully devoid of hope, and he now faces his curse without trying to escape it or dull its effects, living secluded, almost hidden, trying to forget everything in the highest tower of the castle. Unfortunately for him, the terrible powers that caused the convergence were too strong.

Once the Cinders of Lord Lothric have been brought to the Firelink Shrine and placed on their throne, next to those from the other Lords, the Fire Keeper completes the ritual to make the Unkindled a Lord of Cinder. "The five lords sit their five thrones. All thanks to thee, most worthy of lords. Ashen one, with the Lords as thy witness, bend thy knee afore the bonfire's coiled sword. And let the Lords' embers acknowledge

---

214. This term only appears once, in the description for the Soul of Dragonslayer Armor, to refer to these scraggly creatures. We can imagine this is the final form taken by the pilgrims, forming out of the cocoons they wore on their backs all the way from Lordran.

thee as their true heir. A true lord, fit to link the fire." After this speech, the Fire Keeper teleports the player into a replica of the Firelink Shrine, in ruins and devoid of any life. Leaving this sinister place, the Unkindled returns to the Kiln of the First Flame, as in the first *Dark Souls*, were Gwyn linked the Fire to become the first Lord of Cinder. The converging continues: we can see the surrounding buildings have moved in closer, all approaching the Fire. Packed together in a sphere around the point of convergence, they all appear tangled, twisted and broken. These are the last instants of the Fire, placed once again under the eclipse symbolizing the Darksign, waiting for the Unkindled, the only gleam of hope in this accursed place.

The Unkindled has a final challenge to overcome, however: players must defeat the incarnation of all of the previous Lords of Cinder, called the Soul of Cinder. Summoning all of the player's skill, this powerful foe easily wields all of the traditional combat techniques from all of its predecessors, including Gwyn and all of the Undead who sacrificed themselves in the Fire at the end of the first episode.[215] Once the fight ends, the Unkindled peacefully sits at the corner of the Fire in meditation. By linking the Fire, the Unkindled becomes the newest Lord of Cinder, continuing the Age of Fire, until its next decline.

A question remains. Why does the Soul of Cinder protect the Fire from this Unkindled, when the Unkindled is trying to save it? As in the first *Dark Souls*, there are actually several possible endings: four in total. The one we just presented, called "To Link the First Flame," seems the most logical: called by the Fire to lead the Lords of Cinder back to their thrones, the Unkindled has fulfilled the mission. The quest leads the Unkindled to take the Lords' power and then become Lord of Cinder in turn, after the final test with the Soul of Cinder. Through exploration of the game's contents, however, we'll see that other endings are possible—much darker, this time, because they are connected to Dark itself.

The Eyes of the Fire Keeper

When players go beyond the game's traditional path of collecting Lord Cinders and explore other areas, they can access other epilogues. Two relatively similar endings depend on obtaining the Fire Keeper's eyes.

To do this, the player must go off the main path when exploring Lothric Castle. There, they can gain access to the Consumed King's Garden, a path to the den of King Oceiros, whose obsession with Seath the Scaleless caused him to go mad. All

215. The Soul of Cinder description reads, "Since Lord Gwyn, the first Lord of Cinder, many exalted lords have linked the First Flame, and it is their very souls that have manifested themselves as defender of the flame."

of the elements in the room we enter, behind the arena, after defeating the Consumed King, reflect Occiros's fascination with dragons. We find the complete armor set of the "Drakeblood Knights, worshippers of the blood of dragons,"[216] as well as the Path of the Dragon Gesture, which provides access to Archdragon Peak, an isolated area where some formidable wyverns live. In particular, another secret passage can be found in Oceiros's private room, leading to the Untended Graves, which is simply an altered version of the Cemetery of Ash from the beginning of the game, beset by the dark Abyss, the corruption of Dark.

The Untended Graves are shrouded in an Abyss-like dark. Players will easily recognize the space where they first wandered all the way to the boss, still named Gundyr. The whole place seems to be a dark copy of the Cemetery of Ash and Firelink Shrine. However, the only character we find is the Shrine Handmaid, still selling some new items and equipment worthy of interest. A deep mystery surrounds the Untended Graves. Is this a true copy of the Firelink Shrine? Is it a vision of the past or future? It is in the same location, because any message left on the ground using the online features, in either of the Firelink Shrines, will be found in the other. The timeline is still unclear, though. Some clues suggest that this new Firelink Shrine is in the past, a time when it was subsumed by the Abyss, before the Fire sent out its warning, because the bell in the belfry "would not toll."[217] However, the Unkindled already existed at this time and lay in this area. The Queen of Lothric, Gwynevere, took care of these souls who were once sacrificed to the Fire, now resting, waiting for the next call for help. Gwyn's heir respected them and prepared for the future, which already looked grim for the Fire. On several tombs we find powerful objects such as a "Hidden Blessing"[218] and an Ashen Estus Ring.[219] This sense of waiting is echoed in several sentences from the Shrine Handmaid of the Untended Graves: "Tis dark for now, and not a soul stirs. But remember, fires are known to fade in quiet," and "A lost lamb wandereth in, with nary a peep from the bell." These are directed at the player, as if she is accustomed to seeing other Unkindleds.

Gundyr likely once shouldered the role of Unkindled. "Judge" (Iudex) at the game's outset, now he is named "Champion," a term used several times to refer to the player's Unkindled.[220] "Once, a champion came late to the festivities, and was greeted by a shrine without fire, and a bell that would not toll," explains the description of the Soul of Champion Gundyr. Gundyr's lateness was considered unpardonable in this

216. From the description of the Drakeblood Helm.
217. From the description of the Soul of Champion Gundyr.
218. "There is a grave in Lothric that sees no visitors, a dark place where rootless warriors rest. The Queen of Lothric alone cared to wish the poor souls good fortune."
219. "Once a treasure brought before Lothric's Queen, she had it enshrined in the Cemetery of Untended Graves, so that one day an Unkindled might profit from its use."
220. The player is called "Champion of Ash" several times, particularly by Irina of Carim, the blind nun that later becomes the Fire Keeper.

race against the clock (which could still have lasted for thousands of years, per *Souls* standards) to save the Fire. The smallest delay seems to endanger the Fire, due to its constant state of decline. His late arrival meant that Gundyr couldn't assist the Fire Keeper, and the Abyss took over the area.

Several points support this hypothesis. First, the setting is black as night, recalling the area from the first game where we fought the Four Kings of New Londo before encountering Darkstalker Kaathe. Second, the Shrine Handmaid of the Untended Graves sells the Wolf Knight Armor, "Armor of a knight tainted by the dark of the Abyss" (from its description). This knight is none other than Artorias the Abysswalker, as we've seen. Not far from the entryway, we can find the Hornet Ring, which formerly belonged to Ciaran, a lady knight who, alongside Artorias, fought the Abyss in Oolacile[221]: that these objects belonged to the two characters most tied to the Abyss is no accident. Third, in the Firelink Shrine from the beginning of the game, we find the Fire Keeper Soul at the top of the belfry[222] on the desiccated corpse of the previous Fire Keeper. The soul's description indicates that the Fire Keeper "returned from the Abyss"[223] and that she "is said to have soothed and accepted the dark sigil, which has tainted her soul." In addition, "This Fire Keeper preserves the bonfire, and serves its champion." The term "champion" could refer to Gundyr of the Untended Graves, suggesting that she was waiting for him when the Abyss overtook the shrine. Finally, one other item in the Untended Graves supports all of these references to the Abyss and Dark: the Eyes of a Fire Keeper.

"Said to be the eyes of the first Fire Keeper, and the light that was lost by all Fire Keepers to come. It reveals to the sightless Fire Keepers things that they should never see." The Fire Keepers are therefore struck blind and wear a mask over their eyes. The first of them was able to see, however. What she saw with her eyes led her to rip them out, and her future heirs do the same. If the player gives the eyes to the Fire Keeper of the Firelink Shrine, she will describe the vision she sees through them: "a world without Fire, a vast stretch of darkness." Although terrified by this vision, she complies with the player's choice, which she must follow in spite of her reluctance. "Ashen One, is this truly thy wish? Of course. I serve thee, and will do as thou bid'st. This will be our private affair. No one else may know of this. Stay thy path, find lords to link the fire, and I will blindly tend to the flame. Until the day of thy grand betrayal." With the eyes, the Fire Keeper seems to have lost her bearings, as if she has given in to a form of corruption. Thankfully, she seems to view a light of hope in the darkness:

---

221. Moreover, the Hornet Ring can be found at the foot of a tomb, which directly recalls the sad scene in which Ciaran meditates over the tomb of Artorias, her former companion who was tainted by the Abyss, and eventually killed by the player.
222. The bell in this tower can ring, which corresponds to the bell in the beginning, which tolls.
223. The Dark Sigil, which comes into play in the final ending, evokes this return from the Abyss: "there is a tale told of a Fire Keeper who returned from the Abyss."

"In the far distance, I sense the presence of tiny flames. Like precious embers, left to us by past Lords, linkers of the fire. Could this be what draws me to this strangely enticing darkness?"

After this discovery, the Ashen One's initial quest seems compromised. A choice takes shape, between Fire and Dark, similar to the one at the end of the first episode. Rather than prolonging the inevitable decline of the Age of Fire, repeating this desperate act for the umpteenth time, this all can be ended to usher in a new age: that of Dark, and thus of man.

In spite of the warnings from the Lord of Cinder Ludleth of Courland, who is strangely knowledgeable about the existence and visionary power of the eyes of the first Fire Keeper, the rest of the adventure follows a path similar to the previous ending. That is, until the fateful moment when, after fighting the Soul of Cinder, we find ourselves face to face with the Fire. At this point, we can summon the Fire Keeper from the Firelink Shrine using a white summoning sign, as if she were any other character. Thus begins "The End of Fire" ending, with the Fire Keeper. She begins by kneeling by the Fire and gathers a small flame in her hands. "The First Flame quickly fades. Darkness will shortly settle," she says, as the world is suddenly plunged into darkness. Only the tiny ember in the Fire Keeper's hands continues to shine in the dark. "But one day, tiny flames will dance across the darkness. Like embers, linked by lords past." Here, we regain control of the avatar for a brief, almost imperceptible moment. Either we do nothing, and everything goes black, with the flame protected by the Fire Keeper; or, we can attack and kill her, and retrieve the small ember. Then, the avatar raises the minuscule flames up towards the eclipse–the Darksign, and symbol of Dark–as if making an offering, sacrificing the final hope of the Age of Fire to initiate a renewal on behalf of humanity.

Through its parallel with the first game, this conclusion seems to best reflect the spirit of the overall *Souls* narrative. However, doubt sets in when a black darkness literally fills the whole screen: the ending suggests that the Abyss has won, and thus that the world has entered into decay, rather than the age of man. The Eyes of a Fire Keeper are indeed intimately tied to the Untended Graves. As we've seen, this space has all the characteristics of Abyss invasion. So much so that we may start wondering if all this commotion about Dark and the eyes is simply a diversion, an underhand manipulation to influence us. Since *Dark Souls*, we've known how the world works: convinced that the right move is to end the Age of Fire and the reign of the gods, and thus usher in the age of humans; the Unkindled is actually leaving the world vulnerable to the Abyss, the corruptive Dark that destroys all. This is what the ending seems to show: the end of the world, of all things. If the Fire Keeper gathers up the final ember to preserve a small spark of hope that the world will be reborn, her assassination is the worst possible scenario.

For the true rise of Dark, there is another hidden ending, related to the pilgrims and the region of Londor, land of hollows.

Marriage and Dark Sigils

Now we return to the beginning of the adventure for the third and final path, which leads to the hidden ending called the "Usurpation of Fire." After exploring the High Wall of Lothric and fighting Vordt of the Boreal Valley, players reach the Undead Settlement, below the castle. As if blocked by a fallen passage that once led to the fortress, a group of pilgrims kneels there, turned towards the high-perched residence of Prince Lothric. Prostrated in prayer, they remain perfectly still, as if frozen, or even petrified. They remain totally unmoved by the player's interactions or hostility. In one corner, however, we hear sobbing, and suddenly: "Please, grant me death. Undo my shackles." One of them is still alive. "I am Yoel of Londor, a pilgrim as you can see, only... Somehow, I've failed to die as was ordained. Well, perhaps my calling lies elsewhere."

Whether a blessing or a curse, Yoel escaped the death awaiting the pilgrims who came from Londor to reach the kingdom of Lothric. Yoel, a former sorcerer, offers his services to the player, the "Champion of Ash," as he says, before teleporting to the Firelink Shrine. In particular, Yoel grants the player incredible power. "I believe that I can help tease out your true strength," he says. "Those branded by the Darksign possess something quite special..." This new strength takes the form of additional free level-ups: a sacred gift that is not without consequence. This deal with the devil leads to the appearance of Dark Sigils.

Up to five Dark Sigils unlock as many soul levels: the player's inventory slowly fills up with these mysterious items. The appearance of a Dark Sigil is that of a "black gaping hole in the flesh that resembles the brand of an Undead." Indeed, it is a circle, this time outlined in gray, rather than the small flames surrounding the Darksign: "The darkness of humanity seeps from this bottomless pitch-black hole, the gap filled by the accumulation of the curse," indicates the item's description.

As soon as players acquire the first Dark Sigil, the "Hollow" characteristic appears on the status screen. Capped at ninety-nine, it increases every time the player dies, and its only apparent consequence is that the Unkindled's physical appearance progressively changes into a hideous hollow. Without the Dark Sigil, it's impossible for an Unkindled to become hollow. Acquiring the first of these cursed objects profoundly changes the character's nature, with a resurgence of humanity from deep down within.

For purists who don't wish to deviate from their initial quest, the Dark Sigil can be removed. To do so, we must begin by giving the Fire Keeper Soul to the Fire Keeper in the shrine. Then, in exchange for a staggering number of souls[224] (we're dealing with

---

224. The cost corresponds to the number of souls that we would have had to give to the Fire Keeper to unlock the same number of levels as the number of Dark Sigils acquired. For example, to remove four Dark Sigils, we must spend the number of souls required to move up four levels. A high-level hell!

a curse, after all), she will purify her protégé by removing the Dark Sigils, along with any changes they have caused.

Others, curious about what this transformation will lead to, continue on this path of humanity and Dark. Continuing on their quest, players meet another Unkindled, Anri,[225] accompanied by her faithful protector, Horace the Hushed. "Oh, hello. How do you do. I am Anri of Astora. Unkindled, like you. This is Horace. A friend and traveling companion. Are you too in search of the Lords of Cinder?" The tone is cordial; quite the friendly comrade. Anri has stopped to rest along the Road of Sacrifices, on the outskirts of the Crucifixion Woods. With Horace, she is looking for the Cathedral of the Deep to find the Lord of Cinder Aldrich, the "grim" Aldrich, as Anri calls him: it's worth mentioning that Anri and Horace were once both offered up to Aldrich, and just managed to escape.[226] Since then, they have sought vengeance, which is consistent with Anri's fate as an Unkindled.

After eliminating the deacons, and completing the piece of the story of the Cathedral of the Deep, Anri and Horace stop at the Firelink Shrine. They also discovered the small doll in Aldrich's tomb and now plan to head to the city of Irithyll, in the Boreal Valley. "A pilgrim told me that the city lies beyond Farron Keep," Anri confides. With this, we know that she and Horace have also met the pilgrim Yoel in the Firelink Shrine. This detail will prove important when we need to gather the Dark Sigils from Anri's corpse and when Horace turns hollow and highly aggressive. Their meeting with the pilgrim sealed their tragic fate: we'll come back to this.

Yoel eventually perishes, after granting the player the fifth Dark Sigil. He freezes like his fellow pilgrims. No sooner has the pilgrim died than another character appears, next to his body, in the Firelink Shrine: "Oh, prithee...art thou good Yoel's master? I am Yuria of Londor, a close friend of his. Thanks to thee, Yoel's soul is redeem'd. Allow me to express my gratitude, in his stead." Like Yoel, Yuria is originally from the land of hollows. She doesn't appear like the other pilgrims, and seems to hold a higher position. Once Yoel has finished giving away the Dark Sigils and fulfilled his role, while saving his soul, this mysterious character appears to watch over his new protégé: "Thou'rt a Lord, art thou not? Bearer of the Dark Sigil, and our Lord of Hollows. For the time thou remain'st our Lord, we of Londor shall serve thee. And I, of course, am also thine. May the Dark Sigil guide thy way."[227]

---

225. Anri's gender depends on our avatar's gender: a woman if the Unkindled is a man, and a man if our avatar is a woman. To keep things simple, we'll refer to Anri as a woman.
226. Horace's Executioner Helm depicts this terrible past: "Horace is one of only two children to escape Aldrich's clutches." Of course, the other is Anri.
227. Yuria's use of the term "guide" echoes the dialogues from Fire supporters: Anri says, "May the flames guide your way," and the Fire Keeper echoes almost identically, "May the flames guide thy way."

Since the Unkindled are generally considered nobodies,[228] the title of "Lord" is a pleasant and unexpected compliment. Yuria will sell the player many objects originally from Londor, directly related to the hollows, such as the Untrue Dark Ring, which allows players to "retain human appearance while hollow."[229]

A little further on, after defeating the Abyss Watchers, we find Anri deep within the Catacombs of Carthus, and she has lost track of her companion, the hushed knight. Distraught, she asks the player to help her find Horace. As we will discover, the unlucky knight fell to his death while trying to cross the hanging bridge leading to Irithyll. Then, he appears as a hollow, in the throes of madness, lost in the middle of the shallow waters of Smoldering Lake, located below the Catacombs of Carthus. Horace attacks as soon as the player appears, in a duel to the death.

"Knowest thou of a maid named Anri? She is hollow, and will join thee in wedlock. A fellow of mine guides her at this moment. When the time is ripe, thou mayst make thy salutations. For what Lord taketh no spouse?" Such are the strange words of Yuria in a new dialogue with her in the Firelink Shrine. Here, we learn "officially" that Anri and Horace belong to the clan of Londor, as was hinted previously, when the two companions mentioned their meeting with the "pilgrim." Horace died without Anri's knowledge, and she continues to brood around the Catacombs of Carthus. Has she been informed of the marriage that seems to have been planned between her and the player?

Anri's next step is in the Church of Yorshka, in Irithyll, where she tells the player of her latest deeds: "I never managed to find Horace. But my duty must be done, even alone. As an Unkindled Lordseeker. For the children I knew, bless their souls. We all have our reasons, don't we? Ahh, you are brave indeed. To face your duty alone." With determination, Anri helps her new ally (and future husband?) fight Pontiff Sulyvahn. After the battle, she disappears into the fog that surrounds the immense city of Anor Londo.

After a quick trip to the Firelink Shrine to chat with Yuria, we learn that the young woman "awaits thee, in the hidden darkmoon chamber of Anor Londo." She adds that this marriage is necessary for us to become a "true monarch." The place Yuria refers to here is none other than the mausoleum where we fought Gwyndolin in the first *Dark Souls*: an immense corridor at the end of which stands a giant coffin, where Gwyn, the First Lord is said to lie. In a twist of fate, this ultimate symbol of Fire is now

---

228. Words from the introduction ring in our ears, "Nameless, accursed Undead, unfit even to be cinder," and comments from Hawkwood: "We Unkindled are worthless. Can't even die right."
229. From the description of the Untrue Dark Ring. If we take this ring, the Fire Keeper will turn her head away when we arrive in the Firelink Shrine, as if she refuses to look at us now that we have a direct tie with the hollows, and with Dark.

being used to marry two humans, marking the rise of the Lord of Hollows, and thus the antithesis of Fire.

Unfortunately, the marriage doesn't go as planned, at least for the player. Upon entering the Hidden Darkmoon Chamber, we meet a pilgrim who gives us the Sword of Avowal, without any other information. According to its description, the sword is a "ceremonial sword of Londor," and "it is said that a rite of wedlock will presage a true Hollow lord." It's time to honor Londor's traditions. Anri is at the end of the corridor, but to our surprise, she is lying on the floor with her hands crossed over her stomach, a shroud draped over her face. She is dead, and we must perform the avowal in order to retrieve her Dark Sigils. This is when we stab the young maiden's body with the Sword of Avowal, which lets off dark vapors. Three new Dark Sigils are added to the inventory, for a total of eight: this number allows us to reach the final ending.

"When the moment cometh to link the fire, wrest it from its mantle. The Age of Fire was founded by the old gods, sustained by the linking of the Fire. But the old gods are no more, and the all-powerful fire deserveth a new heir. Our Lord of Hollows, it shall be, who weareth the true face of mankind." Yuria finishes consecrating her new Lord, conveying the teachings of Darkstalker Kaathe, upon which her Sable Church of Londor is built. Players are now ready to become the new leader of men, to guide them through the darkness that follows the final fragment of fire. "Away to link the fire, I presume? Think not on thy fears. The Dark Sigil will guide thee. Link the Fire, our Lord of Hollows," she concludes to the player, who leaves to fight the Soul of Cinder within the Kiln of the First Flame.

When we go to link the Fire, we instead witness a different ending, called the "Usurpation of Fire." The eclipse transforms: the glowing orb changes from orange to pale gray, recalling the eight Dark Sigils collected. The character is now surrounded by members of the Sable Church, along with hollows.

We can even see Anri of Astora, back from the dead to acclaim the new Lord of Hollows. "Make Londor whole..." pleads a voice from the crowd. The player has become the leader and representative of all humanity in an attempt to succeed the old gods, diminishing the possibility that the Fire will one day reignite.

Characters

Over the last few pages, we took our time exploring the *Dark Souls III* protagonists. We didn't cover several of the secondary characters, and some only got a brief mention. We'll start here by looking at NPCs from the Firelink Shrine,[230] who join the player throughout the adventure and offer their services.

The Firelink Shrine

As we've seen, the Firelink Shrine is a peaceful oasis for the Unkindled. They can rest, make purchases, and learn new spells, miracles or pyromancies. This is also the location where the five Lords of Cinder were supposed to gather. Three of them went missing, and the fourth refused to link the Fire. Only Ludleth heard the bell's toll and answered its call.

⚜ Ludleth of Courland

Ludleth of Courland is characterized not only by his small size, but also by his somewhat obsequious and pretentious personality. "I may be but small, but I will die a colossus," he says proudly, chuffed to have become a Lord of Cinder. From the beginning of the game, Ludleth takes the shrine's newcomer under his wing. He explains the goal of his quest, along with the reason why the other Lords of Cinder abandoned their thrones. Throughout the adventure, he gets closer to his new protégé, with some nice nicknames like "Lordseeker' and "Lord-Slayer." This relationship is nevertheless superficial, a bit like the tenuous relationship of Fire with the nobodies who are charged with saving it, the Unkindled. "For as we to our thrones, thou art to thy duty.

---

230. This section will be organized by location.

In fact, methinks thou'st helped these poor Lords along their rightful path." He's constantly buttering us up, and congratulating himself on his past act. "Fine kindling for the thrones, is it not, each soul truly worthy of Lordship," he repeats, as if trying to persuade himself of the perfection of his achievement with the Fire. He also fears Dark. We can see this in his reaction when the player retrieves the Eyes of a Fire Keeper from the Untended Graves: "I took the mantle of Lord of Cinder of mine own volition. I speak these words with pride. Choose thy fate alone. All the more, should thy fate entail such foul betrayal." However, he doesn't stop us, leaving us to choose and providing only a warning.

Ludleth's artificial demeanor doesn't prevent him from being an unparalleled crafts-man, knowledgeable about the art of "transposing." This process uses a "Transposing Kiln" to "transpose twisted souls to craft special items."[231] Like Ornifex in *Dark Souls II*, Ludleth can create weapons, spells or equipment from boss souls. Every soul can be transposed into two different items, which reveal additional information about the boss along the way. Transposing is an art straight from the lands of Courland. "Deemed forbidden by those unable to make proper use of it," says the description of the Transposing Kiln. Ludleth also adds: "A forbidden art, that once left a foul stain upon Courland's honor." However, the little Lord of Cinder is highly adept at this forbidden art, which he is happy to demonstrate once we bring the Transposing Kiln back to the Firelink Shrine. To get it, we must defeat the Curse-Rotted Greatwood in the Undead Settlement. "This place is a crossing for all manner of cursed objects," says Ludleth of the Transposing Kiln. This comment refers to the convergence started by the tolling of the bell, after which a person from Courland with a Transposing Kiln was forced to travel the world through to the Undead Settlement. He no doubt was fleeing the kingdom of Courland, in decline after Ludleth's sacrifice to the Fire.

But the precise cause of the kingdom's downfall remains a mystery. Is it related to the maintenance of Fire, like the sad fate of the Profaned Capital, consumed by Yhorm's flames. The Skull Ring suggests a more dreadful fate. This ring is "derived from the soul of a Soulfeeder," and "one of Courland's transposed wonders": "The Soulfeeder was a beast that insatiably absorbed souls to feed its own power. Even after its accursed corpse was burned, it is said that the pungent stench of souls left the air permanently stained." The Skull Ring description seems to attribute the fall of Courland to the barbarous acts of the Soulfeeder, who, once burned, is said to have put a powerful curse on these people. The most troubling aspect is that the Skull Ring appears on Ludleth's throne when he is reduced to ash at the end of the game, once the other Lords have been brought back to their respective thrones. Could the ring be from the transposition of Ludleth's soul, revealing that he is actually the dreaded

231. Description of the Transposing Kiln.

Soulfeeder? This is not certain, and relatively paradoxical considering his behavior, but perhaps he was keeping his cards close to his chest. It wouldn't be the first time a *Dark Souls* character had hidden his past! His alias, "the Exiled," engraved on his throne, seems to refer to a disagreement between him and his fellow men. No matter his past, Ludleth remains steadfastly devoted to the Fire, like the only other character that watches over the center of the shrine: the Fire Keeper.

⚜ The Fire Keeper

One of the story's most important characters is also one of its most discreet and nondescript. All the way down the line, the Fire Keepers have remained similar. One after the other, they guard the Firelink Shrine, waiting for their "champion"–an Unkindled–to save the Fire. However, though this ritual is seemingly eternal, the Fire Keepers aren't really the same as the characters from the first episode, nor do they correspond to the three old, red-clad guardians from the second, disguised as oracles of despair, laughing at the world from their hut in Things Betwixt. No, in *Dark Souls III*, the Fire Keeper plays a central role: that of the player's guide. She watches over the Fire's final hope, serving as an ally throughout the journey. She is the one to teach us how to control Gundyr's Coiled Sword to teleport and leave in search of the Lords of Cinder. She also regularly provides access to new, more advanced skills by allowing us to level up. To be honest, she seems almost too friendly for the *Souls* series. She is deferential and respects our choices with blind trust, even if we decide to unleash Dark over the world. It's only natural for those familiar with the series to be suspicious of her extreme kindness. If anything, it just shows how desperate these agents are to save the Fire, stooping so low as to entrust their cause with a common Unkindled.

Truthfully, the Fire Keepers have been simple servants for ages now. The first of them, at least from this new generation of Fire Keepers, still had her eyes. The Firelink Shrine was shrouded in darkness, prey to the Abyss. Discovering the sad state of the Fire, she saw in it a warning of what would come if Prince Lothric continued to refuse his role as Lord of Cinder. After tearing out her eyes to expunge this vision, she sets out on her task to save the Fire by reigniting the flame at all costs. The Fire Keepers come one after the other for centuries. Their corpses pile up for generations in the tower next to the shrine. We can imagine they worked to make the heavy clapper for the Firelink belfry bell. However, we discover the body of a Fire Keeper just under this famous bell. The description of the Fire Keeper Soul we collect from her body explicitly mentions the Abyss,[232] and we think of when Gundyr was named "the

---

232. This description specifies that this soul's owner "returned from the Abyss."

Champion," when he was "greeted by a shrine without fire, and a bell that would not toll."[233] It's almost as though this Fire Keeper used her last bit of strength to fix the bell so it could toll for the Fire: an act to brighten up the Firelink Shrine and its surroundings, while painting the sky in a pale yellow.

Lastly, we should point out that the Firelink Shrine doesn't exist in the same space and time as the game's other locations. When the eclipse takes place at the end of the adventure, when the player enters Lothric Castle, the Firelink Shrine maintains the same yellow sky as the beginning of the adventure, while the other areas are affected by the Darksign astronomical phenomenon: with the exception of Irithyll, bathed in light from the moon and northern lights, the eclipse is everywhere.

The game presents three different versions of the shrine in reality: the past shrine, prey to the Abyss, which we discover in the depths of Lothric Castle; the "normal" version, in a parallel dimension where the bell once tolled; and finally, the one we find at the end of the game, located near the Kiln of the First Flame. This final version may be the actual present: the eclipse is visible, and not far away is the First Flame, towards which the surroundings seem to converge. From this perspective, we can imagine the normal version of the Firelink Shrine, in order and with all of the NPCs that live in it, as an illusion produced by the Fire to influence us. The ruins of the present attest to the lack of hope of escaping the Abyss, which had already invaded this area in the past. The Fire's bell toll therefore caused this parallel, hospitable version, with the aim of more easily recruiting Unkindleds to the cause.

To leave the Firelink Shrine and seek the Lords of Cinder, we must warp to the High Wall of Lothric using the Coiled Sword, planted in Iudex Gundyr's body.

Iudex Gundyr

The game's first boss, Iudex Gundyr, has left many a player by the wayside. The fight is difficult, and sets the tone for subsequent events, even though the full episode may not be quite as difficult as the others when all is said and done. During the challenging fight, Iudex Gundyr judges the Unkindled's (and therefore our) skills. The colossus likes to rain hits on his foe with his powerful halberd, and if we succeed in reducing his health points by half, Iudex Gundyr transforms into a monstrosity from the Abyss. More aggressive, and with an impressive reach, the new creature teems with jumbled black reptilian bodies, topped off by a giant, serpentine maw. A scrawny, enormous left arm completes the picture of this first boss, who is impressive, if nothing else. His transformation recalls that of the "Pus of Man" from the High Wall of Lothric

233. From the description of the Soul of Champion Gundyr.

(and later in the castle and the Consumed King's Garden): these Undead, sensitive to fire, transform in the same way. They are filled with aggressive rage, while their appearance is reminiscent of the character Manus from the first *Dark Souls*–the Manus who was nicknamed "Father of the Abyss," which corresponds a bit to Iudex Gundyr's story.

Before being Iudex, Gundyr was previously an Unkindled, the Fire Keeper's champion of the time. A time when the Firelink Shrine, and thus the Cemetery of Ash beside it, were under the powers of the Abyss. Too late to help the Fire, he was forced to become the judge of future Unkindleds, so that the error would never happen again: "a steel chain [was] used to restrain Gundyr,"[234] and he was equipped with an halberd that "is said to never crumble," since it seemed that "Gundyr was fated to eternal service from the beginning."[235] The description of his helm[236] indicates that the "Belated Champion [...] became sheath to a coiled sword in the hopes that someday, the first flame would be linked once more." An unavoidable fate, which left him ever under the power of the Abyss. Now judge and prisoner, the colossus is nevertheless very strong, as he is able to resist the Abyss to a certain extent. Indeed, the Pus of Man creatures transform at the player's slightest touch, or remain constantly in this state, just as in the Consumed King's Garden, while Iudex Gundyr fights in the same way as when he was a simple Unkindled, at least during the first part of the fight.

In spite of his chivalrous spirit, Gundyr the Champion doesn't achieve his objective and meets a tragic end. Not only did he not arrive in time to protect the then Fire Keeper, but he has been corrupted by the Abyss, and we eventually kill him.

In the Firelink Shrine, one duo could come straight out of a knightly tale: the knight Eygon and the blind nun he protects, Irina. At the end of her quest, Irina could even become Fire Keeper!

❧ Irina and Eygon of Carim

At the base of the abandoned Undead Settlement, Eygon of Carim accosts the player: "Hmm... Another one of those Unkindled, are you? All you faceless Undead, behaving as if you deserve respect. Hopeless, the whole lot of you. Like little moths, flittering towards a flame." The knight doesn't mince his words, and this first meeting sets the tone for the subsequent relationship. In his behavior, Eygon stays true to his words, acting like a bit of a brute. Besides his austere Morne's Armor and Moaning Shield, his Morne's Great Hammer is what really demands respect: it's

---

234. From the description of the Prisoner's Chain.
235. From the description of Gundyr's Halberd.
236. In its appearance, this helm recalls the mask of Old King Doran from *Demon's Souls*, an important figure of the series symbolic for testing strength: following his arduous test, he gives players the precious Demonbrandt.

a giant mallet, bedecked in small gray stone sculptures, and "imbued with the twisted rage of Apostle Morne."

Morne, known as the Apostle of the Archbishop, is venerated by the Carim Knights. Many of the miracles and pieces of equipment from Carim reference this powerful character. He formerly "served the goddess Caitha,"[237] Goddess of Tears, intimately tied to death, and thus mourning. There are numerous descriptions that emphasize the importance of this divinity for the Carim Knights. For example, we learn the following about the Red Tearstone Ring: "This stone is said to be a tear of mourning of the goddess Caitha, and of course, tears are always more beautiful near death." Regarding the Caressing Tears miracle: "Caressing Tears is a tale of the many deaths surrounding the goddess Caitha." Finally, we read the following in the description of the Tears of Denial: "Tears are shed for the sake of the living, more so than the deceased." Nothing rivaled Morne's devotion to Caitha. When he rejoined the apostles of the Archbishop, the Carim Knights modeled themselves after him. The image of Morne devoted to Caitha inspired them, and they each devoted their life to the service of a lady.

When he was dubbed knight of Carim, Eygon received the Moaning Shield: "The giant woman's face that protects Eygon is that of his sister, some years his senior," explains the description. It's possible that this sister was killed and that the shield was forged in her memory, so that Eygon could draw strength and courage from his mourning, in accordance with the teachings of Morne and Caitha. By becoming a knight of Carim, Eygon took a vow to protect Irina, a nun who wished to become Fire Keeper.

Blind and fragile, the priestess Irina became a saint of Carim, and became one of the most eminent teachers of miracles. "In Carim, the saints give voice to the ancient tales. They memorize countless cumbersome sacred books and read them in sonorous tones," reads the description of the Saint's Ring. Thus were the miracles taught, through sacred texts interpreted by the saints. "Tales of the greater miracles can be quite the epics," says Irina, when players bring her a divine tome in braille.[238] She helps the Unkindled throughout the adventure, sometimes forgetting how unsuccessful she has been.

---

237. From the description of Morne's Ring.
238. Collected throughout the adventure, these books of spells provide access to new miracles, providing regular increases in strength for those who take the path of Faith. This game design choice can be found throughout the game, for all of the different skills found in the Firelink Shrine (blacksmithery, sorcery, etc.), taking away some of the game's surprises. As traditional as this mechanic may appear (maybe a little easy for a *Souls* game?), it means that one location is associated with character management, and makes the spot a haven of peace.

Irina of Carim thus wanted to become a Fire Keeper. Beside her protective knight Eygon, she arrived in the kingdom of Lothric with the hope of aiding the Fire and watching over it as best she could.[239] However, since the bell tolled, nothing has gone right in Lothric. With her great fragility, Irina was overwhelmed by Dark and lost hope. We find her locked in a cell, not far from the entry to the church where Eygon has set up. He shows no signs of tenderness towards the one he is supposed to protect: "Well, she's a lost cause. Couldn't even become a Fire Keeper. After I brought her all this way, and got her all ready. She's beyond repair, I tell you." Did Eygon deliberately lock up Irina so he would be free of watching over and protecting here? it seems likely.[240]

Once freed, the blind woman confides in us: "The dark surrounds me, nibbles at my flesh. Little creatures, they never stop biting. So please, hold out your hand, and touch me..." A simple touch reassures her, and she warps to the Firelink Shrine to dispense her miracles. Eygon, on the other hand, is glad to rid himself of this obligation, and tasks players with looking after her, while throwing in a warning: "My terms are very simple. I am allied to you for as long as you assure the girl's safety." In spite of his rather boorish personality, Eygon remains a Carim Knight, formerly sworn to protect Irina. He eventually returns when things go awry for the saint of Carim.

It's possible to give her some evil tomes. The Deep tome,[241] or that of Londor,[242] for instance, have disastrous effects on the blind saint's mental state. Speaking of darkness and the small, biting creatures she associates with it,[243] she reluctantly agrees to read these forbidden tomes. Then, she disappears from the Firelink Shrine, taken by Eygon. It may first appear as though the Carim Knight has come to protect the nun from us, as we've betrayed his trust by subjecting her to the Dark. However, this isn't the case. When we later find the pair from Carim and kill Eygon, and then put on his Morne's Gauntlets, we can trick Irina by touching her, and, thinking she recognizes her faithful knight, she begs us to kill her, as they once promised to do if she fell prey to the Dark. The saint's quest therefore ends here, in death.

However, if we decide to only give her beneficial divine tomes, and progressively buy miracles from her, her quest will end differently. She also leaves the Firelink Shrine, but this time to stand in the tower with the dead bodies of the former Fire Keepers.

239. Irina and Eygon together are reminiscent of Astrea and Garl Vinland from *Demon's Souls*. They went all the way to the Valley of Defilement to assist the helpless, before falling prey to the corruption of the Colourless Deep Fog and the demons.
240. "I'm sick of looking after her at any rate," he concludes.
241. "Intended to teach divine protection to the deacons of the Deep, but later, dark tales were added to its pages, such that it is now considered a thing profane," says the Deep Braille Divine Tome.
242. The description of the Londor Braille Divine Tome indicates that "this is a forbidden tome, as it offers salvation to all Hollows, and conversely curses all things living."
243. "The little creatures that nibble at me in the darkness..." "The little creatures, how they nip and bite...", "I am frightened. Of the dark that gnaws away at me.": these are a few examples of Irina's comments about the Dark.

She has become one of them, finally achieving her objective. Now we can level up with her. Sadly, in spite of her removed position from the Fire teleportation, she doesn't have all of the other Fire Keeper's skills (removing the Dark Sigils, or accepting the Eyes of a Fire Keeper), which gives us less reason to visit her regularly.

Players who wish to demonstrate some kindness will avoid giving Irina any Dark tomes, thereby depriving themselves of access to forbidden forms of magic. However, we can still bring these tomes to another, darker and less stable character: Karla.

☙ Karla

Like Irina, we also find Karla imprisoned. We meet her much later on in the adventure, in the depths of the Irithyll Dungeon. Her pointed witch hat and tattered dark coat directly echo the characters Yuria in *Demon's Souls* and Witch Beatrice from *Dark Souls*, along with her penchant for black magic. Karla teaches us the game's darkest spells, those that the other scholars (Irina, Cornyx and Orbeck) reject out of fear or ignorance. This witch's singular nature has allowed her to embrace the Dark, and now she is able to channel its strength and secrets. "There is a darkness within man, and I am afraid you will peer into it. Whether the fear will spark self-reflection, or a ruinous nostalgia... is up to you entirely," she explains, suggesting a natural link between players and the Dark. She confirms this in another conversation: "You're a wicked one, aren't you? Very well. Humans are of the Dark, and you are no different. Some may avert their eyes, but the truth remains the truth."

Quite comfortable with her affinity for and connection with the Dark, Karla even considers herself a "child of the Abyss." This is no doubt one of the reasons she was locked up, considering the fear her forbidden knowledge inspires in this Age of Fire. As the description of Karla's Coat indicates: "This stained coat is torn and odorous, telling of a long journey and even longer imprisonment." The burden of this witch led her to lose her self-esteem, as several of her comments show. She calls herself "a skinny little heretic," and says that "this is a land of monstrosities. And I am no exception." Her adjectives also reflect this, with terms such as "wretched" and "detestable."

The similarities between Karla and the witches from other *Souls* games go beyond her attire. To start with, Karla and Yuria (from *Demon's Souls*) are voiced in English by the same actress (Jenny Funnel), and players meet with these witches in similar situations: both held captive for a long time, and likely abused by guards or other prisoners.[244] The ties to Witch Beatrice appear even stronger. In the first *Dark Souls*, Witch

---

244. The Prisoner Chief's Ashes found in Irithyll Dungeon give access to Karla's wide array of attire from the Shrine Handmaid. This suggests ties between the witch and this prisoner, likely due to coercion, considering the context and the description of the ashes: "The prisoner chief used this clout to hoard all manner of things."

Beatrice was a unique NPC with two nagging mysteries. First, she died a number of times, each time supposedly the last. We found her body and equipment in the waters of New Londo. This didn't prevent her from aiding us several times during the episode, particularly in the fight against the Four Kings, in the Abyss of New Londo, a land supposedly only accessible using the ring of Artorias the Abysswalker. However, for the second mystery, Witch Beatrice entered the land easily, and nothing suggests that she wore a ring. The character of Karla seems to echo these two mysteries without providing any solid answers. If players attack and kill the child of the Abyss, they read the following description of Karla's Ashes: "The spurned child of the Abyss never dies, but phases in and out of its fringes. Only, there is no one to search for her any longer." If Karla is none other than the witch from the first *Dark Souls*, this could retroactively explain Witch Beatrice's unique ability to enter into the Abyss and her exceptional longevity (all the way through to *Dark Souls III*): she never actually dies, and is revived after each death.

Karla is also associated with a subtle reference to the second *Dark Souls*. The use of the adjective "*spurned*" ("spurned child of the Abyss") is telling here. Upon entering the Irithyll Dungeon where Karla is held prisoner, players are attacked by a so-called Alva, known as "Seeker of the Spurned." This seems to suggest that Alva's story intertwines with that of Karla. Alva was a character in *Dark Souls II*, known as "the Wayfarer." Her quest was to find a cure to heal Saint Serreta. As if laying groundwork for the third episode, the *Scholar of the First Sin* edition (of *Dark Souls II*) fleshed out Alva's character a bit more: the description of his armor was modified to describe his encounter with a witch named Zullie. After seducing Alva, she persuaded him to give up his quest. Despite his feelings of remorse, he decided to live with her. No one knows what happened between this time and the events of *Dark Souls III*, but Alva eventually went in search of Karla. Few clues link Karla and Zullie, besides the description of Karla's coat, describing her long captivity; the time in prison would have damaged Zullie's noble, beautiful clothing, which looked similar. Another hypothesis is that Karla could instead be Saint Serreta. The ills she suffers would therefore be associated with the Abyss. Aware of Zullie's dishonesty, Alva may have left her to continue his original quest: to heal Serreta. In *The Ringed City*, we can once again cross swords with the famous "Seeker of the Spurned," now anonymous, who attacks when we approach the area with the Black Witch Set, which explicitly references Zullie. We'll come back to this when we present the two *Dark Souls III* DLCs in detail.

Alva and Zullie may only be names mentioned in *Dark Souls II*, but connecting them to Karla is still an interesting pursuit. In doing so, Karla's personality can be intertwined with all of the *Souls* witches who employ black magic. From this perspective, Karla can serve as a bridge between all of the *Souls* games. Yuria, Witch Beatrice, Zullie and Karla: could they all be the same person?

✤ Cornyx of the Great Swamp

In the Firelink Shrine, not far from the alcove where Karla teaches her black magic, Cornyx of the Great Swamp offers to teach us pyromancy. He's therefore an essential character for any pyromancers, sharing his knowledge (which we access by bringing him pyromancy tomes) and his improvements for the catalyst, the Pyromancy Flame. Rather old, mostly blind and no doubt a bit old-fashioned, Cornyx views himself a master, eager to surround himself with fawning pupils. His dialogue continually comes back to the importance of this first relationship between master and pupil: "To learn pyromancies, you must vow to become my pupil. I know, I know, but such is the way of the world. Respect your elders, and so on. And pyromancy, of course, is no exception." We first meet Cornyx in the Undead Settlement, locked up in a hanging cage. Certainly, this recalls our encounter with Big Hat Logan in the first *Dark Souls*, or to a lesser extent, Yurt in *Demon's Souls*. We free the pyromancer, and he warps to the Firelink Shrine. Cornyx is fascinated with the history of pyromancy and the city of Izalith, which he calls "the home of pyromancy." According to him, and the other pyromancers of the Great Swamp, Izalith converged towards Lothric at the same time as the other kingdoms. This would explain why the old man is in the region, looking for clues about the legendary city. In his conversation, he suggests that the Catacombs of Carthus lead to Izalith. Indeed, a hidden path in the depths of the catacombs leads us to the Smoldering Lake, and all the way to the Demon Ruins. Later, we'll see what takes place there, but we should point out for now that this location contains the pyromancy tomes intimately tied to Izalith. The Izalith and Quelana tomes provide interesting support for Cornyx's theory. Upon seeing these books of spells, the old master's interest is piqued: "Then you've found the home of Pyromancy. Brilliant. I will never curse being old and Undead again. The primal pyromanices known only to old Master Salaman! The birthplace of pyromancy, Izalith, was scorched by the very fire it created. Undoubtedly, it was a Chaos Flame, tangled by a witch's hand." Cornyx recites the legend taught in the Great Swamp, sketching out the broad history: destruction of the city of Izalith by Chaos, and the rise of Master Salaman. Quelana's final student,[245] he left to teach pyromancy in his turn. Cornyx seems to worship Salaman, and we don't know if he was Salaman's student, or if the pyromancers of the Great Swamp all venerated him. Later on in the adventure, in the middle of the Smoldering Lake, we meet Cuculus, also originally from the Great Swamp. Although this pyromancer and Cornyx seem related, if we help Cuculus on his quest, we receive Cornyx's set when we return to the pyromancer's former prison.

---

245. This point of the tale is mentioned in the description of the Quelana Pyromancy Tome: "Quelana, the sole surviving witch of Izalith, once accepted a human pupil, but after the pupil moved on, she never took another."

Cornyx's attire, covered in broad black feathers, suggests the appearance of a raven (or crow). Strangely, the description recalls a passage from the first episode: "Ravens are said to have once been Firelink messengers, guiding the Undead to the land of ancient gods." This is a reference to the enormous raven that brought the player's avatar to Firelink Shrine, the land of the gods, from the Northern Undead Asylum. The reference makes sense, given his affinity for crows. The attire's description suggests this: "In the Great Swamp, it was customary to adorn oneself with articles of nature. Cornyx favored the use of raven feathers." When we meet him, he considers himself a "crow in his cage," since he is imprisoned high off the ground. A crow, or raven, is a recurring symbol in the *Souls* games,[246] carrying a number of meanings. In *Dark Souls III*, crows appear more as a totem animal. The pyromancers of the Great Swamp like natural elements, particularly from the animals with which they identify. For instance, *Salaman* is associated with the salamander; cuculus is the Latin word for the cuckoo species[247]; and the name Cornyx is related to the Latin word *cornix*... which means crow.

❧ Orbeck of Vinheim

Like Irina, Karla or Cornyx, Orbeck teaches his craft in the Firelink Shrine. He can be found across from the old pyromancer and guides players along the path of sorcery.

If players have fewer than ten intelligence points, Orbeck will refuse to come to the shrine. His workshop is located in the Crucifixion Woods not far (surely in order to gain information) from one of the Crystal Sages, the eminent sorcerers from the Grand Archives of Lothric. In a rather condescending tone, he presents a deal: "So, you will make me a promise. That in exchange for my teaching, you will bring me knowledge. In the form of scrolls detailing sorcery's secrets". Like for the other masters, these scrolls give access to new spells throughout the game. In reality, Orbeck needs these scrolls to further his own learning, because in spite of his claims, he is nowhere near a true sorcerer from the Vinheim Dragon School.

The description of Orbeck's Ashes says much about the character: "Orbeck was fascinated with sorcery but without means, so offered to serve as an assassin in exchange for acceptance into the Dragon Academy, believing that one day he could reinvent himself as a sorcerer." The Dragon School was an institution from the region of Vinheim, with an excellent reputation. The finest of sorcerers walked its halls,

---

246. This also includes *Bloodborne*, of course, which presents many of these black birds, along with the character Eileen, from the clan of hunters called the "Crows."
247. We should note that she carries the Spotted Whip, venomous as a dangerous snake, which contradicts the interpretations associated with her name.

including great sorcerers such as Big Hat Logan. The legends are quiet on one point, however: that it "held effective sovereignty over Vinheim, with a great many adept assassins at its disposal."[248] Its prestige concealed a despotic undertaking, where any threat was secretly eliminated without hesitation. Orbeck was one of these assassins. He divulges his past bit by bit through the game. This trusting relationship leads Orbeck to give some valuable artifacts to his apprentice, such as the Young Dragon Ring and Slumbering Dragoncrest Ring. The first, as its name suggests, is a smaller version of the true rings of the Vinheim sorcerers—the Bellowing Draconcrest Ring and the Lingering Draconcrest Ring, which increase the strength of spells. The second directly recalls the clandestine side of the school—the assassins—and increases players' stealth. These two rings provide some earlier hints about Orbeck's past, that of a novice magician and murderer, but he outs himself when he has completed his teachings: "In Vinheim, I was an assassin. A sorcerer only in name, a killer for hire. What a fool I was, thinking one day I would learn real sorceries. When I became Undead, I was exiled from the school.[249] But here I am, now, exploring the depths of sorcery. All thanks to you, I might add." After his confession, Orbeck tries to get to the Grand Archives to further his knowledge. Unfortunately, he meets death instead. It's a peaceful death, though, on one of the chairs in the giant library.

Greirat

Orbeck is not the only criminal to walk the halls of the Firelink Shrine; the timid Greirat also has some unfortunate experience in the field. He wears a strange hood, really an old, worn canvas bag with two holes pierced for eyes, similar to a scarecrow, often used for slaves and "occasionally used to shame and humiliate criminals."[250] As with many other characters, we find him locked up in a cell within the High Wall of Lothric.

According to the descriptions of the Cell Key and Greirat's ashes, Greirat once lived in the Undead Settlement, below the High Wall of Lothric. Down there, many thieves would climb to the high wall to grab valuable loot. Greirat was one of these, and he "fancied himself a martyr for the poor, which is what drove him to climb the wall."[251] In other words, the little thief[252] posed as Robin Hood and scaled the high wall to plunder all sorts of valuables, thinking he would be hailed as a savior upon

248. From the description of the Slumbering Dragoncrest Ring.
249. This exile was also imposed upon other sorcerers from the Dragon School, including Rickert of Vinheim from the first episode.
250. From the description of the Thrall Hood worn by Greirat.
251. From the description of Greirat's Ashes.
252. The name obviously recalls "gray rat," which matches the character's small size and his pest-like, pilfering side.

his return. In this old life, he was especially fond of an old woman named Loretta. Unfortunately, he was caught on the high wall, and then thrown in prison. Much later on, when we arrive to free him, Greirat gives us the precious Blue Tearstone Ring and asks us to bring it to his friend Loretta in the Undead Settlement. Alas, Loretta has already lost her life. After learning the news, Greirat decides to remain with us, sometimes selling his personal items.

To renew his inventory, Greirat regularly spirits away from the Firelink Shrine to rob items from the lands explored by the player. He begins with his own land, the Undead Settlement, before returning safely from his treasure hunt. The next step in his journey is more complicated, because Greirat may die, depending on the player's own path. His next destinations are the outskirts of Irithyll, in the Boreal Valley, and then Lothric Castle. Though it is impossible for us to save him, his travels through Irithyll can still go safely thanks to the onion knight Siegward of Catarina,[253] trusty defender of the weak, or with the help of a well-known character for series fans (and not really known for heroism): Patches.

❧ Unbreakable Patches

Patches the Hyena, and then Mild-Mannered Pate in *Dark Souls II*, and even Patches the Spider in *Bloodborne*: he's a recurring character in the series. Whenever he appears, the encounter ends in betrayal placing players in a tricky situation. With a kick in the back into a pit, or a rigged chest, Patches surprises his victims every time, but apologizes profusely when they come back from the dead. In this third episode, Patches is now the "Unbreakable," and has two opportunities to dupe players.[254] the first is during the exploration of the Cathedral of the Deep. Patches masquerades as Siegward of Catarina and cuts off the passage to Rosaria's bedchamber. When we follow the traitor up onto the roof, he grovels and begs for his life. Later on, back in the Firelink Shrine, Patches sneaks up behind us as we explore the Belfry tower and locks us in: the only exit is a dizzying jump down to the base of the tower. "Oh, no matter, I'll look after things," he says. "By stripping every last trinket off your corpse. You're going to make some lucky customer very happy." Once again, players eventually find the scoundrel, now hidden up high in the shrine, not far from the nest of Pickle Pee, Pump-a-Rum Crow: we'll come back to the crow in a bit.

This time, Patches serves us by deigning to sell us some objects from his disreputable business. It's a strangely cooperative move for Patches, suspicious right up to the end of the adventure. However, Patches proves helpful when he helps Greirat

---

253. We'll study this character in more detail later, in the section on the characters of the Profaned Capital.
254. In *The Ringed City*, Patches traps players a third time, as we'll see later.

get out of danger in Irithyll. "Ahh, I see you've met Greirat. The slinking rodent. But he did me a good turn back in Lothric dungeon. Doubtless I should do something about that little debt, or...maybe not. Well, I can hardly believe he's still standing." Patches and Greirat have therefore definitely crossed paths. Though they're not quite friends, Patches shows him some deference, since he helped him out in the past. This means that at a key moment, Patches lends the shy thief a hand. A heroic, unexpected act from someone who loves to betray his associates and watch them die...

❦ Pickle Pee, Pump-a-Rum Crow

As we just saw, Unbreakable Patches' lair is a hideout under the impressive nest of Pickle Pee, Pump-a-Rum Crow, perched above the Firelink Shrine. This corvid character is also present in all of the *Souls* games, with different names: Sparkly in *Demon's Souls*, Snuggly in the first *Dark Souls*, Dyna and Tillo in *Dark Souls II*. In this third episode, its name is never mentioned, but the official guide calls it Snuggly, no doubt in reference to the first episode. Interactions with this character remain the same throughout the series: we leave an item in its nest so it can be exchanged for another. Depending on the game, something "warm and soft," "sparkly, twinkly," or "silky and smooth" is requested. In *Dark Souls III*, the crow never shows itself. Its small voice can be heard, requesting certain items, when players walk near the giant nest. We have to drop something from our inventory to trade for a valuable item, such as titanites, which are essential to make weapon improvements with Blacksmith Andre.

❦ Blacksmith Andre

Andre of Astora is also a character originally from the first *Dark Souls*. He was already one of the most well-known blacksmiths of his time, and now he's the only one who is able to improve weapons and shields. However, he doesn't limit himself just to smithing this time, because he's also responsible for upgrading the player's Estus Flask. As with learning spells, Andre helps us access new levels throughout the game. Unlike in the previous episodes, where players could explore and locate other blacksmiths who specialized in somewhat exotic weapon improvements, Andre is the one and only blacksmith in this game. This fits into the game's logic, since the Firelink Shrine is the hub for players to level up.

Andre is also masterful in the art of "infusion." To "infuse" a weapon is to specialize it. Each weapon can be customized, honing in on properties to reflect the player's avatar characteristics. Bleeding, poison, affinities with Fire or Dark, or automatic recovery of health or magic points, the possibilities are almost endless. We must first gain these skills from Andre, by giving him coal and a specific gem. Since the smithing system is centralized and simple, we can try out a number of different weapons and develop a precise fighting style. Andre is therefore a significant character,[255] allowing players to constantly try new things and explore the gameplay.

On the other hand, the illustrious blacksmith appears only to be a shell of his former self in this episode. No one knows what happened to Andre of Astora since the events of Lordran. His dialogue focuses on the smithy operations and Estus Flasks, peppered by a few mundane salutations. However, he does provide some information about some of the coal when we give it to him, leaving us with some useful conjectures about the kingdom of Lothric. In particular, he mentions a partnership formed between one of the Crystal Sages and Farron's Abyss Watchers when he sees the Sage's Coal, and gives a strange warning about the Abyss when seeing the Profaned Coal: "This is much too dark. I see the Abyss in it... Your fight is for the flame, and for y' fellow kin. Just like mine. A cursed fate this may be, but hope remains, does it not?"

In addition to these asides, he also shows great emotion when he lays eyes on the Giant's Coal. "I miss the old bugger, I do," he confides in the player. This giant was blacksmith to the gods of Anor Londo. In the first episode, he could forge unique weapons using boss souls, a bit like Ludleth with his art of transposition. Unfortunately, he lost his life prior to the events of *Dark Souls III*. He left his friend Andre behind, along with the Giant's Coal on his corpse. There's no indication why Andre was chosen to join the Firelink Shrine, and not the giant, or Vamos or Rickert from the first episode. All of this aside, the blacksmith of Astora works for the shrine as if he was elected by the tolling of the bell, and along with the Fire Keeper and Shrine Handmaid, he works unwaveringly to serve the Fire.

255. In fact, if players attack and kill Andre, he comes back to life to continue his work. He retains his dignity, however, and refuses to forge any more weapons until his murderer atones for his sins by going to see the goddess Velka.

❧ The Shrine Handmaid

At the game's outset, this old, nameless woman appears to be the only merchant in the Firelink Shrine. A bit cantankerous and clad in a long and well-worn dress, she recalls Strowen, Morrel and Griant, the three Fire Keepers in the prologue of *Dark Souls II*. Like them, the handmaid wears a mask over her eyes. Her role is nonetheless very different from that of these Fire Keepers, because her only role is to trade. As with the other residents, her supply expands as the game progresses.

When we bring her Umbral Ashes, she offers new items, which sometimes provide unexpected revelations about characters or the past. For instance, as we've seen, the Prisoner Chief's Ashes raise disturbing questions about Karla's fate, and Yuria's Ashes can be used to obtain all of the lady's set, revealing important information on the Sable Church, where she originated. The most intriguing Umbral Ashes are the Dreamchaser's Ashes. These are the only ashes that cause the Shrine Handmaid to react differently: "Ashen One, what woeful umbral ash is this. This barren dust, stuff of a fool, won't yield aught. Where did'st thou happen upon the stuff? Tell me, for the sport. Clinging to lofty dreams in this dying world... more's the pity. It must come from one most foolish indeed..." The real reason for such criticism is never explained, but one detail from the image associated with the Dreamchaser's Ashes draws our attention. They are represented by a hand—like all of the other ashes—with an old pendant that clearly evokes the first *Dark Souls*. This mysterious item has already been subject to much speculation: as part of the basic equipment when creating a character, it serves no purpose at first glance. However, Miyazaki himself advised players to choose this old pendant at the time. Players left no stone unturned, trying to identify the item's meaning; hypotheses abound about its lore, or how it affects the gameplay. Finally, the game's creator admitted that his recommendation was just a red herring, an obscure joke for a cryptic game. However, five years later in *Dark Souls III*, this notorious pendant reappears in the hand of the Dreamchaser's Ashes, accompanied by the Shrine Handmaid's acerbic dialogue, as she indirectly mocks anyone who looked for meaning in this pendant. Some speculate that the Dreamchaser's Ashes are those of the handmaid's late husband. Her criticism would therefore be directed at him. This hypothesis is somewhat debatable, since we later learn that Holy Knight Hodrick is actually the grandfather of Sirris of the Sunless Realms, therefore possibly the handmaid's husband.[256]

It is therefore unlikely that the Dreamchaser's Ashes are those of Hodrick, because at the beginning of the game, he's still alive in the Undead Settlement. He dies in a fight against the Curse-Rotted Greatwood, and the ashes lie far from there in Farron Keep.

---

256. We'll come back to the ties between these three characters.

It's difficult to link all of these elements, and the handmaid says nothing more on the subject, either in the Firelink Shrine or the Untended Graves.

Finding the merchant handmaid in this location serves as proof of her advanced age: as we've seen, the Untended Graves are an older version of the Firelink Shrine. If we attack her, she disappears forever from the Untended Graves, leaving behind a mysterious Priestess Ring. This ring is connected to one of the Three Pillars supporting Lothric's royal power—High Priestess Emma. If we go a bit further, we'll see that the Shrine Handmaid and Emma have other things in common. They dress similarly, although Emma's clothing is in better shape. In addition, the two old women adopt the same pose, with their left hands draped over their right, seated in the exact same chair. These details suggest that the Shrine Handmaid was once one of the high priestesses of Lothric, and that she once rubbed shoulders with the royal court and the children of Oceiros and Gwynevere. Gwynevere was particularly concerned about the Firelink Shrine and the endangered Age of Fire,[257] so she asked her then high priestess to become Shrine Handmaid and to begin watching over the shrine while waiting for the bell to toll.

The bell tolled at a much later date, strengthening the ties between the handmaid and the Firelink Shrine. Like Andre and the Fire Keeper, who also toiled to protect the Fire, she cannot die in this location. If she is attacked, she reveals that she is "bound forever by the shrine's curse." She takes this opportunity to increase her prices considerably, until (once again) players seek Velka, Goddess of Sin to absolve their sins.

⚜ Hawkwood

Similar to the Shrine Handmaid, Hawkwood is a character we meet at the game's outset in Firelink Shrine. Like the player, Hawkwood is an Unkindled. Once summoned by the Fire, he was also tested by Iudex Gundyr before entering the shrine. Over time, however, he lost all hope of succeeding in his quest. This feeling pervades much of his dialogue: "We Unkindled are worthless. Can't even die right. Gives me conniptions." These are almost the first words he speaks in the game. "We're not fit to lick their boots," he continues, referring to the Lords of Cinder. Later, he adds the following about Aldrich: "Do we have a sodding chance?" We also hear him sigh, "What a sham." Hawkwood excellently fills the role of the "Crestfallen Warrior," found in every episode since *Demon's Souls*.

Unlike his antecedents, this new demoralized character has a bit of a backstory. To start, he has a name; up until now, Crestfallen Saulden of *Dark Souls II* was the only

---

257. We mentioned this when looking at the game's story, specifically when we looked at "The End of Fire" ending.

of his kind to be named. It turns out that Hawkwood was once one of the Undeads of Farron's Legion. Called a "deserter,"[258] he prefers terms like "flying the coop" to refer to his departure from Farron's Legion. Due to his status as an Unkindled and the quest he was assigned, Hawkwood has many details on the Lords of Cinder, and he divulges some of them. We've seen what he tells of Aldrich, but he also supplies information about the Abyss Watchers. He teaches us how to complete the three tasks to access the Wolf's Blood in Farron Keep. Behind his world-weary airs, Hawkwood proves a very handy guide. He's also capable of great empathy: "I pity the sorry souls," he says, remembering the Undeads from Farron's Legion. He repeats himself as he communes beside a large tomb outside Firelink: "The poor wretched souls... Be they lord or legend, the curse shows no mercy. What a sham." He eventually thanks us after our fight against the Abyss Watchers: "I pity the sorry souls. Is that really lordship's last reward? Ah, I failed to thank you. For helping them find their resting place..." In fact, these are his final words before he leaves Firelink Shrine. Hawkwood can also be generous, providing useful items for players. He leaves behind his precious shield, either to Blacksmith Andre or next to the tomb where he liked to sit.

Later on in the adventure, he leaves another object for Andre: a swordgrass. Swordgrass once "quietly identified members of the Undead Legion," symbolizing their "gratitude toward their guardians," according to the description of Wolf's Blood Swordgrass.[259] An additional message, addressed to the player, is written on the one that belonged to Hawkwood: "Come to the mausoleum in Farron. Only one can take the path of ancient dragons."

If we follow the instructions and go to this location, we must duel with Hawkwood. In reality, each fighter has a piece of the Twinkling Dragon Stone: players have the torso[260] and Hawkwood has the head. When either is defeated (even the player), the other will have the chance to become a small dragon. However, this part of Hawkwood's quest seems to have been added later on, because nothing in the knight's discourse refers to this obsession with dragons.

---

258. From the description of Hawkwood's Shield.
259. Swordgrasses are sacred objects of the Watchdogs of Farron covenant, which must be collected to rank up.
260. We can obtain this torso from Archdragon Peak—only after this do we get Hawkwood's message from Andre. We can summon Hawkwood around Archdragon Peak, which gives us a first clue about his fascination for dragons. Upon summoning the crestfallen warrior, we see him worship the giant dragon body at the base of the altar. If we complete this gesture, we can obtain the Twinkling Dragon Torso Stone, the aforementioned duel item.

⚜ Sirris of the Sunless Realms

Also associated with a covenant, Sirris of the Sunless Realms was once a part of the Blade of the Darkmoon. Under the aegis of Gwyndolin the Dark Sun, these knights "punish[ed] the guilt-soaked offenders of the Gods."[261] Sirris's quest is therefore rather traditional, and she is both a graceful and skilled fighter. Although she no longer belongs to the Blades of the Dark Moon, she continues to hunt down scum, such as Creighton the Wanderer, who we also saw in *Dark Souls II*. The Unkindled can help the young woman by being summoned into her world, as for another player. In this case, both fight Creighton at the doors to Irithyll. After the fight, she gives us the Silvercat Ring. This ring is a direct reference to Alvina and Shalquoir, the polymath cats from the previous games.[262]

Later on, when the Lord of Cinder has been defeated, Sirris reappears in the Firelink Shrine. Since Aldrich devoured Gwyndolin, the Blades of the Dark Moon god, the young woman seems to have fulfilled her duty and can now attend to family matters. She leaves a unique blossom with the Shrine Handmaid. Available from among the old merchant's wares, it is a Budding Green Blossom, similar to those found throughout the game,[263] but this time with a peculiar message: "Good-bye, dear Grandmother. I will visit Grandfather, in the Pit of Hollows." In this, we learn that the handmaid, the recipient of this bouquet, is Sirris's grandmother. The grandfather is Hodrick, also known as "Holy Knight,"[264] an ostensibly higher rank than Sirris, a simple knight.[265] "Just as I promised, grandad, remember?" she asks, as the player meets her in the Pit of hollows in the Undead Settlement, before fighting him together. This fight is the last of her questline, fulfilling an old and obscure promise.

It's possible to miss Sirris's quest by following instructions from another character in Firelink, from an enemy covenant: Rosaria's Fingers.[266] The character is named Ringfinger Leonhard, and he opens up a very different journey to the player, who must decide between the two covenants.

---

261. From the description of the Proof of a Concord Kept, a Blades of the Darkmoon tribute item.
262. The Silvercat Ring has this description: "In the Age of Gods, or possibly following it, an old cat was said to speak a human tongue, with the voice of an old woman, and the form of a fanciful immortal."
263. Green Blossoms are common consumables that temporarily increase stamina.
264. A name used in the description of the Sunset Shield, which belongs to Hodrick.
265. A name used in the description of the Sunless Veil, which belongs to Sirris.
266. Sirris's comments about Creighton, and consequently the Rosaria covenant to which he belongs, are particularly scathing: "That Dark Spirit was one of Rosaria's Fingers. Vile bastard offspring who lurk in the darkness. My sworn enemies. Fearsome invaders, to say the least."

⚜ Ringfinger Leonhard

Leonhard descends from an ancient royal family, though the lineage remains unknown. With a noble soldier's upbringing, he learned to wield a sword and use magic, and gained excellent fighting skills. Unfortunately, this didn't prevent him from experiencing a terrible accident, which burned his body and face. Since then, he's worn an evil-looking silver mask and a tricorn, an unusual hat for this world,[267] reflecting his original personality.

Leonhard's appearances in the Firelink Shrine are as timely as Sirris's. Not far from the vacant throne of Prince Lothric, we can spot his black tricorn and sinister figure, contrasting with the young woman's whiteness. As with Sirris, Leonhard's quest can be broken down into two distinct parts.

First, the mysterious member of Rosaria's Fingers invites players to commit murders, and he provides Cracked Red Eye Orbs for this purpose. These objects can be used to invade other Unkindleds in order to eliminate them and collect "Pale Tongues" from their corpses. These trophies serve an important purpose in the Rosaria covenant, because players can use them to rank up. Once players have gotten their first Pale Tongue, Leonhard appears once more in the Firelink Shrine to give them a new mission, now more specific. He provides a key, saying, "Then kill the Darkwraith, survivor of the land swallowed by darkness. He has been a prisoner, for many ages. In the deepest cell in all Lothric..." These words recall the Darkwraiths from the ruins of New Londo, which we explored in the first *Dark Souls*. These ancient lands had fallen prey to the Abyss, and some humans had been transformed into very aggressive, fearful creatures ravenous for humanities. The Darkwraiths were also associated with an old covenant, a cruel one similar to Rosaria's Fingers. Players fight the Darkwraith described by Leonhard and collect a Red Eye Orb straight out of New Londo.[268] This orb, which is much stronger than the Cracked Red Eye Orbs, allows us to invade other Unkindleds anytime we want.

As thanks for successfully obtaining this revolting object, Leonhard congratulates the player thus: "Brilliant. I knew you were no ordinary man. Now invade and pillage all you like. And if you grow weary of your duty, you, too, may become a Finger." With this invitation extended, Leonhard disappears from the Firelink Shrine. The second part of his quest takes place in Rosaria's Bedchamber, within the Cathedral of the Deep.

---

267. Unlike in the *Bloodborne* world, where this type of garb is common.
268. Its description reads, "The red eye orb is rooted in a tiny land swallowed by darkness long ago." In the first episode, this same object was a tribute for the Darkwraith covenant, obtained by offering ten humanities to the famous Kaathe, the group's leader.

The Cathedral of the Deep

✦ Rosaria, Mother of Rebirth

We meet Rosaria, known as the "Mother of Rebirth" within one of the cathedral's chapels. She first appears to be rather impressive: silent, seated on a raised canopy bed, and surrounded by giant cribs, she appears to be a large human-like creature, but with a massive, deformed lower half. As we approach, we can see that she's actually a large woman, surrounded by two of her servants. She strokes one, seated on her lap, as the other lies behind her. Rosaria's servants are the Man-Grubs we see regularly throughout the Cathedral of the Deep, particularly at the entryway to the chapel where their sovereign lives. Some can cast spells, while others use their claws and teeth to wound, when they aren't spewing their bile on players. "The man-grubs have clearly been reborn, but as what?" asks the Man-Grub's Staff. The Man-Grubs seem to come directly from the Mother of Rebirth. As such, they worship her, and protect her from any intruder who dares come too close to her bedchamber lair. The location indeed looks more like a bedchamber than a chapel, with Rosaria's bed at the end of the room, past many cribs strewn around, where the numerous grub "children" were no doubt raised.

Besides the Man-Grubs, other characters worship the Mother of Rebirth, as leader of the Rosaria's Fingers covenant. It's worth mentioning that by joining this group, in addition to the traditional ranking up, we have access to two useful options: we can change our appearance, and reallocate our stats. Though the first option remains cosmetic, the second allows us to totally reshape our character, its strengths and weaknesses, in order to start afresh with a new build. Rosaria thus offers a true "rebirth," both in appearance and in skill.

To get back to Rosaria's covenant members, we meet Leonhard in Rosaria's bedchamber after he disappeared from the Firelink Shrine. He greets us as a new member of the covenant, while revealing his curious mood, far from that of Rosaria, unifying and motherly. "But be warned, my friend. Rosaria's Fingers need only fetch tongues for their mistress. Otherwise, we are free, unchained," says Leonhard. This mysterious attitude marks the beginning of the second part of the Ringfinger's quest.

Later in the adventure, after the fight against Yhorm and Aldrich, Rosaria is assassinated. Next to her body, we find a Black Eye Orb that can be used to invade the murderer, after it is brought to the correct location. This recalls Lautrec of Carim's crime from the first *Dark Souls*, when he killed the Fire Keeper in an act of cowardice. He could be found later within Anor Londo by using a similar Black Eye Orb. Here, after Rosaria's murder, the principle is the same. The orb begins to quiver as we approach Gwynevere's old throne, also in Anor Londo. With it, we can invade Leonhard and engage him in a tough fight. The Ringfinger's motivations are somewhat unclear at first glance. In fact, his goal was to protect the Soul of Rosaria, particularly from this dangerous covenant newcomer. During the fight, he accuses us: "And now you want to ravage her soul, as well. I sowed the seeds. I'll prune the mess. I, Leonhard, swear so upon my vows to the goddess. No one will despoil her soul. [...] What do you want with her soul?" Leonhard, obsessed with Rosaria's soul, went so far as to kill Rosaria to keep it safe. Somewhat paradoxical, but not as definitive an act as it appears: when we bring the Soul of Rosaria to her body, she is revived, "reborn" as if nothing happened.

It's also possible to have Ludleth transpose the Soul of Rosaria to produce the Bountiful Light miracle, closely related to Gwynevere the Princess of Sunlight. Considering that Leonhard absconds to Anor Londo after snatching Rosaria's soul, this suggests a tie between Gwynevere and the Mother of Rebirth. Many theories have attempted to pin down Rosaria's identity. Rosaria could be Gwynevere herself in a different form, one of her daughters, perhaps one of her former maidens. We can rule out the first idea. Gwynevere fled Lothric after the birth of Ocelotte, and there is nothing to suggest she returned to the Cathedral of the Deep. Rosaria is also associated with the moon, as indicated by the Crescent Moon Sword (a type of shotel "imbued with the power of the moon" according to its description), brandished by Leonhard, who "[serves] the goddess as a knight." Leonhard received this sword when he swore allegiance to Rosaria, and it is his preferred weapon. Finally, the moon is a common symbol of rebirth, since it is renewed with each cycle. The elements linking Rosaria and Gwynevere, the Princess of Sunlight, are therefore few and far between.

The idea of Rosaria being one of Gwynevere's daughters or maidens seems more plausible, especially because Rosaria is rather large, similar to the gods of Anor Londo. One interesting hypothesis identifies Rosaria as Gertrude, the Heavenly Daughter. Gertrude is one of Gwynevere's many daughters, formerly locked in a cage under the high ceilings of the Grand Archives in Lothric Castle. Next to this cage lies a Man-Grub, similar to Rosaria's servants. Once again, this type of detail surely can't be random in the *Dark Souls* universe. When we discuss the characters of Lothric Castle, we'll show that the theory tying Rosaria to Gertrude seems the most likely.

Either way, Leonhard's objective was to bring the Mother of Rebirth's soul to the Anor Londo throne, possibly to reveal her divine origins, or maybe simply to protect her from the player or the other Fingers. Leonhard prefers freedom and to act independently, values that are evidently not shared by the Man-Grubs (they protect the entry and exit to Rosaria's bedchamber), nor by the other covenant members. The two other Fingers present have very strong ties with the Mother of Rebirth.

One of them, known as the "Yellowfinger," is named Heysel and has a strong attachment to the family. She's the daughter of a prominent acolyte of Farron (as we learn from the description of the Great Farron Dart), and had previously chosen the way of sorcery, particularly Xanthous magic. Indeed, Heysel wears the Xanthous set: a yellow robe and a large mushroom-shaped hat. "Crown made in imitation of a divine creature of Oolacile, land of ancient, golden sorceries," indicates the description of the Xanthous Crown. We had to wait until this third episode to learn the origins of the Xanthous sorcerers. These revelations also help clarify the story of the mysterious King Jerimiah from the first episode. However, no true golden sorcerers exist anymore, since Oolacile has long been lost. All that remain are followers, attempting to imitate them.[269] Heysel is part of this small group of disciples. She invades players if they haven't yet joined Rosaria's Fingers, and will help them if they have. On this subject, Leonhard says: "Like Yellowfinger, you can choose to believe that all Fingers share camaraderie." This gives us a hint about the familial attachment Heysel has for Rosaria, and therefore about her divergence from Leonhard's proclaimed independence.

The third and final member of Rosaria's covenant that we meet in the game is Longfinger Kirk. He's also known as the "Knight of Thorns" in reference to his armor covered in sharp spikes that inflict damage when he rolls onto his enemies. Kirk recalls the character of the same name from the first *Dark Souls*. Also known as "Knight of Thorns," he took pleasure in regularly invading players and trying to kill them. Beyond his taste for murder, his more subtle side lay in his passion for Quelaan, leader of the Chaos Servant covenant. He would bring her humanities in an attempt to save her from the corruption of Chaos. In *Dark Souls III*, he has the same aims: an unforgiving murderer on one hand, with his oath to Rosaria's Fingers which begins as a band of assassins on the hunt for Pale Tongues, and a possibly romantic passion on the other, for the Mother of Rebirth. No need to explain that this affection doesn't really match Leonhard's general state of mind.

In addition to the Man-Grubs and Fingers, one other individual has sworn allegiance to Rosaria, who certainly has quite a solid following. This final follower, much more than a simple servant, reveres her like a goddess: Klimt, one of the three archdeacons from the Cathedral of the Deep.

---

269. "They were called xanthous scholars, but some foolishly imitate them by simply dressing in yellow," says the Xanthous Ashes description. In passing, we should mention that Oolacile golden magic items can be found throughout the world: in *The Ringed City* DLC, we find the White Birch Bow whose arrows "are enchanted with a golden spell that turns them nearly invisible."

⚜ The Archdeacons

There are three archdeacons in total: these clerics hold a higher rank than simple deacons, and have long reigned over the Cathedral of the Deep. During this period, and under their command, many horrors were committed in the name of Fire and the gods. Their role is therefore parallel to that of the Way of White, a religious sect built by Gwyn and Lloyd in the Lordran era, albeit a more vile and sordid version. The description of the Archdeacon Holy Garb also emphasizes this connection with the Way of White: "A sign of the Way of White's highest rank." It also seems (according to certain item descriptions) that the Way of White covenant, originally from the region of Thorolund, was taken back up by those from Carim. Both the Braille Divine Tome of Carim[270] and Lloyd's Shield Ring[271] associate Lloyd's former small group with the region of Carim. This would explain why there are a number of statues of Velka, the Goddess of Sin worshiped in Carim, in the dark rooms of the Cathedral of the Deep. Finally, according to descriptions of the Deep Ring[272] and the Deacon Skirt,[273] the references to this ominous period are definitely chilling.

The three archdeacons, Klimt, Royce and McDonnell, were chiefly responsible for these abominations. However, little information is available with regard to Klimt and Royce's methods. McDonnell would channel Faith to cast spells. Spells and miracles are two opposing schools, however. The first is based on intelligence and esoteric research, and the other is based on faith, since miracles generally come from the gods, or from divine intervention. "The Archdeacon McDonnell's trespass, the sin of channeling faith for sorcery, transformed what was once merely a symbol of ecclesiastic authority into a catalyst of sorceries," indicates the description of the Archdeacon's Great Staff. This means he sins by using spells (considered heretical by more pious sorts), and casts doubt upon the sincerity of the beliefs held by the religious authorities of the Cathedral of the Deep. But he's not really fooling anyone, considering the atrocities committed in the cathedral: Faith has always been a relative concept here. The most notorious atrocities associated with the Cathedral of the Deep are tied to

---

270. "A sacred braille tome from Carim. [...] In the Way of White, there is a tradition of placing great faith in the words of the blind, and braille tomes are not unusual," indicates the item's description. As we've seen, this braille tome is intended for Irina of Carim, who wears a white dress (the Maiden Set) in a direct reference to Reah of Thorolund, the priestess of the Way of White from the first episode. We should also mention that we get the Maiden Set by exploring the Cathedral of the Deep, where former members of the Way of White reside.
271. "Much time has passed since the worship of Lloyd was common in the Way of White. The clerics of Carim had always strongly asserted that Lloyd was a derivative fraud, and that the Allfather title was self-proclaimed," reads the item's description. In addition to Carim's reappropriation of the Way of White's teachings, Lloyd's very all-power is called into question.
272. "In the Cathedral slumber things most terrible, and as such, the deacons require a grand narrative, to ensure they do not falter in their duty. A philosophy, to ward away the madness beckoned by the grotes-queries at hand."
273. "In time, those dedicated to sealing away the horrors of the Deep succumbed to their very power."

Aldrich, calling the churchly image into question once more: the archdeacons fed Aldrich only on human flesh, from adults or children. Then, they made him link the Fire—to die and become a Lord of Cinder. They built a giant, square black tomb in his memory, like a sinister Kaaba[274] in which Aldrich would lie until the bell tolled much later, and he would be resuscitated. With help from Sulyvahn, Aldrich then fled from the Cathedral of the Deep with the goal of devouring the gods, the very ones worshiped by the deacons.

Then, Royce watched over the tomb while waiting for its occupant's return; he eventually adopted McDonnell's heretical sorcery. Indeed, we later learn that we can cast the Deep Soul sorcery by transposing the deacons' soul we receive from the fight with Royce and his deacons. This spell "fires dark soul dregs," according to its description. We may be tempted to trace the origins of this type of spell to the atrocities committed on humans in the past (and therefore on their Dark Souls). However, there's another theory that's more interesting to us, which ties the Deep to the Abyss. Here's what the Deep Soul sorcery says: "Souls which swell from the deep pursue their target, drawn towards life." Visually, the "soul dregs" recall the humanities from the previous episodes, with long, black silhouettes surrounded by white light. In the first *Dark Souls*, they were in the shape of the Chasm of the Abyss, the location of Manus, Father of the Abyss. The humanities corrupted by the Abyss would float towards players (due to their vital energy?), moving slowly but in great numbers, so that it was hard to shake them if we got stuck in a corner. But another detail ties the Deep to the Abyss: the large black marks under McDonnell's eyes. These marks (like little branches) can be found on the Abyss Watchers' attire. Finally, *The Ringed City* introduces new creatures with strong ties to the Deep and the Dark: the Murkmen, which we'll come back to when we discuss the DLC. It's hard to deny that there's a connection between the Abyss and the Deep. Both entities appear distinct, however, even if the Deep may have drawn some of its power from the Abyss, before separating from it to take its later form, worshiped by members of the Cathedral of the Deep.

For his part, Klimt eventually renounced his faith to join Rosaria, no doubt breaking his archdeacon vows in the process. The reason for this reversal is unknown, but perhaps he felt a small pang of guilt from seeing the horrifying experiments conducted under his watch.

Archdeacon McDonnell also left the cathedral after Aldrich, to follow this creature to Irithyl in the Boreal Valley, where he founded the Aldrich Faithful covenant. McDonnell allied with Sulyvahn to protect Aldrich during the slow feast where he ate the god Gwyndolin.

---

274. A large cubic structure located in Mecca, towards which Muslims bow down when praying.

The Boreal Valley and Anor Londo

❧ Aldrich

Since Aldrich is one of the tale's central characters, we've already delved into his story quite a bit. Formerly known as the "Saint of the Deep,"[275] he was fated to become the "Devourer of Gods," in the highest room of the magnificent city of Anor Londo—a remarkable ascension any way you look at it, geographically, physically and spiritually.

Aldrich started out as an ordinary cleric. We don't know if he became a cannibal out of his own volition, or if this resulted from the experiments conducted on him by the archdeacons. Either way, it was the archdeacons who fueled this man-eating tendency, taking it to the extreme: in the grips of insatiable hunger, Aldrich, who only fed on humans at this point, eventually transformed into a shapeless, slimy blob that would devour anything that passed nearby.

Against his will, he became a Lord of Cinder due to the power he had accumulated through his feeding, and he reached an honorable status after his death. When he was revived by the bell's tolling, instead of returning to sit on his throne in the Firelink Shrine, Aldrich got to thinking. He had risen from the status of cleric to Lord of Cinder, and saw that it was possible to ascend to the greatest heights even after starting from the very bottom. After his sacrifice, hadn't the archdeacons of the Cathedral of the Deep built an immense, ornate tomb for him, a simple cleric, which they watched over as a place of worship? In his reflections, he thought of the Fire, and "it inspired visions of a coming age of the deep sea."[276]

Aldrich began toying with the idea of ending the Age of Fire by using the strength he had acquired when he became Lord of Cinder. For him, this didn't mean entering the Age of Dark. The future would be that of a deep sea. Although the exact meaning of "deep sea"[277] is unclear, this plan to bring on a new age of his own design says much about Aldrich's ambitions, which were as vast as his appetite. Human flesh had given him enough strength to become Lord of Cinder, and the next stage would be accomplished by devouring the gods.

In the meanwhile, Sulyvahn had returned to the Cathedral of the Deep. The story doesn't indicate how this newcomer would influence the megalomaniac vision of Aldrich. Sulyvahn was the one to summon the old Lord of Cinder to follow him to

---

275. In any case, this is his official title with regard to the Fire, engraved on the throne that awaits him in the Firelink Shrine.
276. From the description of the Soul of Aldrich.
277. That said, it's tempting to associate this reference with the entity of the Deep, from the Cathedral where Aldrich lived. As we've seen, the Deep is somewhat tied to the Abyss. Considering the vile creatures engendered by the Abyss, his project is quite ominous.

Irithyll of the Boreal Valley, and then to the summit of Anor Londo, where he offered the god Gwyndolin to him on a platter. Aldrich started his feast, which would take him a long time—really until we interrupt him. If Sulyvahn provided him with this long-lasting feast, it was above all to keep him far from the intrigues and quest of the Unkindled.

After eating Gwyndolin, Aldrich's strength grew enormously. "Aldrich dreamt as he slowly devoured the God of the Darkmoon. In this dream, he perceived the form of a young, pale girl in hiding," says the description of the Lifehunt Scythe miracle, retrieved after transposing Aldrich's soul. This refers to the scythe named after Crossbreed Priscilla in the first *Dark Souls*. It seems the Devourer of Gods saw her in a dream and took advantage of this to assimilate her life-hunting powers. These two characters, Gwyndolin and Priscilla, are reflected in Aldrich's appearance and attitudes. His pose recalls that of the Crossbreed (the two hands holding a scythe-like object) and his head is very similar to Gwyndolin: pale, with white hair, topped with the renowned Crown of the Dark Sun. The crown only has five branches now, though, and is a different color, as if Aldrich has taken on some of Gwyndolin's appearance, in a corrupted yet symbolic way.

The former Lord of Cinder's appearance recalls a third character from the first episode, who is never mentioned in any of the descriptions or dialogues; the following is therefore purely speculation. We're referring to Nito. The end of Aldrich's scythe is strikingly similar to the massive, bony sword wielded by Nito, First of the Dead. The skeletons mixed into the Devourer of God's black robe recall the many more covering Nito. With no other clues, however, it's difficult to determine whether or not a connection exists.

❦ Yorshka

Not far from the immense and majestic steps in Anor Londo that lead to Aldrich's lair lives a strange woman named Yorshka. Everything about her—her pale hair and skin, and especially her tail—recall Crossbreed Priscilla. Not far from Yorshka, there are also many pieces of equipment associated with the Painting Guardians, referring to those who protect the Painted World of Ariamis where Priscilla lived in *Dark Souls*. Yorshka's precise location, though geographically located in Irithyll, also corresponds to the Anor Londo cathedral, which no longer exists in this part of the city that once converged towards Lothric. At the time, the painting that led to the Painted World of Ariamis was in this cathedral.[278] In addition to their physical similarities, Priscilla

---

278. A fun detail: to reach the Painted World of Ariamis, we needed the "Peculiar Doll;" in *Dark Souls III*, we need the "Small Doll" to pass through the barrier into Irithyll.

and Yorshka are located in analogous places. The two women have nothing else in common, because unlike the Crossbreed and her obscure origins, Yorshka's background is clearer, if unexpected.

"Father Gwyn and Sister Gwynevere," she says during her dialogue with the player. Up until this point, we were only aware of three of Gwyn's children: the nameless firstborn, Gwynevere and Gwyndolin. The latter was supposedly the family's youngest, but Yorshka reveals that he was her older brother! This strange revelation is supported only by Yorshka. Is she telling the truth? Her tail, inherited from the dragons (judging from Priscilla's origins), indicates that Yorshka is also a "crossbreed," and therefore that she has a different mother from Gwyn's other children. However, Gwyndolin also had a strange feature, with the lower half of his body made up of many snakes. The identity of Gwyn's children's mother or mothers has remained a mystery since the beginning of the series, and this seems to be why! Like Gwyndolin in the Lordran era, Yorshka is the current captain of the Blades of the Darkmoon, a covenant of which Sirris was a member, as we mentioned above. "Lamenting the waning of the fire, [Gwyn] became cinder of his own will. Now, the fire is linked, by the champions who have come in his stead. Such is the will of father, and the gods. And so the Darkmoon knights took arms, to watch over those who link the fire," says Yorshka, presenting her covenant as the defender of Fire and the gods. Unfortunately for her, members are few and far between, and since Gwyndolin disappeared, she has felt lonely with all of the responsibility on her shoulders. Moreover, when capturing Gwyndolin to feed him to Aldrich, Sulyvahn isolated Yorshka from the rest of the world, at the top of an unreachable tower,[279] thus preventing her from finding any new recruits. Sulyvahn's plans are clearer, now that we know of his intentions and determination to stave off the Age of Fire.

⚜ Pontiff Sulyvahn

After removing Gwyndolin from Anor Londo and locking up Yorshka, Sulyvahn proclaimed himself "Pontiff,"[280] a title to fit his level of influence.

As we've seen, the Pontiff's influence can be felt throughout the *Dark Souls III* story. From the dark past of the Profaned Capital, to the bad influence on Prince Lothric's education when he acted as the First of the Scholars in the Grand Archives, to the manipulation of the powerful and unpredictable Aldrich, Sulyvahn definitely left

279. In reality, it's not totally inaccessible. To get there, players have to (cautiously) cross an invisible bridge that connects the Anor Londo elevator to where Yorshka lives.
280. The title of "Pontiff" carries religious connotations. The term comes from Middle French, "*pontife*," meaning a high priest. Now, it generally refers to the Pope.

his mark on the story. The kingdom of Lothric's present state, and the current state of Fire, is the Pontiff's doing.

His precise reasons for fighting against Fire remain unknown. Was he driven by an old grudge against the gods? Was he simply testing the limits of his power? Although many questions remain, everything suggests that Sulyvahn has a proclivity for domination. In Irithyll, he was a true tyrant, and feared by his subjects above all else. This seems to be the case for the beast that attacks players on the bridge leading to the Boreal city: a type of enormous watchdog with the head of a crocodile. The creature is so aggressive that it's tricky to land a hit; however, when it's about to die, it lies down on its back and begins to pray, in terror, as if it prefers death to the punishment it will receive if it can't carry out its master's orders.

However, Sulyvahn hasn't always been a tyrant. Long before he arrived in Lothric, he traveled the world as a young sorcerer. In the *Ashes of Ariandel* DLC, the Frozen Weapon and Snap Freeze sorceries indicate that Sulyvahn originated from a painted world: Ariamis or Ariandel.[281] A variety of clues suggest that it was the second of these worlds. The first is the location where we find the two sorceries. Then, the Painted World of Ariandel is populated by lots of different types of crows: Crow Villagers, the Corvian Settler, and other Corvian Knights. Before the DLC was released, one part of Sulyvahn's appearance raised a number of questions: black, featherless wings appeared on his back during the second phase of the fight. Some drew a connection with the pilgrims of Londor transformed into butterflies, like those within the walls of Lothric Castle. But after experiencing the DLC, it's clear that this is more of a "family" trait: a crow's wings. In their armor and shape, the Boreal Outrider Knights also echo the Corvian Knights: long limbs, a hunched posture and metal, "spine"-like armor. Could this be more than a coincidence? Finally, Yorshka makes an enigmatic comment that makes sense once we have more information about Sulyvahn's origins. When we cross the empty space separating us from Yorshka, she asks if we can fly. If we say "yes," she says: "Then thou'rt a dragon, or perhaps a crow? Well, whatever thou beest, thou'rt wondrous strange, yet strangely familiar, visitor." Referencing the crow and a "strangely familiar" person, Yorshka is thinking of Sulyvahn. Much later, she mentions Sulyvahn and his tyranny, after players have gained her trust and are promoted to the second rank of her covenant. It's almost as if she wanted to keep his secret out of fear or shame, while dropping a clue (at first incomprehensible) during their first meeting.

---

281. Though only one painted world existed prior to the release of the *Ashes of Ariandel* DLC, we now know that there are at least two, and maybe more.

Sulyvahn was therefore a crow from the Painted World of Ariandel. "Sulyvahn was born and raised inside the painting yet had little use for his frigid homeland." This description from the Frozen Weapon sorcery could not be clearer on the subject, and it finishes with: "since he had not yet experienced loss." That's certainly one way to describe the mind of a young, carefree sorcerer leaving his homeland to travel the world. It's unclear what is meant by "experienced loss," but it's probably a life ordeal, one that leads to growth. This experience may be related to his discovery, much later on, of the Profaned Flame, which led him to embrace the Dark and showed him Fire's hopeless state, causing him to question all of his prior convictions. Once he had reached the royal court of Lothric, Sulyvahn preferred to keep his sorcerer's past quiet, along with his origins.[282] He hid his crow wings and changed one of his weapons, the Greatsword of Judgement, in order to lessen his affiliation with sorcery by associating himself with the moon, symbol of the softer magic found in the Painted World of Ariandel. The sword represents "the judgement of the moon, but with magic far closer to sorcery than any existing lunar power. Its dark blue hues, deeper than the darkest moon, reflect sorcerer Sulyvahn's true nature."[283]

Based on information from the DLC regarding Sulyvahn's origins, we can make another hypothesis about the Dark. It was when Sister Friede (Elfriede of the Sable Church of Londor) arrived that the Painted World of Ariandel was overtaken with Dark. We'll cover the painted world's backstory in greater detail. For now, we'll simply assume that Sulyvahn had already been overtaken by Dark before he left his homeland. This would mean he was also the one to corrupt the Flame of the Profaned Capital, and not the other way around. Unfortunately, although this theory answers some questions, the timeline is still hazy. Did Sulyvahn leave the Painted World before or after Friede arrived and began wreaking havoc on it? We can't know for sure. The "loss" Sulyvahn had not yet experienced could also be an allusion to the decline of his people, the crows, precipitated by Friede. Once again, with a murky timeline and scattered information, plenty of mystery still revolves around this important character in the story. At the same time, we get some essential clues to get us thinking: an exciting narrative balance, and a fascinating enemy!

❦ Vordt and the Dancer of the Boreal Valley

Under Sulyvahn's tyrannical rule, many "outrider" knights were spread out to strategic areas of the kingdom of Lothric, such as the Road of Sacrifices or the castle.

---

282. The group of crows on the roofs of the Grand Archives (which Sulyvahn helped build) makes more sense in light of the DLC's revelations.
283. From the description of the Greatsword of Judgement.

They prove formidable enemies, who we must fight to complete the quest. Like these outriders, Vordt and the Dancer were charged with stopping the Unkindled from reaching the old Lords of Cinder. At the game's outset, Vordt blocks the exit to the High Wall of Lothric, while the fight with the Dancer takes place towards the end of the game[284] in the cathedral of this same area, just before players can enter Lothric Castle. "Vordt served as an outrider knight, never far from the fleeting Dancer." They were inseparable; but the question of whether they were bound by friendship or love is unclear. The arenas of the two bosses are located only a few dozen meters from each other.

Just like the Boreal Outrider Knights, who look like the Corvian Knights of the Painted World of Ariandel, Vordt and the Dancer have something bestial about them. "But beware. The dog keeps a close eye on things. The vile watchdog of the Boreal Valley." This is from Emma's description of Vordt. The "watchdog's" movements are that of a rabid dog, particularly in its second form, when it becomes more aggressive. It's harder to say which animal the Dancer looks like, but her stance and long limbs recall those of the Corvian Knights, with more grace.

"The knights were given the eyes of the Pontiff, but the eyes transformed them into savage, raving warriors who only knew how to serve as mindless guards," reads the description of the Outrider Knight Helm. The Dancer's Armor adds that "the black eyes of the Pontiff eventually transformed the Dancer into a beastly creature, her armor fusing with her own hide." Subjugated and dehumanized, the Outrider Knights, with Vordt and the Dancer at the helm, had no choice but to serve Sulyvahn's tyrannical orders. Though we know nothing of Vordt's past, the Dancer wasn't destined for this life of suffering.

She came from a long line of royalty. There are two hypotheses we can make on this subject. As we saw when looking at the game's story, she could be Gwynevere's daughter. Transposing her soul produces the Soothing Sunlight miracle, formerly created by the Princess of Sunlight. We can imagine that when Sulyvahn, as scholar and member of the royal court, served as Prince Lothric's mentor, he was able to convince Gwynevere's daughter to follow him to Irithyll. Or it's possible that the Dancer descends from Yorshka, Gwyn's hidden child, and that Sulyvahn forced her to serve him when he appointed himself Pontiff. The only support for this theory lies in the geography, since Yorshka lived in Irithyll of the Boreal Valley, the region from which both the Dancer and Vordt originate.

Either way, Sulyvahn gave the Dancer his enchanted swords and dubbed her an Outrider Knight. Mirroring those of the tyrant, these swords symbolize her devotion to him: "These blades, symbolic of the Dancer's vows, are enchanted with dark magic in the right hand, and fire in the left, mirroring the Pontiff," indicates the description of the Dancer's Enchanted Swords, attesting to the trust Sulyvahn had placed in her.

---

284. We can fight her at the beginning of the game, by killing Emma in the cathedral; of course, this makes for a challenging fight at this point in the adventure.

Phantoms of the Outrider Knights wander the streets of Irithyll. They appear for players from time to time in their non-bestial form, large and majestic, walking calmly through the streets of their city, before disappearing into thin air. These phantoms are reminders of former times, when knights hadn't yet seen the black eyes of Sulyvahn, and didn't yet know what bestial lives they were to lead. Not far from the Church of Yorshka, we can spot two ethereal silhouettes, walking side by side. One, thinner than the other, appears to be a woman. She wears a veil–the Dancer's Crown. However, it's hard to get a good look at them, because the Fire Witches (more of Sulyvahn's minions) are simultaneously doing their best to cast spells on us. Their magic comes directly from the Profaned Flame, which Sulyvahn brought back from the capital of the same name.

The Profaned Capital

⚜ Yhorm the Giant

Yhorm is the Lord of Cinder from the Profaned Capital, the city destroyed in an explosion after the giant linked the Fire. We won't retell this part of the story, but there's more about Yhorm to discuss.

First, in spite of being called a "giant," Yhorm is not related to the giants of the second episode. He's closer to the giants of the first or third episode–the blacksmith from Anor Londo, the archer from the Undead Settlement, the giants from the battlefield located behind Irithyll's cathedral, and those imprisoned in the Cathedral of the Deep and Irithyll Dungeon. Yhorm seems even larger and more imposing. This is a constant throughout the *Souls* series: size equals strength. Large beings are generally stronger than the others. Thus, Yhorm is a giant among giants. Ambitious and proud, "the descendant of an ancient conqueror,"[285] he wields a large machete and shield, heavy and terrifying. The fight against this exceptional being has its fair share of challenges, because without an adequate weapon, it's hard to deal any damage. Thankfully, the Storm Ruler sword is nearby in the boss room, amid the charred bodies and unscathed valuables of the Profaned Capital. Yhorm was not popular with his people when he reigned over the city, and he gave this weapon "to the humans that doubted him,"[286] in order to regain their trust and defuse the tension. Also known as the Giantslayer, the sword is a lifesaver for players, because it deals significant damage to this force of nature.

285. From the description of the Soul of Yhorm the Giant.
286. From the description of the Storm Ruler.

In the middle of the fight, Yhorm loses his temper and draws on Fire for supernatural strength. All of the Lords of Cinder have this power, and use it in the second phase of their fights. Linking the Fire gave them this ability, and they don't hesitate to use it when in danger. With this power, Aldrich combines his violet magic with Fire; the Abyss Watchers are revived after losing all of their health points and work together as one fighter, with a flaming sword and renewed health; finally, Yhorm lights up in flames, without changing his attack strategy. Unlike his fellow Lords, Yhorm burns throughout the entire fight. From the beginning, his arms and stomach glow red, a bit like the bodies of the Unkindleds when they consume an ember and recover all their abilities. This may be a hint that the giant is at the height of his ability, unlike Aldrich, who is much too occupied with devouring Gwyndolin, or the Abyss Watchers, plagued by the evil in their kingdom and attacking one another during the fight. Yhorm is perfectly prepared to fight, waiting for players calmly on his lord throne in the Profaned Capital.

The giant is also waiting for an old friend, to whom he once gave another Storm Ruler sword; a "dear friend"[287] who promised him he would return to the Profaned Capital to kill Yhorm if he ever came back from the dead. No doubt, becoming Lord of Cinder ended his solitary reign as his people's unpopular leader. In some ways, the giant Lord's act of linking the Fire can be seen as an attempt to redeem himself. Though he had no idea his people and city would be burned to the ground after his sacrifice, he did predict he would be brought back to life. This is why he gave the sword to his faithful friend and began waiting for him once he was revived by the bell's toll. Refusing to sit on his throne in the Firelink Shrine, he preferred to wait on his own, in his now-ruined city. The man who made him a promise stayed true to his word: Siegward of Catarina would come back to kill him.

⚜ Siegward of Catarina

Siegward is the onion knight from this third episode. His name, his chivalrous bearing, his long quest, and of course his armor, are all references to the excellent Siegmeyer of the first episode. Siegmeyer, later joined by his daughter, had arrived in Lordran in search of new adventures after the death of his wife. He crossed paths with players on a number of occasions. Although he was bent on being generous and helping players out, this often backfired, and players had to save him. His jovial and kind manner, common for people from the region of Catarina, made up for his flaws. Strangely, there were no knights from Catarina in *Dark Souls II*–players can simply

---

287. From the description of the Storm Ruler.

choose to wear onion armor. Nevertheless, the armor's description ("the old tales speak of brave Catarina knights wearing this armor as they rushed courageously into battle") raises a temporal inconsistency, since Siegward appears in the third episode. No matter! The timeline is admittedly a little wonky.

The first meeting with Siegward takes place in the church of the Undead Settlement, where he helps us fight a powerful demon. Some of Siegward's character traits are already clear: optimist, a bit thick, and a little timid around danger, he nevertheless throws himself into the fight with courage, addressing players thus: "I, Siegward of the Knights of Catarina, fight by your side!" After the demon's defeat, he cheerfully takes out a bit of Siegbräu (literally "victory beer") to celebrate the moment with his new friend, before settling in for a little nap.

This good-natured camaraderie continues to the entryway of the Cathedral of the Deep, where we find Siegward stuck at the bottom of a well... totally naked. "Someone's swiped my armour," he says. Of course, it's up to us to find it. This is when, in the cathedral, Unbreakable Patches succeeds once again in trapping us. We nevertheless retrieve the poor guy's armor and bring it back to him in the well. Once he's been saved, Siegward starts off on his quest once more, ending his dialogue with "No need to worry about me."

Later on, in the Irithyll kitchens, we find the Catarina knight snoozing. Between two naps, he shares a succulent estus soup and a swig of Siegbräu. It's a nice, peaceful moment in the middle of all the hostility. Siegward takes advantage of this to reveal the goal of his quest, the promise he made to Yhorm, the "reclusive giant lord," as he calls him. But before he can return to the Profaned Capital, Siegward is locked up in a cell in Irithyll Dungeon.

Once again, we come to his rescue, by finding the key to his cell. This time, we get a nice reward for our help—a Titanite Slab, the rarest of the upgrade materials—, suggesting that his quest is nearly at its end. Siegward finishes his dialogue with, "I've [...] a duty to fulfil, very soon..."

Finally, in the depths of the Profaned Capital, the two companions begin their fight against the giant. "Yhorm, old friend. I, Siegward of the Knights of Catarina, have come to uphold my promise! Let the sun shine upon this Lord of Cinder." Faced with two adversaries each armed with the Storm Ruler sword, Yhorm doesn't last long, and succumbs to their repeated assaults. However, Siegward can also die definitively in this fight. And even if he survives, he'll thank the hero and make one final toast before settling into a final nap: once his quest has been fulfilled and his promise kept, Siegward dies.

This is not a common occurrence in the *Souls* games. Siegward's fate echoes that of some Japanese ghosts, who can't leave the world of the living until they perform certain tasks. Perhaps the knight's soul remained tied to the promise he made to Yhorm, and it can only rest in peace once it has accomplished the task. Taking this into account, it's possible that the timeline is actually consistent: the region of Catarina could also belong to a far-off past. Only Siegward would have continued to wander this hostile labyrinth, striving unsuccessfully to reach Yhorm's throne. With players' help, he finally arrives. In days of old, the two comrades would have visited many lands, from the Undead Settlement to the Profaned Capital, covering the kingdom of Lothric with optimism and solidarity.

Lothric Castle and the Grand Archives

❦ High Priestess Emma

Outside of the Firelink Shrine, Emma is the first non-hostile NPC we meet, in the cathedral of the High Wall of Lothric. She's not exactly friendly, focusing on the importance of Fire, but her dialogue is comforting for the Ashen One in its insistence on the importance of the quest: "Are you not a Lordseeker? Head to the base of the High Wall and seek the Lords of Cinder. Is this not the calling of your kind, since ages past?" In addition to this interesting temporal indication, which suggests that much time has passed since the bell tolled, Emma helps players leave the area by giving them a Small Lothric Banner. When raised, this banner serves as a signal to winged creatures who escort players to the Undead Settlement below the High Wall. This scene instantly recalls the player's arrival in Anor Londo in the first *Dark Souls*. The gargoyles in charge of transportation are identical, as well as the scene itself, though it goes in the opposite direction. In the first game, we climbed up to Anor Londo, with a stunning panorama from the city's ramparts, while from the High Wall, we have a breathtaking view, and descend with help from the gargoyles as the scene narrows in on the Undead Settlement.

Emma is also leader of the Way of Blue covenant, in co-op with the Blades of the Dark Moon, attesting to her unwavering support for Fire. As a high priestess and wet nurse for Prince Lothric, she continues to hope that he will link the Fire and become Lord of Cinder. When players have collected cinder from all of Lothric's predecessors, she summons them and begs them to reason with the prince, or to kill him if reason is not sufficient: "Prince Lothric is in your hands. Please save his soul. Tell him what he must be... A Lord." These are her last words. Then, she disappears, with wounds from a fight, likely inflicted by the Dancer of the Boreal Valley, who also attacks players point-blank to prevent them from reaching Prince Lothric.

❦ The Twin Princes

One of the great surprises of *Dark Souls III* arises during the fight with Prince Lothric. Plot twist: there are not one, but two princes. Lorian is the older, and Lothric the younger.

Long before the intrigues of the Fire, and before hopes were placed in his brother, Lorian was a talented knight. His most glorious achievement was when he "single-handedly slayed the demon prince," according to his weapon, Lorian's Greatsword. This sword remained eternally scorched with the flame associated with the demons: Chaos. The Demon Prince's identity is somewhat vague: he's likely the heir to the Old Demon King we fight near the Smoldering Lake. We'll come back to the demon's story in a section devoted to him. Pleased with his victory over the Demon Prince, Lorian was one of the most lauded princes of his kingdom.

At the same time, his younger brother Lothric was being groomed to become Lord of Cinder. He was given Lothric's Holy Sword, a sword of champions blessed by High Priestess Emma, along with a Hood of Prayer, which he would wear for the rest of his life. Though "born into illness, a frail and shriveled child,"[288] Prince Lothric was considered a savior, the one who would sacrifice himself to renew the Age of Fire. Born to King Oceiros and the goddess Gwynevere, just after his twin Lorian, he was the last in the line of Gwyn, the first Lord of Cinder. "Holy King Lothric, Last hope of his Line": this is inscribed on the back of Lothric's throne in the Firelink Shrine. The prince's arrival was long-awaited, even turning to an "obsession," as Lothric's Cinders of a Lord indicate, adding that "the path to linking the Fire is a cursed one indeed." All this reflects the heavy burden that weighed first on the royal family, before settling on the frail shoulders of the young prince. The word "curse" haunted Prince Lothric–so much so that Lorian left his order of chivalry to assist his cursed brother. Together, they faced their terrible fate. The decision had dire consequences for Lorian, who was "left mute and crippled by his younger brother's curse."[289]

Later, swayed by Sulyvahn, the First of the Scholars, Lothric and Lorian refused to link the Fire. They nevertheless bore the full brunt of the curse, which continued to irreversibly weigh upon them and their line. During the twins' fight, Lothric refers to this terrible curse a number of times: "The fire linking curse, the legacy of lords, let it all fade into nothing," he says upon our arrival, clearly setting the scene and laying out his position. Addressing his defeated brother on the ground, he adds: "Rise, if you would... For that is our curse," referring to the call of Fire that revives the former Lords of Cinder. Finally, once the twins have been defeated, Lothric admits to us: "Mark my words, Ashen One... You remain among the Accursed." These final words invoke the game's first ending, when the player's Unkindled links the Fire and becomes the next Lord of Cinder.

---

288. From the description of his Hood of Prayer.
289. From the description of Lorian's Helm.

The prince's repeated words echo like a theatrical song's grim refrain. Once the fight's introduction has concluded, the battle takes place in two acts, accompanied by fascinating music, both epic and profoundly sad. And if Lothric presents the verses and choruses, silent Lorian performs the choreography until his death. Then, Lothric enters the scene, reviving his brother, who bears him on his back. The mind and body become one, and we must kill the younger prince in order to end their performance: Lothric acts as an unlikely puppeteer, continually bringing his twin back to life to postpone the inevitable. The fight is unforgettable, a climactic moment in this third *Dark Souls*. The boss fight uses original attack patterns, and mixes new story revelations, memorable visuals and emotion.

The brother remains well hidden throughout the adventure, offering up an excellent surprise for players. It requires extensive attention to detail, since the rest of the adventure is quite traditional: four Lords of Cinder must be fought (each with a specific backstory and environment) and their long-awaited cinders must be returned to the Firelink Shrine. Of course, most will detect something strange about Lothric, but no one expects that, upon opening the door,[290] a twin brother will emerge suddenly by his side to fight in his stead. From the beginning of the adventure, everything led us to believe that Lothric was Fire's last hope, as if Lorian had never existed. This plot twist also leads us to reconsider the perspective of Oceiros and Gwynevere when the twins were born. They had so desired an heir, and henceforth had two. This unexpected event required them to make a difficult choice, with Gwyn's divine legacy at stake. They chose the younger twin, whom they named Lothric, like the kingdom he was intended to save. He was raised in faith and doomed to a sacrifice,[291] while his brother Lorian was raised as a knight. They were therefore separated, chosen to walk different paths according to their parents' decision. But Lothric proved weak, and his brother became strong. Everything was done to raise up the younger prince by inscribing his name, without his twin brother's, in the kingdom's annals.

Dark Souls III thus presents a pessimistic vision of destiny, a forced fate chosen by the parents in the name of the state, which leads only to despair and the kingdom's downfall. Lorian returns to aid his brother, thus sacrificing himself and losing his physical prowess in the process. Back together, the twins fight the Fire's decline with unexpected passion and strength, blowing away all predictions. These two brothers, once acting as one,[292] were responsible for the tolling of the bell. Though a direct

---

290. This superbly wrought door contains the Three Pillars of the kingdom of Lothric, referring to a time when these entities worked together.

291. Many statues of Lothric Castle represent knights attempting self-decapitation, and others hold their own head in their hands. This morbid decor depicts the idea of sacrifice, as if Oceiros and Gwynevere had devoted their entire kingdom to Fire, until death.

292. In players' second time around (New Game+), we can fuse Loran and Lothric's swords, each obtained by transfusing their souls, to forge the Twin Princes' Greatsword.

descendant of Gwyn, the Fire's last hope proves to bring about the end of the world in a highly ironic twist, confirming that it's really time for the Age of Fire to end.

⚜ The Black Hand

The Black Hand was a secret organization charged with protecting Prince Lothric. Made up of hunters, it acted in the shadow of the Three Pillars of the kingdom. As for each of the Three Pillars, there is a Hunter's Ring (in addition to the Priestess, Scholar and Knight's ring), the description of which reveals the Black Hand's machinations. "The hunters serve Lothric on the fringes and in the shadows. For generations, rulers of Lothric have relied especially upon the Black Hand hunters to punish enemies in ways that the king's Three Pillars cannot." However, there are few hunters. To enter their ranks, one must serve several generations of sovereigns, demonstrating exceptional prudence and longevity. In fact, since the creation of the Black Hand, "no more than three such individuals have borne this distinction."[293] During the adventure, two of them are identified: Gotthard and Kamui. The identity of the third member of the Black Hand remains a mystery, but we can assume it is the corpse on which we find the Hunter's Ring.

Gotthard[294] is an NPC we can summon for help against certain bosses. However, he breathes his last near the end of the game; we find his corpse lying in front of the door to the Grand Archives just after defeating Dragonslayer Armor. Gotthard was one of the few who held a Grand Archives Key: the archives were home to scholars who were declared heretics, and access to this location was sealed off by the high priestess and the knights. The description of the Gotthard Twinswords, a characteristic weapon for the Black Hand hunters, indicates that the twinswords' owner once "fled the castle." His flight, and ownership of a Grand Archives Key, could suggest that he decided to remain faithful to King Oceiros after the king's decision to join the heretical scholars, in spite of the sovereign's descent into madness, while the conflict between the Three Pillars initiated the kingdom's rapid downfall. On the other hand, his sidekick Kamui pledged allegiance to the prince.

Kamui can be recognized by his two unique katanas, Onikiri and Ubadachi, each a different length. The backstory of his first blade isn't provided, but we learn that the second was forged by Kamui himself in the Undead Settlement, which allowed him to join the proud ranks of the Black Hand. When the Three Pillars came into conflict, he decided to support the prince and was posted not far from the room where Lothric

293. From the description of the Black Hand Hat, distinctive with its broad, rounded brim.
294. "Gotthard" recalls the name Leonhard. The suffix "-hard" comes from an old German word meaning "courage." Though they aren't necessarily from same family, Leonhard also has noble origins, and both characters certainly come from the same region.

lived, charged with preventing anyone from entering. He carried out this mission alongside the Daughter of Crystal Kriemhild and Lion Knight Albert.

❦ Lothric's Personal Guard

Albert protects the twin princes, with help from Kamui and Kriemhild. These three powerful enemies put up a good fight against the lonely player. However, this isn't the first time we can meet Albert. He is one of the characters who can be summoned during fights. In particular, he helps players defeat Vordt of the Boreal Valley. There's an amusing yet significant detail: if we decide to kill Emma at the beginning of the game, Albert will refuse to be summoned by the high priestess's killer, evidence of his loyalty towards Fire and the royal family. Bearing a Greataxe and Golden Wing Crest Shield, his Faraam set is what especially distinguishes him from other knights. Faraam is the god of war of the people of Forossa; this is a reference to the second game in the series, and in particular the *Crown of the Ivory King* DLC. The far-off kingdom was destroyed,[295] but some (indestructible) armor from the knights stood the test of time. These soldiers were known as the "lion knights," and Albert, here known as "Lion Knight Albert," is one of their direct descendants. No one knows how he survived up until the era of the kingdom of Lothric, but his strength and courage are a testament to the olden days and knights such as the valiant Vengarl in *Dark Souls II*, giving him a prominent place among the prince's guard.

Next to the skillful Kamui and solid Albert, Kriemhild plays an important role in this trio of fighters, bringing sorcery to the table. Kriemhild's presence in the Untended Graves, as an invader this time, along with her Fire Keeper set, suggest a particular affinity with the Firelink Shrine. The exact reasons are unclear—perhaps she was close to the Shrine Handmaid, who seems to have served formerly as high priestess. The spellcaster's other unique feature, which earned her the name "Daughter of Crystal," is her Sage's Crystal Staff. The staff's description indicates that it was "presented as a gift from the Crystal Sages to their favorite pupil, Kriemhild": it's a powerful staff, allowing her to wield a variety of spells from the Grand Archives, the spells of her masters, the Crystal Sages.

295. The description of the Faraam Helm tells this legend: "The armor of the Forossa Lion Knights was preserved even after the destruction of their homeland."

❧ The Crystal Sages

Like the princes, the Crystal Sages are twins. These two enemies are associated with the Grand Archives, where they studied the old experiments of Seath the Scaleless and the magic of the famous Big Hat Logan. The Crystal Sages are Logan's self-proclaimed heirs, and they wear the same distinctive hat. They even go so far as to rewrite the legend of the Vinheim magician: "According to the Crystal Sage, old Big Hat achieved enlightenment within the Regal Archives, where he came to find the quintessence of sorcery in the facets of a certain crystal."[296] It's important to remember here that Seath was the originator of magic; he invented it using a strange mixture of crystals and souls. The crystals were also the fruit of his productive mind, as he worked to recreate the scales of his fellow dragons, which he himself lacked. Though the Crystal Sages lauded Seath and Logan's merits centuries later,[297] neither met a very glorious fate.

Indeed, we meet Logan in the first *Dark Souls* as he studies in Seath's archives. However, he seems to slowly go mad throughout the encounters, likely due to his unhealthy obsession with science and the types of discoveries he makes in his reading. Eventually, Seath also lost his mind. They both surrendered themselves to total isolation, and were slain by the player. The school of the Crystal Sages was built on the lofty legends of old. Alongside Lothric's scholars, these two sages worked within the Grand Archives for many years.

One of the two twins (considered a heretic in the kingdom) continues to live in this location. The other left for the region of Farron to help the Undead Legion, providing teachings from the school of sorcery. It's likely that Sulyvahn was responsible for overseeing the Grand Archives with the Crystal Sages, and that he influenced them: later, outside of Lothric, one of the brothers continued to watch over the archives' secrets, while the other assisted Farron's Legion.

Under the watchful eye of their protector, many vestiges remained locked in the Grand Archives. The large bookcases covering the building's walls were haunted by many ghosts, whose arms would pop out of books to assault anyone who gets too curious. To address this problem, the scholars would dunk their heads in a basin of soft wax before browsing the bookshelves: for some reason, this pacified the ghosts. That's why wax is everywhere in the Grand Archives, where it coats every nook and cranny. It's so pervasive that even the statues of scholars reading books are dripping with wax, rendering them misshapen and unsettling.

---

296. From the description of the Homing Crystal Soulmass.
297. The Crystal Scroll, necessary for producing crystal magic, says: "These sorceries are the work of the paledrake, Seath the Scaleless, whom Logan is said to have met, a branch of sorcery that has been carried on by the Crystal Sages."

Another statue in the Grand Archives depicts a Primordial Serpent. Is this a reference to Kaathe or Frampt from the first episode? Or maybe a newcomer? The Primordial Serpents all have identical faces, which makes them difficult to identify. It's still unclear why this type of statue would be inside the Grand Archives. One detail stands out, however. The body of the being in this statue is different from the body of the Primordial Serpents. He almost seems anthropomorphic, except that in place of arms, he has little, perfectly formed wings, very different from Pontiff Sulyvahn's featherless crow wings, or those of the corvians we encounter in the Grand Archives. Could there be a connection between this Primordial Serpent statue and the almost divine angels of the kingdom of Lothric? The angels are affiliated with Gertrude, the Heavenly Daughter, and the large cage full of feathers that hangs above the Grand Archives.

❦ Gertrude, the Heavenly Daughter

Gertrude's name appeared earlier when we identified one of Gwynevere's daughters, but we didn't mention her affiliation with the heavens or with angels, simply because this isn't a central part of the story of the kingdom of Lothric. Also, the scant information we have about the angels means we have to speculate quite a bit.

Gertrude's story is rather simple, though fairly mysterious. It's perfectly summed up by the description of the Divine Pillars of Light miracle: "The Queen's holy maiden Gertrude was visited by an angel, who revealed this tale to her. Despite losing both her sight and voice, she was determined to record the tale. Ordinary men cannot decipher her fragmentary scrawl, nor comprehend how it became the foundation of the Angelic faith of Lothric." The identity of the angel who visited Gertrude is not revealed, but we could guess that it's the Primordial Serpent depicted with angel wings in the Grand Archives. He appeared to Gertrude, sharing some information that would change the young woman's vision of the world. In the first episode, Kaathe easily swayed the Four Kings of New Londo towards the Dark, while Frampt did the same for Gwyndolin with Fire. The Primordial Serpents adore influencing the powerful from the shadows. Following this divine intervention, Gertrude began to develop the Angelic faith in the kingdom of Lothric. Of course, this upset the Three Pillars, and the Angelic faith was declared heretical. The Heavenly Daughter was imprisoned in the Grand Archives, as her winged servants and knights began to wage civil war within the kingdom. Later on, players can see the damage caused by the battles between the knights of Lothric and the winged knights, particularly in a small spot on the High Wall, where a formidable winged knight still roams among the corpses of dozens of the kingdom's soldiers.

Three of the winged soldiers were assigned to protect the route to Gertrude's cage. They developed small wings and increased physical strength, and then donned magnificent gold attire and giant weapons. Posted on the roofs of the Grand Archives, they kill any visitors without hesitation. The three of them together are as strong as they are tough, and they put up quite the challenging fight.

Unfortunately, once we reach the cage, we see that Gertrude is no longer there, or at least that she's no longer alive. In her place lies a desiccated body, some scattered white feathers, and the marks of the famous Divine Pillars of Light miracle. Time may have gotten the better of her, or perhaps the scholars got to her in their experiments, as suggested by the description of the Crystal Chime, found not far from the first wax basin: "A sacred chime, once the possession of Gertrude, the Heavenly Daughter, and defiled by the scholars of the Grand Archives." They affixed crystals to Gertrude's chime, so it could be used to cast both miracles and sorceries. It's unclear why Gertrude died, even though a Man-Grub can be seen on the beams below her cage. As we've seen, the placement of Rosaria's servants isn't random, and it's likely that the Mother of Rebirth and the Heavenly Daughter are one and the same, silent and worshiped. If this is the case, then Gertrude was able to escape her cage, and faked her death (the corpse bearing the miracle), and went to the Cathedral of the Deep. In this, she was perhaps even helped by Sulyvahn, who was also in exile at the time.

Strangely, the angels themselves are considered heretics, like the scholars of the Grand Archives. It's pure speculation, but their opposition to the Fire may be why the high priestess called them "heretics" in the first place. Apart from the close ties between Sulyvahn and the Dark, it may have been Darkstalker Kaathe himself who appeared to Gertrude and was considered an angel!

⚜ Gwynevere, Princess of Sunlight

The mother of Gertrude and queen of Lothric is often mentioned but never appears in the game. She didn't really appear in the first *Dark Souls*, either, since players only view the illusion of her created by Gwyndolin. In Lothric, too, the Princess of Sunlight seems to have recently vanished as we explore the kingdom. The Divine Blessing description indicates that "After giving birth to Ocelotte, her youngest, she quietly disappeared." The same item also describes when Gwynevere was in her prime: "The Queen of Lothric, married to the former King Oceiros, was initially revered as a goddess of fertility and bounty." The queen was loved and started a family in order to perpetuate the teachings of her father Gwyn, first Lord of Cinder. Unfortunately, she only had daughters, and it seems that only sons are allowed to link the Fire. However, it may not be impossible... The game doesn't go into how women and men are different on this level; we can play the game with a female avatar and still link the Fire, becoming the next Lord of Cinder, both in *Dark Souls I* and *III*. The rule is a bit unclear, but either way, Gwynevere did everything she could to produce a male heir, and eventually she did. After Lothric and Lorian, she gave birth to Ocelotte. The latter was not a natural child, but rather resulted from the experiments conducted by King Oceiros, who was obsessed with the crystals and dragons of the Grand Archives. This madness led Gwynevere to leave her children and her fallen kingdom, just as she fled from Anor Londo in the age of its downfall.

⚜ Oceiros, the Consumed King

No one knows what King Oceiros's life was like, or the customs of the kingdom of Lothric, prior to Gwynevere's arrival. The story only mentions their marriage, family and gloomy fate, which led to the kingdom's collapse. The Soul of Consumed Oceiros tells of the devolution of the king, after his son, Prince Lothric, refused to become Lord of Cinder: "Oceiros went mad trying to harness his royal blood for a greater purpose, leading him to the heretics of the Grand Archives, where he discovered the twisted worship of Seath the paledrake."

Besides meeting Gwynevere, his discovery of Seath's experiments was the most pivotal event of his life. In his madness, he disowned his progeny and convinced his wife to bear a final child: Ocelotte. Ocelotte was born part-human, part-dragon. After Gwynevere's flight, Oceiros decided to hide below Lothric Castle, taking Ocelotte with him. Assassins were hired to put a stop to this madness. Though none returned to confirm that the Consumed King had been killed, he was nevertheless declared dead. In reality, he continued to hide away in the Consumed King's Garden, as we can see when we go through this location and fight the boss Oceiros.

With the exception of his supposed death, the rest of his life is confirmed during the fight. Oceiros is raving mad, now partly transformed into a pale, scaleless dragon, like Seath. He's lost his son Ocelotte, and searches for him desperately: "Ahh, dear little Ocelotte. Where have you gone? Are you hiding from me? Come out, come out, don't be afraid. You were born a child of dragons, what could you possibly fear? Now, now, show yourself, Ocelotte," he says mid-fight, paying little attention to the intruder he is currently battling. His son occupies all of his thoughts. He confesses before the fight that "he is all that I have," which explains his great distress. A baby's cries can be heard from time to time during the duel: is this a memory from a former time (since Ocelotte was born long ago), or are the small cries produced by the Consumed King before he launches one of his powerful attacks? Either way, Ocelotte no longer lives in this area. Some clues in the room next to the boss location provide an idea of where the small dragon is possibly hidden: Archdragon Peak. In addition to the Drakeblood

Set, which indicates that these knights were "worshippers of the blood of dragons,"[298] the "Path of the Dragon" gesture provides supporting evidence for Archdragon Peak. This optional (well-hidden) area is accessible using the "Path of the Dragon" gesture in a precise spot in Irithyll Dungeon, which offers an unobstructed view over this mysterious peak that rises above the fog. Players are then teleported to the imposing ruins of Archdragon Peak, the final refuge of the wyverns and dragons, and seemingly a good spot for a young dragon gone astray. Nothing on the peak supports this hypothesis, however, and the fate of Oceiros and Gwynevere's son remains unknown.

Archdragon Peak

The secondary area of Archdragon Peak contains many references to the previous episodes. For instance, using the "Path of the Dragon" gesture when facing the statue of a black dragon produces the Calamity Ring, a ring with "no useful powers": it causes wearers to take double damage without providing any benefits. The item is a reference to Kalameet, the crafty boss from the *Artorias of the Abyss* DLC. Farther on, players are attacked by a knight who wears the attire of Havel the Rock, armed with the mythical Dragon Tooth, whose description says that the weapon was "created from an everlasting dragon tooth that will never break," likely taken from the enormous dead dragon lying in the fight area: this serves as quick and easy fan service, allowing players to pick up a weapon with totally excessive properties, as in all of the games. Finally, two familiar characters appear, or are mentioned, after we have explored Archdragon Peak: the Nameless King, who is none other than Gwyn's firstborn, and Dragonslayer Ornstein.

⚜ The Nameless King, the Firstborn

The Nameless King is the frightening boss in this area: it's a difficult fight, with two phases: before fighting him we must first defeat the dragon he rides, called the King of the Storm. But the challenge posed by these two enemies is less interesting than the identity of the Nameless King. Though he remains nameless, many clues suggest that he is actually the firstborn of Gwyn, the former god of war, whose name was forgotten after he was disowned by his father.

---

298. From the description of the Drakeblood Helm.

"The Nameless King was once a dragon-slaying god of war, before he sacrificed everything to ally himself with the ancient dragons," reads the description of the Soul of the Nameless King.

The Lightning Storm miracle continues this description: "Once a slayer of dragons, the former king and God of war tamed a Stormdrake, on which he led a lifetime of battle. This miracle is likely a tale of their bond."

"Crown of a nameless king who was ally to the ancient dragons. This golden crown, buried amidst long strands of bristling ash, is said to closely resemble that of the First Lord," according to the Golden Crown worn by the Nameless King.

The Dragonslayer Swordspear has something to add on the subject: "A dragon hunting weapon from the age of the gods. The earliest form of the cross spear, serving as both a sword and a spear. Its owner was the Nameless King, a deific hunter of dragons. The swordspear is imbued with lightning, of which he was the heir."

Finally, the firstborn was also known for having created the Warrior of Sunlight covenant. This covenant rewards cooperation between players with its famous sunlight medals, decorated with an image of the sun. Interestingly, this sun symbol can be seen at various points on Archdragon Peak, particularly in the bottoms of containers hidden throughout the environment.

By analysing information on the items associated with the Nameless King, we can guess at his history. First, he was the heir of Gwyn, the First Lord, who held the power of lightning. As part of the dragonslayer regiment, he fought the dragons alongside his father, before betraying him and joining forces with his enemies. Notably, he forged ties with the King of the Storm, a dragon who had an affinity with lighting, according to his name and the description of the Lightning Storm miracle. This element was much feared by many of his fellow dragons, who were vulnerable to lightning. This betrayal led Gwyn to renounce his firstborn, and his name was expunged from the records.

Some fans have suggested specific identities for the Nameless King. Of these various hypotheses, two seem particularly intriguing. Some think he is Faraam, God of War from the region of Forossa. In addition to the fact that both are gods of war, the engraving on the Faraam Helm is what most catches the eye. It depicts a knight facing a dragon, recalling the ancient battle waged by the Nameless King alongside Gwyn and the dragonslayer knights. The second theory is a bit more convoluted: it posits that he is the eponymous god of Sen's Fortress from the first *Dark Souls*. This supposition is based on the many serpent men we can find around Archdragon Peak: this species is hardly found in the other areas of the game, but is common in Sen's Fortress. And yet, we know that this fortress was built by the gods to secure the only entry point to the city of Anor Londo. It is certainly possible that it was constructed by Gwyn's firstborn and named after him, before he decided to team up with the dragons.

⚜ Dragonslayer Ornstein

After the battle against the Nameless King, we can reach the end of this location. Here, we find Ornstein's set, from the captain of the dragonslayers and the emblematic boss of the first episode. This appears to be another instance of fan service: it introduces an inconsistency, since Ornstein left long ago. However, we don't find the equipment on a body: it's simply lying on the ground. The Sacred Oath miracle, which we receive by ranking up in the Warrior of Sunlight covenant, also cryptically suggests a tie between Ornstein and the Nameless King: "This is the tale of the Sun's firstborn, his faithful first knight, and the brave dragonslayer who served them both."

The "Sun's firstborn," refers to the Nameless King, "his faithful first knight" could be Solaire from the first game,[299] and Ornstein could be the "brave dragonslayer." In addition to the reference planted for series fans, Ornstein's armor is justified by this relationship he had with the Nameless King at the beginning of the age of gods. The dragonslayers used similar combat techniques and some affinity with lightning, due to their former allegiance with Gwyn's legions.

The Undead Settlement

⚜ Holy Knight Hodrick of the Mound-Makers

This character has already come up in previous paragraphs as the grandfather of Sirris of the Sunless Realms. We already know some of his story, but the path we take to find him at the beginning of the game is original, to say the least. In the Undead Settlement, a hidden path leads players to face a formidable creature armed with a two-man saw, bearing a cage on its back that appears identical to the one holding Cornyx of the Great Swamp not far from there. Instead of jumping head first into a rough fight, we have to sneak nimbly up onto his back, and climb in the cage! This action doesn't come spontaneously to many, but it allows us to discover Hodrick's lair, which is none other than the Pit of Hollows where we later face the Curse-Rotted Greatwood. Hodrick has joined the Mound-Makers covenant. This covenant is a group of hollows who have chosen to team up in response to the conflict between gods and men, due to the decline of the Age of Fire and the rise of the Age of Dark. The Warmth pyromancy sorcery, obtained by ranking up in this covenant, succinctly describes the situation: "They feared separation from the gods and sought a familial bond." In

---

299. Of course, it could also be another Warrior of Sunlight, but the allusion to Solaire is all the more interesting since he can be summoned prior to the fight with Ornstein and Smough.

reality, this new "family" of hollows is a group of death-crazed fanaticists.[300] The covenant's purpose is to collect as many Vertebra Shackles from corpses as possible. "Only one such bone is found in the vertebrae, and the Mound-makers believe it to be a shackle of the gods. In their minds, each victim is another connection, an addition to the family," reads the description of this unique item, recalling once again the Mound-makers' separation from the gods and their newly formed, tight-knit community.

Hodrick is one of these madmen, and in the brief time we spend with him, the Mound-makers' reputation for madness is not disproved. "Come here to pile up your victims, for that will form your anchor. You'll see when you go mad. They'll be your family," he says in the first encounter. It's creepy commentary, especially considering that the Pit of Hollows is crammed with corpses. Later on, Hodrick is even called the "mad dark spirit" when he invades us during our exploration of the Road of Sacrifices.

The Curse-Rotted Greatwood

Boss of the Undead Settlement, the Curse-Rotted Greatwood appears to us in the heights of the Pit of Hollows before the ground gives way, killing Hodrick in the process. The Greatwood is a tree full of curses, a source of many cursed souls. And, "eventually the curses took their toll."[301] The soul of the Curse-Rotted Greatwood is actually many small souls; transposing them produces the Hollowslayer Greatsword and Arstor's Spear, two weapons that once belonged to two different people. The first was that of a masked knight from Mirrah; the second belonged to Earl Arstor of Carim, whose name appeared in the first *Dark Souls*. These items' sinister descriptions suggest that these men served the Mound-makers. The Hollowslayer Greatsword "harbors the fears that lurk within the mind of Hollows," and the spear owned by Arstor, nicknamed the "Impaler," "is enwreathed in rotten, heavily poisonous meat." With a bit of speculation, it's possible that most of the cursed and corrupted souls of the giant tree belonged to the bloody Mound-makers, whose altar was located below the boss area, in the Pit of Hollows.

The Giant Archer

Another giant is hiding in the Undead Settlement. Perched atop the church's bell tower, he shoots enormous arrows at anyone wandering through the area where young white birch trees grow. However, we can meet him and make peace with him.

300. The term "mound-maker" on its own suggests a fascination with death.
301. From the description of the Curse-Rotted Greatwood Soul.

He gives us a Young White Branch, which we can use to pass risk-free through areas where he shoots his arrows.[302] Birches and branches are also connected to a character from the first episode, Princess Dusk of Oolacile. Indeed, one of the descriptions of the Young White Branch indicates that "Little Dusk's first sorcerer's staff eventually became a seedling, and then three white birch saplings." Oolacile was known in particular for its transformation sorceries, especially the Chameleon sorcery that "Transforms into something inconspicuous." Using the Young White Branch will turn players into branches, so the connection with Oolacile seems only logical!

Farron Keep

☙ The Abyss Watchers

Although we've generally looked at the Abyss Watchers' tale, the Farron Keep area deserves some attention: the area is vast, and highly detailed. The area reminds us of *Demon's Souls'* Valley Of Defilement, and to a lesser extent, Blighttown from *Dark Souls*, with its omnipresent poison. Since the level is particularly expansive, it's easy to get lost and die of poisoning if healing items become scarce, or to be struck down by the powerful tree-like enemies, the Ghrus, or the Darkwraiths. The Darkwraiths are first seen in *Dark Souls* and, as we mentioned in the section on Leonhard, they are closely tied to the Abyss, which tainted the area in the past.

According to the description of the Exile Mask, "Farron was consumed by a festering wood." No one knows how—perhaps due to a similar phenomenon to the convergence following the bell's toll–, but this "festering wood" was incorporated into the region of Farron. It brought the corruption of the Abyss, and condemned the ancient lands of the Undead Legion. As we saw when looking at the game's story, this forest is almost certainly the Darkroot Wood of the first episode. Items associated with Darkroot are relatively common, in fact. For instance, Pharis's attire, dropped by the Ghrus, comes directly from the famous *Dark Souls* archer who we met in Darkroot Wood. Also, many elements from Farron Keep refer to the Oolacile region. This isn't a coincidence: Darkroot Wood and Oolacile are the exact same place, in very different time periods. A little cave in Farron Keep was home to a sorcerer from Oolacile—the golden scroll, found in the cave, says as much. When given to Orbeck, the scroll allows us to learn some golden sorceries of the xanthous scholars, Oolacile's former sorcerers. In the cave, we also find an Antiquated Skirt that directly recalls the attire

---

302. The Giant Archer is no doubt a nod to Gough, the giant we met in the first *Dark Souls'* DLC.

worn by Princess Dusk of Oolacile from the first episode. A bit further on, the Crown of Dusk lies next to a white birch tree. The description reminds us that it was blessed by "guardian Elizabeth." Elizabeth was Dusk's godmother, whom we met at the beginning of the *Artorias of the Abyss* DLC. Her appearance was particularly striking: an anthropomorphic mushroom, like those we could spot in Darkroot Basin. Farron Keep contains the bodies of these "mushrooms" from Oolacile.

Everything we discover in Farron Keep seems to have ties to Darkroot or Oolacile. The Abyss Watchers have the same fate as Artorias (they battle the Abyss, then are corrupted by it); the area is strewn with vestiges of the ancient people of Oolacile; and in the upper levels of the area's central tower resides the Old Wolf of Farron, in a reference to Great Grey Wolf Sif, the unforgettable boss from Darkroot Basin.

⚜ The Old Wolf of Farron

The Abyss Watchers draw their strength from Farron's wolf's blood. They were able to develop enough power to become Lord of Cinder.[303] Afterwards, Farron Keep was overcome by corruption, forever transformed by the Abyss. The old wolf didn't disappear, however: he now leads the Watchdogs of Farron covenant, keeping watch over the "sleeping warriors," as they are called in the Exile Mask description. Its members ensure that nothing tarnishes the legends of the Abyss Watchers, who have fallen to great dishonor. As with Artorias, the dark truth would sully their good name, and the Watchdogs of Farron thus work to conceal the sinister truth. The keep's entry is jealously guarded by two robust watchers in their Exile Armor, bearing giant, ultra-powerful weapons. Though they must be defeated to continue the adventure, players are free to subsequently join the Old Wolf of Farron's ranks to prevent others from learning the sad fate of the Abyss Watchers.

⚜ The Farron Followers

The Farron Followers chose a different path from the previous group. "When a warrior of Farron fell to the Abyss, the tall, lean Followers, with their hollowed eyes, quietly appeared in groups to hunt them down," indicates the Follower Gloves. Armed with torches and shields strong enough to resist the Abyss, the Farron Followers hunted down those who had fallen prey to corruption. For unknown reasons, their

---

303. This episode is told in the description of the Abyss Watchers' Cinders of a Lord: "The Abyss Watchers swore upon their shared wolf's blood, which also served as their mandate as lords."

battle led them to the Painted World of Ariandel (which we see in the *Ashes of Ariandel* DLC). Perhaps they were chased from their land by the Watchdogs of Farron or by the ever-progressing Abyss, which they could no longer contain; or perhaps they were transformed into errant hollows, as the Follower Gloves suggest: "Farron and its Watchers fell to ruin, but the Followers survived as a wandering pack of hollows." Their roaming path must have led them to Londor, land of hollows, but they eventually discovered the entrance to the Painted World of Ariandel. This frozen, unchanging world was watched over by a former dignitary of the Sable Church of Londor, but we'll come back to this in a detailed presentation of the DLC. Regardless, the Farron Followers left the area forever and let the Abyss Watchers and Farron Keep fall into ruin.

The Catacombs of Carthus–Smoldering Lake

Past the Watchers' fight area is the entry to the Catacombs of Carthus, vestiges of a lost Sand Kingdom. As with Farron Keep, the Abyss came and brought with it destruction and damnation. There's nothing to suggest that the Catacombs of Carthus were originally right alongside Farron Keep–when the bell tolled and the lands converged, these regions may have also come together. In the same way, a tunnel within the lower catacombs leads to Smoldering Lake, home of the Demon Ruins, even though these areas are quite distinct.

⚜ High Lord Wolnir

Wolnir was once a conqueror of foreign lands. From Wolnir's Crown, we learn his story: "The Carthus conqueror. Once upon a time, such things were bequeathed judiciously to each of the rightful lords, until Wolnir brought them to their knees, and ground their crowns to dust. Then the crowns became one, and Wolnir, the one High Lord."[304] Demonstrating unrivaled courage, Wolnir also led an army of agile, loyal warriors. Their combat practices, made more effective by their singular curved swords, helped maintain this supremacy.[305] Wolnir and his disciples eventually controlled all

---

304. Wolnir's stature as great conqueror recalls the origins of Yhorm, the giant from the Profaned Capital, whose soul description labels him as "the descendant of an ancient conqueror." Could Wolnir and Yhorm be connected in some way? It's worth noting that their respective kingdoms are both tied to the Abyss or to the Dark.
305. "The sword technique of Carthus allows for fluid movement with a curved sword. Masters of the technique are said to dazzle their opponents by moving as weightlessly as a grain of sand": this explanation from the Carthus Milkring naturally echoes the exploits of the warriors of the Sand Kingdom. When this ring is worn, players disappear momentarily in mid-roll.

of Carthus and its surrounding areas. The sovereign's cruelty was such that he "sentenced countless souls to gruesome deaths, keen to outlive them all."[306] This desire to "outlive" all others went even beyond death: in *Dark Souls III*, we can fight him in the form of a giant skeleton, as he continues to lead the empire of the Catacombs of Carthus. His army also became skeletons, and its members claimed the title of "the grave wardens of Carthus." Since there are very few clues about the Sand Kingdom, it's hard to know if they've always been in skeletal form, or if it resulted from their transformation.

After the Catacombs of Carthus were drawn towards Lothric, the Abyss reached the lair of Wolnir, who could not fight Dark's corruption in spite of all of his past victories and conquests. Wolnir's Holy Sword tells us that "When Wolnir fell to the Abyss, he was gripped by a fear of true darkness, and pleaded to the gods for the first time." However, he succeeded in shutting himself away (no doubt with help from his warriors) with the Abyss in a magic chalice that players must interact with to continue the adventure towards Irithyll, the border of which is marked by the Catacombs of Carthus: players touch the chalice and fight Wanderer in a pitch-black setting overtaken by the Abyss. Thankfully, the lighted bracelets worn by the high lord allow us to see the area during the fight, and prove that Wolnir has not totally succumbed to corruption. This is also clearly a weak spot for him, and striking the skeleton's bracelets is one of the surest ways of defeating him. Without his lighted bangles, Wolnir disappears into the darkness of the Abyss.

⚜ The Old Demon King

Just before the room with the magic basin that leads to our fight with Wolnir, there's a curious hanging bridge. As an interesting side note, players can cut the bridge's ropes, and when it falls, use it to climb down along the steep wall to Smoldering Lake. With the giant sandworm[307] straight from the kingdom of Carthus[308] and the shower of bolts that rains down from an enormous ballista, this zone seems to be one of the most hostile. However, it does present some interesting features, particularly the Demon Ruins not far away. They're interesting more for their storyline value than as part of the gameplay: they're quite onerous to explore, and somewhat unrefined artistically.

---

306. From the description of the Soul of High Lord Wolnir.
307. This is clearly a reference to the sandworm from Frank Herbert's *Dune*. The creature's use of lightning also evokes the electric bolts that preceded the arrival of the sandworms in the deserts of Arrakis in David Lynch's film adaptation.
308. The description of the Yellow Bug Pellet tells us: "The grave wardens of Carthus used these to repel a great sand worm. The worm tumbled to the catacombs and proceeded to dominate its new home in the Smoldering Lake."

The Demon Ruins are the home of demons of old. Could these be the ruins of the legendary city of Izalith, subsumed by lava in the first episode? It's difficult to say. If this is indeed Izalith, it would be the demons' birthplace, created from Chaos when the Witch of Izalith attempted to relight the First Flame. Although the architecture doesn't really match, the Demon Ruins contain many relics with ties to the city of Izalith and the witch's daughters. For instance, many statues of the Taurus and Capra Demons from the first episode adorn the area's hallways. We can also find two pyromancy tomes: that of Quelana[309] and that of Izalith, which, as we've seen, will make Cornyx of the Great Swamp very happy.

These ruins are home to the last living demon. He's the Old Demon King, and his soul tells us that: "The shriveled Old Demon King is now like a clump of burnt ash, but he is the last living witness of the Chaos of Izalith." The king serves as this area's boss, but this foppish character, the last of his kind, doesn't stand much of a chance against players. Weak, almost pathetic, the Old Demon King tries to take his opponent with him by triggering a final explosion of the Chaos Flame, which leaves him mostly paralyzed and vulnerable to a final blow. It's a strange fight, inviting players to end this line of creatures for no apparent reason.

The Hopes of Londor

Far from these regions under Chaos's control is Londor, Land of Hollows. We've already mentioned it on countless occasions, but this place remains one of the most mysterious. We know only that it's located to the south of Lothric, and that it teems with hollows. They await a lord to lead them, in accordance with the Sable Church of Londor, the towers of which rise above the desolation in the distance.[310] This powerful religious organization no doubt originated the prophecy from the game's introduction, pushing the pilgrims to head north: "The fire fades, and the lords go without thrones." The Sable Church continues the line of Darkstalker Kaathe. In the first episode, this Primordial Serpent advised players to end the Age of Fire to usher in the Age of Dark. The pilgrims therefore made their way towards Lothric to watch the downfall of Fire. Yoel was one of them.

---

309. This tome can be found on the petrified corpse of a giant spider who also looks like Quelaag, another of the Witch of Izalith's daughters and formidable boss of the first game.
310. The Morion Blade with its eight small, jagged lateral blades, was made "resembling the towers of the Sable Church of Londor."

❧ Yoel the Pilgrim

At one end of the Undead Settlement, amid a troop of petrified pilgrim corpses, we find Yoel, who also waits for a death that will not come. "Please, grant me death. Undo my shackles," he says to players, who are the first to stumble upon him. Then, changing his mind, he sees hope in this Unkindled who bears the Darksign, and begins using the honorific "Champion of Ash." He dedicates himself to the service of his champion and offers us Dark Sigils: once we collect all eight of them, we can become the long-awaited Lord of Hollows of Londor.

Yoel also offers his service to another Unkindled, Anri, and her companion Horace.

❧ Anri and Horace

We won't go back over the questline of these agreeable characters: instead, we'll take a look at an intriguing parallel with the first *Dark Souls*. Anri of Astora's path is strikingly similar to the quest that would have been taken by Oscar of Astora from the first game. We met this knight at the beginning of the game, when he put us onto the Chosen Undead quest before dying suddenly. Originally, (according to information from the game's files) this character was going to play a greater role, with his path crossing the player's on multiple occasions. He was actually also attempting to complete the Chosen Undead prophecy before eventually losing his mind and becoming hollow. The parallel with Anri is interesting from this perspective, because in addition to their common geographic origins and the fact that they both have the exact same equipment (and never show their faces), they play the same role as the player: Unkindled or Chosen Undead.

One detail upsets this comparison, however. In an old trailer from the first game, a knight in Astora Armor appeared, as if players were playing as Oscar. We see him retreat from the campfire in the Firelink Shrine, where he lets others rest, and addresses them with a hand signal, his back turned, with a resolute fist. Anri teaches this same gesture to players: it's called the "Quiet Resolve"!

❧ Yuria, Liliane and Elfriede, Mentors of the Sable Church

Once Yoel has given his Dark Sigils to players and to Anri, and having accomplished his mission, he quickly decides to return to the other resting pilgrims. This is when Yuria arrives at the Firelink Shrine. Dressed in all black, with her face hidden under a metal veil—an ornately decorated beak mask—, she explains our destiny as Lord of Hollows and guides us on our quest. At certain points throughout the game she puts on her Pale Shade Robe,[311] and helps us beat some difficult bosses. The members of the Sable Church of Londor who wear this garb are none other than the church's assassins; this reveals Yuria's double role, both as eminent founder (black robe) and a simple executioner (white robe).

The Sable Church of Londor was founded by three sisters. Yuria, whom we have now seen many times, was "the second eldest," one of the "three mentors of the Sable Church of Londor."[312] Liliane, the youngest, is only rarely mentioned: the description of the Londor Braille Divine Tome tells us that the texts were "first spoken by Liliane of the Sable Church," and the Dark Blade miracle says that she "is said to recount tales that portray the suffering and conflict of Hollows." The eldest sister and "leader of the Sable Church"[313] remains anonymous in the original game, and appears as Elfriede in the first DLC *Ashes of Ariandel*, which we'll examine now.

311. The term "shadow" is another way to refer to Londor's inhabitants. For example, when we create our character at the beginning of the game, we can choose Londor as our kingdom of origin, by selecting "Londor Shadow of Death" from the list.
312. From the description of the Beak Mask.
313. From the description of the Onyx Blade.

DLCs: Ashes of Ariandel and The Ringed City

Although the DLCs provide some new ideas and some interesting information regarding the main story (particularly Sulyvahn's origins for the first, and the pygmies in the second), the story is actually independent from the rest of the game and split into two parts in *Dark Souls III*'s DLCs. This is why we felt it was better to look at this diptych separately, with its story of the quest of Gael, the wandering slave knight, searching for two elements required by a Painting Woman: first, an Unkindled (called "Ash" in Gael's world) to inspire her, and the pigment she needs to paint her next painting. *Ashes of Ariandel* presents the setting and covers the first part of the quest, while *The Ringed City* allows players to go to the end of the world looking for the desired pigments, all the way to the Dark Soul. The famous and mysterious (eponymous) Dark Soul is thus brought back into this second DLC, bringing the series to a terrific end.

The Painted World of Ariandel

❧ New Perspective on the Painted Worlds

The Painted World of Ariandel (mirroring Ariamis's world in the first game) attests to the existence of portals within paintings. The paintings share several characteristics: their frigid cold and snow, certain architectural structures,[314] the fragile rope bridge for accessing the painting's central area, and finally, all of the scythes and reptile scales.

The Painted World of Ariamis primarily served as a prison for renegades, especially Velka's followers who plotted against the gods. Conversely, Ariandel's is quite

---

314. The fight with Priscilla in the first *Dark Souls* took place in an arena similar to the one where we face off with the livid pyromancer Dunnel from *Ashes of Ariandel*.

different. We'll start by pointing out that the painting that contains this world was restored by a giant, Father Ariandel, using his own blood: "Ariandel, being the restorer of the Painted World, knew that it was painted with blood, and only blood could protect the secret," explains the description of the Rose of Ariandel, a flail he used in his frequent self-flagellation to save the painting. We'll add that this painted world has acted as an adoptive home for many different refugees. We've already mentioned the Farron Followers, but we also find the Millwood Knights (secondary characters in this DLC[315]) in this area, along with the Forlorn, an anthropomorphic crow people of whom we saw a few in the main game. They are in an uncommon situation: they are waiting for their world to catch fire and regenerate, a painful yet necessary cycle from their perspective. One of the village's Forlorn states it clearly: "When the world rots, we set it afire. For the sake of the next world. It's the one thing we do right, unlike those fools on the outside."[316]

❦ Elfriede's Arrival

Long ago, the Forlorn had no idea the "flaming" destiny could be compromised. The legend said that all it took was an Ash–inspiration personified, such as an Unkindled, who would produce the spark of destructive fire–and pigments to produce a new painted world and revive the cycle of regeneration: an offering for a Painting Woman idolized within the village. She had set up her studio in the cathedral's attic. One day, a woman named Friede appeared in the Painted World of Ariandel.

This was Elfriede, of the Sable Church of Londor. A former Unkindled, or Ash, she used her status to gain the villagers' trust, which opened the kingdom up to her. She influenced and manipulated the area's leader–Father Ariandel–to get him to banish the Painting Woman. Friede also persuaded the Corvian Knights to subjugate the Forlorn people[317] and protect the painting from the dangers to come. A symbol of Fire support, like the belfry of the Firelink Shrine, the village's church bell was

---

315. Before landing in the Painted World of Ariandel, these great, strong knights once lived in a legendary forest, worshiping the Ethereal Oak. One day, the Millwood Knights disappeared mysteriously—perhaps this disappearance was inspired by the mysterious vanishing on the island of Roanoke (rhyming with "oak") of the first British colony in North America, the only vestige of which was the inscription on a fence post of the word "Croatoan" in reference to a local Native American tribe. In the ruins of the painted world, the Millwood Knights continue their past quest: hunting the Abyss Dragon. This dragon (perhaps a reference to the black dragon Kalameet from the first game) never reappeared, but the knights retained their beliefs and attachment to the land, from which they draw strength and courage.
316. The outside world is governed by a similar rule: when the Fire is on the verge of going out, the Lords of Cinder sacrifice themselves to regenerate it for a time. The Forlorn speaks of the Fire's bell toll and convergence, a consequence of Prince Lothric's rejection of his fate of Lord of Cinder.
317. "In their infatuation with Sister Friede, the Corvian Knights swore to protect the painting from fire, and to this end, took to the execution of their own brethren," according to the Crow Quills and Crow Talons weapons.

dismantled and left wedged in the ground so it could no longer toll. Sister Friede, an acolyte of the Sable Church of Londor, had a secret purpose: to prevent the regenerating fire from reaching the Painted World of Ariandel, so it would be overcome by rot and Dark.

Through sneaky maneuvering, her control grew over time, and rot settled in. The population continued to view Friede as an Ash, while the prophecy evolved and named several Ashes to provide the Painting Woman with her inspiration. However, not all residents of the Painted World of Ariandel were taken in by Friede's cunning. Well aware of the Friede's double play, a man named Gael was able to escape the painting.

⚜ Gael's Quest

Gael was a slave knight in his world. According to his armor, these warriors were "used as fodder in the bleakest of battles." Considered a nobody, a bit like the Unkindled in the normal world, Gael nevertheless maintained a close friendship with the Painting Woman, who regarded him as an "uncle" figure. They held a deep, mutual respect for one another. When Gael saw that his protégée was being persecuted by Friede, he understood the sister's intentions. His uncommon passion and courage allowed the slave knight to escape Friede's guards to flee the painted world.

Hidden behind his red clothing and a profuse beard, Gael was able to slip by his fellow knights. Once outside the painting, he took a piece of it with him ("Well, rotted scrap of it, that is," to cite the game) and set out for the kingdom of Lothric. In the Cathedral of the Deep, we find him chanting a prayer for his singular land: "Ahh, merciful goddess, mother of the Forlorn, who have no place to call their own... Please, bear witness to our resolve... Fire for Ariandel... Fire for Ariandel... And the ash to kindle flame..." He gives us this new quest: "Now, Ashen One, I have a kindness to ask of you. My lady lives in the cold land of Ariandel. I need you to show her flame. A proper flame, that will burn the rot away. If you truly are Ash, then it must be fire that you seek?" By touching the piece of painting Gael holds,[318] players are teleported to the Painted World of Ariandel, where they reach the DLC's true beginning.

---

318. If we decide to start with the second DLC, *The Ringed City*, where the final boss is Gael himself, this encounter in the Cathedral of the Deep could not take place logically. In this case, Gael will not be there to beg: players simply find a fragment of the painting on the altar where the slave knight was praying, which they can use to travel to the Painted World of Ariandel—another example of the *Souls* creators' great attention to detail!

✤ The Second Ash

After traveling through the painted world, and spending some time fighting the Farron Followers and Millwood Knights, players eventually meet the Forlorn, oppressed by the Corvian Knights. A massacre is taking place in the Corvian Settlement, where the residents—relatively peaceful crows—are hunted and killed by Friede's executioners.

"Surely you've seen the rot that afflicts this world. But that witch fooled the good Father, and buried the flame," says one of the villagers. Aware of what is happening, he implores: "Oh wondrous Ash, grant us our wish. Make the tales true, and burn this world away. My Lady must see flame, and you have only to show her." The "Lady" here is the Painting Woman, who we meet later on, locked away by Friede's right-hand man, Sir Vilhelm, in a room of the archives among the vast libraries. In the player's avatar the captive recognizes the hope promised by her ally, Gael: "I feel the scent of ash upon thee." This also reminds us of the ties between the Unkindled and Fire. "Thou'rt the one of whom uncle Gael spoke. The one to show me flame," she adds. Once freed, the painter goes back to her workshop in the cathedral's attic, and we meet her there soon after. We find her seated on a wooden stepladder, facing an immense canvas that is almost entirely blank. It's her next work—a future painted world that will replace that of Ariandel when it has been consumed by flames. "I wish to paint a picture. Of a cold, dark, and very gentle place. One day, it will make someone a goodly home. That's why I must see flame." The woman reveals her fate and that of her painting, following in line with the themes of the other painted worlds: snowy landscapes, atmospheric moonlight, a welcoming refuge, etc. But as long as the flame of this place remains hidden, guarded closely by Father Ariandel, under Friede's control, the painting will remain blank.

In this same cathedral, a few steps from the ladder that leads to the workshop, we find Sister Friede. From her comments, she appears charitable and devoted to her people.[319] She does seem to be sincere, and if that's the case, it would attest to the character's double nature, considering the terrible acts she's committed towards this same people. She tells us to leave her people be and to return to the land from whence we came. During this exchange with Friede, we can hear the deafened sounds of a cracking whip. Father Ariandel can indeed be found in a room below. Securely tied to a chair, the giant flays himself with the Rose of Ariandel, a large whip-like flail with sharp claws. He spills his blood to slake the flame burning inside an immense cauldron. The blood indeed works to "appease the flame,"[320] which is fanned by the new Ash's presence in the painted world.

319. "I have long stood beside our blessed Father, and the rest of the Forlorn," and "Should this world wither and rot, even then would Ariandel remain our home. Leave us be, Ashen One."
320. From the description of the Rose of Ariandel.

"I see flame, flame, flickering, once again. Not enough blood yet shed. My flail. Bring me my flail.[321] Ahh, Friede. What stops thine ears? Please, my flail, right away... Ahh, oh. Bring Friede to me, please. Canst thou not see? The flame, flickering once again. Soon it will surge. Soon will it surge. I can see it, feel it..." Such are the terrible words of Father Ariandel when we approach, preparing for one of the trilogy's most intense fights. Then, Sister Friede appears, responding to Father Ariandel: "Fear not father, we have no need of thy flail. Tis only the flame, quivering at misguided Ash." Then, she attacks. Friede's first defeat fills Father Ariandel with frenzied rage. He knocks over the cauldron and sets the room on fire. The next part of the fight therefore takes place amid the flames. The unrelenting giant uses the immense cauldron as a weapon against us. Like Friede, he exhibits ambivalence: he has worked for years to snuff out the flames per his mentor's guidance, but appears relieved when he admits to losing. Then, he cites a prophecy from his people: "'When the Ashes are two, a flame alighteth.' Thou'rt Ash, and fire befits thee, of course." This brief comment reveals the father's thoughts. He knows he was manipulated and that his people were duped, but he still holds hope that the old prophecy will be realized, and that the Ashes will rekindle the flames. Sister Friede then reveals her true nature, known as "Blackflame." We fight her in a final, bitter fight, and once it's over, Fire returns naturally to the Painted World of Ariandel.

The Painting Woman draws inspiration from the flames rekindled inside Father Ariandel's cauldron. "I can hear the fire crackle... And soon, I will see it... My thanks, Ashen One. I will finish the painting," she utters, relieved. Outside the cathedral, the Forlorn can finally see their world consumed by flames to be replaced by a new work. One villager thanks us[322]: "Ohhh, my, thank you. I can hear the crackling from here. The sound of my home, the painting of Ariandel, burning away..." Such are the strange and fascinating customs of the painted worlds.

The flames renew the painter's inspiration, which had been lacking since the time of Sister Friede's arrival, but she still lacks the pigments she needs to paint. Her final words in the game prefigure future events: "Soon, uncle Gael will bring me the pigment, I wonder if he has found it... the dark soul of man..." In other words, the Dark from a human must burn in order for her to paint a new world. We must also note the homophonic[323] nature of the words "pigment" and "Pygmy"... the ancestor of the human race in the *Dark Souls* mythology! A fitting connection and conclusion for the DLC, introducing the second: *The Ringed City*.

---

321. Between the time when players first meet Friede and this scene, Father Ariandel lost his flail.
322. By giving us another Titanite Slab!
323. The words sound similar, but have different meanings.

The End of the World

Although *The Ringed City* reveals some important events that took place at the dawn of the Age of Fire, the common theme is still Gael's quest, as he looks for pigments for the Painting Woman in the World of Ariandel. This completes the diptych offered by the two DLCs, the second of which is a pretext to present the end of the *Dark Souls* world. Throughout the DLC, players follow this ghostly Gael using messages he has left, notes on the ground, along with pieces of red cloth from his slave knight attire scattered throughout. In this way, we explore the Dreg Heap, and then the Ringed City.

☙ The Dreg Heap at the End of the World

The first location appears to be the end stage of the convergence: it's a similar setting to the Kiln of the First Flame, where we fight the Soul of Cinder at the end of the game. The atmosphere is apocalyptic, under the omnipresent eye of the eclipse symbolized by the Darksign. All of the locations in the series converge on this final point, with twisted landscapes and buildings crumbled into a chaotic jumble. "At the close of the Age of Fire, all lands meet at the end of the earth. Great kingdoms and anaemic townships will be one and the same. The great tide of human enterprise, all for naught. That's why I'm so taken by this grand sight," declares the Stone-Humped Hag, a pilgrim located in the heights of the Dreg Heap, where the view is quite impressive.

In the pile of debris, parts of Lothric Castle are visible. Among the rubble, we can see several of Lothric's knights, along with some well-known sculptures, like the one with the self-decapitating knight, and some items related to the fallen kingdom, like the Projected Heal: "A miracle discovered in the last days of Lothric," according to its description. The bodies of two giant black snakes lie in the middle of a square: could this be the final form of the "Pus of Men," the Undead who fell prey to the Abyss, seen around Lothric Castle? The locations are now teeming with the "Murkmen," "who rise from the depths" according to the description of the Murky Hand Scythe. Over time, the depths, or the Deep,[324] created these foul, aggressive creatures that have been fully corrupted by the Dark. Some Murkmen use the Great Soul Dregs, an improved version of the magic once used by Archdeacons Royce and McDonnell. The description of the Great Soul Dregs indicates that it is "a sorcery that fires great dark soul dregs that have stewed for ages, far within the deep."

---

324. Remember, the Deep is affiliated with the Abyss.

Of the many enemies we face in *The Ringed City*, the Angels are particularly fearsome. To survive their cascading Pillars of Light, it's important to avoid being struck by hiding behind obstacles. If we stay in the same place for too long, we may also receive a curse, which means instant death. The Angels are summoned by well-hidden monsters, atop the shells of the former pilgrims of Londor. The Angels are likely these pilgrims[325] in flying form, a bit like the "Pilgrim Butterflies" in Lothric Castle. The Pilgrim Butterflies may have been scrawny, but the same can't be said of the Angels—they're celestial warriors, with broad white wings and their attacks of light. The empty shells of the pilgrims suggest that they were transformed into Angels against their will by the hidden creatures controlling them. Judging by their placement and their aggressiveness, their role seems to be to block off access to the Ringed City and therefore to watch over the Fire. The pilgrims of Londor have no interest in serving the Fire, however, because they are on the side of the hollows and Dark. This supports the theory that they were transformed against their will by the strange creatures that summon them.

Below the rubble of Lothric Castle are the windmills and poisoned swamps of Earthen Peak, which we explored in *Dark Souls II*. Here, we find the final descendant of the seductive desert sorceresses: Desert Pyromancer Zoey became an "unassuming queen."[326] The ubiquitous ruins in disarray, and the crushing eclipse, remind us that we're still in the Dreg Heap. Farther along, a place identical to where Primordial Serpent Frampt lived in the Firelink Shrine of the first *Dark Souls* marks the transition to the final stage of the trilogy's adventure: the Ringed City.

❦ Shedding Light on the Past

Before we continue telling the story of *The Ringed City*, it makes sense to go much farther back, to just after the fall of the dragons, when the Age of Fire was just beginning. The DLC provides some significant clarifications, shedding new light on a hazy piece of history, particularly regarding the famous Pygmy, keeper of the Dark Soul and father of humanity.

Contrary to what is taught by the founding myth of *Dark Souls*, there was not just one Pygmy—rather, there was a whole tribe of these individuals, the first humans. Perhaps the name "pygmy" was given by the gods, who were much larger than the humans' ancestors. This doesn't change the story's essence, because the Pygmies had the Dark Soul, one of the four Lord Souls. The other three Lord Souls were held by the Witch of Izalith, Nito and Gwyn. The Pygmies were governed by eight Pygmy

---

325. An Angel appears not far from the Stone-Humped Hag when she dies, as if she just transformed.
326. From the description of the Flame Fan pyromancy, received after the fight against Zoey.

kings,[327] who must have shared the immense power of the Dark Soul. Moreover, *The Ringed City* indicates that Gwyn and the Pygmies were seemingly friendly with one another, which goes against the idea that the Pygmies deliberately withdrew as soon as the Age of Fire began (it seems this didn't happen).

Faced with the corruption of the Abyss and the Hollow Curse, Gwyn eventually decided to cut ties with the Pygmies. He "gifted" them the Ringed City, as the Small Envoy Banner describes: "For the pygmies, who took the dark soul, the Great Lord gifted the Ringed City, an isolated place at world's end, and his beloved youngest daughter, promising her that he would come for her when the day came." He sent one of his own daughters, Filianore[328], as a messenger, protected by guards and the Spears of the Church, knights who took an oath to watch over her. The group also contained Judicator Argo, an agent of the Spears of the Church, and Midir, known as the "Darkeater," "descendant of the Archdragons [...] raised by the gods."[329] In reality, "the forsaken Ringed City was walled off by the gods to contain the pygmies."[330]

Surrounded by steep cliffs, the city of the Pygmies was literally ringed off. However, occasionally people came or left–some in particular left to explore the world. They settled in different places, as far away as Lordran, land of the gods where they brought the Hollow Curse which led to the events of the first *Dark Souls*. Expeditions were also led towards the Ringed City, as the Ruin Helm attests: "Helm of the company of knights who were sent to the Ringed City on an old king's orders. The knights sought the dark soul." The Antiquated Plain Garb also corroborates this: "When a mission visited the Ringed City long ago, one of its younger missionaries elected to stay behind." The Harald Curved Greatsword indicates: "Giant gold-decorated curved sword wielded by warriors of the Harald Legion, who sought the dark soul."

Most of the Pygmies had chosen to remain in the Ringed City. It was, after all, a gift from the all-powerful Gwyn, who had ended the reign of the dragons and had left his daughter Filianore with them. Everyone in the city appreciated this womanly presence: the Pygmies called her "Princess" and the kings viewed her with goodwill. Gwyn's plan had worked perfectly, and the first humans suspected nothing. In spite of the promise to his daughter, the Lord of Sunlight never came back to get her from the Ringed City. Filianore found refuge in eternal sleep within a church at the center of the city, its heavy doors guarded by Judicator Argo and his Spears. The fearful dragon Midir was tasked with his own mission and "owing to his immortality was

---

327. The Pygmy kings were also known as "Pygmy Lords," according to the description of the Blood of the Dark Soul.
328. Like Yorshka in *Dark Souls III*, she is a child who was never mentioned in the previous games. The first *Dark Souls* named three children, but Gwyn actually fathered at least five offspring, not necessarily with the same mother.
329. According to the Soul of Darkeater Midir.
330. From a dialogue with the Stone-Humped Hag, the strange merchant from the beginning of *The Ringed City*.

given a duty to eternally battle the dark, a duty that he would never forget, even after the gods perished."[331]

This final sentence gives us an idea of how much time went by within the Ringed City. Though some of the residents eventually came to understand the trap they were in–like the Locust[332] who speaks to us: "Many of us are by the fire forsaken. I speak of thine kind, and mine"–it was already too late: the Ringed City was already frozen in time. That is, until we arrive.

✤ The Rest of the Ringed City

"I know what thy want. The dark soul, no? Why else wouldst one deign to visit this dung heap?" These are the first words to greet us in the Ringed City, spoken by an old, sickly resident with no name, who is intrigued by this newcomer he first mistakes for an enemy, a servant of the gods, before changing his mind: "Worry not, I am a true friend to thee. If thou'rt yet human, the urge will soon begin to swell. To curse the gods, and bring ruin upon this accursed heap of dung." The first moments in the heights of the Ringed City are beautiful, but also quite strange. This curious character's following words are even more intriguing: "If it is the dark soul thou desirest... Then seek Filianore's church, at the base of the cliff. There wilt thou the sleeping Princess awaken. Her slumber is a deceit... a lid covering an overgrown privy: a prop to keep thee from the dark soul of thine desire." This monologue presents two essential elements of the DLC: Princess Filianore and deception.

Before they find the princess sleeping in the church, players explore the Ringed City, where they discover many details on the lives of the Pygmies, insidiously controlled by Gwyn and his fear of the human species. There were knights among the Pygmies, for instance, who were ruled by the Lord of Sunlight, as the Ringed Knight Armor indicates: "The armor of early men was forged in the Abyss, and betrays a smidgen of life. For this reason the gods cast a seal of fire upon such armor, and those who possessed them." These Ringed Knights were forced to assist the gods in hunting the last fire breathers, as we read from the Dragonhead Shield: "The Ringed Knights, by command of the gods, stood amongst the ranks who set out to slay the dragons, but their contributions were never lauded." They were constrained by the famous seal of fire cast upon their armor: this symbol can be found all throughout the *Souls* games,

---

331. According to the Soul of Darkeater Midir.
332. A creature who is half-man (the head) half-cricket (the body), with close ties to Dark and the Abyss: "The white-faced locusts were meant to beckon men to the dark with sermons, but most of them are unable to think past their own stomachs," says the description of the White Preacher Head. Each dialogue with Locusts in the Ringed City corresponds to the tale of one of the characters from *Dark Souls III* (Orbeck, Irina and Eygon), before finishing with their famous tirade: "Fear not the dark, my friend. And let the feast begin."

since it's the Darksign. This sign, taken from the Dark Soul and placed on all humans to protect them from death, is a black circle (the Abyss, created when the sign was affixed) surrounded by a ring of fire. The sign thus ties each human to Gwyn's Fire, and to the Abyss of the Pygmies. The sign's appearance is not the only detail to suggest this. When humans die, they respawn as Undead at the nearest bonfire, where they fill their Estus Flasks, the description of which evolved through the series to reflect this idea of the ties between humans and Fire.[333]

Though humans are not gods, they can still sacrifice themselves to maintain the Fire by becoming a Lord of Cinder. Humans are able to answer the bell's toll and wake up as an Unkindled, "with the strength of Fire."[334] As we've seen, the Darksign also suggests the form of an eclipse. The red light of Fire surrounding the black circle drips like a tear, as if it no longer has the strength to contain man's Abyss: this symbol eloquently evokes the coming end of the Age of Fire.[335] The seal of fire can be seen in various places, particularly in the Ringed City, on the ancient statues showing a Pygmy buckling under the weight of the seal on his back, like the Christian Jesus bearing his heavy cross.

Other statues are noteworthy within the city, starting with the Primordial Serpent, probably in the likeness of Kaathe. In the series' first episode, Kaathe didn't hide his relationship with the Pygmies. He was the one to tell us of the first humans and the role intended for their descendants: end the Age of Fire by inaugurating the Age of Dark. This conflicts with another unique sculpture placed atop a pedestal: Gwyn crowning a kneeling Pygmy, submissive to the divine power. This is very likely one of the eight Pygmy Kings mentioned above. This representation, immortalized in stone, attests to the Pygmies' great respect for the Lord of Sunlight. The crowning scene also recalls the gift made by Gwyn to the Four Kings of the first episode: sovereignty over New Londo, Lordran's human city, and a fragment of his Lord Soul, which gave them great strength. Also, remember that Kaathe had visited the Four Kings, who he rallied to his cause with the help (corruption?) of the Abyss. It seems that the same was the case centuries earlier in the Ringed City. Did the Abyss appear in the city because of Kaathe? Or perhaps, on the contrary, the Primordial Serpent's affinity with the Abyss can be traced all the way back to his encounter with the first humans,

---

333. The first episode vaguely defined the Estus Flasks as "An emerald flask, from the [Fire] Keeper's soul." The sequel referred to a mysterious link between the flasks and Fire: "The nature of the link between the Estus flasks and the bonfires that illuminate the world of the Undead is entirely unknown." In the third game, it closely associates the Undead's quest with bonfires: "The journey of an Undead has always traced the bonfires." We must also recall that Estus Flasks considerably increase health points. They come in limited quantities, but can be recharged at each bonfire, and they are a vital resource for players.

334. From the description of an ember, an item that restores an Unkindled's abilities.

335. The eclipse from the "Usurpation of Fire" ending looked a little different, with a gray circle instead of the normal red one: this marked the beginning of the age of hollows, led by a new lord (the player). The red Fire gives way to gray ashes, symbolizing the disappearance of the seal of fire and the end of the gods' reign over humans.

whose Dark Soul tied him to it? There are many hypotheses out there, but one thing is for sure: Kaathe, the Abyss and the Pygmies are all closely linked.

Gwyn's coronation of the Pygmies was clearly manipulative. As with New Londo's kings, his only goal was to ensure this species' loyalty and maintain control. For in spite of the Pygmies' fragility, they held the Dark Soul, a Lord Soul like his, from the original Fire during the Age of Ancients. To seal this duplicitous alliance, Gwyn sent his youngest daughter, Princess Filianore, to their land. When players begin exploring the Ringed City in the DLC, the goddess is still in a deep sleep. Her guards complicate the task of meeting her—we must face the dragon Midir and Judicator Argo, flanked by formidable warriors from the Spears of the Church covenant, the final obstacle before we reach Filianore. "Unknowing visitor, return from whence thou camest. The Abyss runneth deep. By the King's decree, none may disturb our mistress's slumber," says Judicator Argo when we approach the heavy church doors. This warning echoes Gwyn's fear of humans, their Darksign curse and their close ties to Kaathe.

Once Judicator Argo has been defeated, the sleeping goddess can be reached. We find her in peaceful slumber, like a Sleeping Beauty surrounded by dense vegetation, holding a strange, large egg with a hole broken in the top. The princess's face has a disturbing detail: strange black marks, similar to those of the Abyss Watchers or Archdeacon McDonnell, run down to her cheeks from her closed eyes, as if the corruption of the Abyss has reached Filianore in her sleep. However, when we "touch the embraced shell" (the only interaction available here), everything changes. The egg, the shell of which was already open and cracked in many places, crumbles to pieces when the Unkindled's hand lightly brushes it. The illusion is lifted: Princess Filianore has been dead for ages, and her body is now totally desiccated. She looks like the old man who met us upon our arrival in the Ringed City—the one who spoke of "a lid covering an overgrown privy" when speaking of the "sleeping Princess." Outside the church where Filianore's corpse lies, the surroundings have also changed a great deal. The Ringed City is now buried in ash, and only a few of the taller ruins can still be seen rising above it. At the same time, the characteristic architecture of Lothric Castle and Anor Londo appear in the distance. The city of the first men was nothing but a vision of the past, an illusion maintained by the strength and aura of the princess clasping the egg (a symbol we'll discuss later on). All is now ash, and never has the end of the world been so near.

"Ohh, Filianore, help me, please... the Red-Hood is come to eat us... To eat our dark souls...," says one of the Pygmy Kings, climbing up through the ash towards us. Though Filianore has long been dead, the threat of the devouring monster appears imminent. The Red-Hood refers directly to the armor of the Slave Knights worn by Gael. Gael is not far, and his quest is reaching its end, along with the diptych formed by *Ashes of Ariandel* and *The Ringed City*.

⚜ The End

The plot that began in *The Ringed City*, as we followed Gael's messages through the maze of runs, reaches its conclusion. The Slave Knight appears older, much older even. We recall the words of the Stone-Humped Hag from the DLC's beginning: "The Ringed City is said to be at world's end. Past this heap of rubbish, as far as one can go." For countless years, Gael sought the pigments for the Painting Woman,[336] and his quest led him to the end of the world, where the Pygmy Kings shared the Dark Soul. As we've already seen, the Dark of humans burns well, and what better than the Dark Soul itself to serve as the painter's pigments? In the flame she could find inspiration for her next painted world. In reality, Gael sought the blood of the Dark Soul, the blood of the Pygmy Lords who possessed the Lord Soul. Unfortunately for him, too much time had passed and the blood had dried up. This seems to be a common occurrence in the Ringed City, whether the first old man who is white and dried out, devoid of any bodily fluids, or the princess and the Pygmy Kings, with equally leathery, dry skin. This didn't faze Gael, though. He consumed what remained of the Dark Soul's dried-up blood before moving on to the Pygmy Kings. We witness the end of this massacre, with the Slave Knight mid-feast. Thus begins the final fight. We battle Gael, much more imposing now than in the Cathedral of the Deep, where we first met him.[337] When we defeat him, we gather the blood of the Dark Soul, the final vestige of the original Lord Soul: "Blood of the Dark Soul that seeped from the hole within Slave Knight Gael." Another piece of the description also catches the eye: "Used as pigment by his lady in Ariandel to depict a painted world."

Back in the painter's workshop in the Painted World of Ariandel, we soon notice some changes. The painted world has begun to burn, and small flames flicker across the ground. These reflect the artist's inspiration and thus an impending renewal. However, she still lacks the pigment she needs to translate this inspiration into a painting. If we choose to give her the Blood of the Dark Soul, the narrative arc of the DLC ends. In the past, Father Ariandel used his own blood to restore the painting, but now the young woman has a high-quality pigment with which to paint her work. "My thanks, Ashen One. With this will I paint a world. Please tell me thy name. I would name this painting after thee." Then, we can choose to provide a name, or claim we don't have one. If we remain anonymous, the painter replies: "I see. We are much alike. Then I will name this painting 'Ash.'" Then, after a final thought for her dear Gael, she busies herself with her future painting, the Painted World of Ash,

---

336. Gael's set hints at the length of his search. The blade of his greatsword "is heavily chipped and stained with the blood of countless battles," and his Repeating Crossbow is described as being "used in the battles of an endless journey, this crossbow is covered with twists and dinks, rusted with blood, and made extremely brittle from overuse."
337. Of course, this is a constant for *Dark Souls*: power affects size!

"a cold, dark, and very gentle place [...] a goodly home." Though the end of the regular world has never been so close, the cycle of painted worlds is saved on this occasion.

This sheds some light on the residents of the painted worlds,[338] who seem more inclined to destroy and rebuild, to sacrifice themselves for a better world, than to keep living eternally in a world devoid of hope.

338. "I'm so terribly frightened, of timidly rotting away... Like those... Like those fools on the outside," and, "When the world rots, we set it afire. For the sake of the next world. It's the one thing we do right, unlike those fools on the outside." The harsh words of the villager from the Painted World of Ariandel take on a different meaning once we've finished *The Ringed City*.

Characters

Ashes of Ariandel

⚜ Gael

A clear reference to Guts, the hero from the manga *Berserk*, Gael is armed with an enormous sword and a crossbow. He also wears his distinctive red cape and hood—that of a Slave Knight. This status makes him a nobody, but he demonstrates his determination and courage throughout his quest to the end of the world. He does all he can to please the Painting Woman, and thus begin the painted world's regenerative cycle.

Gael can be summoned for the daunting three-part fight against Father Ariandel and Sister Friede. First, it's worth noting that we can summon Gael without first having consumed an ember, which attests to the strength of the connection between Gael and his precious painted world, which he works tirelessly to protect. Also, the summoning is not immediate: Gael only appears during the second phase of the fight, when Father Ariandel joins the battle alongside Sister Friede. It becomes an epic battle with two against two, and we can see Gael use the emblematic miracle of the first DLC, the Way of White Corona. This inconspicuous item provides us with some significant information. It's a "lost Way of White miracle" that we discover in the Forlorn village church.[339] This is no coincidence. Members of the Way of White practiced the Rite of Kindling, which consisted in bolstering the Fire by using the Dark in each human, and specifically their humanity. Gael and the Forlorn were looking for just this type of fuel—to burn down their world so it could be reborn. However, there are few "intact" humans left: between the hollows, who have lost their humanity, and the Unkindled, whose Dark has already fed the Fire, none is really suited to the task.

---

339. When we encounter him in the Cathedral of the Deep, Gael is praying next to the altar that is almost identical to the one in the Forlorn village church. Since we know that Archdeacons are from the Way of White, there's clearly nothing random about Gael's presence in this sinister place.

However, the Unkindled are also Hosts of Ember, and therefore maintain a special relationship with Fire and Dark, due to their former lives as humans. In addition, any Unkindled that comes into possession of a Dark Sigil regains new signs of humanity, or some affinity with the hollow state. Thus, the Unkindled are appropriate Ashes to light the regenerating flame. This process contains an original metaphor: Gael's protégée must paint the future painting to replace the last one. For this purpose, someone needs to "show her flame" as inspiration, and then she paints the canvas with "pigment."

Gael finds a viable Ash in the Cathedral of the Deep, a fortuitous coincidence for the Slave Knight, since it is one of the final bastions for former members of the Way of White. His path leads him to the Ringed City, in search of pigment: "Soon, uncle Gael will bring me the pigment [...]. I wonder if he has found it. The dark soul of man...," says the Painting Woman at the end of the first DLC. Indeed, Gael seeks the Dark Soul. He eventually seizes it, devouring even the Pygmy Kings in a grotesque banquet of sorts. Corrupted by the Dark, his quest ends in tragedy: killed by the very Ash he persuaded to save the painted world. In a troubling detail, the Soul of Slave Knight Gael description reads, "The red-hooded, wandering slave knight Gael sought the blood of the dark soul as pigment for the Painted World. But Gael knew he was no Champion, that the dark soul would likely ruin him and that he had little hope of a safe return." Gael had therefore already accepted the idea that he wasn't coming back. On his way, he left instructions to guide the one who would complete his quest: his messages and the pieces of his red garb mark the path to the Ringed City, to his own doom. Knowing that he would never come back from his trip, and hoping above all to save his painted world, Gael does everything in his power to ensure the pigment gets to the Painting Woman.

⚜ The Painting Woman

In some ways, the Painting Woman recalls Crossbreed Priscilla: her white skin, the scales on her feet and neck, and her red eyes all refer back to the central character of the Painted World of Ariamis. Additionally, the statue located deep within Father Ariandel's room appears to depict Priscilla, with her fur and reptilian tail. Was the Painted World of Ariamis the previous painting, before Ariandel's? If so, Priscilla would have painted the Painted World of Ariandel using blood, in accordance with all painted worlds. This would have given her a venerated status, as the statue would suggest. With the same reptilian attributes, the Painting Woman from the Painted World of Ariandel could be a descendant of the Crossbreed. In one of his monologues, she speaks to a "mother": "Those who aren't ken to fire cannot paint a world. Those absorbed by fire, must not paint a world. Don't worry, I haven't forgotten, Mother..."

The character's strikingly long hair recalls Rapunzel from the Brothers Grimm, except that instead of the perfectly braided tresses from the fairytale, she sports a disheveled jumble of grey hair. However, the two women share a certain juvenile charm, and are held hostage up in a hard-to-reach space, waiting for a "savior" to come free them. Access to the Painting Woman is guarded by Sir Vilhelm, knight of the Sable Church of Londor who follows Friede's orders.

☙ Sir Vilhelm

Originally from the lands of Londor, Sir Vilhelm is a hollow. He once served the three sisters who founded the Sable Church. His barbarous acts (which remain a mystery) earned him the description "cold-blooded hangman," according to his helm. We know only that he followed the oldest sister, Elfriede, into the Painted World of Ariandel. He was more devoted to her than to the other sisters, and they left Londor together in search of new horizons. In the painted world, Elfriede and Sir Vilhelm ended their relationship: to put her devious plans in motion, Elfriede had to remove all traces of her past, down to her very name, going by Sister Friede. Sir Vilhelm received the Onyx Blade from her, and it may have been her sword to begin with. The blade is imbued with the Blackflame, "born of the similarly-hued flame that smolders within her," according to the weapon's description. The knight accepted this present, which marked the end of his oath to her. He was later entrusted with guarding the location where the Painting Woman was locked up, a task that he took very seriously due to his former loyalty: "After Sir Vilhelm led a white-haired woman to the attic of the library, he kept this key as if it were his life."[340]

Sir Vilhelm meets us later on, and recognizes us as the Lord of Hollows if we've chosen the corresponding path. He throws himself into the battle tooth and nail to defend the only entryway to reach the Painting Woman, and thus find out the truth about Sister Friede, his former mistress.

☙ Sister Friede

As we've seen, Elfriede of Londor and Sister Friede are the same character. This intriguing character has many distinct, and even conflicting traits. On the one hand, her Sable Church of Londor beliefs have led to her adamant rejection of the rejuvenating Fire; and on the other, her new religious role as Sister Friede leads her to take care of

340. From the description of the Contraption Key.

the Forlorn, or at least she claims this is the case. "After renouncing everything, Friede discovered a people that she wished to protect, and assumed the precise form that they yearned for," says the description of the Ordained Hood worn by Sister Friede.

Some of her dialogue also suggests this: "I have long stood beside our blessed Father, and the rest of the Forlorn," and "Should this world wither and rot, even then would Ariandel remain our home. Leave us be, Ashen One." Finally, the description of the Chillbite Ring specifies: "This ring would never grace Friede's hand, for the painting and its frost became her home." This caring demeanor could certainly be a ruse,[341] as part of Elfriede's mission to fight the Fire and spread Dark. Either way, Sister Friede doesn't hesitate to speak to players in this way if they reach the Dark Sigil ending: "Lord of Hollows, I know not the missteps which led thee to this painted world. But thy duty is all, and thy duty lieth elsewhere. Return from whence thou cam'st." She offers up the Chillbite Ring, calling us the "Great Lord of Londor," before ending with: "Thou'st a place in that world, and that alone is cause to rejoice." In the end, if we decide to rekindle the flame of the Painted World of Ariandel, she willingly defends her home, going so far as to reveal her true nature as the Blackflame, in a direct reference to the Sable Church of Londor.

This duality makes her a fascinating character. On the one hand, she enslaved the Forlorn with the cruel Corvian Knights; on the other, she appears to watch over the painted world with a kindly eye. Even her name change is intriguing. "Friede" is a German name that means peace, while "Elfriede" could be derived from the name Ælfþryð in Old English (Aelfthryth), made up of the words ælf (elf, a creature of Germanic folklore) and þryð (strength). A talented swordswoman whose very name evoked strength, Elfriede changed her identity upon arriving in the Painted World of Ariandel, selecting a similar name, but this time associated with peace.

Why Elfriede left Londor remains unclear. If we give the Soul of Sister Friede to Yuria in the Firelink Shrine, Yuria will say: "'Twas the soul of my sister. Elfriede... a poor wench turned to Ash,[342] who would abandon Londor..." a seemingly unexpected fate for the eldest of the sisters of the Sable Church of Londor—her sacrifice in the Fire forced her into exile. Her new ties to the Fire allowed her to enter the Painted World of Ariandel, where her intent was helped along by the prophecy of the Ash, who would spark the inspiration of the Painting Woman, and then literally the whole world. Elfriede left the world to rot, frozen and waiting for the flames to come. To do so, she

341. That said, item descriptions generally have an omniscient perspective and don't attempt to lead players astray. At most, they may allow some lingering doubt. The descriptions of the Ordained Hood and the Chillbite Ring are not very debatable: they tend to depict Elfriede as relatively sincere.
342. The term "Unkindled" is not used (as when Anri says "I am Anri of Astora. Unkindled, like you"), but rather "Ash," which is logical in this context. Of course, the term "Ashen One" is often used throughout the game—this title is similar to the "Chosen Undead" of the first game, and echoes the idea of being selected. Every word and every detail is significant in the *Souls* series!

needed to gain the trust of Father Ariandel, the leader revered by all of the Forlorn, and to manipulate him.

❦ Father Ariandel

Committed to restoring the painting with his own blood, Father Ariandel is a martyr. Tied to a chair, this scrawny giant engages in frequent self-flagellation sessions and pours his blood into an immense cauldron to maintain the painted world and contain the destructive flame, which continues to grow in the presence of the Ashes. Having worked with Sister Friede for a long time, he has spilled ample blood over the years. The arrival of a new Ash in the painted world doesn't improve his sad lot. After the Ash defeats Sister Friede, Father Ariandel loses control. His suffering has rendered him a mere skeleton, but he breaks through his chains and stands, furious, to seize the enormous cauldron, which he knocks over. The flames begin to grow when his blood mixes with that of Friede on the floor. Sister Friede appears to join the fight, and they support each other to defend their world. Like Friede, Father Ariandel is an ambivalent character: although he protects his companion until the end, he also expresses his relief after his defeat against the player, who can now fulfill the prophecy. These two characters that controlled the Painted World of Ariandel are certainly among the most interesting in this third episode, and they make for one of the most intense fights!

The Ringed City

❦ The Stone-Humped Hag

The Stone-Humped Hag is the first character we meet in *The Ringed City*. Positioned in the Dreg Heap, she takes in the chaotic view that spreads out for miles around her. Her presence from the beginning of the DLC and her pilgrim-like appearance hint that we might finally get to explore the lands of Londor, as many fans expected. Not so... And we find out later that she is not who she may have seemed at first glance. "What is it you want from this old stone-humped hag? I've nothing for you, not a smithereen. I just like to stand here, and take in the view." If the Stone-Humped Hag first appeared to have nothing to offer up or tell, she eventually surrenders, if we insist. To begin with, she offers to sell some items, echoing the character Melentia from *Dark Souls II*, a strange, stooping merchant who carries a small wood hut on her back, just as the Stone-Humped Hag drags her pilgrim shell. The similarities don't stop at their appearance, since their names both contain the epithet "hag": Melentia is known as "Merchant Hag Melentia." In addition to selling inexpensive and useful embers, the Stone-Humped Hag proves to hold a great deal of useful information. She tells us of another Wanderer, the "tin can" as she likes to call him: she's referring to Lapp, who we'll come back to soon. If we agree to help Lapp in his quest, we can ask for a new line of dialogue from the Stone-Humped Hag: "Inquire of the Ringed City." The old merchant is surprised by such a request,[343] and shares her knowledge as she reveals some important information. "The Ringed City is said to be at world's end. Past this heap of rubbish, as far as one can go." She goes on to say, "The forsaken Ringed City was walled off by the gods to contain the pygmies... and the dark soul is better left well alone." These comments may first seem meaningless, but later we can see that this seemingly minor character has presented the DLC's overarching plot lines. In the end, she's not so minor after all.

When she dies, the old woman leaves ash behind with the following intriguing description: "Things that have dreadfully run their course accrue at the great dreg-heap. This old woman was once the wet nurse of royalty." The image paired with this description shows a hand lying over a pile of ash. Notably, the hand wears a Priestess Ring, which is "a ring engraved with a portrait of the high priestess."[344] Could this be Emma, high priestess and wet nurse to Prince Lothric? She supposedly disappeared just before the fight against the Dancer of the Boreal Valley, in the cathedral of the High Wall of Lothric. However, death doesn't always work as we expect in the *Souls* games, and it often comes with a number of paradoxes. Another detail supports the idea that she was indeed wet nurse to the twin princes. She speaks of Prince Lorian and the demon he once fought: "Far below, there's a deep, dark hole carved out of a tree. From time to time, voices brim from the depths of the cavity even now. Mutterings of the very demon that Prince Lorian spoke of, I'm sure. Horrible sounds, of an afflicted thing yet cursing men." The demon is none other than the DLC's first boss, the Demon Prince that Lorian's Greatsword referenced: "Before Lorian embraced his brother's curse, he was a knight who single-handedly slayed the demon prince."

But how can we explain the fact that she seems to have later joined the pilgrims? Did she flee the court intrigues and keep a low profile by donning a disguise, or use a camouflage spell? This doesn't seem likely, because a new Angel appears in the sky when she dies, not far from her corpse. The Angel attacks us only if we have killed the Stone-Humped Hag. If we haven't killed her, she dies anyway at the end of the game, and the Angel shows no sign of aggression. It does seem most likely, therefore, that the Stone-Humped Hag turned into this Angel,[345] leaving behind her former body along with the secrets of her past.

---

343. "Why, where did you hear that name, love?" she asks.
344. From the description of the Priestess Ring.
345. Is there any connection here with the Angel who visits Gertrude? Did the former high priestess have something to do with the story of the heavenly daughter? It's hard to believe, but this is the only connection between the Angels of Lothric and the Angels of the Dreg Heap.

⚜ The Demon Prince

As we just saw, *The Ringed City* adjusts the side narrative of Lorian and the Demon Prince by making the latter the DLC's first boss. Though he was defeated by Lorian, this imposing demon is reborn through the paradox of the Dreg Heap, calling into question the legacy of the Old Demon King, once considered to be the "last living witness of the Chaos of Izalith."[346] However, the Demon Prince seems to be nothing but a figment of the past, as the setting and descriptions associated with the boss imply.

At the beginning of the fight, we face two minor demons, the Demon in Pain and the Demon from Below.[347] It's only when these two have been defeated that the Demon Prince finally appears. It's worth noting that the Demon Prince's attacks depend on the order in which his predecessors were killed: he attacks either with fire or a type of laser beam—it's an interesting gameplay element, but not especially consistent with the game's universe. The text describing the Soul of the Demon Prince shares the following: "The demons, birthed from a common Chaos, share almost everything between them, even the pride of their prince, and his nearly-faded flame. So that the last demon standing may rekindle it." In other words, the demons share all of their inheritance, seemingly because of Chaos. Lost at the world's end, these two anonymous, final representatives of their kind were able to recreate the flame of their fallen Demon Prince.

To complete this long, hard fight, we can summon a major character from this DLC— he's significant not because of his role in the *Dark Souls* universe (indeed, his name has only appeared once in this book so far), but because he is present at every stage of the player's exploration of the world's edge. This character is Lapp.

⚜ Amnesiac Lapp

The "tin can," as the Stone-Humped Hag calls him, is an amnesiac knight clad in heavy armor from the helm on his head down to his toes, "without even slight gaps."[348] There's no way to know what he looks like, and he has no memory of anything: "I haven't a clue about my past. Who I was, or what I lived for. Not even my own blessed name. That's why I've come here, searching. For the purging monument, said to be in the Ringed City." With this, Lapp has told us of all of his problems, and his mission— to find the Purging Monument where he can regain his memory. He accompanies us in our exploration of the Dreg Heap all the way down to the Ringed City below. As Lapp

---

346. From the description of the Soul of the Old Demon King.
347. In the French version of the game, "Demon from Below" is translated as *"démon abyssal,"* a reference to the Abyss not found in English.
348. From the description of Lapp's Helm.

himself says: "This really is a dreg-heap at the world's end... Mangled remnants from every age, and every land... it actually sort of lends credence to the old rumours. That the Ringed City rests below it all." Lapp demonstrates great skill, as when he succeeds in unearthing the Titanite Slab in the poisonous swamp on Earthen Peak, which is all the more difficult to cross since it's monitored by Angels. During the first portion of the DLC, he's the one to take us under his wing, giving us items and even helping us fight the Demon Prince.

The roles are reversed in the Ringed City. "How goes things? I'm rather running in circles, I'm afraid. I can't find the Purging Monument. And I've searched high and low...," Lapp tells the Ashen One later on. However, this monument is not far. If we decide to tell the knight where it is, he answers with an outpouring of sincere thanks.[349]

Further along, Lapp speaks with us a final time: "Oh, finally, you've come. Now I know exactly who I was. And for that, I've a little thanks to be giving." Luring us with talk of treasure, he traps us with a violent kick to the back, causing us to fall down below. We discover that Lapp is none other than Patches the Hyena! Though it's a bitter pill to swallow, one of the last men to survive at the world's end was one of the worst. We retain his final words, though, as he snares us in his trap: "Every age, it seems, is tainted by the greed of men. [...] maybe it's the way we are." Is Patches right after all? Are humans instinctively led by their vices, symbolized by Dark? Patches' words are not without significance: *age, tainted, greed, the way we are*... In any case, they give us pause and a reason to reflect broadly on the *Souls* series. First, we can reflect on the accumulation of souls (or humanities in the first episode, and embers in the third) that made us stronger over time. Then, we can consider the fragments of Manus, Father of the Abyss, represented by the queens of *Dark Souls II* and *The Lost Crowns* DLC. These queens in particular personified Manus's deepest drives: desire and loss (Nashandra), anger and vengeance (Elana), abandonment and solitude (Nadalia), and even fear and anxiety (Alsanna). These purely human emotions and feelings engender dangerous monstrosities, starting with the being that Manus himself became. The profound nature of man–"the way we are"–the Dark itself, is somewhat formidable. Maybe Patches isn't wrong when he speaks of human vice as a common thread throughout the age of man. Either way, his words (need we remind you that they're coming from a manipulator?) still give us something to think about!

Though finding out the amnesiac's identity may come as a kick in the pants (literally), there were some clues along the way, before the final betrayal. He toasts several times with Siegbräu, Siegward of Catarina's preferred drink. Considering Lapp's stout size, it seems unlikely he could be Siegward; in the Cathedral of the Deep,

---

349. However, if we don't tell him where it is and reload the game several times, Lapp will totally forget his quest and his friendship with us, and eventually attack. The sad fate of the hollows...

however, Patches trapped Siegward, and pilfered his armor and equipment (and thus some of his Siegbräu). Another clue regarding his identity: after Lapp has touched the Purging Monument, we find the knight crouching, hands on his knees, in an uncomfortable stance Patches would often take. His memories and attitudes must have come back quickly.

The Purging Monument, the target of Lapp's quest, is a strange altar covered in skulls and white flowers: like Velka's statue, it can be used to absolve sins and to heal hollows, like the purging stones purchased from Yuria. It can also be used to "reinstate the King's decree," meaning that it can resurrect Judicator Argo so we must face him once again as a boss.

⚜ Judicator Argo

There are several judicators to be found in the Ringed City. Recognizable by their great height and ample robes, these giants can summon several allies (archers, sorcerers and knights). No one knows if these are all different judges, or if they are just copies of one Judicator Argo. That said, those they summon during the fights are more intriguing.

The many archers are the knights of the runs who "sought the dark soul, but were so soundly crushed, they had little choice but to swear themselves to the Judicator Giant."[350] Subjugated for the rest of their lives, they are charged with enforcing Gwyn's decree: containing the Abyss and defending the Ringed City.

Silver Knight Ledo is summoned to lend a hand to the archers with melee fighting. He's armed with his Great Hammer: "by far the heaviest weapon amongst those wielded by the knights of Anor Londo," according to the weapon's description. "Ledo, an eccentric who traveled across the outskirts, became a close friend to the giants and even Havel, the Rock." Ledo was therefore a Silver Knight from Anor Londo (the city of the gods), who joined the ranks of judicators to help them rule the Pygmies. Ledo's ties with Havel are intriguing, though.[351] The first *Dark Souls* revealed many things about this legendary character (his agreement with Gwyn, the plot he hatched against the gods, the betrayal by one of his own, followed by his imprisonment in an old tower where he turned hollow), but one mystery remained: who could have betrayed the powerful Havel? *The Ringed City* may finally provide an answer to this

---

350. From the Ruin Helm's description.
351. This connection runs deeper than the comment in Ledo's Great Hammer description. Ledo surrounds himself with rocks to deal more damage. This ties back to Havel's nickname, "the Rock." Also, Ledo's weapon is described as the heaviest wielded by the Silver Knights; however, Havel's equipment is also some of the heaviest found in the trilogy. Havel's Ring increases maximum equip load, allowing players to carry heavier equipment; there's an improved version of it (+3) in the Ringed City, not far from where we fight the dark spirit of Ledo.

question: it may have been Ledo, friend of the rock knight, who betrayed his fellow knight on Gwyn's orders. However, there are few clues that lead to this conclusion. It's nevertheless nice to think that this final DLC, which ends the full saga, could provide some clues and answer questions that have left us hanging since the first episode? Of course, these details are somewhat incidental, but isn't that what makes the *Souls* games so exciting?

To support Ledo and the archers, the judicators summon a witch. We've seen her already: they summon Zullie, the witch from *Dark Souls II* who we discussed when we looked at Karla. Some of her Black Witch Set can be found in the alleyways of the Ringed City following the fight with the dark spirit of the Seeker of the Spurned. This is the alias of Zullie's companion, Alva. Zullie's Black Witch Garb tells us that she "intended to seduce Alva the Wayfarer, but eventually became his closest suppor-ter, spending her entire life with him." Since the couple's story was presented prior to the third episode, it's surprising to find Zullie and Alva in this second DLC, and in such a blatant way. Alva became a dark spirit, while Zullie serves the judicators, but we know nothing more about their relationship which began in *Dark Souls II*, or why Alva appears at the entrance to Irithyll Dungeon. A somewhat unsuccessful reference to the previous episode...

The fight against Judicator Argo is different from previous fights in some notewor-thy ways. To start with, Argo doesn't summon archers, sorcerers or knights, but rather members of the Spears of the Church, also known as "Princess Filianore's Knights." Two Spears are thus summoned to fight the invader violating the king's decree: the player. In the online mode, other players who have taken the oath of the Spears of the Church can play as one of these Spears. As with the Old Monk from *Demon's Souls*, this boss fight becomes player-versus-player.

One of the final members of the Spears has kept her distance, however. Her name is Shira, and she is responsible for protecting the dragon Midir, whose unstable behavior suggests the Dark's creeping influence.

❧ Shira and Midir

The giant dragon Midir was tasked with containing the Dark of the Ringed City—essentially the Pygmies. "Midir, descendant of Archdragons, was raised by the gods," says the description of his soul. "Owing to his immortality [he] was given a duty to eternally battle the dark, a duty that he would never forget, even after the gods peri-shed." This superior soul can be used to create the Old Moonlight sorcery, which uses an older version of the Moonlight Greatsword, described as a "memory of an old sword found deep within Midir" from a far-off time, "from not long after the Beginning." This is definitely not something we've seen before: the Beginning. Was it the first moments of the world, from the beginning of the Age of Ancients that saw the beginning of the dragons, or the transition to the Age of Fire? Or perhaps it's a cryptic reference to the origins of the Moonlight Sword, a recurring reference to FromSoftware's games since the *King's Field* series.

Apart from this clever allusion to the rest of this series, Midir teaches us very little of note.[352] His nickname "Darkeater" didn't prevent him from being overtaken by the Dark, as Shira explains: "He once railed against the dark, but was by dark afflicted." The Spear of the Church asks us to "put the dragon to rest. Afore the dark consumeth him, and his vows are forgot." She shows us her den and even comes and helps us fight the dragon. The fight against Midir, the final optional boss, is long and difficult, and any help is welcome! Shira seems to be well prepared to fight the fire breather, as if she has known for a while that her former ally's death is inevitable. She employs the Lightning Arrow miracle, used for "dragonslaying" according to the description. The description also indicates that "the lightning arrows offer a great improvement to the range of the spears, and were said to have been used to pierce the eyes of the dragons from afar." Shira's mastery of this technique says a great deal about her skills and foresight.

Another piece of Shira's equipment is noteworthy: the Crucifix of the Mad King, a spear on which a Pygmy's body remains skewered. Once, a mad king was born to the pygmy royalty and Shira, knight of Filianore, put him to rest. But Shira's cross spear, unable to kill the undying king, only pinned itself to him." Serving the princess, well respected by the Pygmy Kings, Shira was close to the court. At the slightest whiff of danger, she was ready to intervene. This was the case with the Pygmy Mad King, who was executed without a second thought. Shira actually condemns the Dark and the beings who come from it, or those who fall prey to it. In the final area of the DLC, she attacks us after saying the following: "I've searched for thee, dark-stricken creature. I am Shira, daughter of the Duke,[353] descendant of gods, and trusted friend to Midir. At once, I am the honour of the gods, the glory of fire, and the fear of the dark. Thou shalt not go unpunished. For thy treachery, thy profanity, and thy shameless yearning!" At this point in the adventure, we've just reached Filianore's space, and caused the slumbering princess to disappear.

---

352. For the umpteenth time since *Demon's Souls*, the dragon appears without warning while burning a bridge.
353. She is likely speaking of Seath the Scaleless, former ally of Gwyn, who raised him to the rank of duke. This would make her a crossbreed like Priscilla and Yorshka. Shira's appearance is no less similar to that of the humans. The other well-known duke in the series is Tseldora, from *Dark Souls II*, but that's an entirely different storyline, because the gods are not even mentioned there.

☙ Filianore

Gwyn's (hidden) daughter, Filianore, was sent by her father to the Pygmies as a token of goodwill from the Lord of Sunlight. Of course, this was a bluff, sacrificing his daughter to get the Pygmy Kings on his side and protect himself against the dangers of the Dark Soul. This wouldn't slow the proliferation of humans throughout the world, or prevent the downfall of the gods. Filianore nevertheless continued to live in the Ringed City. As she slumbered for centuries, the city itself languished in temporal lethargy. The city of the Pygmies therefore defied the effects of time thanks to Filianore, but in reality, it had been in ruins for a long time, under a thick layer of ash.

The coexistence of these two realities shows how much the *Dark Souls* universe likes to play with space and time. The rules wear away even more as the Age of Fire is in its last moments, producing aberrations like the three variants of the Firelink Shrine we've already seen, and this example of the Ringed City. Two versions of a single space can exist at once, and the border between them depends on the character of Filianore, with the egg she continues to cradle. On the one hand, a vision of the Ringed City's past goes back to the beginning of the Age of Fire; on the other, the site's future ruin is bathed in a dusky light (present day), where we can see Lothric Castle from afar, along with Anor Londo, brought together by the convergence. This second version of reality corresponds to the landscape we see in the game's introduction, with its pilgrims walking, almost collapsing from the weight of the ash. Their path takes them from the lands of Londor to Lothric, in accordance with the prophecy they follow.

There are many hints in *The Ringed City* that suggest that the Sable Church of Londor, Land of Hollows, was built on the relics of the Ringed City. Londor's symbol can be seen everywhere—the omnipresent orb separated by a vertical bar in the center, perhaps a stripped-down representation of the Pygmy bearing the crushing seal of fire on his back, as depicted in some statues we see while exploring the city. It's also the symbol on the Sword of Avowal, used by players to sacrifice Anri during the "wedding" ceremony and acquire the Dark Sigils. We can imagine that the members of the Sable Church once found the ancient statues of Kaathe amid the ruins of the Ringed City. Did they also find the teachings bestowed upon the Pygmies by the Primordial Serpent? Did they really meet the Darkstalker, or did the remaining Pygmy people share with them the important pieces of the religious order, which would one day seek the Lord of Hollows to guide the last humans? A final hint links Londor to the Ringed City: the Purging Monument resets the player's hollow level, like the purging stones sold by Yuria of Londor. Did these stone draw their powers from the Purging Monument discovered by the members of the Sable Church?

The DLC's final area, where we confront Gael, looks like a place where Londor's beliefs were forged. However, the scene seems to take place at a very different time from the time of introduction. We arrive in this place from the Dreg Heap, the topsy-turvy spherical space where everything physically converges towards the Kiln of the First Flame. From a chronological standpoint, we find ourselves in the future, following the events of *Dark Souls III* and the bell's toll. The scene takes place long after the lords' cinders were brought back to the Firelink Shrine. One indication of time appears in the Iron Dragonslayer Helm: "The Armour, defeated by the Champion of Ash in Lothric, was left ages to rust, until it slipped into an abyssal swamp, where it was possessed once again by the memory of the hunt." The "Champion of Ash" of course refers to the player—we're called that many times during the adventure. The "Armour" references the Dragonslayer Armor boss we fight in Lothric Castle, just before entering the Grand Archives. Since we receive this item after the fight against another dragonslayer, in the depths of the Ringed City, this means that *The Ringed City* takes place centuries after the quest to retrieve Prince Lothric's ashes. But is the Ringed City just an illusion of the past?

One thing is for sure: touching the egg projects us into the future. The young princess ages instantly, and the egg disintegrates at the slightest touch, transforming the magnificent Ringed City into an apocalyptic landscape. But is this really an illusion like in the first episode when we attacked Gwynevere (another of Gwyn's daughters, what a coincidence!) and Anor Londo's sky darkened? The spell was broken, and the city plunged into darkness until a new game was started. In *The Ringed City*, once the egg is touched we can return to the city using the bonfires to warp there, as if the bonfires also allow us to move from one space-time continuum to the next. However, Princess Filianore is no longer there: only her desiccated corpse remains in the city, as though the egg produced a temporal breaking point. Could the egg be a representation of the Ringed City itself, surrounded by cliffs, like the egg's ring of broken shell?[354] If the egg and city are actually connected, then the collapse of the former indeed sent us into the flat expanse buried in ash, devoid of its former cliffs.

---

354. The egg's rich symbolism already invites reflection. The dark interior of the princess's egg could symbolize the Abyss, and the shell the fragile seal made by Gwyn, now breaking and turning to ash at the slightest touch. The egg can also be seen as an allegory of creation, and its disappearance as the end of the world: if Filianore's egg dates back to the dawn of the Age of Fire (the new world), it projects us to the end of time when its shell falls apart.

DARK SOULS

ダークソウル

BEYOND THE GRAVE

CHAPTER THREE
THEMES

The Myth

With *Dark Souls III*, Hidetaka Miyazaki wrapped up his project, picking up the story and themes from the previous episodes. In many ways, *Dark Souls III* seems to simply repeat ideas from the original game. The Fire is similarly on the verge of going out, and parallel symbolism appears.

Everything feels a little familiar: patterns we've seen before are woven together to form the series' complex and compelling thematic tapestry. Fire is synonymous with warmth and destruction, death and rebirth; the dark is associated with human vices, their complexity, and in some ways, a rejection of divinity; royalty reflects the spreading of institutions and societies, but also greed and power. We spent time examining all of these themes in the first volume of *Dark Souls: Beyond the Grave*, and we won't rehash them here. Instead, we'll simply mention some of these parallels with the different mythologies (Greek, Scandinavian, Buddhist, etc.) that we covered in the first volume.

As a sequel, *Dark Souls III* takes place in the same world as the first episode. However, though many topics from the first game can be found in the third, this final saga brings its own unique components to the table, to strengthen and enrich the series' major themes.

Like the great myths of past civilizations, the *Souls* stories are built using metaphors and allegories. Poetic, strange, enigmatic or glorious, mythologies have always served multiple purposes. They cement societies and influence rituals and moral values. They serve as inspiration, offering spiritual answers to human questions about nature, the way things are, and the origins of existence. Myths often revolve around the same images, even in diverse, far-off civilizations. The common images are called "archetypes," a phenomenon named by psychoanalyst Carl Jung at the beginning of the 20th century. These archetypes are universal symbols that exist in the psyche of each individual: they help explain the countless connections between mythologies and religions throughout the ages.

Myths, by attempting to bring meaning to the indescribable and inexplicable, share many fundamental concepts, starting with cosmogony, the origin of the universe, often associated with creator divinities or concepts such as chaos. Recurring figures from mythologies the world over[355] also appear in the *Souls* series. The FromSoftware games have their own cosmogony (the appearance of Fire, the Age of Ancients, etc.), their own pantheon of gods, their own heroes, and the legends and stories of their heroic exploits. At the heart of these myths is the fate of humans. Inferior, fragile and mortal, the human race is denied access to the glory of the heavens, but aspires to find its place in the world. In the *Souls* games, which employ the language of melancholy and morbidity common to dark fantasy, humanity is less significant than ever, corrupted by its own dark nature. And yet, the age of the gods is reaching its end, as the age of man nears. As in most mythologies, the *Souls* series isn't satisfied with simply presenting its cosmogony and stories of gods and men. Any beginning also marks the end of all things—more than in *Dark Souls*, the third episode shows the end of time, or rather the dusk that precedes it.

Eschatology[356]

Since humankind has been aware of its ephemeral existence and of the circle of life, we've pondered the end: of civilizations, of the world, of time, but also our own end, death. It goes without saying that this theme permeates the entire *Souls* series, with its temporal uncertainty, the Fire's imminent demise and the many deaths that lead to the hollow state. Death is omnipresent in the games, and suffuses their atmosphere. *Dark Souls III* takes this even farther, though, with a concrete representation of the end of time.

The Twilight of the Gods

Even in the first *Dark Souls*, the Age of Fire was in decline. It could be preserved by rekindling the Fire, or definitively ended by ushering in the Age of Dark (the age of man). *Dark Souls III* is more literal in its depiction of this decline, however.

---

355. For a study in comparative mythology that's scholarly and complex, *The Hero with a Thousand Faces* by Joseph Campbell (New World Library) is also very interesting, and focuses primarily on the "hero's journey" and the cosmogonic cycle common to myths and popular beliefs. Campbell was highly influenced by the work of Carl Jung.
356. From the Ancient Greek ἔσχατος (*eschatos*, "last") and λόγος (*logos*, "the study of"), eschatology is the study of the end of time.

The yellowish light that washes over Lothric Castle is that of a pale and weak sun, which evokes an evening twilight. The metaphor is obvious: the world of kings and gods is drawing to a close. The game offers up a clear vision of this in its final moments, at the Kiln of the First Flame, where we can see buildings of the kingdom of Lothric, warped due to the convergence: we explore this setting in *The Ringed City*, the conclusion of which presents the world after it is buried in ash—the vestiges of human civilization.

Unlike in the first *Dark Souls*, we can now see the consequences of the rise of Dark, by giving the Fire Keeper the eyes, and reaching the corresponding ending. In the same way, the Untended Graves provide a glimpse into a world overcome by the silent Abyss. The description of Aldrich's vision, in which he sees a "coming age of the deep sea," recalls the great flood, a recurring myth of destruction found in a variety of civilizations, from the Mesopotamians to the Greeks, and of course in the Bible.

Whether shrouded in darkness, covered in sand, or transformed by water, the world of *Dark Souls* will eventually reach a breaking point. This change is continuously postponed, as the primordial Fire is maintained: society won't face up to its decline and fears its downfall.

In our own world's mythologies, the end of time is represented in a number of ways. In addition to references to the flood, which always marks the end of an era, there's Ragnarök from Scandinavian tales, which depicts the final battle between the gods and giants, where most of the Norse pantheon and almost all humans meet their death. The Bible's Book of Revelation describes the catastrophes that are unleashed on humanity by the four horsemen and God's judgment, as well as by the battle pitting the divine forces against Satan.

The Christian Apocalypse depicts the coming of seven angels, and the sound of each of their trumpets causes acts of destruction: hail, fire, seas turned to blood, water poisoned by wormwood, etc. *Dark Souls III* uses similar imagery, with the mysterious Angelic faith and the presence of the winged creatures in *The Ringed City* DLC, called "angels" by the Stone-Humped Hag.

Whispers of the End

Unlike Ragnarök or the Apocalypse, *Dark Souls'* end of time doesn't involve clashing weapons or an onslaught of cataclysms. Rather, the remaining civilizations are slowly festering. This echoes beliefs of Hinduism, particularly the fourth and final age of the cosmogony, the Kali Yuga. The Kali Yuga is the spiritual and material disintegration of humanity over several hundred thousands of years, until a new avatar of the god Vishnu intervenes, bringing back happiness and renewing the cosmogonic cycle.

The world of *Dark Souls* is literally rotting away. The gods are now only far-off memories or illusions. Humans are slowly sinking into madness. The kings have all deserted their thrones. Those who rejected the Fire, like Friede, have taken refuge in a glacial, decaying world, where they now wallow.

The last moments of the *Dark Souls* world recall the famous ending of T. S. Eliot's poem, *The Hollow Men*,[357] published in 1925:

"This is the way the world ends

Not with a bang but a whimper."

In an inconspicuous piece of dialogue, Hidetaka Miyazaki invites us to think more broadly about the meaning of civilizations and human evolution. The Stone-Humped Hag greets us at the beginning of *The Ringed City* with the following: "At the close of the Age of Fire, all lands meet at the end of the earth. Great kingdoms and anaemic townships will be one and the same. The great tide of human enterprise, all for naught." A clever way of summing up the quest for power that drives humanity, and the numerous resulting conflicts; these comments extend beyond the world of *Dark Souls* and ring true for our time, and even on a universal scale. The end of time is not just a concrete representation of the fear of death; it also sheds light on life itself, allowing us to take a step back and gain a new perspective.

However, though this end may be difficult to accept, it's also just a new beginning.

The Cycle of Rebirth

The *Dark Souls* games have continually employed symbolic duality: life and death, fire and cold, shadow and light, beginning and end. These pairings can be found even within the series' most essential concepts, revealing their ambiguities. The image of fire itself falls within this gray area: both a source of heat and comfort and of pain and destruction, fire is also associated with the fragility of existence and ever-elapsing time. Flames waver, and could go out at any moment; the Fire consumes itself, and cannot burn forever. The *Ashes of Ariandel* DLC uses a snowy landscape to provide a thematic contrast, reflected in the character of Friede who renounced the Fire. The fight with Friede juxtaposes the two elements: Friede uses ice attacks while the surroundings burn. And yet, in this DLC, fire is also shown to be purifying. It ends this decrepit world by engulfing it in flames, to better make a purified new world.[358]

The destruction doesn't appear to be absolute—rather, it's a step in a process of rebuilding the world on a better foundation. This is the meaning of the Hindu cycle,

---

357. Note the interesting use of "Hollow" here, also an important descriptor in the game.
358. Ambiguity remains, however, in the future Painted World, because once again it will be "cold" and "dark," but also "gentle."

also found in Norse mythology: Ragnarök spares two humans, Líf and Lífþrasir (a woman and man respectively), who are hidden in the wood of Hoddmímis holt at the end of the world. They can therefore renew humanity. The cataclysms of the Christian Apocalypse eventually give way to the victory of God's army over Satan, and the descent of the heavenly Jerusalem, as humanity is welcomed into a state of bliss.

The fears of the end of time are thus offset by these promises of renewal, or access to a higher existence. Though *Dark Souls III* sows doubt, in keeping with its dark fantasy register and romantic aspirations, it nevertheless leaves us with a faint glimmer of hope. Though it's still possible to maintain the Fire and prolong (perhaps in vain) this declining age, ending it doesn't necessarily imply the end of all things. In the ending where players allow Dark to invade the world, everything goes dark. And yet, in the darkness, the voice of the Fire Keeper resonates. She has said it many times: in her vision, she saw a tiny, dancing flame—embers that will reappear one day. Light amid the dark.

Of course, we can choose to eliminate all hope by killing the Fire Keeper at the last moment. This places the burden of her responsibilities on us. The ending in which we become Lord of Hollows is just as open-ended: the end of one era, and the beginning of the next, an uncertain one.

By presenting the end of time, *Dark Souls* invites us to reflect on the cyclical dimension of existence. In the ancient civilizations of Mesopotamia and Egypt, the ourobouros (a snake in a circle, swallowing its own tail) stood as a symbol of this cyclical nature. The circle motif can be found throughout the game, even in the series' main symbol—the Darksign. It's also in the image of the eclipse or in the shape of the Ringed City.[359] The sun is fading, like the primordial Fire. But what is an eclipse, if but the temporary passage of one celestial body behind another?[360]

By confronting the inevitability of death and obliteration, *Dark Souls* may be asking us to accept this fate as part of a larger whole. And yet, the idea of a predetermined course of events may also be viewed as an affront to our personal liberty.

---

359. Circles also recall the shape of an egg, and specifically the cosmic egg, a recurring symbol in world mythologies (Greek, Egyptian, Chinese, etc.) and associated with the birth of divinities or the world's creation. The cracked egg cradled by Filianore at the end of *The Ringed City* is perhaps a reference to this symbol of life—here, it's broken and falls to pieces at our touch, lifting the veil from the illusion to reveal the world's current desolate state.

360. In Egyptian mythology, Apophis, god of the night, chaos and dark forces, waged a perpetual battle against the sun god Ra, with the aim of overturning his sacred barge. Eclipses were seen as brief victories for Apophis. Interestingly, Apophis was generally represented as a large serpent. Is there a parallel to be seen here with Kaathe and his fight against the Fire?

Rejecting Fate

"... This is your fate."

These heavy words wrap up the introduction to the first *Dark Souls*. The Chosen Undead prophecy guided our steps through the chessboard, and we knew neither its rules nor what was at stake. The same goes for *Dark Souls III*, where we receive a new prophecy: "The fire fades, and the lords go without thrones. [...] the Lords will abandon their thrones, and the Unkindled will rise. [...] And so it is. That ash seeketh embers. Nameless, accursed Undead, unfit even to be cinder."

It seems the wheel of fate has once again begun its relentless spin. However, fate is portrayed differently in this episode: the game's action results from Prince Lothric's refusal to accept his fate: becoming Lord of Cinder. This foundational act calls into question the very notion of fate itself.

The Order of Things

Several myths have personified fate—Greek mythology in particular, through the Moirai,[361] or Fates. These three female divinities, often depicted as weavers with old features, held the fate of men and gods alike in their hands.[362] The Fates split up their tasks: Clotho spun the thread of life, which was unspooled and measured by Lachesis, and cut by Atropos. The gods themselves were subject to their work, and couldn't escape their own destinies.

The same idea can be found in Scandinavian myths. The Norns also spun the thread of fate, seated at the foot of Yggdrasil, the tree of life at the center of the cosmos and connecting the nine worlds.

Fate was thus an inherent part of the culture and existence[363] of the Greeks, Romans and Scandinavians. Stoicism, a branch of philosophy developed in Greece during the third century BC, taught that we must accept our fate, since happiness cannot arise from struggling in vain against immutable forces.

In addition, since we've looked at the recurring image of the circle in the *Dark Souls* series, we can also draw a connection with the wheel of life, the Buddhist representation of *samsāra*, the cycle of reincarnation that ends only when nirvana is reached, with the soul's awakening and liberation. The suffering we endure when we remain

---

361. The Parcae were the Roman equivalent.
362. As we pointed out in the first volume, *Dark Souls II* references these Fates with the three ancient Fire Keepers of Things Betwixt, who meet us at the beginning of the adventure.
363. The Greeks consulted oracles to learn of their fate. The practice of divination was also present in Mesopotamian civilizations (the Babylonians and Sumerians).

tied to *samsāra* is closely tied to our karma. This Buddhist idea can also be found in Hinduism and Sikhism, corresponding to the sum of each individual's actions. In Buddhism, acts of our past and current lives influence our fate. We are impacted by the positive or negative character of the being we are or were.

Fate therefore manifests differently in different cultures and under different systems of belief. It's a philosophical idea that opposes our free will and results from our conflict with the world and its inevitabilities, between us and the natural order of things.

In the storylines, the terms "prophecy" and "chosen one" have familiar connotations. It's a narrative motif inherited from a long tradition of myths and epics, which has supplied much of popular culture, from *The Lord of the Rings* to *The Matrix*, along with *Harry Potter* and *His Dark Materials*.

In video games, and namely *Dark Souls*, it serves as a framework guiding players to a set objective. The *Souls* games have such impenetrable storylines that these familiar motifs are welcome and give us some bearings. However, isn't it also true that laying out a predestined route for players also goes against the idea of free will that governs most role-playing games?

Refusal as a Way of Upsetting the Established Order

In *Dark Souls III*, as the centuries roll by, the Lords of Cinder succeeded one another without ever really forestalling the Fire's slow decline. King Oceiros's descendant was expected to be the kingdom and world's savior. Hopes were so high that his very birth had to be brought about unnaturally. The hand of fate was thus forced. Unable to produce a male heir, the royal family seems to have resorted to dubious methods to produce Lothric and Lorian. When you're born with the fate of the world on your shoulders, and when you had no say in the matter, what can you do? Especially when saddled with a puny, weak body, far below the expectations of your forbearers and a disappointment to your status...

Lothric's choice to abandon his role, though influenced by Sulyvahn's teachings, is understandable. However, such a choice is also potentially responsible for the end of time. His decision to reject his fate turned the world upside down: the game represents this visually through its dangerous environments and crumbling kingdoms, and through the way it jumbles space and time.

In *Dark Souls III*, Lothric is no longer the only one to abnegate his fate. First, there are characters who go against their very nature, such as Orbeck, who assumes the fake role of sorcerer, or Oceiros, whose body reflects his obsessive fascination with his Seath's research. In the same way, the Lords of Cinder, with the exception of Ludleth, have decided not to answer the bell's toll. And we can't forget Friede:

after becoming Ash, she abandoned Londor and the Sable Church to take refuge in the Painted World of Ariandel.[364]

With this central theme, *Dark Souls III* seems to invite us to contemplate our role and the impact we can have on the world. Unlike the first episode, in which we were prophesied as the Chosen Undead, we're now a nobody, an Unkindled: "Nameless, accursed Undead, unfit even to be cinder." And yet, though "unfit," we're destined to prove our value by ending the Lords of Cinder and become the new savior of the Fire. It's an interesting paradox, which reminds us that the player's journey is above all a journey of discovery. We're a simple human who triumphs over demons, dragons, kings and gods. The prophecy, whether or not it's invented, isn't fulfilled automatically. It depends entirely on the character's heroism, perseverance and exploits. Fate has to be set in motion.

There's a parallel here with Gael, who was willing to go to the end of the world for his painter, and this is the price he eventually pays. Aware that a dark fate awaited him, he nevertheless remained unwavering. Perhaps he had already planned for the Unkindled's arrival, to free him of his madness and bring the Dark Soul pigment to the Painting Woman. This would explain the messages he left for us at the beginning of *The Ringed City*. Having accepted his terrible fate, Gael is a true tragic hero, in the literary sense, in that he is destined for downfall.

Players, on the other hand, have everything they need to forge their own destiny. In the end, faced with the Fire, we alone decide the future. Or do we just maintain the cycle, no matter what we do? The Primordial Serpents may still be there, somewhere, playing with the world's chessboard.

The Soul's Corruption

By digging deeper into the notion of fate, and thus the individual's place within the world, *Dark Souls* focuses heavily on human nature itself. Like many dark fantasies, the series depicts despair, resignation and degradation. The darkest corners of the human soul are bared. After all, doesn't "humanity" (a term that can lead to confusion) also contain the Dark Soul in this context? *Dark Souls III* continues its overview of the poisons that consume the soul, starting with the malevolent religious institutions.

---

364. Ariandel's prophecy reveals the presence of two Ashes who cause the painted world to go up in flames. Acting thus, did Friede unwittingly walk straight into her destiny? The same question can be asked about Lothric and the Lords of Cinder, since their refusals echo the prophecy of the lords that "go without thrones."

The Death of the Gods

Dark Souls III draws up a bleak portrait of religious degradation. Comments on the subject are somewhat ambiguous, but numerous. First, followers of the Angelic faith in Lothric were persecuted, oppressed by the royal powers in a civil war. This situation recalls the difficulties faced by Christianity at the dawn of our era, when the Christians were persecuted within the Roman Empire during the third century. In *Dark Souls III*, the faith's leader is ironically none other than Gertrude, one of Gwynevere's presumed daughters, and thus one of the final representatives of the gods from the Age of Fire.

Dark Souls III's storyline has parallels with the end of paganism in our history. When Christianity began to grow, some of the old pagan beliefs were lost, while others were assimilated.[365]

This reference echoes Aldrich's fate. Once venerated as a saint in the Cathedral of the Deep, he is now known as the "devourer of gods." In many ways, Aldrich can be viewed as an allegory of the Catholic Church as an institution. His followers are deacons and archdeacons; that is, they are representatives of the Church.[366] Aldrich feeding on Gwyndolin, a divinity comparable to Greek and Roman gods, playfully evokes the historical assimilation of pagan cultures. This religious cannibalism takes on new dimensions when we discover that the deacons went so far as to feed Aldrich children. This form of maneating may be a metaphor, referring to the indoctrination of young people or the sexual abuse scandals that have shaken the Church.[367] The deacons in *Dark Souls III* use pyromancy and sorcery outside the realm of miracles,[368] a heresy that suggests the perversion of their own religion.

The Decline of the Monarchy

The religious parallels are in line with the changed perspective of this third *Souls* episode. If the first game was about killing gods, and Gwyn in particular, here

---

365. For example, Christmas was set for December 25, which was the celebration of the Roman sun god Invictus, as well as the birthday of Mithra, the Indo-Iranian sun god.
366. There are many parallels with Christianity. The Cathedral Evangelists (a name recalling the writers of the four Christian Gospels in the New Testament) are Aldrich's servants from the Cathedral of the Deep—they go all the way to the Undead Settlement, apparently to preach the good word. However, in reality they gather to sacrifice poor wretches to their saint. The Road of Sacrifices served to lead the sacrificed Undead to the Cathedral of the Deep, where Aldrich and his followers lie in wait. The Road of Sacrifices also goes through the Crucifixion Woods, another foray into Christian terminology. And indeed, the woods contain crucifixions: the Undead we find attached to wooden crosses.
367. Of course, the child-eating monster is also an allusion to the ogre, a cruel giant found in a variety of tales. In psychoanalysis, the ogre is a symbol of the fear inspired by a paternal figure.
368. A quick reminder: in the game's world, miracles issued from divine words.

the primary targets are kings.[369] The figure of power and authority has been taken down a notch. The ancient divinities are no longer celebrated as such; the kings (who embody human power in a broad sense) now rule the world.

And yet, the kings themselves no longer reign. Their thrones remain empty, whether those of Oceiros and Lothric or the Lords of Cinder. Many times near Lothric Castle, we see the statues of kings with their angel wings.[370] This divine attribute also appears on the statues of the Primordial Serpents. The winged kings seem a fitting image of their self-proclaimed divine nature.

The former divinities have passed on; the kings have succeeded the gods, and the world rests on a new foundation, symbolized by the Three Pillars of Lothric. Yet these very pillars now crumble, once again marking the end of an era. With no place to turn, humanity has plunged into chaos.

However, the prominent image of the declining royalty must also serve a purpose. Philosophers and artists have often cautioned against the downward spirals caused by greed and the thirst for power. From this perspective, one of Dark *Souls III*'s most emblematic enemies is Sulyvahn. He who was the "First of the Scholars" from the king's court only every really worked for himself, instilling doubt in thef the future royal figure, Prince Lothric. He also proclaimed himself Pontiff. Considering the ties to Catholicism and Sulyvahn's role with Aldrich, we could say that he simply proclaimed himself Pope.[371] Sulyvahn's corrupted soul turns the purple color of his sorceries. As we saw in the "Story" chapter, he was not always such a tyrant. He symbolizes the evil that lurks within those who, due to a weak mind following a trauma[372] or out of desire for conquest, lose their mind in an attempt to raise themselves up.

Science Without a Conscience: Déjà Vu

Sulyvahn's path also reminds us that knowledge alone can lead to corruption. As we've seen before, the theme of knowledge and corruption forms a significant part of the *Bloodborne* plot, but it was already present in the first *Dark Souls*, in the characters Seath and Logan. The archives, a vast library and allegory of knowledge, represent the madness of the beings consumed by their own thirst for knowledge, and by the discovery of secrets that were better left alone. The nature of the universe is beyond

369. Hidetaka Miyazaki said this in an interview for *Edge* magazine in 2016: "If *Dark Souls* was a story of killing a god, then *Dark Souls III* is about killing a lord."
370. Could this be related to the Angelic faith? This same faith is fought by the kingdom of Lothric, however. This religious iconography is thus subverted, leading to ambiguity about the relatively obscure role of the Angelic faith.
371. Though the term "pontiff" was traditionally applied to bishops, the Pope is the "greatest priest," or *pontifex maximus* in Latin.
372. The mysterious "loss" mentioned in the *Ashes of Ariandel* DLC profoundly affected Sulyvahn.

the reaches of the human mind: it relies on principles that cannot be formulated and that transcend our limited understanding. Anyone who seeks to eat the forbidden fruit may eventually lose their mind. The story repeats itself in *Dark Souls III* with the Oceiros's tragic fate. He becomes obsessed with Seath's research, until his very body has the appearance of a scaleless dragon. The imitation perhaps serves to remind us of the individuals who simply repeat past mistakes. Isn't this also the meaning behind the cyclical nature of the *Souls* stories? By repeating themes, patterns, characters and fates, the series maintains consistency and a broader perspective. The *Souls* stories are complex and exciting, revolving around subjects that can both drive and corrupt us: fear, vice, desire and power.

A resolution to these emotions and actions can be found within the gameplay itself, as Miyazaki invites us to literally fight these scourges with the game system. In spite of everything, we're responsible for our choices, and are free to interpret what the game has taught us at will. This is one of the series' strengths: its suggestive power comes down to the suggestion of its themes. It provides fertile ground for imagination and reflection.

DARK SOULS

ダークソウル

BEYOND THE GRAVE

CHAPTER FOUR
MUSIC

T o give *Bloodborne* atmosphere and set it apart from the *Souls* games, FromSoftware called upon a team of American and Japanese composers, to produce an exciting mixture and build the new world. However, the approach for *Dark Souls III*, as it was a sequel, was necessarily different. While it took place in a new kingdom, this third episode nevertheless echoes all of the dark fantasy elements from the first two episodes, while tying back to some of the story and places from these games.

Synthetic and Organic

Music has helped shape the overall identity of the series. It was therefore not too surprising that Motoi Sakuraba once again worked on the soundtrack. However, he no longer acted as the lead composer: this time, the role fell to Yuka Kitamura. She had already written several pieces for the second episode—"Sir Alonne" in particular—and her work on *Bloodborne* made an impression on players, particularly the piece she wrote for Ebrietas. Unlike Sakuraba, who is an independent composer, she works internally for FromSoftware, alongside Tsukasa Saitô and Nobuyoshi Suzuki, her colleagues on *Bloodborne*, who each wrote pieces for *Dark Souls III*.

Kitamura was responsible for much of the work. She composed seventeen tracks for the main game, and Sakuraba only seven: a reversal that suggests Kitamura's increased clout within the studio.[373] In *Dark Souls II*, Kitamura adapted her music perfectly to Sakuraba's style, while nevertheless maintaining a personal touch, both in how she approached melodies and built the pieces. Her mission for *III* was to continue to assert her own style, without throwing players off by moving too far from the characteristic sound of the series.

Unfortunately, while *Bloodborne* was given an orchestra and choir, two orchestrators and several recording sessions, all supervised by different musical directors,

---

373. Sakuraba was perhaps too busy working on the soundtracks for *Exist Archive* and *Star Ocean 5*.

Dark Souls III seems to have had to make do with much less. As for the DLC *Artorias of the Abyss* or *Dark Souls II*, the instruments are synthetic, and it's obvious. It's all the more unfortunate that *Demon's Souls* and *Dark Souls* were given real instruments, at a time when FromSoftware was working with a much more limited budget. This strange decision suggests that this episode, like *II* before it, didn't get the same attention and care in all of its parts.

Since they don't use the same sound libraries, the difference in quality between Sakuraba's pieces and those of the three other composers is noticeable, and has a negative effect on the game. Sakuraba's pieces quickly get muddled when he adds the samples of brass instruments he's used for over a decade. Kitamura, Saitô and Suzuki's pieces are more expansive, even though the synthetic rendering doesn't generate as much power as an orchestra could—there's a distinct difference between these pieces and the compositions of *Bloodborne*.

There's one consolation, however, in the five singers from the Tokyo Philharmonic Chorus: two sopranos, an alto, a tenor and a baritone. With some adjustments to the mixing[374] and when supplemented by synthetic voices, these singers may not produce as much power as a full choir, but they still add undeniable beauty to the game's music, which is more consequential than that of *Dark Souls II*. The singer Kokia also returned for this soundtrack: she had made a name for herself with *Final Fantasy XIII-2* and *Lightning Returns*, but especially *Demon's Souls*. Her return confirms the team's desire to play on the nostalgia of the series' earliest fans.

The use of real voices, even the voice of composer Yuka Kitamura herself, counterbalanced the disappointment of the synthetic instruments. In sum, the result is somewhat off-balance, disappointing some expectations considering the game's high-quality visuals. However, the excellent work of the composers still manages to shine through.

The End of Time

The game's title screen sets the tone straight away. The first episode opened with a silent screen, and the second was accompanied only by the troubling murmur of the wind; *Dark Souls III* begins with a choir and the chiming of a bell. Yuka Kitamura takes us on a magnificent voyage of sound, with epic surges that contrast with the image's simplicity: the game's title appears in white on a black backdrop, as in the previous episodes. As soon as the piece gets going, violins, brass and choir provide the foundation, and a harrowing solo voice soars above. Both majestic and desperate, the music sets the stage for the adventure. As Miyazaki promised, *Dark Souls III*

---

374. *Demon's Souls* used the same technique; with just a few singers, it's possible to simulate a full choir.

takes melancholy to its extreme, leading us to the end of time, and this piece expertly captures this feeling.

The prologue's music confirms Kitamura's direction, pairing cavernous voices, a low cello, and violins that hold long notes with a slow, percussive beat. And then, from the depths, a spectral voice rises amid the dissonance. The growing power builds into a spectacular choral explosion as the Lords of Cinder are presented, before an imploring soloist supported by violins ends the piece in harmony with a bell's tolling, as if to signal the characters' dark fate.

Though Sakuraba was no longer the primary creator behind the *Dark Souls* "sound," Kitamura proves after just a few minutes that the series is safe in her hands, even though few of the musical features seem like they came straight from *Bloodborne*, with troubling similarities that break slightly with the uniqueness we expect for *Souls*. However, the *Dark Souls III* soundtrack does an excellent job conveying the game's atmosphere of profound melancholy. As soon as the character-creation screen appears, depressing and anxious strings begin to play, contrasting with the soft, dreamlike piece that accompanied the same phase in *Dark Souls*, as if to signal that the trilogy will end on a bitter note.

On the other hand, "Firelink Shrine" is very similar to the pieces used for other hubs in the series. A harp and violin give way to long silences, as in *Demon's Souls* and *Dark Souls*, emphasizing the desire to maintain artistic continuity through the games. Slowly, a sinister yet calming melody builds with the cello and a woman's voice.

The atmosphere is solemn, transforming into despair in "Secret Betrayal," the second piece played in the Shrine, which begins when players decide to give the eyes to the Fire Keeper. We hear diffuse chords on a piano as bells chime and a deep cello forms the foundation. The melancholic voice of Kokia soars above it all, plunging us into a dark atmosphere, casting doubt on the decision that was just made. What if the Dark isn't the solution? However, we can't let this languor undermine the Unkindled's determination: our quest drives us to destroy all of the monstrosities along our path.

At the Gates of Hell

Tsukasa Saitô gets the ball rolling with the boss fights. "Iudex Gundyr" propels forward with the expected arsenal: choir (synthetic here), brass, violins and even harpsichord, all supporting a melody that oscillates between tragedy and heroism. As in most of the game's fights, the music is divided into two parts. The first flows into the second to mark the two phases of the fight. Though we can feel the orchestra's absence, the mixing nevertheless does justice to the compositions. The pieces intensify the fights, stopping us in our tracks, where in *Dark Souls II* their impact was diminished by the jumbled sound.

Here, music regains the original role Miyazaki wanted for it. It only comes in at crucial moments, during boss fights, and it elicits strong reactions, taking us on an emotional ride. Motoi Sakuraba is the composer who ventured the most into the horror register, continuing his experiments from the previous episodes.

In "Curse-Rotted Greatwood," dissonance blends with murmurs, strange chants and a raspy voice. The music sounds off-key, with a strident violin. The overall impression is a formless and grotesque cacophony, perfectly suited to this enemy. Wolnir gets similar treatment in "High Lord Wolnir," where deep brass and warped violins mingle with a more nuanced choir, which brings majesty to this hellish atmosphere. In "Crystal Sages," Sakuraba melds harpsichord, gypsy violin, dissonant and raspy strings, and brass to sow a feeling of discomfort and insidiousness, reflecting the corrupted sorcerer, and echoing the approach Sakuraba took for Pinwheel in the first *Dark Souls*.

"Old Demon King" is also replete with dissonance, built up by a piano, a spectral voice, a relentless rhythm from the violins, along with some brass and a monstrous choir, for a chaotic, trying ambiance. Through its rhythm and patterns, the piece evokes "Bed of Chaos" from *Dark Souls*—a logical connection, since the Old Demon King is the final demon created by the Chaos Flame.

Sakuraba thus circumvented the limitations of his sound library by pushing his compositions into dissonance, and even atonality, thus giving the boss fights a nightmarish quality. Though this approach may not be quite as refined as in the first *Dark Souls*, it gives the third episode's soundtrack quite a bit of depth. "Deacons of the Deep," written by Nobuyoshi Suzuki, reflects this, conveying the heretical side of this black mass through bells, an organ and a choir, but also a flute (wind instruments are rare enough that they're worth pointing out). The violins and choir blend to produce an unexpectedly poignant and dramatic moment, confirming Suzuki's talent which he had already proved in *Bloodborne* with "The One Reborn." We're left feeling that it's too bad he only composed one piece for this game.

Nobility and Disappointment

Despite his taste for horror, Motoi Sakuraba still went for some more epic surges. "Vordt of the Boreal Valley" is a bit clumsy to start, with stifling brass and violent percussion, but the second part builds on this chaos to reach apocalyptic heights in an aggressive rhythm, crushing us with an imposing choir and sinister percussion. For "Nameless King," he composed a piece of great stature, with a harpsichord to evoke royal authority, to support the piece's predictable instrumentation: a tempest of strings to reflect the setting, imposing brass and a heavy bass male choir.

Yuka Kitamura nevertheless composed the music that had the greatest impression on players, staring with Sulyvahn's theme, "Pontiff Sulyvahn." After the female choir and melancholic strings enter in a religious tone, it grows in power with the addition of brass, harpsichord and massive percussion. No other piece could more expertly express this character's hieratic quest for grandeur. The composer pushes the emphasis even further in "Dragonslayer Armor" and "Yhorm," reflecting the sublime and heroic energy of these fights with full instrumentation—still using brass, strings and choir— and complex instrumental and vocal sections that build throughout the pieces.[375]

And if the music feels a little too similar from one track to the next, Kitamura doesn't hesitate to provide pieces that play more subtly on our emotions. For instance, "Oceiros, the Consumed King" depicts his terrible fate with a mournful voice, while the darting violins seem to evoke the king's mental distress: the music is magnificent, donning more ostentatious trimmings in the second half without abandoning the profoundly sad atmosphere. It's a true requiem, counterbalancing the angry side of the fights and washing over players with mixed emotions. This music ties back to the pieces that allowed us to overcome fights against Astrea and Garl Vinland in *Demon's Souls*, or the Great Grey Wolf Sif in *Dark Souls*, as the series transcends the simple pleasure of gaming.

A similar emotion tugs at us in the fight against the Abyss Watchers: the piece also uses the heartbreaking lament of a soloist accompanied by violins, with a male choir to add solemnity and grandeur: yet another unquestionably great moment in the game's soundtrack, emphasizing the cruel fate of the Watchers, caught in an endless battle against the corruption of the Abyss. On the other hand, the fight against the two princes is profound and dramatic: on top of the brass and solo violin, a majestic chorus sings a funereal melody for these two pathetic brothers, linked until their death. This just makes the fight all the more emotional. "Dancer of the Boreal Valley" has some Eastern touches, opening on sustained notes from the violins and cold female choir, echoing the wintry atmosphere of Irithyll. The second part of the piece is more tragic, which says much about this character who fell under Sulyvahn's influence, and the bestial grace of her movements, supported by poignant notes, becomes troubling.

The composer didn't hold back emotionally when depicting the battles of the two DLCs. If "Demon Prince" wins the award for the most horrifying music in the DLCs, with the aid of cavernous voices, dissonance and orchestral swells that inspire both admiration and fear, the compositions associated with the other bosses maintain a feeling of sadness, even in their most grandiose moments. The array of instruments is predictable (choir, brass and strings), ensuring musical

---

375. A different version of "Dragonslayer Armor" has made its way around the Internet. Absent from the game itself, it's a longer version of the final theme, and even more impressive. Its length suggests that the fight was modified during development.

consistency with the main game. However, it's hard to resist Yuka Kitamura's weeping violins and the soprano in "Champion's Gravetender" and when she conveys the majesty and unfortunate fate of the dragon corrupted by the Dark in "Darkeater Midir." Even more dirge-like, the "Halflight, Spear of the Church" theme melds an organ, harpsichord and bells, supporting the mixed choir and the violins to portray the religious dimension of these enemies.

Gael's music emphasizes the tragedy of the character as the music ramps up through the three stages of the fight, until it erupts in an apocalyptic finale, which nonetheless doesn't refrain from dramatic asides, particularly some poignant soprano-violin duets. "Father Arandel and Sister Friede" is even more surprising—especially in its delicate and melancholic opening. The first section is carried by piano chords, bells and a cello, with tremolo strings and an imploring solo voice that covers the sound of a woman's breathing, recalling breezy cold air and thus the fight's setting. The second part of the piece, which is much more traditional in its instrumentation and accents, is necessarily a little disappointing, even though it will still cause many to break out in a cold sweat.

Full Circle

Dark Souls III is comfortable with its role as a conclusion, even as its compositions play on our nostalgia and memories of the earlier games. Composed by Sakuraba, the fight with Aldrich ("Aldrich, Devourer of Gods") also reuses Gwyndolin's superb theme from the first episode,[376] since the lunar god was literally devoured and absorbed by the Lord of Cinder. An immeasurable sadness emanates from the plaintive theme performed by the female choir, making the full piece all the more terrifying. In the background, strange voices alternate between crying and sick laughter, as the dissonance complements the organ, harpsichord, brass and violins to better depict Aldrich's abominable nature, musically corrupting Gwyndolin's theme. The arrangement is especially well thought out, liable to give players goosebumps.

The final battle against the Soul of Cinder provides a similarly brilliant accompaniment. Composed by Kitamura, the piece opens on a powerful first half, conveying a feeling of relentlessness through percussion, bells and an imploring male choir, amid strings and brass. Between dignity and despair, the theme plays on light and dark until a piano enters, playing Gwyn's disillusioned theme,[377] reviving the memories of the final fight in *Dark Souls*. In this way, players understand that they're fighting a reincarntion of Gwyn and even of the Lord of Cinder who they become in

---

376. We also heard this when we fought the Moonlight Butterfly.
377. Composed for the first episode by Motoi Sakuraba.

the canonical ending. The poignant dialogue between the piano and violin is interspersed with the tolling of a bell. The uninterrupted cycle of the *Souls* story is perfectly embodied here.

Our final moments in *Dark Souls III* are inevitably melancholic. For the end credits, Kitamura composed a sad piece highlighting violins, harp, bells, and the enchanting voice of Kokia in slow, moving vocals.[378] The final pieces are aesthetically tied to the melodies that conclude the other *Souls* games, a tie that is strengthened by the return of the singer from *Demon's Souls*. It allows the games to come full circle, while reminding us that the series centers more on solitude and dreaminess than horror.

In conclusion, the *Dark Souls III* soundtrack isn't really that full of surprises: the tone is relatively uniform, and it's used in a fairly traditional way throughout the game. The soundtrack doesn't deviate from the traditional blueprint of progressing through the game without music until the boss fights, though it could have, as with the Ash Lake in the first *Dark Souls*, or the Unseen Village in *Bloodborne*. Plus, the change in the music for the hubs has been present since *Demon's Souls*. However, Kitamura breathes fresh air into the compositions, while allowing Sakuraba to focus his efforts on the most dissonant works, and to find the inspiration for Aldrich that he lacked a little in *Dark Souls II*. Kitamura, Saitô and Suzuki once again demonstrated the creativity they had shown in *Bloodborne*, without hesitating to come up with complex compositions that could have only been made better through an orchestra's interpretation. In spite of the technical limitations, the music of *Dark Souls III* presents numerous moments of bravery and delicate emotional swells, providing a significant contribution to the tomb-like, depressing atmosphere of the game.

---

378. At the end of *The Ringed City*, the epilogue's music has a slightly different arrangement: in particular, we can hear that a piano replaced the harp accompanying the melody.

DARK SOULS

ダークソウル

BEYOND THE GRAVE

BOOK III
DECRYPTION

BY GROWING, and by taking new unique paths like *Bloodborne*, a series reveals its particularities, singularities and its place within the videogame cultural sphere. This "Decryption" section, a companion to what is presented in the first volume of *Dark Souls: Beyond the Grave*, is an opportunity to enrich our analysis of this extraordinary series. We hope that this cross-disciplinary section will give you a more perspicacious view of the series' exciting complexity, and what these games can tell us about video games in general. We'll look at such diverse topics as the influence of Romantic and Gothic painting on the *Souls* and *Bloodborne* games, the way in which game promotion evolved over time, how the worlds were built differently, and how outsourcing affected game development.

Connecting Gameplay and Story

Video games aren't content with simply imitating the codes used in other narrative arts; they benefit from a unique feature: interactivity. In the first volume of *Dark Souls: Beyond the Grave*, we commented on the virtues and potential of environmental storytelling. This form of narration makes use of videogame assets to build a story and create an atmosphere simply through a backdrop, relying on player observation. Though at times it seems that video games have had trouble moving past their arcade game predecessors, particularly with respect to action and violence, and the concepts of victory and reward, increasing numbers of games have toyed with the idea of taking down the boundaries between storytelling and gameplay.

Storytelling Through Interactivity

With interaction, the goal is to better integrate players' actions into the game storyline, to give the overall experience more consistency and depth, while also limiting the gaps between the cinematic moments and the game phases.

Fumito Ueda's works led the way[379] (*ICO, Shadow of the Colossus*), and independent games fully embraced this approach. The games were necessarily based on simpler concepts with smaller production teams, allowing their creators to focus on the ideas that took full advantage of this narrative potential. *Braid* and *Life Is Strange* are notable for their use of traveling back in time; *Journey* for its anonymous, silent connection that players build with another player; *Brothers: A Tale of Two Sons*, which allows players to control two brothers at the same time, each assigned a thumbstick on the controller; or the numerous "walking simulators" including *Gone Home*, *The Stanley Parable*, *Firewatch*, etc.

Interactivity is no longer seen as a simple tool for amusing players. Rather, it can be used to immerse players and tell them something through the objectives laid out for them, even using an action as simple as walking.

The greatest difficulty is successfully adapting this approach to games whose primary purpose is still to entertain. The *Souls* games, and what they inherited from Western RPGs and Japanese precision, fall into this category: they appear to be pure entertainment at first glance. *Souls* and *Bloodborne* are epic, packed with exploration, complex menus, and difficult and violent fights. Their many storytelling components are often scant allusions, scattered throughout and forming an understated backdrop.

Moreover, the series owes its success primarily to the sound yet radical nature of its gaming experience, even more than to its captivating atmosphere. As early on as *Demon's Souls*, many gameplay elements were tied directly to the storytelling, starting with the perpetual deaths. "Game over" is an integral piece of video game history, but in *Souls*, it's never actually the end. There's no true "game over": the game doesn't stop when players are defeated. The character dies, but is reborn in "Soul" form (or an Undead in *Dark Souls*), without a transition, and without returning to the home screen. In particular, players can retrieve the souls they lost, while maintaining the items they found in other areas of the game: death is but a continuation, directly connected to the curses that weigh over the various *Souls* kingdoms.

In *Dark Souls*, humanity points are also tied to the game's world, in which Undead humans slowly lose their humanity through successive deaths, losing their mind until they become hollow. The asynchronous connection with other players fits perfectly within the game world, where time and space clearly obey different laws than in our world. *Bloodborne* took the world/gameplay connection even further.

---

379. See *The Works of Fumito Ueda: A Different Perspective on Video Games*, from the same publisher.

In the Mouth of Madness

Bloodborne does more than just adapt Lovecraft's works into a game; it makes his works part of the game's very structure. Thus, getting captured by an Amygdala, or falling under the gaze of a "Winter Lantern" (enemies with a monstrous brain in place of their head) or the Brain of Mensis increases Frenzy, which means considerable damage when the meter is full. Frenzy is directly tied to the concept of Insight.

Analogous to the levels of humanity in *Dark Souls*, Insight points are first and foremost practical, because they give players access to online features such as summoning other players (as well as NPCs). Insight can also be used to pay for items or equipment in the Hunter's Dream. Their actual value is directly tied to the game's storytelling, however, because the level of Insight corresponds to the spiritual evolution of the character, who ascends ever closer to the eldritch Truth, like Lovecraft's narrators, who become aware of a higher reality.

The higher the level of Insight, the greater players' access to various elements within the *Bloodborne* universe. For example, with over 30 points, players can hear a sinister song from the Winter Lanterns. At 40, they'll see the Amygdalas perched on Yharnam's buildings before the Red Moon rises. At 60, they can hear the cries of a baby from time to time in the background.

The ways in which we can obtain Insight points is also interesting to consider. Without getting into the specifics of gaining Madman's Knowledge or Great One's Wisdom, it's worth emphasizing that Insight increases when players simply see a boss (or defeat it), or when they arrive in an important place. In particular, echoing Lovecraft's work, the higher a player's Insight, the more vulnerable they are to madness—and conversely, they move away from their beasthood.[380]

Frenzy, or madness, is an essential parameter when adapting Lovecraft's works. For instance, the tabletop RPG *The Call of Cthulhu* introduced levels of sanity into character traits. Other video games with a strong Lovecraftian influence have similarly drawn from this concept of madness. *Eternal Darkness*, for instance, uses a sanity meter which causes random hallucinations and starts the health bar. *Amnesia: The Dark Descent* uses a similar system—characters become more vulnerable and their vision becomes troubled if their sanity wanes (when they stay too long in darkness, or witness strange events).

Bloodborne therefore follows in line with these works that have used interactivity to reflect their themes. Miyazaki's game goes even farther, making it the focus of the game's progression. In the "Universe" and "Themes" chapters, we looked closely at the about-face that takes place halfway through *Bloodborne*, after the fight against Rom. In retrospect, with the overall game in mind, we can better understand

---

380. In *The Old Hunters* DLC, *Bloodborne* allows players to become a Beast or a Lumenwood, the two facets of human evolution.

the evolutionary logic of the game's fights. The first noteworthy bosses are all beasts, or they become them (like Gascoigne); then, players confront the experiments that tried to raise humans to the level of the Great Ones (Rom, the Celestial Emissary, the One Reborn), and eventually cross swords with the true Great Ones, including Amygdala, the Moon Presence, Ebrietas and Mergo's Wet Nurse. In sum, the game's progression is presented as a vast allegory for the process of intellectual and spiritual elevation.

With regard to the Lovecraftian inspiration, however, any true connoisseur of the American author would point out a huge "betrayal"; that is, how the game answers a simple question: "Can you kill Cthulhu?"

Killing the Nightmare

One of the common threads through Lovecraft's short stories is the undesirable fate of the main characters, who either die or succumb to utter madness. Such is the inevitable consequence of their encounter with the Great Old Ones, whose boundless reality is impossible for any human to comprehend.

Though *Bloodborne* respects all of this intelligently and to the letter, with disastrous repercussions striking all who try to access the eldritch Truth, players are nevertheless able to eliminate the Great Ones, the beings whose terrifying appearance alone is enough to stop us in our tracks. In truth, we were already defeating Lovecraftian monsters in the *Souls* games, but things get stickier in *Bloodborne*. The game makes such deft use of the author's ideas and approach, leading us to wonder about this deviation and Miyazaki's intentions.

First, it's worth recalling the designer's *modus operandi*, and the objective he has always emphasized during interviews since *Demon's Souls*: his desire to foster a strong sense of achievement. He has reiterated at every opportunity that, beyond what they represent in his vision of the world, elements of horror and difficulty were primarily means by which players could gain this sense of accomplishment.

He didn't concoct these creations just so they would crush players. The intent of placing players in uncertain or incomprehensible situations is to have them push their limits and triumph over these nightmares—in fact, this is reflected in the very expression that appears onscreen after Mergo's Wet Nurse and the Moon Presence are killed: "Nightmare Slain." Since the interactivity requires a certain amount of activeness on our part, the videogame experience is much different from that of reading a book.

The game imposes its own storytelling rules, while sticking to some gaming standards for an action and adventure game. *Bloodborne* therefore doesn't content itself with simply transposing Lovecraft's ambiance and approach to a different medium. It adapts his works, in the fullest sense, to maintain their essence while remolding them using a different artistic language. Hacking up Cthulhu with an ax would be incoherent and ridiculous in Lovecraft's literature, but not so in *Bloodborne*—here, it's the heart of the player's journey. What Miyazaki seems to be telling us is that we're capable of slaying our nightmares and overcoming our fears within the "dreamy" world of video games, so maybe we can also do so in real life, following the lessons learned in the game: patience, observation, analysis and learning from our mistakes. With this in mind, what if the Plain Doll's words were directly for players rather than the Hunter?

"Farewell, good hunter. May you find your worth in the waking world."

Bloodborne and the Victorian Gothic Influence

Gameplay isn't the only element that was thoughtfully linked to the story. The visuals also benefited from exceptional attention, immersing players in a rich, coherent world. In a world where real and supernatural intermingle, *Bloodborne* uses imagery well known to fans of vampire stories, drawing from Gothic, Neogothic and Victorian styles. While several centuries separate the Gothic movement from the Victorian era, they are closely related from an artistic standpoint.

Fantasizing the Past

The Victorian era refers to the period in the United Kingdom that took place during the reign of Queen Victoria, from 1837 until her death in 1901. This period marked history for several reasons: the industrial revolution, the theories of Charles Darwin on evolution, the explosion of English literature, the murders committed by Jack the Ripper, and the aesthetic that is associated with the period.

Victorian London, as it is represented in the collective unconscious, is that of street lamps that shine gloomily through thick fog. We picture men in top hats and tailcoats, cane in hand, and women in long dresses with bare shoulders, round skirts, and dainty waists held in by corsets, their heels clicking on the cobblestones at the foot of Big Ben, a parasol resting on their shoulder.

In fact, the *Bloodborne* costumes are very respectful of Victorian fashions: we see the short capes typical of the aristocracy, women's hats,[381] frock coats, vests, and of course, male characters can sport a mustache, beard or sideburns. In the same way, the street lights illuminating the streets of Yharnam are fairly typically Victorian.

With its chic yet dark character, this aesthetic has fostered an entire imaginary world. This is particularly visible in Arthur Conan Doyle's character of Sherlock Holmes, who remains popular to this day. However, the primary literary reference for the Victorian era was the Gothic novel. The Romantic period, from the end of the 18th to the middle of the 19th century, was defined by its nostalgia for the past. The Gothic movement, which had been scorned along with everything from Medieval times, was redeemed. Many authors became enamored of the imposing Gothic buildings and their religions and gloomy atmosphere.

The Importance of the Gothic Novel

Historically speaking, the first Gothic novel was *The Castle of Otranto*, written by Horace Walpole in 1764. It reflects an obvious penchant for Medieval intrigues and supernatural oddities—the novel contains modern horror stereotypes like unsettling noises or doors that open on their own. The Gothic novel was further developed by authors such as William Thomas Beckford (*Vathek*), Ann Radcliffe (*The Mysteries of Udolpho*), Matthew Gregory Lewis (*The Monk*), John William Polidori (*The Vampyre*) and Charlotte Smith (*The Old Manor House*). The genre uses a characteristic gloomy atmosphere and recurring settings (churches, cemeteries, castles, abandoned ruins, etc.), which fit with the Gothic novel's themes of religiosity, persecution and the demonic. The heroes are often frail and naive, and find themselves thrown into dark and disquieting places, where morals are transgressed; as they encounter ghosts and Satanists, they're plunged into horror and fascination. In 1818, one of the most famous Gothic novels, *Frankenstein*, was published by Mary Shelley. The work raises ethical questions about hubris and the limitations of science. Some years later, many Victorian writers cited the Gothic novel as an influence, such as Charles Dickens (*Oliver Twist*), Arthur Conan Doyle (*Sherlock Holmes*), Edgar Allan Poe (*The Fall of the House of Usher*), along with the French writer Victor Hugo, in his works *The Hunchback of Notre-Dame* (written in 1831) and *The Man Who Laughs* (1869). Throughout the 19th century, various authors wrote serialized stories to appear in the booklets known as "penny dreadfuls," with tales of detectives or criminals in sordid and supernatural settings. The penny dreadfuls were called thus because they only cost a penny at the time;

---

381. The hat worn by the doll is particularly authentic.

they were targeted at poor people from the working classes. During the next century, similar magazines would be developed in the United States, like the Pulp magazines.[382]

The end of the 19th century and the Victorian age was also marked by the Neogothic trend: authors drew inspiration from Gothic novels and gave them a modern twist. They included Robert Louis Stevenson (*Strange Case of Dr. Jekyll and Mr. Hyde*), Oscar Wilde (*The Picture of Dorian Gray*) and of course Bram Stoker and his *Dracula*.

From Shelley to Lovecraft, to Edgar Allan Poe and Bram Stoker, these authors all helped sow the seeds for modern horror and develop a collective imagination so strong it now is part of our cultural heritage. The myth of the aristocratic vampire is intuitively associated with the Victorian era, along with a number of Gothic horror tales, like *The Legend of Sleepy Hollow*, written by Washington Irving and published in 1820. Though the story takes place in the United States, it was written during the time he spent in England, and it's clear that the English countryside left an impression on him. Tim Burton directed an excellent movie adaptation in 1999, with a rural vision of the anxieties crouching in the shadows of this century of the industrial revolution. The Hemwick Charnel Lane area of *Bloodborne* is its successor, with its dilapidated windmill, deformed trees, ochres and blacks, insane peasants, and witch who hides in the depths of the woods.[383] Above all, the FromSoftware game draws inspiration from the other side of the Victorian Gothic—settings directly inspired by the Medieval world.

Gothic and Neogothic Architecture

Though the street lamps and costumes are a direct reference to the Victorian era, Yharnam is above all a Gothic city, from the style of the houses to the immense towers and buildings that stretch up towards the sky, not the least of which is the Healing Church Cathedral. The buildings reflect the ancient features of Prague, capital of the Czech Republic, which the FromSoftware team visited. Eastern Europe, famous for being the home of vampire legends, served as a model for the artists, who also visited Romania. They focused specifically on Transylvania, where Gothic art grew during the Middle Ages.

However, it was in France that the Gothic movement took off in the 12th century; at the time the movement was known as *opus francigenum* (literally "French work"). The term "Gothic" didn't appear until four centuries later in Italy, during

---

382. See "Cosmic Horror: Lovecraft's Shadow" from Book I.
383. In an interesting detail, there are actually two Witches of Hemwick, a surprise that echoes Burton's *Sleepy Hollow*. Is this a coincidence or direct inspiration? We know that Miyazaki has sometimes drawn inspiration from films, such as *Harry Potter* for the Duke's Archive and *Avatar* for Ash Lake in the first *Dark Souls*.

the Renaissance, to disparage this artistic movement by referring to the sack of Rome in August 410 by the Visigoths. Before falling into disgrace, Gothic art flourished across Europe up until around the 15th century. In the 19th century, it was rediscovered by the Romantic movement, in particular with the emergence of the Gothic novel. Many architects began creating buildings inspired by this old tradition, giving it a modern interpretation.

Like Romanesque architecture, which it followed, Gothic architecture is primarily associated with religion, with the construction of churches, chapels, cathedrals and other basilicas. Romanesque churches used barrel vaults, with arcs composed of a single, uniform curve. In contrast, Gothic churches used the distinctive rib vaulting—in the beginning, the ribs were in the form of an arc, connecting two support points. Crossing ribs to support the vault's weight made it possible to build much higher than with the Romanesque vault structure.

Gothic architecture became associated with ribbed vaults, with the two touching arcs pointing skyward, a figure also reflected in the long and narrow stained glass windows in Gothic churches. These buildings were also distinctive for the flying buttresses positioned at the side of the vault to support it, generally topped with a conical or pyramid-shaped pinnacle. The pinnacles that rise above Gothic cathedrals are often adorned with several flowers, which make them look serrated—an architectural detail we can spot in *Bloodborne*.

Other remarkable decorations have also entered into the collective unconscious, such as highly detailed sculptures and the gargoyles used to flush out rainwater. Gothic churches placed great importance on light and its diffusion: they used large stained glass and rose windows, and the windows were much taller in general.[384] Light was seen as a manifestation of the divine, also translated through symbolism—circles, in particular, representing the universe, eternity and perfection.

This quest for God drove the construction of Gothic cathedrals and their elevation towards the sky. This architecture plays on the interaction between the horizontal (the nave's length, thanks to the ribbed vaults) and the vertical (the increasingly high ceilings, and pointed and pyramid-shaped figures).

Bloodborne is highly attentive to details in the design of its Gothic buildings. The game makes use of all of the features we've just discussed. For instance, Cainhurst Castle takes us straight to Romania, recalling the great Gothic castles such as Hunedoara, built in 14th-century Transylvania. All of Yharnam's architecture uses this verticality, the ascension towards the heavens, like the great Clocktower, which looks like a warped Big Ben. Its pendulum is a cross between a clock and a church rose window, with numerous circles that let yellowish, sepulchral light filter through, a sinister omen.

---

384. It was also during this period that candles began to replace oil lamps for practical reasons.

Spirals and Distortions

Research of the divine and the cosmos is one of *Bloodborne*'s central themes, but as we saw in the "Hubris and Knowledge" section, this hubris led to downfall and destruction. This is why Yharnam and its surroundings aren't just facsimiles of the Gothic and Victorian aesthetics; they offer a grotesque and nightmarish vision, where exaggeration is juxtaposed with architectural oddities, all bathed in dusky, pale light.

The city is like a living organism—chaotic, built from tentacular growths, where characters are lost among the mazes and multi-level structures. The jumbled vision of Yharnam in *The Old Hunters* resembles a manifestation of its true nature, and of the madness that has taken hold of its residents.

Thus, in *Bloodborne*, architecture is generally chock-full of meaning. This was already the case in the first *Dark Souls*: the character's quest revolved around verticality, from the deepest depths, and up into the skies and light. The aim of this epic adventure was to reach the kingdom of the gods, seemingly spared from the decline of the Undead humans, but we discover that the light filling the city is nothing but an artificial divine light. The *Dark Souls* world was replete with meaning, and the same goes for *Bloodborne*. The world resembles a sick mind where players dive in head first, searching for an unknowable truth.

The sprawling nature of the city, which takes shape through its various branches and shortcuts, feels like it's foreshadowing the appearance of the Great Ones. The heights of Yharnam's ruins tower suffocatingly overhead. We could view the city itself as a character, or at least the body of this world—the sinuous architecture is literally swallowing up its inhabitants, as we discover on the walls of Yahar'gul in which humans are embedded and petrified.

In many ways, and particularly in places like the laboratories with their many spiral staircases, some *Bloodborne* levels recall Giovanni Battista Piranesi's *Imaginary Prisons*, engravings from the 18th century depicting improbable and illogical monumental structures, sprawling with footbridges, drawbridges, ladders and spiral staircases; humans are insignificant here, dwarfed by the immensity of these prison-like fortresses.

The connection between grandeur and absurdity is at the core of *Bloodborne*, which contains numerous dreamlike layers (dreams, nightmares, and an "intermediate" reality), along with towering structures to make the world a vertical labyrinth, a reflection of human hubris, cleverly twisting the meaning of Gothic architecture: in this place of terror, communion with the divine can take place. *Bloodborne* brilliantly adapted the major characteristics of the Victorian Gothic, with visuals depicting 19th-century England, and mixed them with the artistic, literary and architectural obsessions from this period, without forgetting to give them a modern spin: the game demonstrates a proclivity for the macabre and twisted religiousness, which comes from an authentic approach to the visuals.

Horror and Beauty:
The "Dark Romanticism" of Souls

"What we want to communicate to the fans is that there's an inherent beauty that can be found within everything, beyond all the withering and decay."[385]

Under dark fantasy's tattered rags, its cursed characters, sepulchral atmosphere and flickering flames, does the *Souls* series, and by extension, *Bloodborne*, really offer a quest for beauty? This is the most striking piece of Miyazaki's comment—how he supervised the artistic direction of all of the games, starting with *Demon's Souls*, as well as the player experience. Even for those who aren't prone to contemplation, it's hard not to notice the attention paid to the visuals in each game, from expressive panoramas, to diffuse lighting, to monsters that are both repugnant and elegant. So what is this beauty that can be found in everything?

Aesthetics in Visual Art

The term "aesthetics" is commonly associated with visual perception, but it also denotes a philosophical discipline that studies this form of perception: that is, the notion of beauty itself. This practice dates back to long before the word "aesthetic," which was coined in the 18th century: it first took root in Ancient Greece. For Plato and his theory of forms, according to which the true nature of things is not found in the physical world (what we perceive with our senses) but in the world of ideas (non-physical forms, concepts), beauty falls within the second category. Beauty pushes man to rise up and see beyond appearances. Beauty is thus of the intellectual order—transcendent, even. Plato regarded artistic beauty as artificial, in that he felt art aimed to reproduce

385. Interview with Hidetaka Miyazaki by Sayem Ahmed for the site *Vice*, published March 1, 2016: http://www.vice.com/read/on-the-sublime-and-beautiful-a-conversation-with-dark-souls-iii-director-hidetaka- miyazaki-400.

the beauty of nature. However, the concept of beauty has been constantly reevaluated over the centuries. One after another, artistic movements have redefined their vision of beauty and what is pleasing to the eye. Much debate and confusion has ensued: where can we draw the line between absolute beauty and the beauty of judgment and taste? Does an objective beauty actually exist that meets universal criteria? Philosophers of the 18th century tore one another to pieces over the question.

On one end, thinkers such as John Locke, George Berkeley and David Hume (well-known representatives of England's modern empiricism) defended the idea that taste is relative, tied to each individual's affect and psychology. In *Of the Standard of Taste*,[386] Hume writes: "Beauty is no quality in things themselves: it exists merely in the mind which contemplates them; and each mind perceives a different beauty."

His contemporary Emmanuel Kant added some perspective to his position, however, noting that it confused beauty with the agreeable. The latter is indeed a product of subjective judgment, while beauty corresponds to an aesthetic feeling independent of taste, as he explains in the *Critique of Judgment*: "Beautiful is what, without a concept, is liked universally." He thus reiterates Plato's thoughts, reminding us that the quest for beauty in art relies on processes, while natural beauty is pure, as it is laid out for humankind to see.

The word "concept" from the quote thumbs its nose at the classic concept[387] of beauty, which presented beauty as a quest for simplicity and respect of rules, order and symmetry. Classicism celebrated the supremacy of reason over passion. However, art history is nothing but a back-and-forth between movements with contradictory conceptions of beauty. Classicism was developed in response to the Baroque, and then Romanticism made passion the driving force behind art, and then Naturalism took art back to precise, documented reality. Symbolism then rejected rational understanding, focusing instead on the existence of an ineffable reality. And so forth.

Every new aesthetic model contradicts its predecessor, and philosophers have continued to clash over ideas of art and beauty. At the beginning of the 19th century, Hegel refuted the Platonic vision of art, placing it above nature in his *Introduction to Aesthetics*: "By as much as the mind and its products are higher than nature and its appearances, by so much the beauty of art is higher than the beauty of nature."[388] For him, art is a quest for truth which allows us to glimpse the intelligible. Nietzsche took this farther during the second half of the 19th century, extolling the superiority of art over truth itself. He felt that art is a force of life, embellishing it.

386. Published in 1757.
387. In France, Classicism was a movement born in the mid-17th century, and which lasted up until the beginning of the 18th century. In other countries, rather than referring to a specific cultural and artistic movement, the term refers to the recurring tendency of the Western world to take Greco-Roman Antiquity as a model—a trend that appeared once again in Europe during the 1750s with Neoclassicism.
388. From *Introductory Lectures on Aesthetics*, Penguin Books, 1993.

But how is beauty created? Does it depend on rules such as perspective, proportions, geometry, harmonious colors? Many movements, such as abstract art, surrealism, symbolism, and contemporary art, freed themselves of these restrictions. Art transcends the ages, centuries, and therefore also transcends styles and fashions. Today, we celebrate artists from past ages, and contemporary audiences can perceive beauty in a work from the Renaissance and from the Cubist movement. We should also add that colors and symbols vary from culture to culture, and country to country. The quest for universal characteristics within art seems futile, due to the very nature of the human mind. Taste is not negligible, either. Artists are always in search of beauty: their own conception of beauty, which they attempt to convey through their art. People may be profoundly moved by an artist's work, even if their own tastes or sensitivities are fundamentally different.

It's also important to remember that art is predominantly a question of sensitivity and education, and not just education in its primary sense, but also an empirical education of the mind. Exploring different forms of art requires time and teaching, learning its subtleties and refining one's perception.

There are nevertheless works whose beauty seems more immediate and obvious, that seem to have an immediate effect on us, in the same way that nature requires no particular understanding in order to be admired. From this perspective, it's possible to consider the limitations of beauty. Is it really just a question of form? In this case, we'd be back at Kant's conception of the distinction between beauty and the agreeable. The notion of aesthetics refers back to this idea of perception; and yet, we can find beauty in an object or creation that is not actually art, but rather its primary expression: crafts. We can praise the beauty of a chair or piece of clothing, without feeling an emotion or reflecting much on it.

Art is a matter of meaning, of representation and affect. The most important part is probably not form itself (for a painting, its brushstrokes, colors, general composition, rules of composition, etc.), but rather the feelings, emotions and thoughts elicited by the form, the way in which viewers project their own cultural and aesthetic baggage on it, their interpretation of the world and anything they take away from the artist's vision. In this case, art is a matter of interaction, and maybe also of the mind and ideas, blending the Platonic, Hegelian, Kantian, and even Nietzschean conceptions and transcending their conflicts.

In 1911, in his treaty *Concerning the Spiritual in Art and Painting in Particular*, painter Wassily Kandinsky wrote: "Is beautiful what proceeds from an inner necessity of the soul." Is this what Hidetaka Miyazaki is aiming for here: guiding players to experience this inner beauty? In many ways, the aesthetics in *Souls* draw from an artistic movement of the soul and passions: Romanticism.

In the Dark of Romanticism

Though it began at the end of the 18th century, Romanticism really flourished during the second half of the 19th century. This movement, which rejected the standards and academic forms of Classicism, spread throughout all of the arts: music, poetry, painting, etc. It exalted the profound sentiments of artists, and nature was a primary focus of their work: not a calm and serene nature, but unpredictable nature, even in its most violent manifestations. Nature in all of its grandeur was also a mirror for the artist's soul, with its torments and passions.

Caspar David Friedrich is a representative example of this, and his work had a great influence on the *Souls* games (whether conscious or not). Painted around 1818, *Wanderer above the Sea of Fog* is one of the most famous Romantic paintings. On a rocky outlook, a man dressed in black stands overlooking a vertiginous landscape with no clear horizon line, where silhouettes of boulders and mountains rise above the titular sea of fog. The colors are soft, and the blues fade into grays. We can feel this man's solitude and languor as he takes in the splendor and immensity of nature. The beginning of *Dark Souls III* leads players to similarly experience a view before going to the Firelink Shrine, with a panorama of snow-capped mountains lost in the fog, which extends as far as the eye can see.

Other paintings by Friedrich are also echoed in *Souls*, like *The Abbey in the Oakwood* (1809-1810[389]), where the ruins of a church sit amid a small grove of gnarled, dead trees. Its atmosphere is desolate, and the scene is bathed in a dusky, phantasmagoric light, which gives off a strong feeling of solitude and darkness. The setting recalls this period's literature: the Gothic novel and its gloomy backdrops. The twisted trees, darkened and withered would later inspire visuals from films such as Tim Burton's, and of course the *Souls* and *Bloodborne* landscapes.

Other parallels can be drawn with Friedrich's paintings, such as *Winter Landscape with Church* (1820): the contours of an enormous Gothic cathedral rise up in the background above the fog. Another, *Moonrise by the Sea* (1836), is also disquieting, with its surreal and threatening sky. His works depict splendid, desolate landscapes, eerie trees and dreamlike fog.

The imagery is similar to some of Ernst Ferdinand Oehme's pieces, with his *Procession in the Fog* (1828), or Carl Friedrich Lessing's *Rocky Landscape: Gorge with Ruins* (1830). In the way that they depict nature, its mystery and beauty, and their use of melancholic autumnal and wintry colors, these works are uniquely evocative, and *Souls* used this same imagery to build the musty, melancholic atmosphere.

---

389. Or another variation, *Monastery Graveyard in the Snow*, a painting that was sadly destroyed in 1945.

The FromSoftware games seem to draw from the darkest manifestations of this movement and what followed it, starting with Symbolism.

In 2013, the Musée d'Orsay in Paris held an exhibition called *The Angel of the Odd*[390]: *Dark Romanticism from Goya to Max Ernst*. The show presented lots of opulent pieces, drawing fascinating connections between several so-called "dark romanticism" painters–the title is more an approach to pictorial art than a specific movement. They reflect a certain affinity for melancholy and the macabre, terrifying mythological figures, desolation, and religious perversion (witches, demons). In addition to works by Friedrich, many of the other paintings in the show echoed the characteristics we see in the *Souls* games, staring with the impressive *Pandemonium* by John Martin (1841), inspired by John Milton's poem *Paradise Lost* (1667). In his glowing, apocalyptic landscape, the rocky ground splits apart, spewing lava, surrounded by hundreds of columns that wall off a gigantic structure. The setting evokes the ruins of Lost Izalith from the first *Dark Souls*–John Martin also specialized in these dramatic works, where stormy, supernatural skies hang over powerless human cities.[391]

Bloodborne and *Souls'* use of captivating morbidity also recalls the works of Johann Heinrich Füssli, and particularly his famous *Nightmare* (1781): a demon perches atop the body of a sleeping woman, while the ghostly head of a white-eyed horse appears from behind red curtains. The plays of light and dark, which we find in other Füssli paintings such as *Between Scylla and Charybdis* (1794-1796) or the dark *Silence* (1799-1801), plunge spectators into a surreal, disquieting world, shrouded in impenetrable darkness: these are excellent examples of the suggestive power of painting. The empty and dark areas are also areas for the imagination to run wild, with intimate and visceral feelings. *Souls* and *Bloodborne* play with light in this way, too; whether the source is the moon, candlelight, or a pallid, listless sun, the scenery is awash with this eerie lighting. Rays of light may strike a sculpture, like that of Prince Lothric, not far from the kingdom's cathedral in *Dark Souls III*. The light draws our attention, and sometimes acts as a visual clue (shining on a ladder, for instance) or a tool to support the scenery.

Keeping with Gothic literature, several painters also depicted the paranormal or sorcery, often both elegant and unsettling. *The Witches' Sabbath*, by Louis Boulanger (1830[392]) references the sabbath, the nocturnal meetings of witches to engage in their ceremonies and orgies. The painter presents these rituals as a supernatural and diabolical dance, where dozens of men and women (many naked) form a human whirlpool that rises into the air, turning around what is likely a satanical church prelate.

---

390. The title *The Angel of the Odd* comes from a short story by Edgar Allan Poe, pioneering author of Romantic literature. The story is steeped in tropes from the Gothic novel.
391. See the extraordinary *The Destruction of Pompeii and Herculaneum* painted in 1822.
392. Also the year when Hector Berlioz composed *Fantastical Symphony*, the last movement of which is entitled "Dream of the Night of the Sabbath."

A parallel with the fight against the deacons of the Deep in *Dark Souls III* is not out of the question here: players have to identify the right enemy among the masses of monks engaging in their satanic ritual. The enemy is encircled by a red aura and wearing a miter (the hat on the prelate in Boulanger's painting is more reminiscent of the first papal headpieces).

In waxy, sinister tones, Serafino Macchiati's *Visionary* (1904) depicts the ghost of a woman walking through a table, watched by a terrified man. The pallid ghost dressed in a white dress is a common trope today; however, Macchiati's strength lies in his ability to convey a sadness in the phantom that is both frightening and poignant. The ghost is not just a vengeful, malevolent being, but above all a dead woman condemned to wander among the living: this idea is also reflected in *Bloodborne* in Cainhurst Castle, where we fight similar-looking female ghosts, lit by a pale light, whose cries echo through the building. They exude a form of elegance that makes them much different from the ghosts that have populated recent movies. This is probably the artistic approach that Miyazaki is referencing when he refers to a "sense of dignity" in the game.

A famous illustrator from the 19th century, Gustave Doré (1832-1883), demonstrated similar expressiveness in his works. He illustrated numerous stories, including Charles Perrault's fairy tales, La Fontaine's fables, and works from Rabelais and Shakespeare. One of his most monumental works is the set of illustrations for Dante's *Divine Comedy*: the depictions of *Hell* in particular have held up over time and inspired many other artists. His plays of light and dark reinforce the dismal and timeless atmosphere of the story. The illustrated journey of Dante and Virgil is imbued with mysticism, through a cavernous underground where the tortured damned suffer for eternity. We see beings who have been turned into trees, writhing in pain or begging, recalling the Undead from *Dark Souls III* who turn into trees. Arachne,[393] with her bare breasts and spider legs, may have inspired Quelaag from the first *Dark Souls*, who also mixes eroticism and dread.

Gustave Doré was cited as inspiration for Coppola's *Dracula*, along with many symbolist and expressionist painters (Gustav Klimt, Edvard Munch, Henry Payne and Alfred Kubin). This film adaptation of Stoker's novel shares other visual parallels with *Bloodborne*, including its baroque yet modern approach: Japanese costume designer Eiko Ishioka was hired to create unexpected costumes for the film, which convey the emotions of the characters.

A Japanese sensibility runs as an undercurrent through the environments of all of the *Souls* games. The Japanese aesthetic influences are subtler, but present nevertheless. The fight against the skeleton king Wolnir can be compared to the *Takiyasha*

---

393. A weaver from Greek mythology, turned into a spider after she offended the goddess Athena.

the Witch and the Skeleton Spectre, a woodblock print from artist Utagawa Kuniyoshi (1798-1861). The triptych depicts said witch going up against a *gashadokuro*, a giant skeleton of Japanese folklore. According to tradition, these skeletons are spirits– *yōkai*–, born of the bones of those who have starved to death. They can be spotted in many Japanese video games (*Muramasa: The Demon Blade*, *Ôkamiden*, *The Legend of Zelda: Majora's Mask*, etc.); in *Dark Souls III*, Wolnir inspires terror while also emanating majesty.

Towards the Sublime

Once more, this giant skeleton blends macabre, poetry and splendor: a combination that was the lifeblood of Romanticism, which mixed feelings and themes of death, mourning, melancholy, love and contemplation. The FromSoftware artists weren't necessarily directly inspired by the works we've described above. Their nearest sources of inspiration were from within Miyazaki's library[394]: his collection includes fantasy and science fiction novels, dark fantasy mangas like *Devilman* and *Berserk*,[395] essays, works of art, and of course the four-part game book *Sorcery!* and guides from the world of Titan,[396] and even the *Dragon Pass* board games. Though the designer has always said that his primary literary influences were from his childhood, when he read works that were too advanced for his age and used his imagination to fill in the gaps, the world he has built nevertheless has its roots in the art movements we've seen, which form the foundation for modern Gothic imagery and dark fantasy in general.

We could have also mentioned the symbolist paintings of Gustave Moreau, whose mythological power and colorful intensity are extremely evocative. However, the most important thing to remember is the aesthetic inheritance handed down to *Souls* and *Bloodborne*. This predilection for the beauty that emanates from darkness and rot is first and foremost a mirror of the soul, of a state of mind, which is reflected in various themes. The primordial flame in *Dark Souls* aptly illustrates this idea of dusk, where the duality between life and death is blurred. From the viewer's perspective, this flame carries a philosophical ambivalence: the dying fire can represent imminent death, or

---

394. He described some of his influences in an interview with James Mielke for *Rolling Stones*, on October 4, 2016: http://www.rollingstone.com/culture/news/dark-souls-creator-miyazaki-on-zelda-sequels-w443435
395. *Berserk*, as explained in the first volume of *Dark Souls: Beyond the Grave*, has many visual similarities and even themes in common with the *Souls* games. Kentarô Miura's manga, which has been published since 1989, already provided a perfect example of syncretism, revisiting the Western dark fantasy genre, as seen through a Japanese lens. Miura also cites similar sources of inspiration to Miyazaki, such as Robert E. Howard's *Conan the Barbarian*, or Lovecraft's stories.
396. This is the universe for several game books from the game books in the "Fighting Fantasy" collection published by Puffin Books.

alternatively a fragile hope, which must be kept alive. There's something fascinating in this image of the dying flame, both a source of warmth and danger.

Through their customs, the Japanese have a unique approach to aesthetics that revolves around two fundamental concepts. *Wabi-sabi* is characterized by ideas that may be considered negative from a Western perspective: *wabi* (solitude, austerity, melancholy, nature, etc.) and *sabi* (the passage of time, decrepitude, rotting). However, this world view also reveals a new dimension: we humans must be modest and accept our smallness with relation to nature; we must also respect the passage of time and what it means for change and creation. The idea is to accept the imperfection of the world and human nature, and to find beauty within these principles. A similar idea is that of *yūgen*, characteristic of Japanese art. This concept refers to the profound and mysterious beauty of things–a reality that artists can express through their pieces.

This refined aesthetic mission is an apt characterization of Miyazaki's games.[397] When we discover the lifeless body of a dragon at the beginning of *Dark Souls III*, with fine particles wafting up through the air to signal its slow decomposition, we feel respect and admiration. The beast is frightening, but remains unwaveringly majestic even in death. The Moon Presence's appearance at the end of *Bloodborne* also elicits fascination: this sprawling, nightmarish creature is nevertheless captivating. The setting, with the blushing red moon and the dreamy field of flowers, reinforces the paradoxical feelings of horror and awe. In this tenuous, indescribable in-between space lies mystery and a profound beauty, related to another major aesthetic concept: the sublime.

In his work *A Philosophical Enquiry into the Origin of Our Ideas of the Sublime and Beautiful*, written in 1757 (well before the rise of Romanticism), Edmund Burke contrasted beauty (which results from aesthetic pleasure, whether visual or auditory) with the sublime, an extremely powerful and destabilizing feeling, tied loosely with emotions that are greater than the individual: immensity, infinity and death. Unlike beauty, which he argued requires precise rules, the sublime can arise from asymmetry or alienation, from excessiveness or dread. Isn't that one of the advantages of art: it can shake us up, disturb us, raise questions, and ultimately enrich our vision of the world?

The sublime goes much further than what is agreeable–it levels us by placing us in the presence of the immeasurable. *Wabi-sabi* and *yūgen* for the Japanese seem to lead to a similar conception of the world. The sublime may raise humans up, while simultaneously reminding us of our mortal nature, our insignificance. The word "sublime" comes from the Latin *sublimis*, which in fact means "uplifted" or "elevated,

---

397. The Japanese language uses three terms to characterize beauty. *Utsukushi* describes beauty which is fragile and small, worthy of attention and protection. *Kuwashi* conveys a refined aesthetic with an astute sense of detail. Finally, *kiyoshi* is the beauty of purity and simplicity, without embellishment. In an interview with *Eurogamer* in 2016, Miyazaki came back to the first word when describing the aesthetics of his games: "The term 'utsukushi' is really difficult to translate in English. It doesn't necessarily mean simply beautiful. Sadness, loneliness, withered—all those things can be explained using this term too."

raised." For Burke, the sublime procures both pleasure and fear. His writings heralded the Romantic aesthetic.

True beauty, which nears the sublime, goes beyond appearances. Gloom, macabre and melancholy all certainly have negative connotations, recalling the dark side of human nature, but they are also the beginning point for understanding a world that transcends binary conceptions. To contemplate death is to comprehend the passage of time and one's own demise, but also the miracle of existence. Ugliness is not the antithesis of beauty—rather it complements and mirrors it.

Souls and *Bloodborne* draw inspiration from the visual legacy of the romantic and symbolist painters, but also from all of the components that make up a videogame experience—music, storytelling, interaction, progression, temporality. They invite players to confront madness, rot and death to better rise above it and seize the fleeting and subtle beauty of the swirling ashes, flickering flames, sinister and silent landscapes, old, majestic creatures, and the gods that cling to their lives with all their might. Even better, through powerful symbols and by fostering uncertainty, these games lead us to experience the sublime, even momentarily.

Evolution in the Worldbuilding

The series' aesthetics owe much of their impact to the highly developed environments, and the way in which they lead players to grow intimately familiar with all of their nooks and crannies. However, more than the complexity and excitement of each level, the most impressive piece is the way in which the universe seems to grow right before our eyes as we explore it, giving us a glimpse into a plausible, coherent world. The first *Dark Souls* was particularly adept at interweaving the different layers of its world together—so much so that all of the other episodes were compared to it on this point. None of the sequels were able to match it, but it's still interesting to look at how the worldbuilding changed over the different games.

From Division to Continuity

Demon's Souls kicked off the series with a world divided into five large, independent regions, accessible from the Nexus (Latin for "bond" or "tie"). Each of the regions is divided into several stages marked by Archstones, the carved stones that appear after every victory against a boss that allow players to return to the Nexus. The division of levels is fairly classic, though after players have defeated the first boss, Phalanx, they can reach any of the other areas. Of course, it's better to follow a logical order to avoid drastic increases in difficulty, but it's still possible to explore the five areas in any order. In particular, there were many who discovered that powerful weapons could be pilfered from the beginning of the fourth world, the Archstone of the Shadowmen, as long as they had the mettle to defeat the highly aggressive skeleton knights. These weapons make the game's earlier progression easier—a liberty that makes up somewhat for the lack of connections between the levels.

Moreover, though it's impossible to create a mental map of the kingdom of Boletaria without having any points of reference, the world's divisions also heighten the feeling that we've been dropped into an otherworldly, timeless place. The exploration of the Tower of Latria or Valley Of Defilement is strengthened by this feeling of isolation, which gives the feeling of a hell with no end: a different type of immersion.

Dark Souls nevertheless completely overhauled the concept, abandoning this segmentation to offer an open world concept that is more realistic. It's not as wide an open world as in the Rockstar games (*GTA*, *Red Dead Redemption*): here, there's no immense central area where we can frolic around freely or enter the dungeons of our choice, as in a *Zelda* game. On the contrary, the world is narrower and more restrained, which gives the layout a denser and cleverer feel, as if whole new levels to explore are always right around the corner. The kingdom of Lordran is a far cry from the immense *Elder Scrolls* games, and this is quite intentional. The goal is to give players a rich exploration experience, with no empty spaces. This is not about contemplative peregrination, but rather permanent progression.[398]

In the beginning, it's possible to go to New Londo or to the catacombs. Of course, as for *Demon's Souls*, it's better to follow a logical order, and thus to start the adventure with the Undead Burg. The fact that we can access other areas of the game is of interest later in the game, when we retrace our steps and continue the exploration.

Dark Souls' stroke of genius was that it didn't offer teleportation until the final third of the game, after the defeat of Ornstein and Smough. This obliges us to complete all of our travel on foot, thereby unearthing shortcuts and secret passages and forming a mental map (unlike in *Demon's Souls*), while feeling more immersed in this interconnected world.

On the Internet, the *Souls* community had fun designing world maps for each episode of *Dark Souls*. The maps detailing the first episode's world show how the environments overlap, and attest to FromSoftware's ingenuity. Several levels are indeed connected—the Undead Burg with Darkroot Basin, which is connected to the Valley of

---

398. Keeping in mind that *ICO* was a videogame revelation for Hidetaka Miyazaki, it's interesting to note that his approach is at the opposite end of the spectrum from Fumito Ueda's pared-down design, which removes as many superfluous elements as possible from the game design to keep only the essentials. In particular, Ueda loathes complex menus and NPCs who loop through the same dialogues.

Drakes, which links to Blighttown and the ruins of New Londo. The layout is brilliant in how it leads players to come back through familiar areas with several hours in between, allowing us to see how we've progressed. There are many points of reference to help with this. From Sen's Fortress, we can see the Undead Burg; in the darkness of the Tomb of Giants we get a glimpse of the glowing lava of the Demon Ruins; in Anor Londo, the Duke's Archive tower above, and so forth. The game uses verticals exceptionally well, adding to Lordran's coherence. This is the only episode to take this vertical approach, however.

Adding Complexity

Dark Souls II provides the most different environments of any of the *Souls* games, by far. Its worldbuilding techniques may appear similar to the first episode, but this isn't the case in practice. *Dark Souls II* uses Majula as an open hub, making it conceptually similar to Firelink Shrine. From this central point, it's possible to reach the Shaded Woods, the Forest of Fallen Giants, and even the ruins of Heide and the Huntsman's Copse. However, each branch leads to a separate route with a dead end. There are no shortcuts for reaching far-off areas,[399] which would connect the different areas through one movement.

There are still several landmarks that can be spotted from afar, but it's rather difficult to come up with a mental map, especially since (for practical reasons) we can warp from one bonfire to another from the beginning. Unlike those from the first *Dark Souls*, all of the lit bonfires in *Dark Souls II* can be reached, which limits the number of back-and-forth trips, but also makes it tedious, and even impossible to visualize the full kingdom of Drangleic.

As a visualization aid, progression through *Dark Souls II* looks like a tree with many branches, which sometimes splits off into other branches, each of which remains independent of the others. This design seems to stem primarily from the desire to offer lots of different environments. This sacrificed the incredible feeling of connectedness from the first episode, and led to some oddities, such as the ascending platform used to access the Iron Keep, which is nonetheless surrounded by flowing lava, as if located in a volcanic space underground.

Bloodborne attempted a return to the *Dark Souls* approach, while borrowing things here and there from *Demon's Souls*. Its separate hub, the Hunter's Dream, is similar to the Nexus, and we must warp to another place from a tomb. However, unlike in *Demon's Souls*, it isn't possible to reach other significant areas. Exploration takes

399. The Crow can be used to reach the Lost Bastille from the Forest of Fallen Giants, but this isn't a land-based shortcut.

place gradually. And though the game's sprawling city and nightmare and dream dimensions can lead to confusion, the worldbuilding is no less brilliant. As in the first *Dark Souls*, several shortcuts or branches link to areas that were explored much earlier. For instance, there's a secret path in the Forbidden Woods, which leads past a poison swamp, and then to a ladder that takes us to Iosefka's Clinic–the same place where we began the game. There's also a connection between Yahar'gul, the Graveyard of the Darkbeast and Old Yharnam. In this episode, the Grand Cathedral serves as a hub: it is surrounded by the Forbidden Woods, Hemwick Charnel Lane, as well as the Lecture Building. In sum, the world appears to be fully coherent, but then manages to baffle players with its surprising branches, vast spaces and regions removed from all temporality and tangible landmarks, such as the Nightmare Frontier, the Chalice Dungeons, and the Nightmare of Mensis; not to mention the oddities of *The Old Hunters*, with its warped version of Yharnam and the disconcerting entrance to the Fishing Hamlet through the Clocktower. *Bloodborne*'s very world is built in a way that reflects the game itself: access to a truth that transcends physical laws and our mind's limitations.

Simplification

After the chaotic branching of *Dark Souls II* and the sophisticated labyrinths of *Bloodborne*, *Dark Souls III* went with a much clearer approach. Miyazaki stated that he wanted to recapture the approach from the first *Dark Souls*, proposing an interconnected world, but players weren't fooled: *Dark Souls III* is much more linear than its predecessors. There are several branches, such as the Road of Sacrifices, which can be used to reach the Cathedral of the Deep and Farron Keep, or Irithyll, where we can go down to the Profaned Capital or climb to the heights of Anor Londo. But the progression is no less delineated by an obvious path that forces us to move forward, without other connections between the different areas. Retracing our steps is indeed quite tricky, which explains the teleportation at the beginning of the game.

On the other hand, the levels are vaster and are excellently built, as in the rest of the series. But the fact that this episode was unable to reproduce the approach from the first *Dark Souls* shows how hard such an approach actually is. *Dark Souls III* nevertheless maintains its own internal logic. In the story, the kingdoms of each of the Lords of Cinder are (physically) pulled towards Lothric Castle. This can also serve as a reference point as we progress: every time we find ourselves outside, the giant silhouette of the building is visible with its ramparts, which makes it easier to determine the location of the rest of the areas. Echoing the story's cyclical dimension, the game starts on the High Wall of Lothric, and ends beyond the Grand Archives of the castle–

we return to the starting point, teleported by Emma after defeating the three Lords of Cinder. Our fate ends where it began.

The construction of this third world is somewhat obvious: the kingdoms have converged and several regions have melded together, such as Farron Keep and the forest of Oolacile, Smouldering Lake and the Demon Ruins, and Irithyll and Anor Londo. It's enough to play with our memories a little without losing us entirely, since Lothric Castle always rises tall on the horizon to guide us like a beacon.

Dark Souls III focuses on the essentials by striving for simplicity. The progression often leads us to breathtaking panoramas–particularly the view from the Cemetery of Ash, but also when we arrive in Irithyll, where we can contemplate the splendors of the wintry city, bathed in the blue light of a crescent moon, or the dizzying views upon our arrival in the Ringed City. It almost seems as though the outlooks are placed along our path to lead us to take in these unobstructed views. The same type of radiant setting greeted us in the first episode, heightening our spectacular arrival in Anor Londo, and in *Bloodborne*, with disorienting phantasmagoric visions.

Though *Dark Souls* is always cited as the standard bearer for layout in a virtual world, every episode followed its own logic, taken from its world and atmosphere, but also the aesthetic and gaming objectives from the designers. And if Boletaria, Lordran and Yharnam are just as fascinating today, it's not just because of their visible construction, but also because of what they conceal–their shadowy and mysterious parts, which we glimpse behind the rays of light that pierce the clouds, or beyond the craggy outlines of the mountains reaching up above the fog.

Storytelling and Illusion

The games may all have taken different worldbuilding approaches, but they all maintain the same method of storytelling. We've already looked at Miyazaki's method in detail in the first volume–the pleasure he takes in letting players piece together the puzzles of the plot and fill in all the gaps with their imagination. We also saw how this led to misunderstanding for some: many thought that the *Souls* games lacked real stories, since they were never explicitly presented outside of the introduction and conclusion using traditional storytelling techniques. We hope that the "Universe" chapters in this and the previous volume of *Dark Souls: Beyond the Grave* have demonstrated the wealth of these games and their mythologies, built up by the FromSoftware teams. It's still understandable that some players never really get into the stories of *Souls* or *Bloodborne*, since the games never make it easy.

In Search of a Lost Past

For those who are less given to role-playing, or who prefer a clear set of guidelines, the *Souls* experience can certainly be off-putting. Unless we spend an improbable amount of time analyzing the introduction sequences, our immersion in the world is somewhat hazy. The objectives are hardly outlined at all, and are incomprehensible for *Bloodborne*, which could justifiably be considered a flaw in the game. *Dark Souls III* is perhaps the clearest of the games, with the five Lord of Cinder thrones and the quest to find them all (except Ludleth) and bring back their cinders to prevent the Fire from going out; however, this proves to merely be a distraction.

The actual goal of the adventure requires player observation and deduction: we must start by listening carefully to dialogues, and read as many item descriptions as possible. This is the only way for the bigger picture to form, and for actions to have meaning. Although the *Souls* and *Bloodborne* stories are closely tied to the path taken by players (the environments and enemies they face), the storytelling is almost entirely unspoken: narration is largely image-driven, and can only be decoded with prior knowledge of certain elements. This means that when many of the boss fights take place, players are ignorant of what is really at stake, and even of these enemies' roles and pasts. These elements are only revealed in retrospect, through souls collected or items found nearby. Even more troubling: several major bosses remain mute for no apparent reason.[400] This just reinforces the false impression that the games have no plot, and that the bosses are nothing but empty shells scattered imposingly along our path. It's also worth noting that the *Bloodborne* and *Dark Souls III* bosses are more talkative than in the previous episodes, almost as though Miyazaki eventually decided that it was important to add story elements into the fights themselves.[401] Are these the exceptions that confirm the rule?

In reality, this laconic style resulted from the desire to leave most of the interpretation up to players, with plenty of space for role-playing and imagination. The story is suggested in the ways the fight is presented—i.e. the settings, the music, the boss's appearance and name, etc. However, it's harder to be moved by the tragic fate of an enemy if we don't know anything about its past until later. But isn't this also a constant in the series, as players are pushed to commit acts without asking questions, and only later become aware of their responsibilities?

---

400. A few examples are the false King Allant XII in *Demon's Souls*, Seath in *Dark Souls*, Sulyvahn in *Dark Souls III*, etc.
401. *Demon's Souls* had already adopted this approach, with Maiden Astrea and Garl Vinland. This scene contrasted with the other fights, unsettling players and highlighting the importance of these characters.

A Pawn on the Chessboard

Thrown into a new world with very few points of reference, players exploring a *Souls* game or *Bloodborne* for the first time have only their sense of observation to help them decode the story unfolding around them. But the trickery doesn't stop there; even the most meticulous of players are unlikely to grasp the whole picture during their first game. Here, we're talking about NPC questlines. They often require actions to be completed in a very precise order and at a specific time, and this necessarily takes a bit of luck the first time around. It's common to finish a first game having discovered less than half of the questlines, even for players who take their time to explore. On the other hand, the longest and most complex questlines are also often those that offer the greatest reward—not necessarily material rewards, but narrative.

The "sense of achievement" at the core of Miyazaki's philosophy is therefore not limited to fights. It's applied to anyone who takes risks to explore, or invests fully in the game's world. We could almost consider the illusory walls, which go so far as to hide complete levels (such as Ash Lake in the first *Dark Souls*), as a metaphor of the games' storytelling approach. Searching always leads to satisfaction. And by promising many secrets, the *Souls* games invite players to jump right back in for a second game. This is what draws players to the community and to the shared experience of discovery: players want to immerse themselves again in these decrepit environments to figure out what else is hiding behind the veil.

The series takes this so far that it drives the very stories themselves. Players who don't pay enough attention to the descriptions and dialogues will simply abandon themselves to the fate outlined for them by higher powers. And how can we blame them? The terminology in the games can be misleading, and the familiar dualism tends to numb players, cutting short any questions they may pose about their quest. Why, as a "Chosen One," would we want anything but to save the Fire (symbol of life) to prevent the Dark from spreading? And yet, in *Dark Souls*, *Bloodborne* and *Dark Souls III* in particular, if players are content with following the path laid out for them, they are simply playing into the hands of those who dominate the world, who will do anything to preserve it.

Though the alternatives may be succinct and evasive, they aren't just a role-playing gimmick to reinforce the chosen illusion. They can be very difficult to arrive at,[402] and they exist to allow players to affirm their freedom and reject the dogma imposed on them. The only way to achieve them is to understand how the world works, with its history and rules. Reaching this "understanding" must be earned, but it's also the only way to end the ceaseless decomposition of the declining world, held together by dominating powers whose sole objective is to protect their own interests.

---

402. *Bloodborne* is one example, with the Thirds of Umbilical Cord. Another is *Dark Souls III* and Yuria's questline.

The paradox lies in the fact that this victory is rarely possible for players during a first game (unless, of course, they cheat). The *Souls* games invite us to start again from the beginning—after all, don't the stories themselves revolve around the idea of cycles? To break free of the illusion[403] and discover the truth, it's not just a matter of *wanting* it. We have to equip ourselves with the means of doing so—learn from our mistakes and use everything at our disposal. In sum, we need to apply what we learn from the fights to decipher the story.

Criticism of the *Souls* story writing is entirely understandable. Not all players will be seduced by such a convoluted storytelling format and the significant effort it requires. However, it's impossible to deny the integrity of the approach, which never made concessions for clarity over five whole games. In many ways, and in spite of the series' ever-growing reputation, the *Souls* games never compromise their creator's vision. This is a difficult balance to strike, especially considering that the development teams were composed of several hundred people, many of whom worked for external studios.

Outsourcing and the Creative Vision

When developing the first *Dark Souls*, a bigger project than *Demon's Souls* which already had the support of a larger internal team, FromSoftware enlisted some special studios for subcontracting work to help with game development, including the Chinese branch of Tose Software (based in Hangzhou) and the Taiwanese Movanova. These were significant additions to the team, both in terms of graphics creation and programming, and art design. Outsourcing is a common trend in videogame development, and has grown a great deal over the years.

A Call for Help

A careful examination of the *Dark Souls III* or *Bloodborne* credits reveals the many external employees and subcontractors. Some appear in both games, like Visual Flight, Tose Software, Lemon Sky Animations, XPEC Art Center, Sunchos Software, and Kusanagi. For each game, over ten specialized companies are listed.

---

403. Sometimes in a literal sense, as with Gwynevere in the first *Dark Souls*.

These Japanese, Chinese and Taiwanese studios have generally been working in the field for many years, on a large number of projects. Tose Software, in particular, is one of the biggest in the field.[404] In 2006, in an interview with *Gamasutra*, the company revealed that it had worked on over one thousand games—most of the time without being named (a policy that suits them as well as their clients, who are happy to take all of the recognition). Ten years later, Tose's unofficial games list must be absolutely massive.

These ghost studios have grown exponentially since the industry exploded during the 2000s, and even more since the Xbox 360 and PlayStation 3 generation. Development costs, time and difficulty increased significantly with the ever-changing technology, the financial crisis and a more crowded and competitive market. Medium-sized studios could hardly survive, as a gap formed between independent and AAA games, the latter of which are on par with Hollywood blockbusters and monopolize the full marketing space, and with it, players' expectations. This cutthroat environment is tough on "intermediate" games—each new release seems to be swept aside the week after, and entirely forgotten if it wasn't able to make a breakthrough during this short time.[405] Studios therefore face multiple financial, logistical, and technical obstacles, and the race for graphics weighs on much of the industry.

In this brutal environment, even large studios have trouble striking a balance between productivity, overall quality and profitability. Without intending to tarnish the reputations of the biggest studios, we should specify that most of them now use outsourcing. Ubisoft, Crytek, Electronic Arts, Capcom and Square Enix[406] all hire specialized companies to boost development and stay within their budget.

Profitability and Efficiency

After the worldwide success of *Dark Souls*, FromSoftware's budget increased, and they decided to sell *Dark Souls II* like a Triple-A game, in their words, which was not entirely accurate. Of course, the internal FromSoftware team grew considerably following Miyazaki's success, which allowed the company to design several large projects at once. However, to compete with the largest studios producing high-quality games, several hundred employees are necessary. To cut costs, FromSoftware turned

---

404. In the last several years, their official collaborations include games as different as *Sims 3* and *4*, the handheld console versions of *Dragon Quest*, and *Resident Evil: Revelations*.
405. The fact that *Demon's Souls* was so successful after being advertised primarily by word of mouth is all the more miraculous.
406. *FFXIII-2* and *Lightning Returns* required over ten subcontractors (including familiar names like Kusanagi, also listed among *Dark Souls III* and *Bloodborne*'s credits). The same goes for *Final Fantasy XV*, of course, and games such as *Star Ocean 4* and *5*—the smaller Tri-Ace team only did some of the work.

to outsourcing–Chinese and Taiwanese labor is less expensive, and outsourcing is more efficient in terms of recruitment and training.

Money is an important consideration for outsourcing, of course, but not the only one. In video games, programming, visual modeling (2D and 3D) and animation are also taken into account. Outsourcing can present many short- and long-term advantages for companies.[407]

Salaries for internal employees can be problematic during periods between projects, because they're paid to sit around and wait for the next one. The more in-house employees there are, the more compensation is paid "into the void," not to mention the need for extra office space if there are too many new recruits. This problem is addressed by using contractors, who provide more flexible agreements, which can be easily be terminated if the client isn't satisfied, and the business owner can easily choose the most efficient and proactive subcontracting studio. From an employee standpoint, having fewer short contracts (project-length contracts, for instance) can lead to more stability and less stress.

Outsourcing also saves lots of time in development. On the one hand, since subcontractors have worked in the field for years, and on all games consoles, they already have the skills required and are ready to put them to use–this considerably reduces the time spent on some internal research and development stages. They are specialized, and their role is to share this expertise.

Delegating more trivial design elements to other studios also theoretically means that in-house teams can be used more effectively. These teams can work on the most complex and exciting tasks, which can only boost office morale. With fewer people to manage, the leaders of each division can also focus on the essentials, and maintain better team unity.

With these many advantages in mind, it's clear why most studios and publishers choose to outsource, whether officially or not. With development now stretching over several years and becoming increasingly costly, it makes sense to save time in this way. However, this idyllic picture we've drawn obscures some potential problems, which have less to do with industrial logic and more with how we conceive of artistic creation.

407. We've based our discussion on accounts from people who work for or with subcontracting development studios. From Saigon Dragon Studios: http://saigondragonstudios.com/outsourc- ing-in-the-video-game-industry/, and Anton Wiegert, who supervises outsourcing for Guerrilla Games: http://www.gamasutra.com/blogs/AntonWiegert/20140726/221960/

Is There Still Room for the Auteur?

Are AAA video games, like most Hollywood movies, business productions rather than *auteur* visions? This topic has fueled many debates. As in cinema, the video game industry involves collaborative creation: creating characters, settings, monsters, music, lighting, animation, artificial intelligence, plot, questlines, producing trailers, fight phases, menus, etc. With so many technical and artistic divisions, several hundred internal employees are required, along with different subcontracting studios. So how can they maintain cohesion, an all-encompassing vision, without watering it down?

In the first volume of *Dark Souls: Beyond the Grave*, we insisted on Hidetaka Miyazaki's omnipresence in the design of *Demon's Souls* and the first *Dark Souls*; he wanted to oversee every detail, to picture the full story and world, something he didn't try to hide in interviews. His role was similar to a film director with control over a project–a person who wants to bring an idea to life, and draws out resources from each member of the production team to ensure that all talents converge towards the same goal, while taking their relevant proposals and initiatives into account.

However, Miyazaki worried about the size of projects, as he showed in an interview with *Official PlayStation Magazine* in 2015: "I see advantages to having a smaller team, a smaller, more conceptual project. [...] I get down to the details when it comes to direction–the story, the art and everything. I'm a pretty anal person. I tinker with every little thing. In five or 10 years, my guys aren't going to want to work with me. At that point, maybe it will be smarter for me to work on my own little idea."

We'll add another perspective to this discussion, from another well-established game designer Suda51 (*No More Heroes, Killer7*). He explained the following in an interview with David Roberts for *GamesRadar* in 2015: "I want to think that the real core of game development hasn't changed. But put simply, what's changed the most in the past 20 years or so is, back in the day, if you wanted to make a game, you had a meeting, and you talked about what kind of game you wanted to make, then you made the game. Nowadays, to be blunt about it, there's all these pointless-ass meetings, where you've got to report every single thing to a bunch of people, and all these people who don't even need to be there have to be in the meeting, and constantly talking about stuff. There's not really the opportunity to just talk about a game and make it anymore. [...] It's a real bitch to have to go through this whole entire process for every single little thing."

The question of outsourcing also raises an important issue: how do developers make sure the work of subcontractors is at the same level of quality as that of inhouse employees? Between language barriers, interpreters and representatives, with everything passing through meetings, it's easy for things can get lost in the shuffle. Everyone needs to make sure expectations are clear and well understood. This means regular feedback, which can impact internal production, since internal employees sometimes need to wait for outsourced pieces to be completed in order to continue.

The game *Deus Ex: Human Revolution* provides a telling example of this. Though the game met with success, it was criticized for its boss fights, which were considered inferior to the rest of the adventure. It turned out that these sequences were created externally, by the studio Grip Entertainment: this studio's boss admitted he wasn't very familiar with the *Deus Ex* world, and that he was more of a shooter guy. But who should be blamed in this situation? Grip Entertainment, because they didn't meet fan expectations, or Square Enix and Eidos, who decided to use this studio to complete these pivotal sequences?

However, with the exception of some graphics that clash with *Bloodborne*'s[408] overall feel, and attest more perhaps to a lack of time or less polished work from the subcontracting studios, the game is clearly the work of an *auteur*. Miyazaki once again conceptualized the entire world, the story and the primary concepts of the gameplay—the essential elements for any artistic vision in a video game that set the tone for his teams. *Bloodborne* presents the same cohesion and artistic integrity as any of the previous *Souls* games. It offers an aesthetic and intellectual point of view, which is the defining feature of a work of art.

Dark Souls III seems to counterbalance this approach slightly. Though the work is inspired in its own way, the sequel arose primarily from a market demand, with a specific, well-defined list of specifications. For promotional reasons, Miyazaki put himself in the forefront of the game design, thus obscuring the presence of two co-directors. Does being the work of a single, well-known creator make a game more valuable? We've sometimes argued for this opinion, but it also may be the source of some misunderstandings, particularly in video games where collaborative creation is extremely important. The creator's place has to be determined on a case-by-case basis, and no matter the context, creators need artists and other skilled workers to bring their ideas to life.

Perhaps Miyazaki realized that fans' real disappointment regarding *Dark Souls II* was just that he had left the project, and that even though he couldn't invest himself fully in the third (since he had to help complete *Bloodborne*), he needed to appear as the mastermind of the episode regardless. The approach feels like more the act of a FromSoftware president than an artist trying to maintain his integrity.

The situation recalls that of Suda51, who, when his studio Grasshopper Manufacture took off after the success of *No More Heroes*, decided to step away from his position of creative director, while still supervising the creation of each new game and giving it his stamp, his "Suda51 touch," which is more of a superficial label than the true *auteur* approach that motivated his former creations.

---

408. This is particularly the case for the exteriors of Cainhurst Castle: the modeling and textures lack precision and subtlety. The streets of Yharnam provide a telling contrast.

Nowadays, between collaboration, the creator's vision, outsourcing, detailed specifications and marketing expectations, it's much more difficult for large productions to strike the right balance. Some games have so many people on board that their credits can feel like they go on forever! In these circumstances, it seems almost impossible to maintain true artistic cohesion, in the highest sense, without having a strong personality at the helm to tie everything together and impose a vision. This can even be quite unhealthy, as Ken Levine (*BioShock* and *BioShock Infinite*) explained to *Rolling Stones* in 2016, referring to *Infinite*'s long and difficult development process: "It changed my life in terms of what it did to my health, and what it did to my view of making games, and my relationships with people. Managing 30 or 40 people where you know everybody's name is a very different process than managing 150 people. You walk by people in the studio and you don't know who they are." This is rather alarming, and says much about how difficult it is to reconcile large productions with human relationships and creativity.

There's reason to wonder what will happen with future FromSoftware creations. Nevertheless, *Bloodborne* is fairly reassuring when it comes to Miyazaki's position, and his desire to remain at the core of game development, as he told *GNN* in 2016: "I can guarantee, I will stay as a game director for at least another five years. [...] If I'm not allowed to make games then I'd rather not be a president." And right before *Dark Souls III* came out, he told *Vice*: "I'm happy that I have a greater budget for the third game, as well as the creative freedom to make my own decisions. But if there were some restrictions about what I was creating, I definitely wouldn't want to work on it." He's pretty clear about it, but there's no way to be one hundred percent sure that these aren't just fine-sounding promotional speeches, to gloss over a more nuanced reality.

Game Promotion

How do you sell a *Dark Souls* game? This was a thorny topic for Bandai Namco's marketing department with each game—they had to strike a balance between pleasing the series' earliest fans and enticing new players. Their balance didn't always quite work, particularly in the marketing campaign for *Dark Souls III*: it was a perfect illustration of the expression "walking on eggshells."

On Difficulty

We covered this subject in depth in the first volume of *Dark Souls: Beyond the Grave*, the series was a surprise success, mainly due to the way it broke with convention of the time. With its very demanding style, pushing players to their limits, the series banked on the "old-fashioned" approach, which drew players who were tired of player-friendly games. However, the game's difficulty soon confined it to a narrow category of hardcore games, known for being punishing and uncompromising: the type of game that isn't for everyone. Though the *Souls* games may be synonymous with repeated deaths, the approach is not so much that of a mindless "die and retry"; players are instead encouraged to learn from their failures, in a clever and generous way.

The game's reputation is often hijacked. But in some ways, that's probably for the best, because this same acceptance of the perverse difficulty is what ensured the international success of the *Souls* games—between battles of the egos and strength competitions, everyone's pride is flattered. Finishing a *Souls* game is an "achievement," even though it's within anyone's reach if they invest a little time in it.

Namco Bandai fully embraced this niche for the release of the *Prepare to Die* edition of the first episode—the title could not be clearer. For the occasion, the publisher uploaded a trailer with the title *Hardcore*, showing death after death and the full spectrum of violence from the game's different enemies and bosses.

More interesting, the *Dark Souls II* campaign was not so much focused on the "game over" aspect, as on the idea of surpassing oneself, like the trailer presented at E3 2013, which used a voiceover to explain that death is not a finality, but just a step along the way. The video was entitled *Go Beyond Death*. The damage was done, though, and the series' reputation never rose above the image of a game "for real players," with legendary difficulty. The *Super Meat Boy* and other *Titan Souls* games understood this well when entering this niche.

However, with each new *Souls*, the production budget got bigger, and so did the communications budget. This made it even more important to reach the niche audience, but also the general public. The marketing for *Dark Souls III* no longer took on the topic of difficulty head on. On the other hand, what better way to attract new players than to produce videos that would really blow them away?

Death in Music

The first *Dark Souls* got the ball rolling with two trailers that were released in August and September 2011, each accompanied by a different piece from the rock group the Silent Comedy: *Bartholomew* and then *All Saints Day*. The video has all of the ingredients for a hip promotional clip–a driving beat, fades to black, cool music–, even though the tone has nothing to do with *Dark Souls*.

This type of trailer, with its modern, flashy style, generally appeals to neophytes without deterring the game's devoted fans. In 2007, the trailer for the launch of the first *Gears of War* made a splash through its use of Tears for Fears' *Mad World*, sung by Gary Jules.[409] The soft, melancholic song gave the images a unique feel, and contrasted with the fury depicted in the game. Following this success, many games tried their hand at the musical trailer, going so far as to introduce new artists like Woodkid with one of the trailers for *Assassin's Creed: Revelations*.

After the success of the trailer using the Silent Comedy's song *Bartholomew*, the *Souls* games made this a recurring element in their marketing campaigns. *Dark Souls II* used three different songs, for instance: *I'm Undone* by Nitzer Ebb, *Hollow Lullaby* by Greg Downs and *Locomotive Breath* from Jethro Tull. *Bloodborne* got its own stylized trailer with the song *Hunt You Down*, written by the Hit House Music,[410] and performed by Ruby Friedman. The undeniably poser side of these videos may contrast significantly with the games' morbid elegance, but it has always hit the nail on the head.

Dark Souls III didn't change the formula: the promotional clip was paired with a cover of *True Colors* sung by Richie Kohan. The video is full of visual effects (such as text that remains glowing onscreen) and a series of fade-outs to present the third episode's world. Then, it shows fight scenes from spectacular camera angles that couldn't be from the game, but which give the trailer a strong feeling of dynamism: it's quite the dramatization, heightened by the contrast with the slow, gloomy music.

And Namco Bandai went even farther for this episode, asking film director Eli Roth (*Hostel*), known for horror movies, to produce a short animation to promote the game for the three weeks between the Japanese release and the wider release. The resulting animation is about two and a half minutes long. It echoes the visual themes from the series (the three "witches" from *Dark Souls II*, the hues of *III*, the cursed woods, the knight hero), but without understanding them, devoid of subtlety and with an ambiance that feels unrelated–at one point, it falls into crude gore, as the poor knight's face gets pecked apart while he's still alive. It's animated in a jerky fashion (reminiscent of Flash animation) and a little cheesy. The clip has trouble paying tribute to

---

409. Arrangement produced by composer Michael Andrews for the film *Donnie Darko* in 2001.
410. Music production company that specializes in trailers and advertising.

the game it's trying to promote, and lacks an artistic identity that would make it interesting outside of this context. It was a nice intention, but the result fell flat. Could the publisher itself have misunderstood *Dark Souls'* true essence? Or does marketing follow a totally different logic? One of the greatest difficulties is still to make the target audience happy–that is, the fans from the very beginning.

The Sequel Dilemma

Though *Dark Souls II* sold quite well, the game didn't fully satisfy all players, even though it was a rich game in many respects. Some didn't think its quality was as high as the two previous *Souls* games, especially with regard to the bosses, level design and general atmosphere. People's fears of seeing the series suffer increased with the announcement of *Dark Souls III*. *Bloodborne* was going to apply the approach to a different world, but another *Souls* sequel seemed like a risky bet, not so much in terms of sales, but because of the weariness it could induce. As some games such as *Call of Duty* and *Assassin's Creed* and sports games series wring their concepts dry by churning out new games practically every year, it seemed as though one of the most exciting and original games of the last few years was falling into the same trap.

In part, the communications goal of *Dark Souls III* was therefore to reassure fans. In addition to Miyazaki's comments, which emphasized that the errors made in *DS II* had been understood and accounted for (particularly in terms of the worldbuilding), everything else also supported this idea. For instance, as early as three months following the game's announcement, the Dancer was revealed, a boss with gracious movements and rich in detail.

Miyazaki's return as creative director also reinforced this idea (though he was not alone in this role), along with the first trailers released with Yuka Kitamura's sublime music, glimpses of the world and the ties to the Lord of Cinder mythology, the many visuals that solidified the connection with the first episode's graphics, the aesthetic elements, the livelier combat system that recalled *Bloodborne*, and so on. All of the communications elements came together to make *Dark Souls III* into the long-awaited epic conclusion. The expectation was really shaped by the campaign–the two previous episodes didn't really need a sequel. The marketing team had to drum up interest while giving the impression that it had been there from the start.

With the hope of rediscovering the sensations of the first *Dark Souls*, fans turned to this third (or rather, fifth) episode. Namco Bandai took this even farther, organizing a contest that would reward the person who could best explain the *Souls* story.

To sweeten the pot, $10,000 were at stake.[411] The marketing strategy was designed both to butter up the series' fans, exciting their spelunker spirits as they dove into the games' cryptic stories down to the tiniest detail, and to spark the curiosity of newcomers who would thus have access to clear and concise summaries.

The difficulty lay in selling *Dark Souls III* both as the conclusion of a trilogy, and as an independent game that could be played without experience of the previous ones. The new-generation console also required such positioning. *Dark Souls II*'s *Scholars of the First Sin* edition and *Bloodborne* could have served as a point of entry, but it was obvious that many players would first discover the series with *Dark Souls III*. In these circumstances, how could they satisfy both neophytes and regulars, which seemingly require different marketing approaches? Namco Bandai attempted this balancing act, but lost its way a bit.

Spoiling the Discovery

Did they worry they wouldn't be able to reassure those who were disappointed with *Dark Souls II*? Or that newcomers would not be tempted by the game? Either way, as the trailers continued to be released, more and more important pieces of the game were revealed, reaching a pinnacle with the game's launch trailer. The launch trailer didn't hold back: it showed glimpses of the fights with the Nameless King, Lorian, Sulyvahn, the Abyss Watchers, Yhorm, and so on. Basically, it presented most of the game's major fight scenes, accompanied by some crucial dialogues, as if to highlight the game's narration and suggest traditional scriptwriting to those new to the series.

In contrast, and in spite of Sony's intensive promotion, *Bloodborne* had maintained the secrets of its world—the Great Ones and Lovecraftian mythology—up until the very end, content with only revealing the first bosses and game environments.[412] On the *Dark Souls III* side, the beginning of the promotional phase revealed screenshots of sunny Archdragon Peak, a place whose appearance was likely to surprise those familiar with the series. Of course, no one was ever forced to watch the trailers, or look at the press images. You can close your eyes when an advertisement comes on, or refuse to click an article about a game, though this only really applies to those who are already sold on the game: those who are undecided have to read the first reviews, or watch the trailer, and thereby deprive themselves of the pleasure of discovery.

---

411. Steven Dixon won the grand prize for his video *Biography of the Chosen Undead*.
412. With the exception of the *Project Beast* trailer, which showed Ebrietas. This video resulted from a leak, and was never officially released.

The pleasure of discovery is essential in the *Souls* games, and intensified by the community movement that takes place with the release of a new episode. On forums, wikis, social networks, or at bars, everyone likes sharing their experiences, their progress, observations on the world, secret paths, etc. The collective dynamic is particularly invigorating and enjoyable. The collective enjoyment was partly spoiled for Westerners by Bandai Namco. The game came out on March 24, 2016 in Japan, before the end of the fiscal year, but three weeks later in the rest of the world, while *Dark Souls II* and *Bloodborne* were released almost simultaneously everywhere, and for all consoles.[413]

The wait would have been less frustrating if Namco Bandai hadn't decided to send copies of the game to some video creators and streamers (people who play live on platforms such as *Twitch*). What was the point? To ensure maximum visibility for the game's release and reach people other than the game's regular fans.[414] The problem was that the streamers were allowed to go all the way up to the Abyss Watchers, almost a third through the adventure. The Internet was quickly swarming with *Dark Souls III* videos, prompting spoilers and irritating those who couldn't understand why streamers should have access to the full game before everyone else.

There again, no one was making people watch the videos or look for secrets about the game. Nonetheless, we can't deny that unless you cloister yourself away, it's hard to avoid the constant flow of information available on the Internet; by just reading a video's title or glimpsing an image on social media, the pleasure of discovery can be spoiled. TV fans know something about this. And sometimes, when our curiosity is high and we have to wait so long, it's hard to resist the temptation. This was the thing that irked some of the community, and the forums on *NeoGaf*, *Giant Bomb* or *Reddit* were soon teeming with heated debates.

The anger of fans reached all the way to Namco, which backpedaled and asked streamers to stop their videos until the eve of the release. This backpedaling felt like an admission of failure, and one that couldn't really stop the bleeding. Some kept on with their videos using the Japanese version—bilingual players like Jayson Love (MANvsGAME) went so far as to interpret the game in English for their viewers. On the day *Dark Souls III* was released in Japan, others discovered that the Xbox One version had English subtitles, and that it could be purchased digitally on a console outside of Japan using a little tweaking. The hack started making its way around social networks, and Namco was powerless to stop it. They still warned players that the version was "not complete" and that it didn't include the contents of a day-one patch. Of course, this didn't temper any enthusiasm.

---

413. With the exception of the PC version of *Dark Souls II*, which was released one month later.
414. In 2016, Sony took a similar approach by sharing with PewDiePie (who has several tens of millions of subscribers) an early release version of the first twenty minutes of *The Last Guardian* so he could create a video of it and reach lots of players who otherwise may not have been interested in the game.

Added to this, there were some other dubious marketing choices, like the Chicken Wing challenge in England, in partnership with the MeatLiquor restaurant chain—the ludicrous goal was to devour 20 chicken wings as quickly as possible (covered in extremely spicy chili sauce) to win a PlayStation 4 and a Collector's or Prestige Edition of the game.

The Prestige Edition raised the stakes quite a bit. *Dark Souls II* and *Bloodborne* had standard Collector's Editions, with an artbook, original soundtrack and metal box, along with accessories in *Bloodborne*'s "nightmare" edition, all sold at a reasonable cost: $140 at most. Though *Dark Souls III* also sold a Collector's Edition at a comparable price and with similar content, a "prestige edition" was also released in limited quantity, proudly containing a 15.5" figurine of Yhorm. This edition cost almost $500, and now sells for exorbitant sums on the Internet, sometimes going for over $2,000. Namco Bandai knew that some fans of the series weren't afraid to spend money, as was evidenced by the crowdfunding success on *Kickstarter* for a *Dark Souls* board game, designed by Steamforged Games with approval from Namco Bandai—the campaign received over £3.7 million (almost $5 million), 7,542% of the initial goal.

A Necessary Evil?

Namco Bandai did all it could to sell *Dark Souls III* in any way possible: advertising, aggressive store displays, big posters at E3, in addition to the marketing we explored above. A free app was also published soon before the Japanese release, in the form of a "choose your own adventure" book. It included several prize drawings for those who made it through the app: T-shirts, keychains, a copy of the game, and in particular, a statue almost 6'5" tall.

However, by hedging its bets, the publisher poorly predicted the reactions of fans. Revealing too much, by all means possible (trailers, live streaming on *Twitch*, press, etc.), was not to everyone's taste. The lag between the Japanese and other release date, the lack of explanation for this decision and the aimless communications regarding the streaming only served to anger some fans more. This wasn't especially surprising: the more passionate the community, the more reasons it will find to complain. However, the numbers offer food for thought. *Dark Souls III* may have broken Namco Bandai's release records, but the overall sales weren't much higher than for any of the other games in the series. As is common in the industry, the publisher sugar-coated the reality a bit, referencing the three million copies distributed around the world. Distributed, yes, but not necessarily sold. Did the aggressive marketing campaign really draw in that many new players? Or did the series' success come from its logical continuity with the previous games, which would explain the similar sales numbers?

It's worth wondering whether all of the money and resources put into promoting the game were actually necessary. Of course, games of this scope can't go without a large ad campaign to ensure strong sales. But is it enough to capitalize on flashy graphics and consumer-driven, collector habits to get the public on board? In this way, the *Dark Souls III* marketing campaign is perfectly symptomatic of our era of overconsumption, in which a game's real value on the market depends heavily on its first week of sales.

The *Souls* games, since *II*, have been sold using the same methods as a Triple-A game, a paradox for a series that owes its success to its singularity and against-the-grain approach. But perhaps it's just a necessary evil that will allow it to endure, giving it prime placement in an increasingly unforgiving market. To this end, the series also has additional content to continually rekindle the flame.

The DLC Approach

It's now part of the videogame landscape, but it still elicits indignation from time to time. We've referring to DLC, an abbreviation for "downloadable content." Whether free or paid, this catch-all term refers to an additional element that can be added to a game, whether a costume pack or a game sequence of varying lengths. The term "expansion pack" also applies here, to employ the term that was used for computer games long before this trend infiltrated the console market. Here, we're specifically talking about expansions—the content that introduces new plot elements, locations and so on. Since the first *Dark Souls* and *Artorias of the Abyss*, the FromSoftware series always provided paid DLCs with the games, acting as mini-adventures to complement the primary game. But are they just a bonus, a little extra treat, or do they serve as a pillar that's indispensable to the work as a whole?

In Search of Quality

As early as the 1990s, and in the early 2000s, the studio Blizzard created high-quality expansions to complement the *Diablo*, *StarCraft* and other *Warcraft* series. This additional content was generally a sequel to the original story, or perfected the games by improving graphics or balancing the systems. Even if there weren't enough additions to justify the title of "sequel," the content was nevertheless welcome, as it extended the game's lifespan on- and off-line. A treat for fans (though not free), and plenty of revenue for the publisher.

When technological changes allowed consoles to do things reserved previously for computers, such as download data or update, designers quickly saw that DLCs could serve many purposes. Many studios soon proved that, for good content, players would take another trip to the cash register. This was true for Rockstar and the two DLC episodic packs developed for *GTA IV: The Lost and Damned* and *The Ballad of Gay Tony*. Each one offered over ten additional hours in Liberty City, from viewpoints related to the adventures of Niko Bellic, with new protagonists. It's a nice example of what can be done with expansions when studios and publishers aren't just focused on the bottom line.

The *Dark Souls* and *Bloodborne* DLCs are similar in many ways. Their content is dense, original, surprising, and even enhances certain elements of the original game. From this perspective, FromSoftware is beyond reproach—the work is commendable. However, the matter isn't quite so clear-cut when we look at what the DLCs actually contribute, and how necessary they are.

The Obligation to Pay

For *Artorias of the Abyss*, FromSoftware's first DLC for the *Dark Souls* series, Miyazaki and his team wanted to add elements that had to be excluded from the main game due to production issues. Artorias's story, a legend literally lost in time, is presented as an appendix that we can explore in full. Obviously, the DLC also expands the game's world, in particular the elements related to the Abyss and Manus, but nothing that is essential in order to understand the main adventure. Things get more complicated with the following episodes, however. The additions to *Dark Souls II* may first appear independent, but they're actually closely tied to the original game's plot. Similarly, though the *Dark Souls III* DLCs center around a sideline plot, Gael's fate still leads players to learn about a central character, Sulyvahn, and especially to enter the Ringed City, a location full of revelations about the Pygmies, the ancestors of humans and essential to the myth of the Dark Soul. And finally, *The Old Hunters* provides vital tools for interpreting *Bloodborne*'s nebulous, complex storyline, to the point where players may wonder why all of it wasn't presented, or at least mentioned in the original game.

If we just consider the main adventures in the games, they all fully conclude in the main game, and the DLCs never add an alternative or enhanced ending. This wasn't the case for the contentious *Asura's Wrath*: its epic ending had to be purchased and downloaded separately for players to experience the story's true conclusion.[415] Another interesting example is that of *BioShock Infinite*. It was a complete work, but the double-episode DLC *Burial at Sea* adds an ending that appears indispensable to

---

415. Another example is *Prince of Persia* from 2008. Its abrupt ending was extended with a new paid DLC.

the story. However, the *BioShock Infinite* plot stands quite well on its own—it doesn't need this addition for comprehension, or to fully develop its themes. In the *Souls* games, however, the goal wasn't to provide sequels in DLC-form, but rather to develop the existing world and provide new elements for understanding.

In these clever, fragmented games that require serious investigative work, observation and reflection to untangle the complex plot and complete the puzzle, isn't it a little frustrating to have to wait for a DLC to piece together the bigger picture? Especially since conjectures arise spontaneously from the gray area surrounding some important points that are barely mentioned in the original game (Kos in *Bloodborne*, the Angels or Demon Prince in *Dark Souls III*, etc.), which can give the unpleasant feeling that this content was indeed concocted by Miyazaki, and that the allusions here and there are simply subtle hints of the DLC and thus planned from the start. Player theories are squelched when the downloadable content is released, invalidating the research and imagination many put into the game, when they may have just preferred to stick to their own version.

Why did most players not feel swindled by the *Dark Souls* and *Bloodborne* DLCs? It must have something to do with the flawless quality of these expansions, which mirror the original games in their meticulous finish and their high ambitions for the artwork and gaming experience. In this instance, it's surely also because the DLCs provide an immense satisfaction with regard to the story's content. They awaken the same sense of discovery and fascination that we get from the primary adventure, offering an escapist pleasure in the dark lands where so much remains undiscovered. In a new space, with new characters and item descriptions, the treasure hunt for clues recommences at full tilt, as theories unravel or solidify, and others are born. The additions are always deep-rooted. And with his sense of the implicit and suggestiveness, Hidetaka Miyazaki is wise enough not to explain and reveal everything. For all the questions that are answered, as many new ones are raised. The pleasure of exploring blindly—scrutinizing the slightest changes in the background, the tiniest details in a set of armor—is rekindled, just like the very first time. On social networks, chats come back to life, the search for meaning starts once again, and *Dark Souls* prolongs its existence in the cultural world, an inestimable treasure for designers.

A Second Life

What is the purpose of an expansion that appears several months after the initial game, if not to gain new visibility in the media? From a marketing standpoint, at a time when numerous video game products are released every week, eclipsing past releases, additional content helps bring a game back into the limelight to ensure greater longevity. This is even truer for the *Souls* games, which rely enormously on the activity of the community. An expansion, as we've already seen, is an opportunity for players to set off once again on a hunt for clues, to struggle alongside their ever-stronger opponents to come up with tips and discoveries: generally speaking, they bring the game to life.

For a continually growing studio like FromSoftware, whose reputation really took off with the first *Dark Souls*, steady visibility is a significant asset. The DLC expansions help keep both the series and the studio in the mainstream. In fact, it's a safe bet that this is what pushed FromSoftware to develop the *Dark Souls II* DLCs, which were not initially planned, at least according to producer Takeshi Miyazoe.[416] At the end of December 2013, *Dark Souls III* had just been secretly put into production, but *Bloodborne* was the only news coming from the studio. It was a Sony exclusive, which limited the audience a bit, and risked losing fans who had played *Dark Souls* on Xbox 360 and PC. Not to mention that the atmosphere was different, potentially putting off fans of the medieval world. They needed to keep the *Dark Souls* series going until the third episode's release, which explains the *Dark Souls II* expansions, and the regular release schedule, which didn't separate the full game releases by more than a year (*Bloodborne* included) starting in early 2014. The DLCs for *Dark Souls III*, each released six months apart, also served this purpose as FromSoftware prepared to announce its plans.

And these DLCs have another advantage. They can be included later on as part of a new, comprehensive version of the game, in a box and generally with the label "Game of the Year," all at a lower cost than that of a traditional release. This package deal can be an enticement for the final undecided players to buy the game and reopen the discussion.[417] *Dark Souls' Scholar of the First Sin* edition pushed the envelope by providing an overhaul of the game, with improved graphics, additional plot elements, updates to item descriptions, and different enemy locations. The approach gave the impression that a whole new experience was available. Fans could justifiably feel that, up until this edition, they had only played an unfinished version of the game. However, *Dark Souls* fans tend to wholeheartedly embrace anything with potential to enrich the initial work, even if it means digging a little deeper into their pockets. After all, considering the prolific contents in the base games, it's hard to sniff at FromSoftware and accuse them of not respecting players. The debate is still open, though.

416. See "Creation" chapter from the first volume of *Dark Souls: Beyond the Grave*.
417. Though nothing rivals the exciting moment when the Internet becomes awash with players all exploring the game at the same time, researching and sharing, as wikis begin to fill up, and many secrets remain out there for the taking.

As it stands, the *Souls* and *Bloodborne* DLCs were nothing but satisfying. Players got high-quality expansions, and FromSoftware got a return on its investment and maintained the visibility of its flagship series, which will let other games take the spotlight, without losing the company's audience. Customer loyalty is essential to the process, and additional content helps preserve the brand image in the long term. With *The Ringed City*, Hidetaka Miyazaki and his team provided fans with a final adventure through the *Dark Souls* world, one year after *Dark Souls III*'s release. A final immersion in the horror and melancholy before turning his focus elsewhere, towards FromSoftware's unknown future projects. It's a conclusion that works with *Dark Souls III* to give us both a feeling of satisfaction and of familiarity.

Dark Souls III: Culmination or Redundancy?

In the press, the third episode of *Dark Souls* was often referred to as a kind of "greatest hits" compilation, in a positive way, from testers' and critics' perspectives, overcoming this status and rising above its basics. Almost as though the game represented the culmination of the formula, the most obvious ending, even though it ultimately offered very few novelties.

In Constant Improvement?

The series has come a long way since *Demon's Souls*. As a perfectionist, Hidetaka Miyazaki always tried to take a step back from his works to figure out what could be improved, and provide players with a richer and more balanced experience. Even for *Dark Souls II*, which he didn't lead, his supervision consisted in explaining his perspective on the series to the two creative directors and pointing out things that needed changing.

Concretely, the changes that took place from 2009 onward are fairly obvious. *Dark Souls* moved away from the healing consumable items, using "replenishable" Estus Flasks instead, to prevent players from having to repeat game phases over and over again to rebuild their stores. *Dark Souls II* aimed to strike a compromise to allow players to maintain health in reserves, while *III* decided to return to the system used in the first game, in response to player feedback. *Bloodborne* went for a new approach, returning to limited consumables, balanced by the option to regain health immediately after taking damage.

Dark Souls also marked a radical shift in terms of worldbuilding, diverging greatly from *Demon's Souls*' independent regions, even though none of the later episodes were able to reproduce the stroke of genius from *Dark Souls*. *Dark Souls II* significantly improved fights, both in terms of movements and skills, particularly with the option of using twinblades. By adding a livelier feel, *Bloodborne* also revamped the fight scenes with a more aggressive angle, an approach that eventually also affected *Dark Souls III*.

With small touches here and there, the series has continued to evolve, to refine elements, take out others, always with the aim of striking the right balance and meeting player expectations. Miyazaki has declared on several occasions that he takes the various comments he reads online to heart. However, though his philosophy as a creator remained the same, every new episode moved away from the austerity of *Demon's Souls* to approach a delicate balance.

A Compromise Between Difficulty and Accessibility

With *Dark Souls III*, the *Souls* formula was used in an interesting new way. While some fights (particularly in the game's final third and the DLCs) were just as perverse and faithful to the series' reputation, the game tends to soften in other ways, in the same vein as *Dark Souls II*.

Elements that have often been poorly understood, like the covenants, were simplified a great deal. Where the online component proved too cryptic for players starting out in the first *Dark Souls*, the second game clarified the concept, providing access to covenants very early on, and providing more explicit instructions for the system and the benefits of joining a covenant, beyond the role-playing elements. The concept of "sin" itself was toned down: in the first episode, players would get one sin point at a time for breaking a covenant, but this concept disappeared entirely from *II*, and *III* basically removed the idea of sin altogether, limiting it to hostility towards NPCs. In this third episode, the covenants themselves can be changed through a simple equipment change, at will, and with no direct consequences. There's no longer the need to go talk with the characters who let you join a covenant in the first place: this saves time, certainly, but takes away from our immersion as a result. We still have to return to the place associated with the selected covenant to bestow items, rank up and gain new items, equipment and information about the game world.

The other element to be drastically modified was the equipment durability. In *Demon's Souls* and the first *Dark Souls*, players had to take care of their equipment, which wore away over time and required the skills of a blacksmith, without which it would become unusable. In *Dark Souls II*, it was no longer necessary to visit a blacksmith to return a weapon or armor set to its maximum durability: resting at a bonfire sufficed. On the other hand, equipment wears down much more quickly, so much so that players had to pay attention to how long they spent between bonfires. In *Dark Souls III*, this feature lost its importance; equipment wears down almost as slowly as in the first episode, but like *II*, it's restored fully at each bonfire! There's practically no risk of breaking a weapon, which makes the durability level pointless. Fights may be just as difficult, but this change is one that makes the series more accessible to the general public: one less parameter to consider during exploration. It meant more efficiency, but took away from the role-playing perspective.

Also with the goal of making the experience more flexible, players can warp freely throughout *Dark Souls II* and *III*, which simplifies players' paths, since they no longer have to go back to a hub to get to another place as in *Demon's Souls* or *Bloodborne*. There's also the consideration of what this does to level layout: unlike in *Dark Souls*, there's no way to go from one area of the map to another using shortcuts, since the kingdoms of Drangleic and Lothric aren't set up for these kinds of paths. This begs the following question: is the teleportation used throughout *II* and *III* a practical tool, or an admission that the designers failed to come up with a world as convincing as in the first *Dark Souls*?

The series clearly evolved quite a bit, but it tends towards greater player comfort rather than a radical shift away from the first games. This approach was confirmed by the online system—though Miyazaki had preferred random, anonymous encounters, *Dark Souls II* moved towards easier collaboration with friends. This was even more noticeable in *Bloodborne* (particularly with the Chalice Dungeons), and in *Dark Souls III*—even Miyazaki had changed his mind. *Dark Souls II* also introduced PvP (player versus player) arenas, to encourage honest dueling, with no option for healing: a part of the game that only took on its full meaning with support from the community, and which had hardly occurred to Miyazaki at the time of *Demon's Souls*. *Dark Souls III* goes so far as to introduce purple phantoms, whom players can summon to shake things up a little, without knowing if they'll be friend or foe.

The creative process of *Souls* and *Bloodborne* was therefore peppered with questions and changes, with a mission to strike a complex balance between difficulty and accessibility, two seemingly contradictory elements that nevertheless arise from an obvious logic: reaching the greatest number of players without betraying the series' inherent challenge.

In spite of the minimal yet numerous changes, however, the overall experience wasn't ever lost. Far from it: the series fosters familiarity. By doing so, *Dark Souls III* met the expectations for the trilogy's conclusion, even though it may have suffered a bit from its strong attachment to the series' fundamentals.

In Familiar Territory

Serving in some ways as a "greatest hits" compilation, *Dark Souls III* uses imagery familiar to all *Souls* buffs. The Firelink Shrine and Fire Keeper are direct references to the Nexus and Maiden in Black from *Demon's Souls*, characters who were already reinterpreted in *Dark Souls II* (Majula and the Emerald Herald), and in *Bloodborne* (Hunter's Dream and the Plain Doll). We can also find the archetype of the Crestfallen Warrior we've seen since *Demon's Souls*: now he answers to the name "Hawkwood."

The first level, on the High Wall of Lothric, brings back memories of Boletarian Palace, down to the traditional dragon who decided to burn everything in its path. There's a slight change here, though: this time, he doesn't burn a bridge.[418] Either way, the *Souls* blueprint remains the same. Evidently, the appetite for novelty isn't as strong. By acting thus, *Dark Souls III* takes the risk of getting stuck in a rut that has haunted the series since the second episode.

Miyazaki may have promised that the second half of the adventure would be more surprising, but it is only partly so. It emphatically references *Demon's Souls*—for instance, the Irithyll Dungeon looks like the Tower of Latria with its guardians that ring their bells. There's even the Storm King's sword, which can be used to defeat Yhorm by sending shockwaves through the air, as in *Demon's Souls*: it's a great idea the first time around, but it loses some of its appeal the second time. And we can't forget Yuria of Londor, whose name is directly taken from the *Demon's Souls* witch.

These are references, certainly, but this may start to feel like obvious fan service rather than a passionate desire for game continuity. Just take the giant wolf we meet in the Painted World of Ariandel: he's a glaring reference to Sif. Even Blacksmith André, a character whose presence in the game is justified by the game's status as a sequel, doesn't have a compelling reason to be in the game. He's disappointingly transparent, serving only to give us tips about forging and Estus Flasks when we talk with him. It's also worth noting that the monsters and locations seem to come directly from *Bloodborne*, like the Undead Settlement, a daytime version of Hemwick Charnel Lane. The aesthetic and thematic inspirations also seem to come straight from *Berserk*, in particular the eclipse, or Gael's appearance and weapons. *Dark Souls III* often resembles a mash-up of the previous *Souls* games, along with their cultural heritage.

Even when the game manages to surprise players with new environments, like the sublime polar setting of Irithyll, it's only to tie back to previous scenes: the Irithyll Dungeon, but also Anor Londo. Of course, it's hard to criticize Anor Londo, with its satisfying discoveries that are well-integrated into the world. Nonetheless, the feeling

---

418. As if to better contradict this little shift, at the end of the game, players can see not one but two dragons burning a bridge at Lothric Castle. And the second DLC adds a third dragon burning a path—here along the side of a mountain.

of familiarity, or nostalgia, in *Dark Souls III* doesn't necessarily work in its favor. In its desire to satisfy fans, while also impressing newcomers, it doesn't innovate and offer a new experience. Comfort and familiarity, which are certainly necessary for players to enjoy themselves, are also anathema to creativity. And yet, creativity has always been central to the series.

Dark Souls III nevertheless meets its primary objectives, with especially strong visuals and music, and high-quality fights (the best of the series), a wide variety of bosses[419] and great overall structure. Without a doubt, the conclusion isn't lacking in determination. This holds true up until the final boss fight, which is just the right blend of intensity, nostalgia and relevance. The final boss employs all of the major techniques that players can use, a concept that Miyazaki had wanted to use for Gwyn at the end of *Dark Souls*, but didn't have time—he got his wish this time, though.

The game may provide a fitting end to the series and meet most expectations, but it also highlights the limitations of the formula. *Bloodborne* cleverly transposed this formula into a new world, with an aesthetic and thematic approach that is both similar, yet very different. It was one way to rejuvenate the series and add some surprises without shaking things up too much; on the other hand, *Dark Souls III* is only sprinkled with rare novelties, mainly drowning in a very sleek but predictable ensemble. In this way, it does represent the turning point described by Miyazaki in his interviews: a major game that synthesizes all of the series' qualities down to the last drop, to better allow FromSoftware to turn towards the future and break new creative ground. Is it a culmination or redundancy? It's a bit of both.

Legacy: An Indelible Mark

The *Souls* series ended eight years after the release of its flagship game, *Demon's Souls*, eight years during which the videogame world continued to evolve, and eight years that allowed the FromSoftware creations to trickle down into the collective consciousness and become a part of popular culture.[420] A cartoon, unfortunately not of the highest quality,[421] was even published in 2016 by Titan Comics. More than ever, *Dark Souls* has become a strong and influential game.

---

419. Even if the flaming sword motif is repetitive—we find it against the Watchers, Sulyvahn, the Dancer, Lorian, Lothric, the final boss—, it's appropriate for the situation, particularly in the case of the Lords of Cinder, who use the power of Fire.

420. *Dark Souls II* even appears in a scene from *Jupiter Ascending*, by the Wachowski sisters, in which a character can be spotted playing the game. The soundtrack was replaced by a different piece, probably due to copyright. The box of this same game also appears in the episode "Playtest" (S3E2) of the TV series *Black Mirror*.

421. Nothing like the awful *Slashy Souls*, a free-to-play 2D game produced by Bandai Namco and GameStop, which came out in February 2016 to keep fans occupied until the release of *Dark Souls III*.

A Source of Inspiration

In the "Legacy" chapter of the first volume of *Dark Souls: Beyond the Grave* we emphasized that Miyazaki's creation, through its harshness and the trust it places in players, upended many trends and awakened a desire for real challenges, risk-and-reward dynamics, and deep, well-thought-out game systems. Many designers and games adopted the form of challenge used in the *Souls* games, drawing from the series' best ideas. We've already mentioned games like *Shovel Knight*, *Titan Souls*, *Lords of the Fallen*, *Salt and Sanctuary*, as well as other more incongruous references like *Zombi U* and *Destiny*. Since then, even though some games seem to be missing in action, like *Deep Down* from Capcom,[422] others have been added to the list of works highly influenced by *Dark Souls*. One prime example is *Nioh* from Team Ninja (*Ninja Gaiden*) and Koei Tecmo, released in February 2017.

The wait for this game was a long one: the development process for this action-RPG was chaotic from its start in 2004. There were team changes, story rewrites and system overhauls, and the eventual game was midway between action and role-playing, a successful hybridization of *Ninja Gaiden*, *Onimusha* and *Dark Souls*, while maintaining its own identity. And if the game managed this feat, it was in large part thanks to Miyazaki's work. At the beginning of the 2010s, the successes of *Demon's Souls* and *Dark Souls* proved that there was indeed a market for difficult, thoughtful action games that don't lead players by the hand. This return to a challenging approach, which was somewhat exclusive to Japanese games in the past, led producer Kô Shibusawa to pass the project along to Team Ninja, whose *Ninja Gaiden* had already taken this approach.

In several interviews, co-director Fumihiko Yasuda (*Ninja Gaiden 3*) was open about the game's primary source of inspiration: For example, when speaking with *Destructoid*: "As anyone can see, we have that influence. We have a lot of *Souls* fans on our design team. It's not something we're trying to hide," and with *Eurogamer*: "There's an obvious inspiration there. Yes, it did have a big impact on the direction this project eventually took. We have very, very high opinions of the *Souls* series and it's captivated a very wide audience, even here in Japan. Also, fundamentally that the game is very difficult, very challenging, yet very well-done and refined as a great action game."

---

422. There haven't been many signs of life since 2013, even though Capcom continues to renew the trademark.

A Major Topic of Discussion

Besides *Nioh*, we can also list *The Surge*, from the creators of *Lords of the Fallen* (Deck13 Interactive studio), which came out in May 2017. They also cited *Souls* as a primary source of inspiration, though the futuristic atmosphere is quite different. The game did well to distinguish itself, at least visually, from the FromSoftware flagship series.

However, the *Souls* effect can't be measured simply by the number of games that have tried to copy them or drawn inspiration from them. Sometimes, the effect is found in a game's general design, as for the creators of the shooter *Alienation*, who have said they based themselves on *Demon's Souls* and *Dark Souls* in the way they push a concept to the max. And other times, a precise element is recycled, as in Taro Yoko's *NieR: Automata*–when players die, they lose their items and must locate their body to retrieve them. If they die again before completing this goal, they lose them for good. This mechanism is familiar to any *Souls* player,[423] and can also be found in *Shovel Knight*. The finesse of *NieR: Automata* lies in the way that this aspect is justified by the plot even more so than in *Souls*, since the player is controlling an android.

Finally, the *Souls* reputation has increased to such a level that they are a major topic of discussion, both for players and developers. Behind the scenes, many question the series' qualities, what made it so popular, and why it resonated so much with a certain audience. That is, what importance the FromSoftware games hold in the videogame landscape.

Between 2015 and 2016, *Kotaku* interviewed several big names in the field to get their take on the series, and its strengths and weaknesses. About a dozen artists and programmers, including Scott Benson (co-creator of the adventure game *Night in the Woods*), Greg Kasavin (*Bastion*, *Transistor*), Brandon Sheffield (*Gunsport*) and Brad Muir (*Massive Chalice*), spoke about the games without equivocating. Some praised the games' empirical learning style, or all of the details that can be missed, while others reproached the technical issues that plagued the games, or the lack of a tactile feel in the attacks. Interestingly, Tanya Short of Kitfox games goes so far as to complain that the *Souls* games monopolize the conversation whenever a new episode comes out. If anything, this serves as definitive proof that the FromSoftware series is the subject of countless discussions, debates and analyses.

Of course, it's not everyone's cup of tea, even as far as designers go. But this wide spectrum of opinions is vital. Video games don't require a single approach, and shouldn't rely on immutable rules. With their surprise success, *Demon's Souls* and its successors proved that players aren't just puppets ruled by the market and trends.

---

423. *NieR: Automata* has another clear reference to *Souls*: a hidden blacksmith in a castle, which we can find by following the blacksmith's hammering sounds.

Onwards to the Future

As we write this, FromSoftware is being very secretive about the company's future. Hidetaka Miyazaki has stated that his company is working on several projects, without revealing any of them. One thing is certain: there won't be another *Dark Souls*. For now, anyways. And he doesn't plan to lead any more *Souls* games—he's finished with the series. For *Bloodborne*, it's not quite so clear, even if his comments suggest that a sequel isn't in the works.[424]

FromSoftware's objective is to forge ahead, to benefit from fans' loyalty to the *Souls* games to try out new things, without fully abandoning what made the company a success from an aesthetic and philosophical standpoint. Having refined and enriched its formula and work practices with each new episode, FromSoftware demonstrated its ability to satisfy the cravings of a friendly yet exacting audience.

The future is therefore unclear, but full of promise. With a creator as inspired as Hidetaka Miyazaki, surrounded by such talented artists, level designers and other programmers, there's little to worry about the quality of future FromSoftware productions. All we can hope for is to get some surprises soon. To experience new, unforgettable adventures. And to see how video games continue to evolve. There's no question about it: the *Souls* games were part of these evolutions, and their echoing influence can still be felt.

---

424. It's still worth remembering that Namco Bandai owns the rights to *Dark Souls*, and Sony has *Demon's Souls* and *Bloodborne*. Both publishers could always decide to continue this series without FromSoftware's help. But considering the important role that fans have played in the success of the *Souls* games, would Sony or Namco Bandai risk "betraying" fans' trust? It may depend on the success of the games FromSoftware currently has in the works.

DARK SOULS

ダークソウル

BEYOND THE GRAVE

CONCLUSION

A Reflection of Their Time

What a trip it is to play *Demon's Souls* after finishing *Dark Souls III*! The differences are glaring: not only visually, but in lots of other little details. *Demon's Souls* is slower and less permissive, and cruder than the most recent episode, both in terms of its artistic and musical direction, and in terms of the gameplay. However, behind this harshness, the foundation had already been laid. The direct ties between the games are undeniable.

This retrospective look also confirms some things. Even if, in some ways, the series evolved away from its initial philosophy (such as the online interactions, which lost some of their asynchronous, anonymous quality), it never caved under the weight of compromise. Even better, the studio benefited from technological improvements and heftier budgets to show the series' qualities in their best light, in particular by using more spectacular visuals. If the tactile environments of *Demon's Souls* and *Dark Souls* are distinctively evocative, *Bloodborne* and *Dark Souls III* are visually staggering, with minute attention to detail, made possible by current-generation consoles and PCs.

Fights in the series were considerably enhanced by many adjustments and new possibilities, even if the original slow *Excalibur*-style duels (John Boorman's film) were slightly altered due to the acceleration of fights.

Either way, in spite of the redundancies we've already mentioned, each episode in the series, including the less popular *Dark Souls II*, has its own distinctive flavor. This also explains why there's no consensus among the player community about which episode is the "best," and everyone has to make arguments for their own favorite. *Bloodborne* also has a prominent place in the series, though necessarily slightly removed. With its graphic violence, dynamic fights and a story that's even more complex and impenetrable than that of *Souls*, it stands out as a veritable *auteur* game, proud of its commitment and lack of concessions.

"*Auteur* game" is a title that could be applied to all of Miyazaki's titles. Each new game only strengthened this belief: the games were designed with determination and vision. *Souls* and *Bloodborne* are models of design and intelligence. It doesn't matter if their radical approach is to everyone's taste; they offer rich storytelling and a depth that most games lack. The beauty of video games also lies in their diversity.

The *Souls* games certainly made waves when they came out; and yet, eight years later, it's clear that they've transcended the basic status of pivotal games. Today, more than ever, we can celebrate these games for what they are, beyond their influence in the videogame industry: exceptional and inexhaustible games, with their unabashed integrity and bitter love for players—players who have mostly chosen to share and celebrate this love unrestrainedly. Let's hope that this Fire doesn't go out.

DARK SOULS

ダークソウル

BEYOND THE GRAVE

AFTERWORD

T HOUGH *The Ringed City* DLC wrapped up *Dark Souls*, the influence of Hidetaka Miyazaki's saga has continued to grow year after year. In 2009, Japanese video games had hit a low point; at the same time, their Western cousin was focused on boosting the "cinematic experience" of increasingly player-friendly games, going so far as to eliminate the very idea of failure.

During this tedious period, when I had lost all faith in the medium, *Demon's Souls* totally jolted me out of this daze. After thousands of hours spent exploring the kingdoms of Boletaria, Lordran, Drangleic and Yharnam, this series profoundly changed the way I think about video games, and my relationship with the medium. In his unique way, Miyazaki built a challenge, achievement, and an adventure: the stroke of genius was not that he simply placed players before an insurmountable wall, but rather that he made each of us a student, a disciple, teaching us the essential lessons of humility, patience and observation, which are necessary for comprehending and surviving in these hostile lands. I'm very aware of this master-student relationship that is built throughout the *Souls* games, and I suppose that it's my attachment to the full series that earned me the invitation to write this afterword, and I'm honored.

It's been eight years since this same jolt shook all layers of the industry, affecting players, journalists, designers, and even marketing teams. Today, everything can be compared to *Dark Souls*, be it a game, a gameplay mechanic, a developer's intent or even events that have nothing to do with video games. Almost any time a stamina bar appears, or a game is not especially lenient, the *Souls* games will come up: it can be pretty funny, or even eyeroll-inducing. Everything is the "*Dark Souls*" of its genre or category... professionals will even unabashedly write things like "*Breath of the Wild* is no doubt the *Dark Souls* of *The Legend of Zelda* saga." It's an absurd response to the chicken or the egg dilemma—*Zelda*, *Castlevania* and *Metroid* all had a great impact on Miyazaki's works. What I take away from this, however, is that there's a clear before and after *Dark Souls*. This series was able to grasp, assimilate and modernize these mechanics to place them in a dark fantasy setting awash with sadness, solitude and despair. To paraphrase the now-president of FromSoftware, players had to be thrown into a bottomless abyss so they could better evaluate the path ahead, and enjoy the journey up to the surface.

Whether we decide to adventure alone or with other ailing souls, one of the main features of *Souls* is that it forces players to always remain alert. Keeping with this objective of emotional intensity, the games don't forgive any bouts of inattention—we could easily evaluate the difficulty of a fight using this characteristic. The most grueling fights are those that punish every error, while more basic enemies leave us alive after two or three attacks. It's not innovative for a game to require this much from players, but this approach had been abandoned by game designers in favor of highly player-friendly games. This is the critical difference between the mindless, mean-spirited difficulty of some titles, and the challenges posed by a *Souls* game. By assuming responsibility for failures and successes, players learn not to blame the games for their hardships, slowly reexamining their own attitude. I've always considered the *Souls* games to be imbued with a Japanese martial spirit, in which the ego must be set aside. When starting a *Souls* game, there's always a period during which players need to unlearn the habits they've developed in other games, in which they were all powerful, to become aware of their fragility. Once this reality has been hammered home by some ax blows to the head, players can take on the adventure more serenely, viewing failures as their own neglect to live up to the game's expectations.

This is also why I insist that neophytes should really try to finish their first *Souls* by themselves, without any guides or companions. The moment when this revelation occurs is often a unique memory, and one that's impossible to relive. No matter which episode you first play, you experience this feeling, which explains the never-ending debates on which is the best game. If we view the first one from this perspective, we're likely to keep a special place in our hearts for this game. Following this logic, we can also understand why the later episodes are progressively seen as less exciting, always presenting "the same thing." Every episode offers a unique variation on the same theme, but since the same learning period isn't necessary, the surprise is also lessened. As a new, non-sequel, *Bloodborne* was spared this critique, while *Dark Souls III* may have disappointed some. However, after placing *Demon's Souls* on a pedestal for many years, I consider the *Bloodborne-Dark Souls III* saga to be the pinnacle of the series.

These two titles are inseparable: they share so many elements that they are really just two sides of the same coin. They were both overseen by Hidetaka Miyazaki in person, and in an interview, he told me that there was quite a bit of commingling between the games. One of the young FromSoftware president's ideas was to work on three projects simultaneously, both to ensure relative profitability, but also to allow each team to benefit from common progress. In this way, numerous ideas that were tested in *Bloodborne* can be found in *Dark Souls III*, and vice-versa. For instance, *Bloodborne* deliberately got rid of the defensive side of *Dark Souls*, going so far as to mock people who hide behind a shield. But rather than creating a divide between the two series, the bestial agility of *Bloodborne* influenced the overall pace of *Dark Souls III*. The third episode is much more dynamic, vigorous and "visceral" than its illustrious predecessor. The true difference lies in their respective fates: where *Bloodborne* brilliantly created a new setting and mythology revolving around nightmares, *Dark Souls III* was duty-bound to provide a conclusion to the saga that began in 2011. And if the flagrant similarities with the first episode have been interpreted as studio laziness by some, I saw them more as a grand design that seemed to have been planned from the beginning. The final fight against the Soul of Cinder is proof for me that the saga is driven by the vision of its creator. For Miyazaki, this universe (and video games in general) is nothing more than a cycle that we can never really escape.

Anyone who's looked death in the face, before finding a bonfire at the very last moment, has experienced intense moments of relief and victory thanks to a simple video game. These emotions aren't conveyed through breathtaking cutscenes; rather, they're won through considerable effort, controller in hand. This video game-specific narration reminds us that we're actors, rather than spectators, in these onscreen adventures. Perhaps the success of *Dark Souls* arose from the fact that so many players were able to (re)discover and experience these emotions. This is why I believe so many people have been inspired to look for signs of *Dark Souls* everywhere, as soon as a game uses any of its codes. Unlike so many others, the saga doesn't try to impersonate film. It uses the medium's own language, and Miyazaki's series asserts a vision of video games that can now be found throughout the industry. By systematically comparing his recent games, we may actually be discussing a specific vision of video games themselves, making *Dark Souls* into a standard-bearer that resembles this overall vision. And after all these years playing and talking about the *Souls* games, I'm convinced that the saga has helped everyone see that video games aren't just entertainment, but are sometimes an art in themselves.

ExServ

Benoît "ExServ" Reinier

Immersed in video games for as long as he can remember, ExServ started his *YouTube* channel in 2011 with a complete guide of the *Dark Souls* games. Passionate about videogame review and making gameplay accessible, his work can be found on *Nesblog* and *Gamekult.com*, where he was hired to lead the video section in 2014. Still active on *YouTube* and *Twitch*, he now works as an independent journalist and writes articles for *Gamekult* and *NextInpact*.

DARK SOULS

ダークソウル

BEYOND THE GRAVE

Acknowledgements

Damien

To Mehdi and Nicolas, for their passion and kindness.

To our collaborators at Third (proofreaders, model maker, graphic designers, etc.) who brought their talent and professionalism to the work.

To Kévin and Benoît, for their excellent, relevant foreword and afterword.

To Sylvain, of course, for his remarkable, in-depth work on the game worlds, his advice and comments, and for the hours of *Souls* and *Bloodborne* discussions.

To readers of the first volume, whose feedback was a joy for us to read, and whose critiques guided us in our creation of this second book.

To my family, my loved ones and friends, for their support.

To Aude, for everything.

Sylvain

I would like to thank:

The FromSoftware teams, for their unremitting work on the series over many years, and especially for *Bloodborne*, which captivated me all throughout my analysis with its unexpected store of treasures and coherence.

The *Soulsborne* community, for all of the brilliant and quirky discussions and theories.

Damien, Ludovic and Hubert, for the long and fruitful discussions and debates on the lore and the details, which are all important in the end.

Mehdi and Nicolas, for their trust.

Jenny, for her patience.

Hugo, for being the funniest kid in the world.

DARK SOULS

ダークソウル

BEYOND THE GRAVE

BIBLIOGRAPHY

Books and Theses

ANONYMOUS. *Bloodborne Strategy Guide*. Hamburg: Future Press. 2015. 552 p. ISBN 978-3-86993069-5.

ANONYMOUS. *Bloodborne: The Old Hunters Collector's Edition Guide*. Hamburg: Future Press. 2015. 224 p. ISBN 978-3-86993072-5.

ANONYMOUS. *Dark Souls III Official Guide*. Roseville (California): Prima Games. 2016. 400 p. ISBN 978-0-74401708-3.

CHEVALIER, Jean and Alain GHEERBRANT. *Dictionnaire des symboles : Mythes, rêves, coutumes, gestes, formes, figures, couleurs, nombres*. Paris: Robert Laffont, 1997. 1,100 p. ISBN 978-2-22108716-9.

COMTE, Fernand. *Larousse des mythologies du monde*. Paris: Larousse, 2004. 321 p. ISBN 978-2-03505526-2.

GOMBRICH, Ernst Hans. *Histoire de l'art*. 16e éd. London: Phaidon. 2001. 688 p. ISBN 978-0-71489207-8.

LOVECRAFT, Howard Phillips. *Dagon et autres récits d'horreur*. Paris: Points. 2016. 240 p. ISBN 978-2-75785144-9.

LOVECRAFT, Howard Phillips. *La Couleur tombée du ciel*. Paris: Points. 2015. 144 p. ISBN 978-2-75785140-1.

REDGRAVE [pen name]. *The Paleblood Hunt: A Bloodborne Analysis* [online since 2015, viewed May 23, 2017]. Available Online: < https://docs.google. com/document/ d/1JL5acskAT_2t062HILImBkV8eXAwaqOj611mSjK-vZ8/ >.

Websites

Bloodborne

Wiki Contributors. *Bloodborne Wiki* [online]. Fextralife. 2017 [viewed May 23, 2017]. Available Online: < http://bloodborne.wiki.fextralife.com/ >.

Wiki Contributors. *Bloodborne Wiki* [online]. Wikia. 2017 [viewed May 23, 2017]. Available Online: < http://bloodborne.wikia.com/wiki/Bloodborne_Wiki >.

Wiki Contributors. *Bloodborne Wiki* [online]. Wikidot. 2017 [viewed May 23, 2017]. Available Online: < http://bloodborne.wikidot.com/ >.

Blog Contributors. *The Lore Hunter: A Bloodborne Lore Blog* [online]. Blogger. 2017 [viewed May 23, 2017]. Available Online: < http://www.thelorehunter.com/ >.

WIKIPEDIA CONTRIBUTORS. "*Bloodborne*" [online]. *Wikipedia, The Free Encyclopedia*. Wikimedia Foundation, 2017 [viewed May 23, 2017]. Available Online: < https://en.wikipedia.org/wiki/Bloodborne >.

Dark Souls III

WIKIPEDIA CONTRIBUTORS. "*Dark Souls III*" [online]. *Wikipedia, The Free Encyclopedia*. Wikimedia Foundation, 2017 [viewed May 23, 2017]. Available Online: < https://en.wikipedia.org/wiki/Dark_Souls_III >.

Dark Souls III Wiki [online]. Wikia. 2017 [viewed May 23, 2017]. Available Online: < http://darksouls.wikia.com/wiki/Dark_Souls_III >.

Dark Souls III Wiki [online]. Wikidot. 2017 [viewed May 23, 2017]. Available Online: < http://darksouls3.wikidot.com/ >.

Souls Lore [online]. Wikidot. 2017 [viewed May 23, 2017]. Available Online: < http://soulslore.wikidot.com/ >.

Online Articles

BARZAN, Ario. "Understanding the sublime architecture of *Bloodborne*" [online]. *Kill Screen*, July 29, 2015 [viewed May 23, 2017]. Available Online: < https://killscreen. com/articles/understanding-sublime-architecture-bloodborne/ >.

BARZAN, Ario. "Worlds Worth Believing In: On *Demon's Souls* and *Dark Souls*" [online]. *Medium*, September 18, 2015 [viewed May 23, 2017]. Available Online: < https://medium.com/@Doshmanziari/worlds-worth-believing-in-on-demon-s-souls-and-dark-souls-8414cb8b9a8e >.

BLAIN, Louise. "Miyazaki says *Dark Souls* 'has been completed by players' so no more secrets then" [online]. *Gamesradar*, December 16, 2015 [viewed May 23, 2017]. Available Online: < http://www.gamesradar.com/miyazaki-says-dark-souls-has-been-completed-players-so-no-more-secrets-then/ >.

CHANDLER, David. "*Bloodborne* and the history of horror" [online]. *Kill Screen*, Thursday, April 30, 2015 [viewed May 23, 2017]. Available Online: < https:// killscreen.com/articles/bloodborne-and-history-horror/ >.

CRAFT, Scott. "*Nioh* Director Says Team Ninja Inspired by *Shogun*, *Onimusha* and *Dark Souls*" [online]. *IDigitalTimes*, June 27, 2016 [viewed May 23, 2017]. Available Online: < http://www.idigitaltimes.com/nioh-director-says-team-ninja-inspired- shogun-onimusha-and-dark-souls-542675 >.

DONALDSON, Alex. "*Dark Souls 3*: Miyazaki explains the difference between 'difficult' and 'unreasonable'" [online]. *VG247*, March 2, 2016 [viewed May 23, 2017]. Available Online: < https://www.vg247.com/2016/03/02/dark-souls-3-miyazaki-bloodborne-interview/ >.

DONNELLY, Joe. "'*Dark Souls* is completely done as of *The Ringed City*,' says Hidetaka Miyazaki" [online]. *PCGamer*, March 31, 2017 [viewed May 23, 2017]. Available Online: < http://www.pcgamer.com/dark-souls-is-completely-done-as-of-the-ringed- city-says-hidetaka-miyazaki/ >.

KHAN, Zarmena. "Hidetaka Miyazaki Says *Bloodborne*'s Limitations Made Him Return to *Dark Souls 3*" [online]. *PlaystationLifeStyle*, September 13, 2015 [viewed May 23, 2017]. Available Online: < http://www.playstationlifestyle. net/2015/09/13/ miyazaki-talks-dark-souls-3-freedom/ >.

Kollar, Philip. "Everything we know about the *Dark Souls 3*: 'Ashes of Ariandel' DLC" [online]. *Polygon*, September 21, 2016 [viewed May 23, 2017]. Available Online: < http://www.polygon.com/2016/9/21/12999624/dark-souls-3-ashes-of-ariandel-dlc-preview-hands-on-everything-we-know >.

Krupa, Daniel. "Production on *Dark Souls 3* began without Miyazaki" [online]. *IGN UK*, November 17, 2015 [viewed May 23, 2017]. Available Online: < http://uk.ign.com/articles/2015/11/17/production-on-dark-souls-3-began-without-miyazaki?%20hub%20page%20(front%20page)&utm_content=1 >.

MacGregor, Kyle. "Bent, not broken: *Nioh*'s flexible rigidity - An interview with Team Ninja's Fumihiko Yasuda" [online]. *Destructoid*, June 25, 2016 [viewed May 23, 2017]. Available Online: < https://www.destructoid.com/bent-not-broken-nioh-s-flexible-rigidity-370774.phtml >.

McWhertor, Michael. "Our first look at *Dark Souls 3* gameplay and its new changes to combat" [online]. *Polygon*, Wednesday, June 17, 2015 [viewed May 23, 2017]. Available Online: < http://www.polygon.com/2015/6/17/8798005/dark-souls-3-e3-2015 >.

Martin, Gareth Damian. "Visions of Hell: *Dark Souls*' Cultural Heritage" [online]. *Kill Screen*, Wednesday, May 11, 2016 [viewed May 23, 2017]. Available Online: < https:// killscreen.com/articles/visions-of-hell-dark-soulss-cultural-heritage/ >.

Matulef, Jeffrey. "*Nioh* director Fumihiko Yasuda on difficulty, player feedback and what's changing" [online]. *Eurogamer*, October 4, 2016 [viewed May 23, 2017]. Available Online: < http://www.eurogamer.net/articles/2016-09-30-nioh-director-fumihiko-yasuda-on-difficulty-player-feedback-and-whats-changing >.

Parkin, Simon. "*Bloodborne* creator Hidetaka Miyazaki: 'I didn't have a dream. I wasn't ambitious'" [online]. *The Guardian*, March 31, 2015 [viewed May 23, 2017]. Available Online: < https://www.theguardian.com/technology/2015/mar/31/bloodborne-dark-souls-creator-hidetaka-miyazaki-interview >.

Patulei, Mike. "E3 2015: World's First *Dark Souls III* Details Revealed" [online]. *HardcoreGamer*, June 16, 2015 [viewed May 23, 2017]. Available Online: < http://www.hardcoregamer.com/2015/06/16/e3-2015-worlds-first-dark-souls-iii-details-revealed/154333/ >.

ROBINSON, Martin. "*Dark Souls 3* isn't the last in the series - but it is a turning point" [online]. *Eurogamer*, Wednesday, June 17, 2015 [viewed May 23, 2017]. Available Online: < http://www.eurogamer.net/articles/2015-06-17-dark-souls-3-isnt-the-last-in- the-series-but-it-is-a-turning-point >.

ROBINSON, Martin. "*Bloodborne*'s two planned DLC packs have been combined in the epic 'The Old Hunters'" [online]. *Eurogamer*, Friday, September 18, 2015 [viewed May 23, 2017]. Available Online: < http://www.eurogamer.net/articles/2015-09-18-bloodbornes-two-dlc-packs-have-been-combined-in-the-substantial-the-old-hunters >.

ROBSON, Daniel. "The Story Behind *Bloodborne*'s Haunting Soundtrack" [online]. *Playstation.Blog*, May 18, 2015 [viewed May 23, 2017]. Available Online: < http://blog.us.playstation.com/2015/05/18/the-story-behind-bloodbornes-haunting-soundtrack/ >.

SCAMMELL, David. "*Dark Souls 3* is being developed by a different team to *Bloodborne*" [online]. *VideoGamer*, June 17, 2015 [viewed May 23, 2017]. Available Online: < http://www.videogamer.com/ps4/dark_souls_3/news/dark_souls_3_is_being_developed_by_a_different_team_to_bloodborne.html >.

SKREBELS, Joe. "Hidetaka Miyazaki not ruling out working on 'Dark Souls-like' games" [online]. *IGN*, September 21, 2016 [viewed May 23, 2017]. Available Online: < http://www.ign.com/articles/2016/09/21/hidetaka-miyazaki-not-ruling-out-working-on-dark-souls-like-games >.

SLABAUGH, Brett. "*Destiny* Inspired by *Dark Souls, Monster Hunter*, Bungie Says" [online]. *The Escapist*, December 18, 2013 [viewed May 23, 2017]. Available Online: < http://www.escapistmagazine.com/news/view/130638-Destiny-Inspired-by- Dark-Souls-Monster-Hunter-Bungie-Says >.

SLIVA, Marty. "Inside the mind of *Bloodborne* and *Dark Souls*' creator" [online]. *IGN*, Thursday, February 5, 2015 [viewed May 23, 2017]. Available Online: < http://www.ign.com/articles/2015/02/05/inside-the-mind-of-bloodborne-and-dark-souls-creator- ign-first >.

Interviews (Magazines)

BITTERLIN, Kevin. "Interview with Hidetaka Miyazaki," *JV Magazine*, April 2016, no. 29.

BROWN, Nathan. "Interview with Hidetaka Miyazaki," *Edge Magazine*, July 2015, no. 281.

Online Interviews

ANONYMOUS. "An Interview with Hidetaka Miyazaki" [online]. *4Gamer*, Wednesday, June 11, 2014 [viewed May 23, 2017]. Available Online: < http://www.4gamer.net/ games/260/ G026038/20140611091/ >. English translation by Zefah [pen name]. *Neogaf*, June 18, 2014 [viewed May 23, 2017]. Available Online: < http://www.neogaf. com/forum/showthread.php?t=840059 >.

ANONYMOUS. "An Interview with Hidetaka Miyazaki" [online]. *GNN Gamer*, April 25, 2016 [viewed May 23, 2017]. Available Online: < https://gnn.gamer.com.tw/2/130902. html >. English translation by Jokingbird [pen name]. *Reddit*, s. d. [viewed May 23, 2017]. Available Online: < https://www.reddit.com/user/jokingbird >.

Anonymous. "An Interview with Hidetaka Miyazaki" [online]. *4Gamer*, Monday, June 13, 2016 [viewed May 23, 2017]. Available Online: < http://www.4gamer.net/ games/305/ G030528/20160526060/ >.

CUETO, Gerard. GameStart 2014 - *Bloodborne*: Interview with Masaaki Yamagiwa - Talks Frame-Rate, Messengers and More" [online]. *PlaystationLifeStyle*, October 29, 2014 [viewed May 23, 2017]. Available Online: < http://www.plays- tationlifestyle. net/2014/10/29/gamestart-2014-bloodborne-interview-with-masaaki-yamagiwa- talks-frame-rate-messengers-and-more/#/slide/1 >.

Dutton, Fred. "A Conversation with *Bloodborne* Creator Hidetaka Miyazaki" [online]. *Playstation.Blog*, Friday, March 20, 2015 [viewed May 23, 2017]. Available Online: < http://blog.us.playstation.com/w2015/03/20/a-conversation-with- bloodborne-crea- tor-hidetaka-miyazaki/ >.

GARCIA, Juan. "Entrevistamos a Hidetaka Miyazaki, director de *Dark Souls 3*" [online]. *IGN España*, March 1, 2016 [viewed May 23, 2017]. Available Online: < http:// es.ign.com/dark-souls-iii-pc/100747/feature/entrevista-a-hidetaka-miyazaki -director-de-dark-souls-3 >.

HINDMAN, Heath. *"Bloodborne* Producer Talks Story, Guns, Armor & Sadness" [online]. *PlaystationLifeStyle*, Tuesday, September 30, 2014 [viewed May 23, 2017]. Available Online: < http://www.playstationlifestyle.net/2014/09/30/bloodborne-interview- director-talks-story-guns-armor-sadness-exclusive-interview/#/slide/1 >.

KAMEN, Matt. *"Dark Souls 3* director: it's about 'accomplishment by overcoming tremendous odds'" [online]. *Wired*, April 12, 2016 [viewed May 23, 2017]. Available Online: < http://www.wired.co.uk/article/dark-souls-3-hidetaka-miyazaki- interview >.

KLEPEK, Patrick. "Preparing for Life After *Dark Souls*: A Conversation with Designer Hidetaka Miyazaki" [online]. *Kotaku*, July 7, 2016 [viewed May 23, 2017]. Available Online: < http://kotaku.com/preparing-for-life-after-dark-souls-a-conversation-wit-1783296404 >.

MAKUCH, Eddie. *"Dark Souls 3* Director Talks Franchise's Legacy, Possible *Demon's Souls* Remaster, More" [online]. *Gamespot*, July 8, 2016 [viewed May 23, 2017]. Available Online: < http://www.gamespot.com/articles/dark-souls-3-director-talks-franchises-legacy-poss/1100-6441636/ >.

NELVA, Giuseppe. *"Dark Souls III* Director Hidetaka Miyazaki Talks DLC; Future Games, *Armored Core* and Much More" [online]. *DualShockers*, September 21, 2016 [viewed May 23, 2017]. Available Online: < http://www.dualshockers. com/2016/09/21/dark-souls-iii-director-hidetaka-miyazaki-talks-dlc-future-games-armored-core-and-much-more/ >.

PALMER27 [pen name]. "Mini Interview with Composer Ryan Amon" [online]. *Reddit*, May 30, 2015 [viewed May 23, 2017]. Available Online: < https://www. reddit. com/r/bloodborne/comments/37wanm/mini_interview_with_composer_ryan_ amon/ >.

ROBSON, Daniel. "Interview with Hidetaka Miyazaki on the *Dark Souls III* DLCs" [online]. *IGN Japan*, September 21, 2016 [viewed May 23, 2017]. Available Online: < http://jp.ign.com/dark-souls-3/7702/interview/dark-souls-3dlc12 >.
English translation by Valfreze [pen name]. *Reddit*, s. d. [viewed May 23, 2017]. Available Online: < https://www.reddit.com/r/darksouls3/comments/53xuso/ign_ jp_ posts_a_miyazaki_interview_of_whats_in_dlc/ >.

SEMEL, Paul. "Exclusive Interview: *Bloodborne* Composer Cris Velasco" [online]. *Paulsemel.com*, April 15, 2015 [viewed May 23, 2017]. Available Online: < http://paulsemel.com/exclusive-interview-bloodborne-composer-cris-velasco/ >.

Videos

GAME DEVELOPERS CONFERENCE, "The Gothic Horror Music of *Bloodborne*" [online video]. *YouTube*, July 08, 2016 [viewed May 23, 2017]. Available Online: < https://www.youtube.com/watch?v=5yncMReF8QA >.

GAME INFORMER. "Unravelling *Dark Souls* Creator Hidetaka Miyazaki's Secrets" [online video]. *YouTube*, September 23, 2015 [viewed May 23, 2017]. Available Online: < https://www.youtube.com/watch?v=r6F5flVQRus >.

GAMEREACTORTV. "*Dark Souls III* - Hidetaka Miyazaki Interview" [online video]. *YouTube*, March 02, 2016 [viewed May 23, 2017]. Available Online: < https://www.youtube.com/watch?v=WUoNrydsYgE >.

IGN. "Making *Bloodborne*: Part 1 - *Souls* Evolved" [online video]. *YouTube*, February 06, 2015 [viewed May 23, 2017]. Available Online: < https://www.youtube. com/watch?v=gExoq4CGDHo >.

IGN. "Making *Bloodborne*: Part 2 - A PS4 Exclusive" [online video]. *YouTube*, February 23, 2015 [viewed May 23, 2017]. Available Online: < https://www.youtube. com/watch?v=oiGPTI06fn8 >.

PLAYSTATION. "*Bloodborne* - Soundtrack Recording Session - Behind the Scenes" [online video]. *YouTube*, February 13, 2015 [viewed May 23, 2017]. Available Online: < https://www.youtube.com/watch?v=NHIkUzmNmc0 >.

SILVER MONT. *Silver Mont* [YouTube channel, viewed May 23, 2017]. Available Online: < https://www.youtube.com/user/SilverMontGames >.

VAATIVIDYA. *VaatiVidya* [YouTube channel, viewed May 23, 2017]. Available Online: < https://www.youtube.com/user/VaatiVidya >.

WOODWARD, Frank H. *Lovecraft: Fear of the Unknown*, [online documentary]. Wyrd Studios, March 30, 2016 [viewed May 23, 2017]. Available Online: < https://www. youtube.com/watch?v=jg9VCf5einY >.